ANTON RAUSCHER (Hrsg.)

Das Eigentum als eine Bedingung der Freiheit

Property as a Condition of Liberty

Soziale Orientierung

herausgegeben von

Anton Rauscher

Band 22

Das Eigentum als
eine Bedingung der Freiheit

Property as a Condition
of Liberty

Herausgegeben von

Anton Rauscher

Duncker & Humblot · Berlin

Bibliografische Information der Deutschen Nationalbibliothek

Die Deutsche Nationalbibliothek verzeichnet diese Publikation in
der Deutschen Nationalbibliografie; detaillierte bibliografische Daten
sind im Internet über http://dnb.d-nb.de abrufbar.

ISSN 0720-6917
ISBN 978-3-428-14169-2 (Print)
ISBN 978-3-428-54169-0 (E-Book)
ISBN 978-3-428-84169-1 (Print & E-Book)

Gedruckt auf alterungsbeständigem (säurefreiem) Papier
entsprechend ISO 9706 ∞

Internet: http://www.duncker-humblot.de

Vorwort

Als das kommunistische Imperium 1989/91 zusammenbrach, wurde die ganze Misere offenbar, in die eine Gesellschaft gerät, die den Lehren von Karl Marx folgt und das Privateigentum von Grund und Boden und an den Produktionsmitteln abschafft. Im Ostblock waren – von einigen Repräsentativbauten abgesehen – die Häuser und Straßen und die gesamte Infrastruktur heruntergekommen; die Wirtschaftsleistung der DDR erreichte im Vergleich zur Bundesrepublik Deutschland nicht einmal 30 Prozent; die Qualität der Güter war dürftig; es gab keine freien Märkte; in besonderen Läden konnten Güter aus dem Westen gegen D-Mark gekauft werden, was vor allem den Funktionären zugute kam. Nur Mauer und Stacheldraht konnten verhindern, dass weitere Millionen Ostdeutsche in den Westen flüchteten. Die Wirklichkeit hatte die Ideologie entlarvt.

Allen sollte Alles gehören und die Ungleichheit in der Gesellschaft überwinden. Schon der griechische Philosoph Platon hatte die Vision einer Gütergemeinschaft, die die Unterschiede zwischen Arm und Reich beseitigen und für alle Menschen gleiche Lebensbedingungen bewirken sollte. Diese Idee wurde im Laufe der Geschichte immer dann lebendig, wenn die Besitzverhältnisse von der Bevölkerung als ungerecht empfunden wurden und die Mächtigen die Kleinen unterdrückten. Auch beim Übergang von der Agrar- zur Industriegesellschaft kam es zu revolutionären Umbrüchen. Die Klassenspaltung der Gesellschaft in Kapitalisten und Proletarier war der Nährboden für die Parole: „Eigentum ist Diebstahl".

Nach dem Niedergang der totalitären Machtsysteme haben sich die Ideen des Rechtsstaates und der Demokratie in fast allen Teilen der Welt ausgebreitet. Sie beruhen auf den Freiheitsrechten aller Bürger. Die Bedingung dafür, dass diese Freiheitsrechte nicht nur auf dem Papier stehen, sondern im konkreten Leben der Menschen in Wirtschaft und Gesellschaft, in der Politik wirksam werden können, ist das Eigentum, das als eine fundamentale Ordnungsinstitution in den wirtschaftlich, sozial und politisch fortgeschrittenen Ländern anerkannt ist, auch wenn die konkreten Verhältnisse, die innerstaatlichen und zwischenstaatlichen Regelungen und auch die gerichtlichen Maßstäbe zum Teil noch weit auseinanderklaffen.

In der Bundesrepublik Deutschland lautet Art. 14 Abs. 1 des Grundgesetzes: „Das Eigentum und das Erbrecht werden gewährleistet. Inhalt und Schranken werden durch die Gesetze bestimmt." Der Grundsatz von der Gemeinbestimmung der Erdengüter ist in Abs. 2 festgehalten, wo es heißt: „Eigentum verpflichtet. Sein Gebrauch soll zugleich dem Wohle der Allgemeinheit dienen." Die Nutzung allen Eigentums muss so erfolgen, dass sie dem Wohl der Allgemeinheit nicht im Wege steht, sondern dieses fördert. Die Soziale Marktwirtschaft war von Anfang an so angelegt, beide Rechtsbereiche aufzubauen und im Auge zu behalten.

Unter der Rücksicht, dass Eigentum Bedingung der Freiheit ist, haben sich in Deutschland und in Europa, wohl auch in Nordamerika, zwei Problembereiche entwickelt. Der eine betrifft die Verteilung von Eigentum und Vermögen. Es ist weitgehend gelungen, dass die Bevölkerung an dem wachsenden Wohlstand teilhat. Auch die Produzenten haben erkannt, wie wichtig es ist, dass die steigende Gütermenge Absatz findet und nicht Absatzkrisen die gesamte Wirtschaft gefährden. Es ist aber nicht gelungen, die Bevölkerung in größerem Umfang für die Beteiligung am Produktivkapital zu gewinnen. In den USA scheint dies trotz der enormen Einkommens- und Vermögensunterschiede besser gelungen zu sein, dass immer neue Schichten sich an den modernen Formen des Produktivkapitals beteiligen. Dadurch verringert sich auch die Gefahr, dass sich in der Gesellschaft der Sozialneid ausbreitet und, wenn er von den Medien kräftig geschürt wird, zu einer Belastung für den Zusammenhalt wird. Die Beteiligung breiter Schichten am Produktivkapital würde wohl auch das Verständnis der Bevölkerung für die notwendigen Innovationen und Investitionen stärken, die in einer zusammenwachsenden Welt eine immer größere Bedeutung haben.

Der zweite Problembereich hängt mit dem Ausbau des Sozialstaates zusammen. Der Sozialstaat ist die Antwort auf die Veränderungen, die mit dem Übergang von der Großfamilie zur Kleinfamilie und zur individuellen Lebensgestaltung eingetreten sind. Früher hat die Großfamilie die Hauptrisiken des Alters, der Verarmung, der Krankheit und Invalidität, der Kinderlosigkeit abgedeckt, was heute die Sozialversicherungen übernommen haben. Während aber die überschaubaren Verhältnisse in der Großfamilie dafür gesorgt haben, dass jeder durch Arbeit, die er leisten kann, zum Wohl des Ganzen beiträgt und auch die Risiken soweit wie möglich mitträgt, wächst im Sozialstaat die Neigung, möglichst viel auf die Gemeinschaft abzuwälzen. Die persönliche Verantwortung, die auch für den Risikobereich gilt, schwindet. Das Eigentum und Vermögen tragen sozusagen immer weniger den Wirtschaftsprozess und werden immer mehr zu Zeichen des Reichtums. Eine Gesellschaft, in der vor allem Reichtum zählt und Freiheit und Verantwortung nicht mehr im Bewusstsein der Bürger lebendig sind, gerät schneller, als man denken möchte, auf Abwege.

Das 12. Deutsch-Amerikanische Kolloquium, das vom 21. bis 26. Juli 2012 im Conference Center in Mundelein/Chicago Ill stattfand, behandelte das Thema „Das Eigentum als eine Bedingung der Freiheit". Der erste Teil befasst sich mit Grundfragen. Aus verschiedener Perspektive wird der Ausgangspunkt des Denkens über das Eigentum betrachtet. Die Tatsache, dass die Menschen als Leib-Geist-Wesen auf die Nutzung der materiellen Güter angewiesen sind, die Natur aber diese nicht bestimmten Personen zuteilt, hat in der christlichen Tradition zum Grundsatz der Gemeinbestimmung der Erdengüter geführt, den die konkreten Eigentumsverhältnisse immer im Auge behalten müssen. Auf der anderen Seite bietet die Natur nur Ressourcen, die erst durch Arbeit und Bearbeitung zu Gütern werden, wie sie die Menschen brauchen. Die Menschen sind dazu in dem Maße bereit, wenn sie auch über die Früchte ihrer Arbeit verfügen. Der zweite Teil wendet sich philosophischen und verfassungsrechtlichen Fragen zu, wobei auch politische Erfahrungen aus Deutschland, aber auch aus der Gründerzeit der USA zur Sprache kommen. Im dritten Teil werden Fragen aufgegriffen, die die Verantwortung des Eigentümers von Unternehmen betreffen. Ohne Risikobereitschaft können weder multinationale Unternehmen noch mittelständische Firmen erfolgreich sein. Die Sozialstaaten müssen dafür Sorge tragen, dass die Freiheit nicht erstickt wird.

Jude P. Dougherty von der Catholic University of America in Washington DC und der Herausgeber dieses Bandes haben im Jahre 1990 die Deutsch-Amerikanischen Kolloquien begründet, die alle zwei Jahre abwechselnd in Deutschland und in den USA stattfinden. Wir waren überzeugt, dass mit dem Ende der Spaltung in Ost und West neue Aufgaben und Ordnungsprobleme in der Welt auf uns zukommen, die auf der Grundlage des christlichen Menschen- und Gesellschaftsverständnisses überzeugende Antworten fordern. Die Kolloquien waren von Anfang an interdisziplinär angelegt. Nach dem 11. Kolloquium im Jahre 2010 in Wildbad Kreuth legte Jude P. Dougherty seine Aufgabe in die Hände von Kollegen William A. Frank, der an der Universität in Dallas TX einen Lehrstuhl für Philosophie innehat und das „Leo XIII Center for Philosophy and Social Issues" errichtet hat. Ich danke meinem Kollegen und Freund Jude für die langjährige fruchtbare und reibungslose Zusammenarbeit, ohne die dieses internationale Projekt nicht zustande gekommen wäre.

Mein Dank gilt meinem Kollegen William A. Frank, der nunmehr die Verantwortung für die amerikanische Seite übernommen hat. Für die umsichtige Planung und Organisation des 12. Kolloquiums, die Pflege der Kontakte zu interessierten Kollegen, die Sorge für die Simultan-Übersetzung der Vorträge und der Diskussionen, nicht zuletzt die sehr zeitaufwendige Betreuung der amerikanischen Manuskripte für den Druck bin ich sehr dankbar.

Eigens erwähnt sei das inhaltsreiche Abendgespräch mit Francis Cardinal George, dem Erzbischof von Chicago. Er berichtete über die Lage der katholischen Kirche in den USA und die Herausforderungen, die sie bewältigen muss. Besonders habe ich mich darüber gefreut, dass Ministerpräsident a. D. und der Ehrenvorsitzende der Konrad-Adenauer-Stiftung Bernhard Vogel, der dem

Deutsch-Amerikanischen Kolloquium von Anfang an verbunden ist und es gefördert hat, seine Einschätzung über die weitere Entwicklung der Europäischen Union dargelegt hat.

Zusammen mit meinem Kollegen Frank danke ich den Autoren für ihre Beiträge. Dank gebührt auch allen Spendern, die die Finanzierung des Kolloquiums ermöglicht haben. Besonders danke ich Frau Wilma Cremer für die Organisation des Kolloquiums auf deutscher Seite und für die redaktionelle Bearbeitung des Berichtsbandes. Nicht zuletzt bin ich dem Verlag Duncker & Humblot in Berlin verbunden, der die Reihe „Soziale Orientierung" betreut.

Mönchengladbach/Augsburg, im März 2013 *Anton Rauscher*

Inhaltsverzeichnis

I. Die naturrechtliche Sicht des Eigentums
The Natural Law View of Property

II. Rechtliche und politische Aspekte
Legal and Political Aspects

III. Wirtschaftliche Aspekte
Economic Aspects

I. Die naturrechtliche Sicht des Eigentums
The Natural Law View of Property

Property as a Condition of Liberty

By Jude P. Dougherty

Attitudes with respect to the acquisition, use, and protection of property are but a manifestation of an unexpressed philosophy of human nature. It goes without saying that absent personal property be it real, intellectual, or monetary, one's scope of action is limited or nonexistent. But there is a deeper aspect to the holding of property that begs to be acknowledged. Ownership is closely tied to one's personal identity. A person is often known by his holdings, by the land that he owns, by the real estate or personal wealth that he has accumulated, and by the use he makes of it. Ownership is often an expression of taste and aspiration, of preferences tied to one's character. Property gives one a sense of independence and enables one to act in a multiplicity of ways otherwise impossible. Recreation, travel, the expansion of social contacts, the support of social and political activity, and the furtherance of one's education become possible. Absent appropriate financial resources, personal acumen is truncated.

If the advantages of property are so evident, how account, in Western societies, for public acquiescence to the myriad government takings, from taxation to currency debasement, that effectively limit personal property and its use? The answer in part is that affirmations of the necessity of personal property usually carry with them an acknowledgment that from a moral point of view property carries with it certain obligations to the other. Given that an individual flourishes only within a community, it is universally recognized that a reciprocal relationship is created thereby, one that entails personal responsibility to the whole. This is the moral basis of taxation that goes beyond ordinary public services, for example, roads, utilities, and public parks, to alleviate the lot of the poor or the unfortunate. The concepts "social justice" and "social market economy" build on this moral mandate, as does public policy which seeks to implement objectives demanded in their name.

Discussions of the rights and duties of property owners date to antiquity. Property is so bound to considerations of human nature that the ancients still speak to us across the ages. Aristotle in his criticism of Plato's communal society recognized that private property, from an economic point of view, is more highly productive than communal ownership. Goods owned in common by a large number of people, Aristotle saw, will receive little attention since people will mainly pursue their own self-interest to the neglect of obligations they can pass off to others. Plato had argued in the *Republic* that communal ownership – or the leveling of property generally – would be conducive to peace since no one would then be envious of the other.[1] Aristotle responds to the contrary, noting that in general, living together and sharing in common all that matters is difficult, and most of all with regard to possessions.[2] To impose communal property on society, he says, would be to disregard the record of human experience. In any communal effort, human nature being what it is, some people are likely to work less than others and yet claim the same entitlement as those who work harder. Such, Aristotle held, can only lead to discontent and to fractional conflict. Aristotle also advances a moral consideration. Only private property enables one to practice the virtues of benevolence and philanthropy. Communal ownership would abolish that opportunity.

Plato and Aristotle apart, the most famous treatise on property from antiquity is that of Cicero, who begins with the observation that there is no such thing as private ownership established by nature. "Property becomes private either through long occupancy (as in the case of those who long ago settled in unoccupied territory) or through conquest (as in the case of those who took it in war), or by due process of law, bargain, or purchase, or by allotment. ... Therefore, inasmuch as in each case some of those things which by nature had been common property became the property of individuals, each one should retain possession of that which has fallen to his lot; and if anyone appropriates to himself anything beyond that, he will be violating the laws of human society."[3] Property, however acquired, Cicero notes, is increased largely by wisdom, industry, and thrift and rightly belongs to its holder. Yet, says Cicero, as Plato reminds us, we are not born to ourselves alone. Our country and our friends make claims upon us. Fellowship requires that we help one another. "In this direction we ought to follow Nature as our guide, to contribute to the general good by an interchange of acts of kindness, by giving and receiving, and thus by our skill, our industry, and our talents to cement human society more closely together, man to man."[4]

Assistance to others must be rationally grounded, he continues. "For many people often do favors impulsively for everybody without discrimination,

---

[1] Plato modifies this position somewhat in the *Laws*, when he writes, "Let the citizens at once distribute their land and houses, and not till their land in common, since a community of goods goes beyond their proposed origin, and nurture and education" [*The Dialogues of Plato, Laws*,740, trans. B. Jowett, Vol. II (New York: Random House, 1937), p. 506].

[2] Aristotle, *Politics*, 1263 a 15–16.

[3] Marcus Tullius Cicero, *On Duties*, trans. Walter Miller (Cambridge, Mass.: Harvard University Press, 1997), I, p. 21.

[4] Ibid., p. 22.

prompted by a morbid sort of benevolence or by a sudden impulse of the heart, shifting as the wind. Such acts of generosity are not to be so highly esteemed as those which are performed with judgment, deliberation, and mature considera- tion."[5]

"The man in an administrative office, however, must make it his first care that everyone shall have what belongs to him and that private citizens suffer no invasion of their property rights by act of the state."[6] "For ... it is the peculiar function of the state and the city to guarantee to every man the free and undis- turbed control of his own particular property."[7] Cicero speaks of destroyed harmony when property is taken away from one party and given to another or when officials intervene to cancel debt.

Although he speaks of the obligations of property holders, Cicero is clear that need does not create entitlement. Even so, he says, "let it [property] be made available for the use of as many as possible (if they are worthy) and be at the service of generosity and beneficence rather than sensuality and excess."[8] "Ac- quire, use, enjoy, and dispose, but rationally" is his time-transcending advice. Cicero's concept of "deserving poor" will be adopted by St. Jerome and St. Augustine and other Fathers of the Church when they speak of obligation in charity. They commonly affirm that charity to be efficacious cannot be mind- less.

Ancient theories of property cannot effortlessly serve as a guide to the for- mation of law affecting property rights today, especially intellectual property, in our age of undreamt of technological innovation. Even contemporary statu- tory law is hard pressed to resolve disputes over intellectual property rights.[9] Yet abstract discussions, ancient or contemporary, are not without conse- quence.

The idea that private property is at the root of political and economic evil is the well-known cornerstone of theories advanced by Marx and Engels. In *The Communist Manifesto*, Marx and Engels proclaim that the basis of communism as a theory may be summed up in a single sentence: abolition of private prop- erty.[10] The declared aim of Marx is the nationalization of economic assets for the common good. In a communist society, he tells us, everyone is to contribute

---

[5] Ibid., p. 49.

[6] Ibid., II, p. 73.

[7] Ibid., II, p. 78.

[8] Ibid., I, p. 92.

[9] The complexity of adjudicating law governing intellectual property is seen in *El- dred v. Ashcroft*, 537 U.S. 186 (2003) also cited below.

[10] Karl Marx and Friedrich Engels, *The Communist Manifesto* (New York: Interna- tional Publishers, 1935), pp. 42–43.

according to his abilities and receive according to his needs. From this principle, the regulation of production is a *conditio sine qua non*.

John Stuart Mill, perhaps equally as influential as Marx, infused his brand of liberalism with the same socialist goal by stressing the overriding importance of the equitable distribution of productive wealth. Many of our contemporary intellectuals find in Mill the moral authority for legislation which curtails the right of ownership in the interest of the common good.[11]

Among the twentieth-century authors who treat property exclusively in moral terms, the most influential is undoubtedly John Rawls. In *A Theory of Justice* Rawls delineates what he believes to be the principles of a well-ordered society based on "fairness."[12] He proposes to reform or abolish laws and institutions, no matter how efficient and well arranged, if they are "unjust." For Rawls, the essence of injustice is inequality. His ideal is perfect egalitarianism, a principle of equality that he applies not only to material goods but also to intelligence and inborn skills. The advantages afforded to the genetically favored ought not bring the fortunate possessor any special benefits. Why? Because they are unearned. From Rawls's moral perspective, the allocation of talents and abilities must be regarded as "arbitrary." Talents should be viewed as "a common asset," and their possessors should profit from them "only on terms that improve the situation of those who have lost out."[13] This principle was contested in an academic debate occasioned by the U.S. Supreme Court's consideration and subsequent ruling in *Eldred v. Ashcroft*.[14] The Court was asked to rule on the constitutionality of the Copyright Extension Act of 1998, which extended the limits of copyright beyond, it was contended, the constitutional specification of a limited time. The Court's ruling is a matter of record, and it is not our intent to review that ruling but to address the question: Does the larger society or community which may benefit from the productivity of an author or inventor have a just claim to the fruits of his labor. Rawls would say, yes.

Marx himself might have been shocked, for Rawls goes far beyond even the most radical of communist theorists in wishing to socialize natural talents by denying to the talented the benefits their talents bring them. Rawls rejects "equality of opportunity" as inherently unfair since it means that the less gifted orless industrious will be left behind. Efficiency must be sacrificed in the name of equality.

---

[11] John Stuart Mill, *Principles of Political Economy* (Oxford: Oxford University Press, 1994), esp. Chaps. I, II.

[12] John Rawls, *A Theory of Justice* (Cambridge, Mass.: Harvard University Press, 1971).

[13] Ibid., pp. 100–102.

[14] *Eldred v. Ashcroft*, 537 U.S. 186 (2003).

It is to be noted that entitlements to what one has earned or otherwise legally acquired have a completely different status in *A Theory of Justice* than do freedom of speech, freedom of religion, freedom of association, due process of law, and the right to vote and to hold office. Property rights are excluded from protection. Economically significant property rights are valued not as conducive to liberty but as indispensable features of an economic system which must be maintained for the benefit of all. Reliance on contract, salary agreements, the payment of interest and dividends is economically essential, but its only moral justification is the good of the whole, not an individual's entitlement to what he has earned or otherwise acquired. What the individual is entitled to is determined by the overall system. Individual property rights are merely the consequence, not the foundation, of a just economic system.

Rawls, of course is not the first in the history of political theory to take this extreme view. He acknowledges the influence of Rousseau and Hobbes, but his social view of property is more akin to that of that of Pierre Joseph Proudhon. In his famous treatise, *What is Property?* Proudhon answers his own question with the memorable declaration, "Property is theft." Proudhon reasoned, as Rawls was to reason more than a century later, "All capital, whether material or mental, being the result of collective labor, is in consequence, collective property."[15]

But is it realistic to speak of the distribution of talents and the fruit of sometimes extraordinary individual or cooperative effort as a common asset? How far should distribution go? In *The Law of Peoples*, Rawls proposes the extension of his principles of justice to the Society of Peoples under the Law of Peoples. "The Law of Peoples," he writes, "is an extension of the liberal conception of justice for a domestic regime to a Society of Peoples."[16] It is not the intent of this brief presentation to offer a detailed critique of Rawls but to suggest that a seemingly benevolent theory of justice, viewed in terms of its consequence, can lead us to utopian ideals far removed from reality. In advancing his theory of justice, Rawls ignores psychological, political, and economic realities as well as recorded history and the findings of anthropologists.

Without explicitly addressing Rawls, the French political theorist, Pierre Manent, meets Rawls's concept of a global "Society of Peoples" head on. In *Democracy without Nation?: The Fate of Self-Government in Europe*, Manent argues that the democratic nation is the irreplaceable political context for human action, the instrument of self-government, the locus for deliberation, and

---

[15] Pierre Joseph Proudhon, *Q'est-ce que la Propriété?* trans. Benjamin B. R. Tucker as *What Is Property?* (New York: H. Fertio, 1966), p. 147.

[16] John Rawls, *The Law of Peoples: With the Idea of Public Reason Revisited* (Cambridge, Mass.: Harvard University Press, 1999), p. 9.

the administration of justice.[17] He shows that after Maastricht the European Union's bureaucratic contrivances have become more and more artificial, detached from the national political bodies that formed the Union, and have taken on a life of their own. Instead of increasing self-governance, Europe's new instruments of governance shackle it ever more with each passing day, promising an indefinite extension that no one wills and no one knows how to stop. In Manent's judgment, Europe's governing classes, without explicitly saying so, hope to create a homogeneous and limitless human world. In fact, he continues, given its intellectual climate, what distinguishes Europeans from one another cannot be evaluated or even publically named. The European value that seems to trump all others is "openness to the other," a universal political creed that relegates to the private sphere religious belief and cultural identity. "We [Europeans] do not possess any particular existence," Manent writes. "We do not want to possess any shape, manner or form, a distinctive character of our own, one that would necessarily be particular."[18] To parry the threat of self-destruction, Manent is convinced that nothing is more important than to get a grip on our centuries-old development, and that means first of all that we must become fully aware of the original Christian character of our nations.

Clearly ideas advanced within the academic sector are not without consequence in the social and political order. The effect of ideologically induced welfare programs adopted in the West in the 1930s and in the post-World War II period are now being felt on both sides of the Atlantic. All such programs required immense monetary outlays that could only be attained through taxation of one form or another. The cultural historian, Richard Pipes, in his authoritative study, *Property and Freedom*, dramatically shows how modern democratic governments have become giant mechanisms for the redistribution of private assets to the disadvantage of personal freedom.[19] He shows that the United States, for example, in its desire to alleviate the lot of the poor has gone beyond that goal in its quest to "abolish poverty itself." In the pursuit of the latter objective, policy has moved from a guarantee of equality of opportunity to equality of results. Pipes dates this transformation to President Lyndon Johnson, whom he regards as the principal architect of the postwar welfare state in the United States. In an address at Howard University, June 1965, Johnson asserted, "Freedom is not enough ... we seek not just freedom but opportunity ... not just equality as a right and a theory but as a fact and as a result."[20] Pipes comments, "It is doubtful that either Johnson and his speech writers or the pub-

---

[17] Pierre Manent, *Democracy without Nations? The Fate of Self-Government in Europe*, trans. by Paul Seaton (Wilmington, Del.: ISI Books, 2009).

[18] Ibid., p. 66.

[19] Richard Pipes, *Property and Freedom* (New York: Alfred A. Knopf, 1999).

[20] As quoted by Pipes, p. 229.

lic at large had any inkling of what a break with the Western tradition these words represented. Social equality can be attained, if at all, only by coercion that is at the expense of liberty. It necessarily requires the violation of property rights of those citizens who possess more wealth or enjoy higher societal status than the majority. Once the elimination of poverty becomes a state objective, the state is bound to treat property not as a fundamental right, which is its supreme obligation to protect, but as an obstacle to social justice."[21] Pipes goes on to point out that "Liberty is by its nature inegalitarian, because living creatures differ in strength, intelligence, ambition, courage, perseverance and all else that makes for success."[22]

Economic historians tell us that those countries that have provided the firmest guarantees of economic independence, especially property rights, are virtually without exception the richest. For most economic historians the determinant of economic growth lies in the legal institutions which ensure to enterprising individuals the fruits of their labors. European history suggests that the rise of the West to the position of global economic preeminence lies in the institution of private property.[23]

Romantic appeals to the common good, such as those of Mill and Rawls, may be fruitful under some conditions, but absent a sense of community, they are dangerous. As Richard Pipes reminds us, when one appeals to a common good separate from and superior to the private goods of individuals, the function of government (be it that of a legislative, executive, or judiciary body) becomes one of conflict management. Given our litigious society, opposing parties are likely to press for state-awarded privileges, bargaining and negotiating for advantage. Under such conditions the state is not likely to represent a common will, but rather it becomes the object of adversarial wills. Thus positioned, the state serves not by defining goals which members of society ought collectively to pursue but by removing obstacles to goods privately defined. The common good becomes the result of negotiations between private political actors. Such a situation can only lead to social and economic disaster. A compliant or weak judiciary is apt to rule in the light of a supposed common good against an individual claimant, perhaps settling the dispute but undermining other fundamental rights.

The issue before us remains: What claim does society have on the individual? Ancient notions of human nature are the foundation of the common law

---

[21] Ibid., p. 229.

[22] Ibid., p. 283.

[23] Cf. Douglas North and E. P. Thomas, *The Rise of the Western World* (Cambridge, Mass.: Cambridge University Press, 1973); Douglas North, *Structure and Change in Economic History* (New York: Norton, 1981); Tom Bethel, *The Noblest Triumph* (New York: St. Martin's Press, 1998.

tradition assumed in the English-speaking world, a tradition that informed the documents associated with the American founding. The U.S. Constitution took for granted that the right to private property is a condition of liberty. It was taken as evident that property rights adhere not only to the individual but also to the individual in his collective arrangements. If a man is entitled to the fruit of his labor, a corporation is entitled to the fruit of its investment. Apart from the judgment rendered by the Supreme Court in *Eldred v. Ashcroft*,[24] cited above, one is brought to the conclusion that Article 1, Section 8 of the U.S. Constitution had it right when it declared its purpose "... to promote the progress of science and the useful arts, by securing for limited times to authors and inventors the exclusive rights to their respective writings and discoveries." The Constitution provides a prudential balance between the protection of property rights and social claims. There may always be a tension between property rights and reasonable communal claims. Resolution in the practical order cannot avoid an appeal to an undergirding philosophy of human nature. Ultimately the conflict may be between the common-sense philosophy of Aristotle and the Stoics and that of Karl Marx and others of the Enlightenment period.

Summary

Attitudes with respect to the acquisitions, use, and protection of property are but a manifestation of an unexpressed philosophy of human nature. It goes without saying that absent personal property, be it real, intellectual, or monetary, one's scope of action is limited or nonexistent. But there is a deeper aspect to the holding of property that begs to be acknowledged. Ownership is closely tied to one's personal identity. A person is often known by his holdings, by the land that he owns, by the real estate or personal wealth that he has accumulated, and by the use he makes of it.

Zusammenfassung

Die Einstellungen zum Erwerb, zur Nutzung und zum Schutz des Eigentums deuten auf eine zugrunde liegende Philosophie der menschlichen Natur hin. Jedem leuchtet ein, dass das Fehlen von Eigentum, seien es materielle oder geistige Güter oder Geldvermögen, den Handlungsspielraum begrenzt oder versperrt. Aber es gibt noch eine tiefere Perspektive des Eigentums, die beachtet werden muss. Besitz ist eng verknüpft mit der persönlichen Identität. Man erkennt eine Person häufig an dem, was sie besitzt, sei es Land, das ihr gehört, sei es Grundbesitz oder Vermögen, das sie angesammelt hat, aber auch an der Art und Weise, wie sie davon Gebrauch macht.

---

[24] *Eldred v. Ashcroft*, 537 U.S. 186 (2003).

Der innere Zusammenhang
zwischen Freiheit und Eigentum

Von Anton Rauscher

Karl Marx war nicht der erste und auch nicht der letzte, der im Eigentum die Ursünde der Menschheit diagnostizierte und der von der Vergemeinschaftung des Eigentums die Überwindung aller sozialen Übel in der Welt erwartete. Auf dieser Linie liegt auch das soeben in deutscher Übersetzung erschienene Schulden-Buch von David Graeber. Der in London lehrende amerikanische Anthropologe ist ein bekannter Globalisierungskritiker und Ideengeber der Occupy-Bewegung.[1] Graeber will die Schuldknechtschaft überwinden, die im Zuge des Wirtschaftsliberalismus entstanden sei, wonach der Mensch von Natur aus ein am Eigennutzen interessiertes Wesen sei. Markt und Geld seien zerstörerisch, wohingegen die Menschen ursprünglich in einem Naturzustand lebten, in dem allen alles gehörte. Bedeutsam für unser Thema ist die Einschätzung bei Graeber, das römische Eigentumsrecht und der zugehörige Freiheitsbegriff seien für die Übertragung der Grundidee einer Schuldenwirtschaft in allgemeine Rechtssätze verantwortlich. Der „Individualismus" des römischen Rechts, Freiheit als Bindungslosigkeit, Eigentum als Egoismus zu denken, sei die rechtliche Fassung von Sklaverei. Der Kapitalismus sei die Ursache für die Bindungslosigkeit des Menschen und habe die Gewaltbereitschaft entfesselt.

I. Eigentum als soziale Grundregel

Älter als alle Theorieansätze über die Entstehung des Eigentums sind die Erfahrungen, wie die Menschen mit den Gütern, die die Natur bietet, umgehen, worüber die Kulturgeschichte der Menschheit Aufschluss gibt. In allen Sprachen, die uns bekannt sind, findet sich die Unterscheidung zwischen „Mein" und „Dein". Noch aufschlussreicher ist der ebenfalls in allen Kulturen vorfindbare Begriff des „Diebstahls", der bestraft wird. Diese Redewendungen setzen voraus, dass nicht allen alles gehört, sondern dass es Eigentum gibt – Güter, über die der Eigentümer verfügen kann. Dieses Kulturphänomen, das auch in

---

[1] Eine aufschlussreiche Rezension des Buches hat *Werner Plumpe* veröffentlicht: Schuldsklaven sind wir alle!, in: Frankfurter Allgemeine Zeitung, Nr. 114, 16. Mai 2012, S. 30.

vorgeschichtlichen Lebensverhältnissen anzutreffen ist, deutet darauf hin, dass Eigentum nicht ein zufälliges Ergebnis der Evolution, auch nicht von Machtkonstellationen oder von rechtlichen Fixierungen einer individualistischen beziehungsweise egoistischen Perspektive, sondern in der Natur des Menschen selbst angelegt ist. Diesem Befund entspricht auch das siebte Gebot des Dekalogs in der jüdisch-christlichen Tradition: „Du sollst nicht stehlen!" Es handelt sich um eine soziale Grundregel, die längst vor der Ausbildung des römischen Rechts im Bewusstsein der Menschen lebendig war.

Die Bildung von Eigentum hängt mit der Bedingtheit und Abhängigkeit des Menschen als Leib-Geist-Wesen von der Nutzung der materiellen Güter zusammen, um leben und sich entfalten zu können. Die Tatsache, dass alle Menschen auf die Nutzung der materiellen Güter angewiesen sind, die Natur selbst aber diese nicht den einzelnen Menschen zugewiesen hat, ließ schon früh die Einsicht aufkommen, dass die Erde mit ihren Gütern allen Menschen, denen Gott das Leben schenkt, anvertraut ist. Kein Mensch darf von ihrer Nutzung ausgeschlossen werden; im Gegenteil: die Menschen müssen dafür Sorge tragen, dass alle Menschen Zugang zu diesen Gütern haben. Auch müssen die Erdengüter so gebraucht werden, dass davon auch die künftigen Generationen leben können.

In der nur dünn besiedelten Agrargesellschaft waren die Besitzverhältnisse, die sich in weiten Teilen Europas herausgebildet hatten, unangefochten, auch wenn es immer wieder zu kleineren oder größeren Streitigkeiten kam. Im Übrigen war der Zusammenhalt in den Großfamilien so eng, dass von einem „individualistischen" Eigentumsverständnis nicht die Rede sein kann. Dies änderte sich in der Epoche des Umbruchs von der Agrar- zur Industriegesellschaft und vom Ständestaat zum Rechtsstaat und zur Demokratie. Die Französische Revolution proklamierte das Privateigentum als ein heiliges und unantastbares Recht; der Eigentümer konnte mit seinem Eigentum nach Belieben verfahren. Mit der „Bauernbefreiung" entfielen alle bisherigen sozialen Bindungen und Abgaben, die mit dem Landbesitz verbunden waren.

Nicht minder gravierend war, dass mit der Beseitigung der ständischen Ordnung auch der Gesellschaftsvertrag, der zwischen dem Handwerksmeister und seinen Gesellen bestand, rasch an Bedeutung verlor. Ähnlich wie die Großfamilie auf dem Land bot der Gesellschaftsvertrag das, was man heute soziale Sicherheit nennt. Die Arbeiter, die vom Land in die Stadt zogen und in den überall entstehenden Fabriken Arbeit und Brot suchten, erhielten keinen Gesellschaftsvertrag mehr. Es gab zunächst auch keinen „Arbeitsvertrag", sondern nur eine jeweils mündlich vereinbarte Einstellung. Erst nach Bildung von Gewerkschaften setzte sich allmählich der Arbeitsvertrag durch.

Der Lohn, den die Arbeiter erhielten, bildete sich am Arbeitsmarkt nach dem Gesetz von Angebot und Nachfrage. Je größer das Angebot an Arbeit war, umso geringer der Lohn. Ob er ausreichte, den Unterhalt des Arbeiters und seiner Familie zu sichern und für die Wechselfälle des Lebens vorzusorgen, das interessierte den Fabrikherrn nicht. Das Privateigentum ohne jede soziale Verpflichtung und Bindung und die Verelendung eines wachsenden Teils der Arbeiter waren der Nährboden für Sozialisten und Kommunisten, die die Abschaffung des Privateigentums forderten.

Als sich in den frühen Industriezentren die Gegensätze zwischen den Fabrikherren und den Arbeitern verschärften, entstanden zwei Gegenbewegungen: auf der einen Seite die christlich-soziale Bewegung, auf der anderen Seite die Sozialisten. Im Mittelpunkt der Auseinandersetzungen stand das Privateigentum. Papst Leo XIII. erkannte, dass die Kirche, die seit der Französischen Revolution ins gesellschaftliche, kulturelle und politische Abseits geraten war, nicht schweigen dürfe, sondern zu der immer drängender werdenden sozialen Frage Stellung beziehen müsse. 1891 erschien die erste Sozialenzyklika *Rerum novarum*, in der der Papst auch zur Frage des Privateigentums Stellung nahm. In Fortführung der christlichen Tradition erklärte er: „Daß aber Gott der Herr die Erde dem ganzen Menschengeschlecht zum Gebrauch und zur Nutznießung übergeben hat, dies steht durchaus nicht dem Sonderbesitz entgegen. Denn Gott hat die Erde nicht in dem Sinne der Gesamtheit überlassen, als sollten alle ohne Unterschied Herren über dieselbe sein, sondern insofern, als er selbst keinem Menschen einen besonderen Teil derselben zum Besitze angewiesen, vielmehr dem Fleiße der Menschen und den von den Völkern zu treffenden Einrichtungen die Ordnung der Eigentumsverhältnisse unter ihnen anheimgegeben hat. Übrigens wie immer unter die einzelnen verteilt, hört der Erdboden nicht auf, der Gesamtheit zu dienen, denn es gibt keinen Menschen, der nicht von dessen Erträgnis lebt" (Nr. 7). Der Papst knüpft an die christliche Tradition der Gemeinbestimmung der Erdengüter an, verteidigt aber das „Sondereigentum", weil die Nutzung der Erdengüter vom „Fleiß", also von der Arbeitsleistung abhängt. Der Arbeiter soll einen Lohn erhalten, der es ihm ermöglicht, „Eigentum" zu bilden und dadurch für sich und seine Familie vorzusorgen (Nr. 4).[2]

Liegt in dieser Sichtweise nicht ein innerer Dissens vor? Entspricht der Gemeinbestimmung der Erdengüter nicht eher eine Gemeineigentumsordnung denn eine Privateigentumsordnung, wie sie manche Strömungen in der Gesellschaft und auch in der Kirche heute noch anstreben? Der Schlüssel, um diese Frage zu klären, liegt in dem Begriff „Erdengüter". Er erweckt den Eindruck,

---

[2] *Leo XIII.*, Rerum novarum (1891). – Diese Position der Kirche in Fragen des Eigentums wurde seither von den Päpsten und vom Zweiten Vatikanischen Konzil wiederholt und präzisiert: *Pius XI.*, Quadragesimo anno (1931), Nr. 45; *Johannes XXIII.*, Mater et magistra (1961), Nr. 104 ff.; Pastoralkonstitution Gaudium et spes (1965), Nr. 69 und 71; *Paul VI.*, Populorum progressio (1967), Nr. 22 ff.; *Johannes Paul II.*, Laborem exercens (1981), Nr. 14; Centesimus annus (1991), Nr. 30 ff.

als ob die Güter, wie sie die Natur bietet, schon in der Quantität und Qualität zur Verfügung stehen, wie sie die Menschen brauchen. Er verdeckt den Tatbestand, dass es sich bei den Erdengütern vornehmlich um natürliche Ressourcen handelt, aus denen erst durch Arbeit und Bearbeitung Güter werden, wie sie die Menschen zum Unterhalt ihres Lebens und zum Aufbau von Kultur benötigen. Wenn heute nicht wenige Menschen in den oft noch weit zurückhängenden Entwicklungsländern über das Fernsehen erfahren, wie gut viele Menschen in den fortgeschrittenen Industrieländern leben, und wenn ihnen niemand erklärt, dass der Wohlstand eines Landes in erster Linie das Ergebnis von harter und qualifizierter Arbeit ist, kann sich leicht eine verhängnisvolle Ideologie einschleichen: Wir sind arm, weil die anderen reich sind. Inzwischen haben eine Reihe von Entwicklungsländern große Fortschritte gemacht im Aufbau von leistungsfähigen Marktwirtschaften. Genannt seien die sogenannten Schwellenländer in Asien (Korea, Singapur, Indonesien) und Lateinamerika (Brasilien). Dass sich dieser Prozess nicht von heute auf morgen vollzieht, sondern nur allmählich vorankommt, hängt von vielen Voraussetzungen ab. Im Übrigen sind die Ressourcen, wie sie die Natur liefert, auf der Erde höchst unterschiedlich verteilt. Einen Ausgleich können nur ein leistungsfähiges Transportwesen sowie die Produktion von künstlichen Rohstoffen schaffen. Am schwierigsten ist es, die Menschen durch Bildung für ihre Aufgaben vorzubereiten, vor allem dann, wenn sie bisher nicht durch eine Hochkultur geformt sind.

Mit der Arbeit kommt der Mensch ins Spiel und damit die Frage, wer über das Ergebnis der Arbeit verfügen kann und wie es genutzt werden soll. Wem gehören die Früchte der Arbeit? In der Agrargesellschaft stellte sich diese Frage nicht nur für die Arbeit auf den Feldern und Wiesen und in den Wäldern, sondern auch für das Wohnen, für die Viehhaltung und das Zusammenleben. Der Besitzer eines Stück Landes entschied darüber, wie der Ertrag genutzt werden soll, welcher Teil der Früchte für den Konsum zur Verfügung stehen und welcher Teil investiv genützt beziehungsweise für die Wechselfälle des Lebens gespart werden soll. Diese Entscheidungen waren in aller Regel nicht vom Egoismus gesteuert, sondern von der Kenntnis und Einsicht in die gegebenen Möglichkeiten und von der Verantwortung für die (Groß-)Familie, von der das Überleben und die weitere Entwicklung abhingen. Auch das römische Eigentumsrecht war in diesen sozialen Bezugsrahmen eingebettet.

Auch wenn der Grundbesitz das Rückgrat in der Agrargesellschaft bildete und die Zuständigkeiten für die Bewirtschaftung des Bodens regelte, gab es auch Formen von Gemeineigentum, wo Wiesen und Ländereien gemeinsam bestellt und der Ertrag geteilt wurde. Die Großfamilie war nicht nur ein Erwerbsbetrieb, sondern zugleich eine Institution der sozialen Sicherheit. Auch die Infrastruktur der damaligen Besiedelung wurde von allen Dorfbewohnern getragen. Es gab gemeinsam genutzte Häuser und Räume, für die nicht selten eine „Stiftung" zuständig war. Kirchen und Kathedralen sind zu einem erheblichen

Teil nicht von den Regierenden, sondern vom Volk erbaut worden. Die Abgaben an die Fürsten und die Belastungen, wie etwa der „Zehnte" an die Kirche oder an die Klöster, waren keineswegs Mittel der Ausbeutung. Die Regierenden sollten für Recht und Ordnung sorgen, die Kirche für ein Grundmaß an kultureller Bildung und für die Bedürftigen. Aber diese Formen sozialer Tätigkeit und Verantwortung setzten die Grundstruktur des Eigentums voraus.

II. Die Entdeckung des Individuums

Eine ganz neue Situation, die vor allem die Sichtweise des Eigentums verändern sollte, kündigte sich seit dem späten Mittelalter an. Neben dem Grundbesitz und dem verbreiteten Naturaltausch gewann das Geld als Tauschmittel und für produktive Verwendung an Bedeutung. Mit dem Ende der Agrargesellschaft und der Entwicklung der Industriegesellschaft, die auf der Arbeitsteilung und auf den Produktionsfaktoren Arbeit, Kapital und Boden aufbaute, erhielt das Geld und in Sonderheit das Eigentum an Produktionsmitteln eine bisher nicht gekannte Dominanz für die Wirtschaft und für alle Lebensbereiche.

Es kam zur Aufhebung der bisherigen sozialen Bindungen und Abgaben auf Grund und Boden („Bauernbefreiung"). Der Bauer konnte jetzt größere oder kleinere Teile seines Besitzes verkaufen, wenn er wollte. Desgleichen wurde die Zunftordnung, die die sozialen Verhältnisse des Handwerks regelte und in die Gesellschaft einpasste, obsolet. Die Französische Revolution verkündete die völlige Freiheit des Eigentums, das jetzt zum *Privat*eigentum generierte. Das Recht auf Eigentum wurde als „heilig" und unantastbar proklamiert. „Eigentum macht frei", hieß ein anderer Slogan. Gewiss: Der Bauer und auch der Handwerksbesitzer waren auch bisher frei, wie sie ihren Grund und Boden nutzten und wie sie die Nachfrage nach handwerklichen Erzeugnissen befriedigten. Wenn sie erfolgreich wirtschafteten, konnten sie ihr Vermögen mehren. Was jetzt anders wurde, war die „Geldherrschaft" und die wachsende Bedeutung der Märkte, auf denen Angebot und Nachfrage die Preise bestimmten. Der Eigentümer konnte mit seinem Eigentum tun und lassen, wie es ihm beliebte, ohne irgendwelche Rücksichten und Bindungen sozialer Art berücksichtigen zu müssen.

Man kann nachvollziehen, dass die Beseitigung der vielen Auflagen und Abgaben, die auf dem Eigentum lasteten, eine Epoche einläutete, in der „die Freiheit von" als die Errungenschaft schlechthin erfahren wurde. Dabei darf man nicht übersehen, dass es zunächst nur wenige waren, die von dieser „Freiheit von" Gebrauch machten. Vor allem die Großfamilien auf dem Lande blieben noch lange den bisherigen Gewohnheiten verbunden und waren auch für diejenigen, die als Industriearbeiter in den rasch wachsenden Städten ihren Lebensunterhalt verdienten, noch lange ein Ort der Zuflucht.

Die Weltanschauung des Liberalismus, der sich im 19. Jahrhundert in ganz Europa durchsetzte, war von der Aufklärung stark beeinflusst. Im Mittelpunkt steht jetzt das „Individuum", das sich selbst genügt und seine Interessen verfolgt. Die bisherigen sozialen Bindungen gelten nicht mehr als eine Erweiterung des individuellen Aktionsradius, sondern als eine von außen auferlegte, die Freiheit des Einzelnen einschränkende Abhängigkeit und damit als Hindernis für den Fortschritt. Die Gesellschaft erweist sich als die Summe von Individuen, denen es freisteht, ob sie sich zusammentun und gemeinsam handeln wollen oder nicht. Je mehr jeder Einzelne seine eigenen Interessen verwirklicht, umso mehr – so dachte man – profitiert davon auch die Gesellschaft. Das „Gemeinwohl" setzt sich zusammen aus dem Wohl der Individuen. Damit das Ganze nicht auseinanderfällt, dafür hat der Staat zu sorgen, der für Recht und Ordnung zuständig ist.

Die Entdeckung des Individuums in der liberalen Weltsicht kontrastierte mit der christlich-mittelalterlichen Deutung des Verhältnisses von Einzelmensch und Gemeinschaft. In der Scholastik folgte man weitgehend den Überlegungen, die schon in der griechischen Philosophie über die Fragen nach dem Verhältnis von Einzelmensch und Gemeinschaft entwickelt worden waren. Man ging von der natura humana aus, an der alle Menschen teilhaben. Der Einzelne entsteht durch die Individuation der natura humana. Alle Menschen zusammen bilden – im Sinne Platons – den „großen Menschen". Mithin erweist sich die Sozialität des Menschen als Teilhabe an der gemeinsamen Menschennatur.[3] Hierin liegt auch die Begründung für den Vorrang des Gemeinwohls vor dem Einzelwohl, auch wenn die Scholastik an dem Eigenwert jedes Menschen unbeirrt festhielt.

In diesem Zusammenhang sei daran erinnert, dass sich die christliche Theologie, die sich seit dem Ersten Ökumenischen Konzil im Jahre 325 entwickelte, nicht in dieses Denkschema einordnen lässt. Um nämlich die Widerspruchsfreiheit der Glaubensgeheimnisse des Dreieinigen Gottes und des Mensch gewordenen Sohnes Gottes, der zugleich wahrer Mensch und wahrer Gott ist, zu klären, bediente man sich nicht des Begriffs der Individuation, sondern des Begriffs der Person. Während das Individuum das Teilhafte betont, ist es bei der Person die Vollkommenheit. An einer markanten Stelle spricht Thomas von Aquin vom Menschen als Person und sagt, sie sei „perfectissimum in tota natu-

---

[3] Diese Erklärung der Sozialität war in der Antike und auch noch im Mittelalter naheliegend, weil der einzelne Mensch sehr viel stärker von der Gemeinschaft abhing. Diese Sichtweise wird noch spürbar bei *Eberhard Welty*, Gemeinschaft und Einzelmensch. Eine sozial-metaphysische Untersuchung, Salzburg u. a. 1935. Dieser Ansatz dürfte auch der Grund dafür gewesen sein, dass die Menschenrechte erst seit der Französischen Revolution eine größere Bedeutung erfuhren.

ra"[4]. In der spanischen Spätscholastik war es der Jesuitengelehrte Francesco Suarez, der von der Personalität des Menschen ausging. Für die Kirche, die in verschiedenen Bereichen mit der liberalen Weltanschauung in Konflikt geriet, wäre es leichter gewesen, eine Brücke zu dem neuen Selbstverständnis des Menschen in der Moderne zu schlagen, wenn sie in ihrer Anthropologie und Sozialethik den personalen Grund ihres Denkens über den Menschen herausgearbeitet hätte.

Was nun den Zusammenhang von Eigentum und Freiheit betrifft, so muss berücksichtigt werden, dass in der mittelalterlichen Gesellschaft die Entfaltungsmöglichkeiten des Einzelnen bescheiden waren. Mit Ausnahme des kirchlichen Lebens gab es wenige Aufstiegsmöglichkeiten in der damaligen stationären Gesellschaft. Das Sprichwort „Schuster bleib bei deinem Leisten" ist dafür kennzeichnend. Erst in der modernen Gesellschaft wuchsen die Freiheitsräume sowohl für die Großfamilien als auch für die Einzelnen. Man konnte sein Vermögen und seinen Besitz dort einsetzen, wo der größtmögliche Erfolg zu erreichen war. Die Arbeitsteilung, die Verselbständigung der Produktionsfaktoren Arbeit, Kapital und Boden und die sich ausweitende Geldwirtschaft, dazu die neuen Möglichkeiten der Bildung, der Mobilität und der Kommunikation haben die Freiheitsräume enorm erweitert. Noch bedeutsamer ist die Tatsache, dass die Menschen ihre Ideen verwirklichen können, auch wenn ihnen die dafür nötigen Eigenmittel fehlen. Sie können bei den Sparkassen und Banken Kredite aufnehmen, um ihre Erfindungen und Verbesserungen umsetzen zu können.

III. Der Streit um das Privateigentum

Das individualistische Credo bestimmte auch das Denken von Adam Smith, des Begründers der Nationalökonomie, und der sogenannten Klassiker. Sie waren fasziniert von den Möglichkeiten der schnell wachsenden Industriegesellschaft. Zwar hielten sie daran fest, dass die Arbeit der entscheidende Produktionsfaktor ist; aber ihr Interesse galt vornehmlich dem Faktor Kapital, der die Produktivität enorm steigerte. Die Märkte waren der Ort, an dem sich die Preisbildung zwischen Angebot und Nachfrage der Güter und Dienste vollzog. Die Wissenschaftler waren ebenso wie die Anhänger des weltanschaulichen Liberalismus davon überzeugt, dass es zum ersten Mal in der Geschichte der Menschheit gelingen werde, Armut und Elend zu überwinden.

Anstelle des erhofften Fortschritts und des Wohlstandes sollte es ganz anders kommen. Die „soziale Frage" erschütterte die Industrieländer Europas. Die

---

[4] Zur thomistischen Anthropologie vgl. *Leo J. Elders*, Die Naturphilosophie des Thomas von Aquin (Schriftenreihe der Gustav-Siewerth-Akademie, Bd. 17), Weilheim-Bierbronnen 2004, S. 296 f.

Verelendung großer Teile der Arbeiterschaft und die Klassenspaltung der Gesellschaft in Kapitalisten und Proletarier lösten soziale Revolutionen aus. Die Angriffe von sozialistischer Seite konzentrierten sich auf das Privateigentum. War es beim französischen Sozialkritiker Joseph Pierre Proudhon noch der Protest gegen die Ungerechtigkeit der liberal-kapitalistischen Wirtschaftsordnung, auf die er sein Wort „Eigentum ist Diebstahl" münzte, so war für Karl Marx das Privateigentum die Quelle allen Übels schlechthin. Es bewirke Ungleichheit und Abhängigkeiten, Ausbeutung und Unterdrückung. Es verhindere eine menschenwürdige Sozialordnung, worin, wie es im Kommunistischen Manifest heißt, „die freie Entwicklung eines jeden die Bedingung für die freie Entwicklung aller ist".

Im Kern entzündete sich die soziale Frage nicht an dem Unterschied zwischen Arm und Reich. Schon im Evangelium heißt es: Arme werdet ihr immer bei euch haben. Der Stein des Anstoßes war, dass die Arbeiter schwer arbeiten mussten und trotzdem einen Hungerlohn erhielten, der nicht ausreichte, den notwendigen Unterhalt für den Arbeiter und seine Familie zu sichern. Auf der anderen Seite waren die Kapitalisten oder Couponabschneider, wie Karl Marx sie verächtlich nannte, die den Arbeitern den ihnen gehörigen Lohn vorenthielten. Was in dieser Perspektive nicht in den Blick kam, war die Notwendigkeit, einerseits gerechte Löhne zu zahlen und andererseits die erforderlichen Investitionen zu finanzieren. Das Privateigentum, das nur noch Reichtum repräsentiert, aber nicht mehr sinnvoll für den Lebensunterhalt und für die wirtschaftliche Entwicklung eingesetzt wird, verliert seine Legitimation.

Was sollte die Kirche in dieser Situation tun, die seit der Französischen Revolution und dem Ende des Heiligen Römischen Reiches deutscher Nation (1806) viel von ihrer früheren kultur- und gesellschaftsprägenden Kraft verloren hatte? Es waren die Laien, die sich in Deutschland, aber auch in anderen europäischen Ländern in der christlich-sozialen Bewegung zusammenfanden und sachgerechte Antworten auf die soziale Frage suchten. Sie wurden ermutigt durch das Engagement des Mainzer Bischofs Wilhelm Emmanuel von Ketteler[5] und von Papst Leo XIII., der 1891 die erste Sozialenzyklika *Rerum novarum* verkündete. Beide wandten sich gegen das individualistische Verständnis des Privateigentums, ebenso gegen die sozialistisch-revolutionäre Forderung nach Abschaffung des Privateigentums, wodurch die Lage der Arbeiter nur verschlimmert würde. Lange Zeit stand die Kirche mit dieser Position allein, da die Wirtschaftswissenschaften in den Sog der Diskussion um die „Wertfreiheit" gerieten. Es ging nicht mehr um Ordnung der Wirtschaft, sondern nur noch um ihre Funktionalität.

---

[5] Dazu *Anton Rauscher / Lothar Roos*, Die soziale Verantwortung der Kirche. Wege und Erfahrungen von Ketteler bis heute, Köln ²1979.

Inzwischen hat die katholische Sozialwissenschaft die naturrechtliche Sicht des Eigentums, seine Begründung und Reichweite herausgearbeitet. Ausgangspunkt ist nach wie vor die Gemeinbestimmung der Erdengüter. Da aber die Güter und Dienste, auf die die Menschen angewiesen sind, erarbeitet und bereitgestellt werden müssen, dies aber mit Mühe und Anstrengung verbunden ist, hängt die ausreichende Versorgung der Menschen davon ab, unter welchen Bedingungen die Menschen bereit sind, die notwendige Arbeitsleistung zu erbringen. Das kommunistische System in Osteuropa ist nicht zuletzt daran gescheitert, dass der Ansporn zur Arbeit, insbesondere zu qualifizierter Arbeit, fehlte und die Betriebe von staatlich eingesetzten Funktionären verwaltet wurden. Auch eine hoch technisierte Wirtschaft wird nur dann den erwarteten Ertrag bringen, wenn der entscheidende Produktionsfaktor, nämlich die Arbeit, und zwar die qualifizierte Arbeit, die Maschinen in Bewegung hält. Und auch die Leistung des Unternehmers wurde lange Zeit nicht erkannt und nicht richtig eingeschätzt.

IV. Ohne Privateigentum keine Freiheit

Was den Zusammenhang von Eigentum und Freiheit betrifft, so ist in der katholischen Soziallehre die Klärung bedeutsam, die die Gesellschaftsauffassung des christlichen Solidarismus mit sich brachte. Die überkommene Denkweise, wonach die Sozialität des Menschen als individuelle Teilhabe an der natura humana erklärt wurde, war hinreichend für eine Zeit, in der die Abhängigkeit des Einzelnen von der Gemeinschaft eine sehr viel größere Rolle spielte als in der Moderne. Zwar ist die Verankerung des Einzelnen in Familie, Gesellschaft und Staat geblieben, aber der Einzelne besitzt jetzt sehr viel größere Freiräume für die Gestaltung seines Lebens und der sozialen Verhältnisse. Was der Liberalismus richtig erkannt hat, ist die Subjektstellung des Individuums. Hier hat die Kirche viel zu lang an dem im Mittelalter vertretenen Modell des Menschen als Teil der Menschheitsfamilie festgehalten. Dies hat auch dazu geführt, dass das Gemeinwohl auch in allen Bereichen über dem Einzelwohl stand und die Idee der Menschenrechte nicht aufkommen konnte. Leider konnten sich die Ansätze, wie sie in der spanischen Spätscholastik vor allem von dem Jesuiten Suarez in die Diskussion eingebracht wurden, nicht durchsetzen. Man kann Suarez als Vorläufer des Solidarismus bezeichnen. Allerdings ist die Gesellschaft nicht eine Summe von Individuen. Der Solidarismus geht aus vom Menschen als Person und erklärt die Sozialität nicht als Ergänzung dessen, was dem Einzelnen fehlt, sondern als Offenheit für den Mitmenschen, als Mitteilung der eigenen Seinsfülle. Die Menschen sind Partner in der Verwirklichung der gemeinsamen Ziele und Zwecke in solidarischer Verbundenheit. Dies kommt in der Formulierung zum Ausdruck, die auf Gustav Gundlach zurückgeht und die Papst Pius XII. in seine Sozialverkündigung übernahm: Die menschliche Person ist Ursprung, Träger und Ziel allen gesellschaftlichen Lebens.[6] Konsequent ging Pius XII. davon aus, dass die personale Würde jedes Menschen Kernbestandteil des Gemeinwohls ist und niemals dem Gemeinwohl geopfert werden darf. Totalitäre Systeme haben sich zu Unrecht auf das Gemeinwohl berufen. Jeder Mensch hat von Natur aus ein ursprüngliches Nutzungsrecht an den Gütern der Erde. Aber erst das Recht auf Eigentum gibt dem Menschen die sichere Grundlage, in Freiheit über die Früchte seiner Arbeit zu verfügen und seinen sittlichen Pflichten, sowohl den individuellen als auch den sozialen, nachzukommen.

Zum Personsein gehören Freiheit und Selbstbestimmung. Für eine biologische Lebensfristung genügte die bloße Nutzung der Güter, wie dies bei den Tieren der Fall ist. Der Mensch ist jedoch mehr und etwas anderes als ein biologisches Lebewesen. Er bedarf der rechtlichen Verfügung über die in seinem Eigentum stehenden Güter. Das Privateigentum verleiht ihm die notwendige Unabhängigkeit und Freiheit, um sein Leben selbst zu gestalten. Papst Pius XII., in dessen Pontifikat die totalitären Machtsysteme des Kommunismus und des Nationalsozialismus/Faschismus aufeinanderprallten, äußerte sich sehr pointiert zu den Kernfragen der gesellschaftlichen Ordnung. In diesem Zusammenhang muss auch seine Lehre über das Eigentum gesehen werden: „Das naturgegebene Nutzungsrecht an den Erdengütern steht in engster Beziehung zur Persönlichkeitswürde und zu den Persönlichkeitsrechten des Menschen. Es gibt mit den genannten Auswirkungen dem Menschen die sichere materielle Grundlage, die ihm für die Erfüllung seiner sittlichen Pflichten von höchster Bedeutung ist. Denn durch die Wahrung jenes Nutzungsrechts wird der Mensch instand gesetzt, in rechtmäßiger Freiheit jenen Bereich dauernder Obliegenheiten und Entscheidungen auszufüllen, für den er unmittelbar vor dem Schöpfer verantwortlich ist."[7] An anderer Stelle betont Pius XII.: Die Anerkennung des Privateigentums „steht und fällt mit der Anerkennung der persönlichen Würde des Menschen, mit der Anerkennung der unveräußerlichen Rechte und Pflichten, die der freien Persönlichkeit unzertrennbar innewohnen und die sie von Gott empfangen hat. Nur wer dem Menschen die Würde der freien Persönlichkeit abspricht, kann die Möglichkeit zugeben, daß das Recht auf Privateigentum (und folglich auch das Privateigentum selbst) durch irgendein System von ge-

---

[6] *Pius XII.*, Radiobotschaft vom 24. Dezember 1942, in: Arthur-Fridolin Utz / Joseph-Fulko Groner (Hrsg.), Aufbau und Entfaltung des gesellschaftlichen Lebens. Soziale Summe Pius XII., Bd. I, Freiburg (Schweiz) ²1954, Nr. 227. – Dazu *Anton Rauscher*, Die soziale Natur des Menschen, in: ders. (Hrsg.), Handbuch der Katholischen Soziallehre, Berlin 2008, S. 25 ff.

[7] *Pius XII.*, Radiobotschaft vom 1. Juni 1941, in: Utz / Groner, Nr. 507. – Zu dieser Aussage des Papstes vgl. *Gustav Gundlach*, Die Ordnung der menschlichen Gesellschaft, Bd. 1, Köln 1964, S. 493–511.

setzlichen Versicherungen oder Garantien des öffentlichen Rechts abgelöst wird."[8]

Markant äußerte sich auch Papst Johannes XXIII.: „Sowohl die Erfahrung wie die geschichtliche Wirklichkeit bestätigen es: wo das politische Regime dem einzelnen das Privateigentum auch an Produktionsmitteln nicht gestattet, dort wird auch die Ausübung der menschlichen Freiheit in wesentlichen Dingen eingeschränkt oder ganz aufgehoben."[9] Das Zweite Vatikanische Konzil erklärte: „Privateigentum und ein gewisses Maß an Verfügungsmacht über äußere Güter vermitteln den unbedingt nötigen Raum für eigenverantwortliche Gestaltung des persönlichen Lebens jedes einzelnen und seiner Familie; sie müssen als eine Art Verlängerung der menschlichen Freiheit betrachtet werden; auch spornen sie an zur Übernahme von Aufgaben und Verantwortung; damit zählen sie zu den Voraussetzungen staatsbürgerlicher Freiheit."[10]

Papst Johannes Paul II., der den Kommunismus am eigenen Leib erfahren hat, betont in der Sozialenzyklika *Centesimus annus* (1991): „Der Mensch, der gar nichts hat, was er ‚sein eigen' nennen kann, und jeder Möglichkeit entbehrt, sich durch eigene Initiative seinen Lebensunterhalt zu verdienen, wird völlig abhängig von den gesellschaftlichen Mechanismen und von denen, die sie kontrollieren. Es wird dem Menschen äußerst schwer, seine Würde als Person zu erkennen" (Nr. 13).

Im kommunistischen System, in dem es kein Eigentum an Grund und Boden und kein Eigentum an Produktionsmitteln gab, waren die Menschen dem Staat, den die Partei beherrschte, völlig ausgeliefert. Der Staat bestimmte die Quantität und Qualität der Konsumgüter und ihre Zuteilung an die Menschen. Es gab keine Landwirte, die auf eigene Rechnung den Boden bewirtschafteten. Die Wohnungen und Häuser verkamen, da sich niemand um notwendige Reparaturen und die Bestandserhaltung kümmerte. Der Staat dekretierte, was die Betriebe produzieren sollten, vergab die Arbeitsplätze und regelte die Lohnhöhe und die Lohnstruktur. Es gab keine Unternehmer, sondern nur noch ernannte Betriebsleiter. Auch die Gewerkschaften verloren ihre Funktion als Sozialpartner und dienten als Hilfsorgane des Staates bei der Verwaltung von sozialen Leistungen, wozu ihnen das Geld vom Staat zugewiesen wurde. Man vertröstete die

---

[8] *Pius XII.*, Ansprache an Mitglieder des Internationalen Instituts für Vereinheitlichung des Privatrechts vom 20. Mai 1948, in: Utz / Groner, Nr. 417. – Siehe auch *Anton Rauscher*, Das Privateigentum in der Soziallehre Pius XII., in: Herbert Schambeck (Hrsg.), Pius XII. zum Gedächtnis, Berlin 1977, S. 381–399.

[9] *Johannes XXIII.*, Mater et magistra (1961), Nr. 109. – Zum Zusammenhang von Person, Eigentum und Freiheit siehe auch *Wilhelm Weber*, Person in Gesellschaft, München u. a. 1978, S. 277 ff.

[10] Pastoralkonstitution Gaudium et spes (1965), Nr. 71. – In der Fußnote wird auf die einschlägigen Aussagen der Päpste Leo XIII. bis Johannes XXIII. verwiesen.

Arbeiter durch Versprechungen derart, dass man dabei sei, die „kapitalistischen Länder" zu überholen. Gorbatschow erkannte, dass dieses System an sein Ende gekommen war. Der Staat war pleite und hatte das Vertrauen der Arbeiter verloren, zumal wenn sie die katastrophale Situation in den kommunistisch regierten Ländern mit den Lebensverhältnissen in den freiheitlichen Demokratien des Westens vergleichen konnten.

Auch der Nationalsozialismus in Deutschland hatte zwar das Privateigentum an Grund und Boden und an Produktionsmitteln nicht verstaatlicht, aber mit Hilfe von Gesetzen und Kontrollmechanismen sowie über eine fatale Allianz mit Großbanken und Großunternehmen die Wirtschaft seinen Zielen dienstbar gemacht. Mit Hilfe der Medien, die nach der Machtübernahme gleichgeschaltet wurden, konnte das totalitäre System aufgerichtet werden.

V. Die Verantwortung des Eigentümers

Die Rechtsordnung des Staates muss gewährleisten, dass das Eigentum an Grund und Boden, an Produktionsgütern, an Gebrauchs- und Konsumgütern, auch an erspartem Geld in investivem Kapital sicher ist. Dabei spielt zunächst keine Rolle, ob es sich um ein großes oder kleines Eigentum handelt. Die Rechtsordnung muss ebenfalls sicherstellen, dass der Eigentümer sein Eigentum frei und nach eigenem Ermessen einsetzen kann. Dabei ist er gehalten, die Eigentumsrechte anderer nicht zu verletzen oder zu schädigen. Darüber hinaus muss er verantwortlich handeln. Freiheit und Verantwortung bedingen sich gegenseitig. Aber was heißt Verantwortung? Der Eigentümer trägt für alles, was er mit seinem Eigentum unternimmt, das Risiko, das er nicht auf andere, etwa auf die Mitarbeiter, auch nicht auf den Staat beziehungsweise die Steuerzahler abschieben darf. Das Risiko und die persönliche Haftung wirken darauf hin, dass der Eigentümer die Voraussetzungen und die Folgen seiner Entscheidungen sorgfältig prüft und keine unübersehbaren Geschäfte tätigt. Man kann sich gegen Risiken versichern, aber man kann nicht jedes Risiko ausschließen. Der Eigentümer muss bereit sein, Entscheidungen, die sich über kurz oder lang als Fehlentscheidungen herauszustellen, zu tragen. Unverantwortlich wäre es, die Gewinne zu privatisieren und die Verluste zu sozialisieren.

Eigentum und Vermögen geben dem Besitzer nicht nur die Möglichkeit, seinen eigenen Lebenszuschnitt zu wählen. Viel wichtiger ist, dass er damit für die Bildung der Kinder und für deren Start ins Leben sorgen kann. Er braucht nicht von der Hand in den Mund zu leben. Besonders ermöglichen Eigentum und Vermögen freie Entscheidungen, sei es bei der Wahl des Berufes oder des Arbeitsplatzes. Vor allem gibt Eigentum Sicherheit gegen unvorhergesehene Schicksalsschläge oder schwere Krankheiten. Unverzichtbar ist Eigentum als Bedingung der Freiheit im Bereich der Wirtschaft. Die Entwicklung einer Firma, Entscheidungen über den Standort, womöglich im Ausland, Innovationen, die Neuland betreten und die für die moderne Wirtschaft von größter Wichtigkeit sind, fallen nicht vom Himmel, sondern beruhen auf der Freiheit des Unternehmers, seiner Fähigkeit, neue Produkte zu entwickeln, neue Produktionswege zu gehen, die Marktchancen ausfindig zu machen und rechtzeitig die Richtung zu ändern, wenn die damit verbundenen Erwartungen nicht erreichbar sind. Freiheit und Verantwortung im Unternehmensbereich sind deshalb so entscheidend, weil davon nicht nur die Zukunft des Unternehmers und seiner Familie abhängt, sondern auch seiner Mitarbeiter und ihrer Familien, womöglich ganzer Stadtteile und Regionen.

Einen weiteren Problembereich bildet der moderne Sozialstaat, wenn er zum Wohlfahrtsstaat mutiert. Dies ist dann der Fall, wenn die Sozialgesetzgebung nicht nur dafür sorgt, dass Freiheit von Not für alle Bürger gewährleistet ist, sondern wenn die Eigenverantwortung der Menschen und ihre Entschlossenheit, mit eigenen Kräften einer Not vorzubeugen, schwinden und die Sozialisierung der Ansprüche auf allen Gebieten vom Staat gefördert wird. Es ist sozusagen ein „sanfter Weg", um das Privateigentum und die Privatautonomie auszuhöhlen.[11] Nicht die soziale Marktwirtschaft, nicht der Sozialstaat, wie er besonders seit dem Ende des Zweiten Weltkriegs in vielen Ländern Europas entfaltet wurde, sondern die schleichende Entwicklung zum Wohlfahrtsstaat bedroht die Freiheit und die Funktion, die das Privateigentum in der Wirtschaft, aber auch in allen anderen gesellschaftlichen Lebensbereichen erfüllen kann. Hier wird nicht nur die Not bekämpft im Sinne der Hilfe zur Selbsthilfe, vielmehr geht man davon aus, dass staatliche Einrichtungen und Institutionen alles besser können. Deshalb nehmen die Steuern überhand und die Abhängigkeit der Bürger wächst.

Oswald von Nell-Breuning, der sich häufig kritisch zur Verteilung von Eigentum und Vermögen geäußert hat und ein Vorkämpfer für die Mitbestimmung der Arbeitnehmer in den Unternehmen war, hielt 1958 das Hauptreferat der vom Deutschen Gewerkschaftsbund veranstalteten 7. Europäischen Gespräche. Darin kam er auch auf den Zusammenhang von Eigentum und Freiheit zu sprechen: Eigentum und Eigentums-Wille sind für die Freiheit „von denkbar größter Bedeutung". Er fährt fort: „Eine Bevölkerung, die ihre ganze Daseinssicherung von den Einrichtungen der sozialen Sicherheit erwartet, mit all ihren Erwartungen sich an den Staat, an staatliche oder andere öffentlich-rechtliche Großgebilde klammert und sich gewöhnt, ständig nur Forderungen an sie zu stellen, ist nicht so sehr aus technisch-organisatorischen Gründen, obwohl auch diese eine Rolle spielen, als vielmehr ihrer inneren Haltung nach in erschre-

---

[11] Vgl. dazu *Alfred Schüller*, Wilhelm Röpke und die Krise des modernen Wohlfahrtsstaates, in: Heinz Rieter / Joachim Zweynert (Hrsg.), „Wort und Wirkung". Wilhelm Röpkes Bedeutung für die Gegenwart, ²Marburg 2010, S. 85.

ckendem Maße anfällig für die Überwältigung durch totalitäre Mächte, um nicht zu sagen: eine solche Haltung macht sie dagegen haltlos. Ganz anders ein Volk, dessen einzelne und dessen Familien an die erste Stelle das ‚Hilf dir selbst' stellen. Auch diese wissen sehr wohl, daß viele notwendige Leistungen nur durch die Solidarität kleinerer, größerer und selbst größter Gemeinschaften erbracht werden können; sie *üben* dann aber auch an erster Stelle selbst diese Solidarität, anstatt sich auf die Solidarität anderer zu verlassen oder gar sie auszubeuten."[12]

Besonders zugespitzt hat sich auch die Frage der Freiheit und der Selbstverantwortung des Eigentümers im Rahmen der modernen Kreditwirtschaft. Solange das Geld- und Kreditwesen auf die reale Produktivität der Unternehmen und Geschäfte bezogen war, hat dies das Wirtschaftswachstum enorm begünstigt. Aber schon die erste Weltwirtschaftskrise, die der New Yorker Börsenkrach von 1929 auslöste und verheerende Folgen für Unternehmen und ihre Belegschaften nach sich zog, war eine Katastrophe. Die gegenwärtige Wirtschafts- und Finanzkrise, die im Immobiliensektor in den USA ihren Ursprung hat und die internationale Bankenwelt erfasste, ist entstanden einerseits durch die Staatsverschuldung Nordamerikas, Japans und der Länder der Europäischen Union, andererseits durch die unbekümmerte Ausweitung wenig gesicherter Kredite durch die Banken sowie durch die weltweit gewachsene Börsenspekulation. Die Gewinne wurden privatisiert, die Verluste hingegen sozialisiert. Da sich nicht wenige Staaten an die Finanzierung neuer Ausgaben durch Schulden gewöhnt haben, ist die Rückführung der Staatsverschuldung schwierig. In früheren Zeiten nahm man die schleichende Inflation der Währung in Kauf, weil sie geräuschloser erfolgte als etwa die Kürzung vor allem von Sozialausgaben oder die Erhöhung der Einnahmen, die womöglich die Investitionen der Wirtschaft gefährdet hätte. In der Eurozone ist an die Stelle der Inflation die Verteuerung der Kredite getreten.

Ist es gerecht, wenn die Länder, die hoch verschuldet sind, auch noch höhere Zinsen für Kredite zahlen müssen, und verletzt dies die Solidarität? „Ja, es ist gerecht", antwortet Udo Di Fabio, „weil es die Voraussetzungen der Freiheit garantiert. Im Prinzip gilt: Wer frei entscheiden will, muss bereit sein, die Folgen seines Handelns zu tragen. Dass der Sozialstaat Ungleichgewichte und Härten für den Bürger abmildert, ist seine zentrale Aufgabe. Aber das geschieht in der Ausgestaltung der Leistungen doch immer so, dass die freie Entfaltung der Persönlichkeit nicht allmählich sozialisiert wird, sondern die persönliche Verantwortung möglichst schnell wieder zurückgewonnen werden kann."[13] Besser

---

[12] *Oswald von Nell-Breuning*, Wirtschaft und Gesellschaft heute, Bd. III, Freiburg i. Br. 1960, S. 301 f.

[13] *Udo Di Fabio*, Das europäische Schuldendilemma als Mentalitätskrise, in: Frankfurter Allgemeine Zeitung, Nr. 143, 22. Juni 2012, S. 9.

kann man den Zusammenhang zwischen Person, Eigentum und Freiheit nicht formulieren. Es wäre wichtig, wenn die Regierungen und ebenso die Parlamente die Lehren von John Maynard Keynes ernst nehmen würden: Die Kredite, die der Staat in Krisenzeiten zur Belebung der Wirtschaftstätigkeit aufnimmt, müssen in guten Zeiten so rasch wie möglich wieder zurückgezahlt werden. Die Politik verliert das Vertrauen der Bürger, wenn sie das Ersparte der Bürger aufs Spiel setzt.

Der Zusammenhang von Eigentum und Freiheit verlangt, dass Vermögen und Eigentum in einer Gesellschaft breit gestreut und gerecht verteilt sind. Diesbezüglich ist eine Aussage von Papst Pius XII. von bleibender Dringlichkeit. Es ist die Einsicht, „daß der wirtschaftliche Reichtum eines Volkes nicht eigentlich in der Fülle der in ihrem Wert rein materiell zählbaren Güter an sich liegt, sondern darin, daß diese Fülle wirklich und wirksam die hinreichende materielle Grundlage bildet für eine berechtigte persönliche Entfaltung seiner Glieder. Wäre dies nicht oder nur sehr unvollkommen der Fall, dann wäre der wahre Zweck der nationalen Wirtschaft nicht erreicht. Trotz der etwa verfügbaren Güterfülle wäre ein solches um seinen Anspruch betrogenes Volk keineswegs wirtschaftlich reich, sondern arm. Wo aber die genannte gerechte Verteilung wirklich und dauernd erreicht wird, kann ein Volk auch bei geringerer Menge verfügbarer Güter ein wirtschaftlich gesundes Volk sein."[14]

Zusammenfassung

Älter als alle Theorieansätze über die Entstehung des Eigentums sind die Erfahrungen, wie die Menschen mit den materiellen Gütern umgehen. In allen Sprachen gibt es „Mein" und „Dein" sowie den Begriff des „Diebstahls". Der Mensch als Leib-Geist-Wesen ist auf die Nutzung der materiellen Güter angewiesen. Daraus erwächst die Einsicht, dass die Güter der Erde für alle Menschen da sind und keiner davon ausgeschlossen sein darf. Aber entspricht der „Gemeinbestimmung der Erdengüter" nicht eher eine Gemeineigentumsordnung? Der Schlüssel zur Beantwortung dieser Frage liegt in dem Begriff Erdengüter. Dabei handelt es sich um die natürlichen Ressourcen, aus denen erst durch Arbeit und Bearbeitung Güter werden, wie sie die Menschen zum Unterhalt ihres Lebens und zum Aufbau von Kultur benötigen. In den Sozialenzykliken der Päpste wird der innere Zusammenhang zwischen Eigentum und Freiheit betont, aber ebenso die Verantwortung des Eigentümers für den Umgang mit seinem Eigentum. In der Industriegesellschaft müssen alle, auch die Arbeitnehmer, in der Lage sein, Vermögen zu bilden und damit für die Wechselfälle des Lebens vorzusorgen.

---

[14] Radiobotschaft vom 1. Juni 1941, in: Utz / Groner, Nr. 510.

Summary

Man's experience in the use of material goods is older than all the theories about the development of property. In all languages we find the words "my" and "your" and as well, the idea of "theft". Man has body and soul and consequently is dependent on material goods. Therefore in reality these goods are for all mankind. One might then ask whether the holding of property in common does not better correspond to this reality. But the material goods of the earth are just natural resources; only by labor do they become the goods men are longing for. The social encyclicals of the popes defend the right to property as a natural right. There is an inner connection between person, freedom, and property. One could say that property is a prolongation of the person into the material world. Therefore the Catholic Social Doctrine demands that everybody, including workers, be able to work and to acquire property.

Personalist Dimensions of Property

By William A. Frank

I. Introduction

Property belongs to someone. A human person can be the owner, or just as well, a collective such as a tribe, corporation, or state. In addition to ownership, property also signifies a set of socially acknowledged relationships pertaining to the use of things we own. Whether material or intellectual, property serves a manifold of individual and common purposes in a community. It is an invariant in human experience. As one scholar put it, "images of a property-less world of 'natural man' are a mirage."[1] These initial observations indicate the complexity of the notion of property. It is a term that expresses an invariant disposition in human affairs to establish commonly acknowledged or defined interrelationships that obtain between persons and things in given communities relative to the production and enjoyment of wealth.

For the purposes of this discussion, I shall consider property and ownership as specifically human phenomena. Nature, however, provides the background to our understanding of property. In the animal world the phenomena of territoriality, possession, and occupation are universal. Animals carve out a place for themselves, limiting their vulnerabilities and securing opportunities for nutrition and reproduction. Many also provide for themselves with the building of webs, nests, lodges, or warrens. It is interesting to note how the English word "to possess," the Latin "possidere," and the German "besitzen" derive from the same Indo-European root *misad* or *mizdo*, which means to nest or to sit. The concept of nesting is suggestive, for it unites the idea of "holding one's place" with that of "nourishing the life of one's kind." Another linguistic point to observe is the connection in English between "to occupy" meaning to hold a certain place and "occupation" meaning an activity that generate one's livelihood. Nature and language show a primitive connection between holding one's place or territory and providing for one's self and one's kind. The specifically human notions of ownership and property that are the focus objects of this inquiry no doubt rise from more primitive, elementary notions of place and the embodied life of animals. I am reminded of Mary Midgely's opening sentence in her *Man*

---

[1] Richard Pipes, *Property and Freedom* (New York: Knopf, 2000), p. 65.

and Beast: "We are not just rather like animals; we are animals." And she continues: "Our difference from other species may be striking, but comparisons
with them have always been, and must be, crucial for our view of ourselves."[2]
As the argument of this paper continues, attention will turn to the more rational
or spiritual dimensions of the specifically human institutions of ownership and
property. The personalist concerns of our inquiry, however, are not intended to
deny those commonalities man shares with the beasts.[3] Its interest, however, is
in the meanings as they have entered into the rational, spiritual sphere of human
existence.

I hope to show how notions of personal freedom and responsibility lie at the
origin of the concept of property. I wish to explore these notions at the conceptual point where ownership and property enter into our ordinary experience,
where the idea of property is bound up in laws and customs of civil associations
that regulate the ownership and use of material things. What takes on the form
of "property" by virtue of legal status, however, is something more primitive or
foundational, namely, an external thing identified as "one's own." The attribute
of ownership is foundationally prior to that of property. The idea of "one's
own," for its part, rests upon or, better, emerges from the even prior notions of
responsible agency and productive activity. These notions, in turn, originate in
even more foundational notions of personal being and a meaningful cosmos.

In developing the argument of the paper, I freely elaborate ideas introduced
by Jacques Maritain in a rudimentary theory of property which he appended to
his book, *Freedom in the Modern World*.[4] Maritain himself recapitulates certain
fundamentals drawn from Thomas Aquinas.[5] In Maritain's overarching intellectual vision, the idea of personal freedom looms large. As he understands it, man

---

[2] *Man and Beast: The Roots of Human Nature*, revised edition (London and New
York: Routledge, 2002), p. xxiii.

[3] For instance, attention to the necessities of animal possession and territoriality
would bring out the attribute of particularity evident in the "belonging" of things and regions that is part of animal life. Such particularity is itself grounded in the more essential particularity of the categories of body and place. If these notions of embodied particularity which are universal features of the natural world become incorporated into the
specifically human experience of property, it is because of man's ability to lift them into
the sphere of human persons. It is the burden of this paper to draw out those personalist
dimensions of property.

[4] Jacques Maritain, "Person and Property," Appendix I, *Freedom in the Modern
World* (London: Sheed & Ward, 1935).

[5] As Maritain organizes it, Aquinas's theory of property unfolds in three stages: the
principle of common destination, appropriation, and civic determinations governing
property. Marcus Lefébure gives a succinct description of Aquinas's doctrine of private
property in his "'Private Property' according to St. Thomas and Recent Papal Encyclicals," Appendix 2 to St. Thomas Aquinas, *Summa Theologiae*, vol. 38, *Injustice* (2a-2ae
63-79) (New York: McGraw-Hill, 1975).

is made responsible for his own well-being and for the care of others. Much of this responsibility is carried out in mankind's making of the world. By virtue of our rationality, men and women enjoy the freedom of creativity to re-fashion material reality to serve our needs and interests. It is this same rationality in the sphere of world-making that, in the ethical sphere, gives men and women spiritual leverage from the determinisms of self-interest. The demands of justice and benevolence inevitably figure into the use of the thing we have fashioned. Both the creativity of *poesis* (making) and the freedom of *praxis* (action) share the common form of independence from being simply determined by what is given in nature. Both the artist and the moral agent introduce into the fabric of the world something new that takes its origin from vision and judgment. The subject of this freedom is the human person.

For an understanding of the person I draw on ideas of the contemporary German philosopher, Robert Spaemann.[6] In his account of human persons, Spaemann holds together several themes with important implications for an understanding of property. First of all, he distinguishes person and nature. Individual humans are both natural and personal beings. As natural, we are members of a species, but "a man is obviously not a man in the same way that a dog is a dog, i.e. simply and solely by being an instance of the species": It is "non-identity with their nature that entitles us to call human beings 'persons.'"[7] As personal, we *have* our natures in such a way that our speech and action need not be determined by the always present external conditions of bodily, psychological, social, or cultural conditions. "Persons exist by being present in each of their acts, but not so inseparably fused with any one of them as to disappear into it altogether."[8] Secondly, essential to Spaemann's understanding of personal being is the primordial act of recognition of other persons. "To be a person is to occupy a place within the field where other persons have their places."[9] "To recognize a person means preeminently to restrain my own potentially unlimited urge for self-expansion. It means to resist the inclination to see the other only as a factor in my own life-project."[10] Finally, these two notions come together in human freedom. "A person 'has' a nature, but that nature is not what the person *is*, because the person has the power to relate freely to it. But this power is not innate; it comes through encounter with other persons. Only the affirmation of other centers of being, through recognition, justice, and love, allows us the distance on ourselves and the appropriation of ourselves that is constitutive for

---

[6] Robert Spaemann, *Persons: The Difference Between 'Someone' and 'Something'* (Oxford: Oxford University Press, 2006).

[7] Spaemann, p. 81.

[8] Spaemann, p. 61.

[9] Spaemann, p. 182.

[10] Spaemann, p. 186.

persons – in sum, 'freedom from self.'"[11] As we shall see, such a notion of freedom, grounded in the distinction between person and nature and tied to an inherent recognition of other persons, sheds considerable light on the personalist dimension of property.

II. Intended for All

"Man-in-the-world" sets the horizon for our consideration of property. Not only do we find ourselves in the world, we adapt ourselves to its necessities and contingencies. And the world for its part proves to some degree pliable. Human life in the world appears as a special, even exaggerated and narrow instance of the broader fact of nature's hospitality to vegetative and sentient life. What mankind adds into the mechanisms of adaptation is self-conscious and self-determining creative reason. Men and women take responsibility for their measure of world-making. The notion of property developed in this paper grows out of this expansive background notion of the world as intended for human life. The original intention does not discriminate among human persons. The potentialities of the world's resources to be developed for the ends and purposes of mankind are potential to any individual of the human species: grain grown on fertile earth nourishes any hungry person, and a house in the city will shelter any man, woman, or child from the elements. Considerations of "property" have to do with rational and social determinations mediating these primordial potentialities or intentionalities of the world to the concrete ways that men and women actually pursue their needs and interests.

The Aristotelian-Thomistic philosophical tradition refers to these ideas as the *universal destination* or *vocation* of the material world to human well-being. Maritain introduces it as the first of what he calls "fundamental principles in the metaphysic of human life and action."[12] He holds that material things have inscribed into them from the beginning a purposiveness to serve the needs and interests of all mankind. "[E]very person by reason of his membership in the human species ought in one way or the other to derive advantage from [the] dedication of material things to the good of the human race."[13] The point here is that despite whatever considerable justification there might be in asserting proprietary rights in the ownership and use of external things, one's individual dominion is conditioned in two ways. First of all, it is relativized by the final causality of external things themselves, that is, by the fact that in the divine act of creation material things are destined to the service of the needs

---

[11] Spaemann, p. 216.

[12] Maritain, p. 193.

[13] Maritain, p. 194.

and interests of every person in the human community. As creator of all, God possesses the things of the world principally or absolutely, whereas man's possession is secondary or relative in that it is received as a feature of the divinely ordered, purposed universe. Secondly, the dominion that man might enjoy over the material things of the world is a share in God's own exercise of providential care for the created world. Insofar as man himself is made in God's own image and likeness,[14] his development and use of material things is meant to advance the good of God's original intention. Along with the transmission of power or dominion over external things comes a due measure or share of providential responsibility. This notion of responsibility informs Aquinas's insistence that, with respect to the use of external things, "man ought not to possess external things as his own, but as common, so that he is ready to communicate them to others in their need."[15] In the mastery over exterior things, the world and its resources, men and women express their personal nature as individuals who take responsibility for their own well-being and that of others who fall within his sphere of responsibility. The limits and the content of that responsibility are not at all easy to see.

In sum, men and women exploit the earth's resources to meet their needs within a larger purposive or teleological pattern of creation. The striking point to the principle is its assertion of a "rightful destination" or ordination of the *good* of material things to any human person in general and to no one in particular. Such purposes "inscribed in the nature of things"[16] are brought to term through human work and action. What subsequently emerge as ownership relationships and even later as property relationships will assume their identities over and against the manifold of the world's teleological potentialities and the various ways mankind's world-making takes up its responsibilities before the world's intentions.

III. Work Generates Ownership

The second stage of the argument builds upon a fact and a claim. The fact is that work is required if the world's material resources are to meet mankind's needs and interests. The claim is that it is work that generates ownership. In making the claim, ownership needs to be understood as more than the simple possession of thing or the mere occupying of a territory. Also, the meaning of

---

[14] Thomas Aquinas, *Summa theologiae*, 1-2, 91, 2.

[15] Thomas Aquinas: "non debet homo habere res exteriores ut proprias, sed ut communes: ut scilicet de facili aliquis eas communicet in necessitates aliorum" (ST 2-2, 66, 2).

[16] Maritain, p. 194.

work must be extended beyond the idea of purposive rearrangement of material resources in the service of life's interests. Drawing on Aquinas again, Maritain proposes the following rationale: because there is a (universally distributed) right to the use of the world's material goods, men and women, as individuals or collaborating as a collective, must therefore have the power to procure, manage, and administer external things.[17] Wheat needs to be milled, grapes fermented, and timber planed. And these goods need to find their way into the human economy. Were men to lack the capability to interfere, change, elaborate, and distribute the external material things, then the world of artifice that feeds, shelters, heals, entertains, and schools us would simply not exist. One sees how such specifically human activities lift things out of the status of "the purely natural state." What needs to be seen more clearly is how ownership, that is, the insertion of the distinction between "mine and thine" among material things, proceeds from the seizing and transformation of material reality for use.[18]

We have already noted that human artifice readies matter for the ends and purposes of human life and fits it into the web of the human economy. But what is it that requires the introduction of the language of appropriation – of possession, ownership, "one's own"?[19] How does "mine/ours" – precisely as opposed to "yours/theirs" come to belong to material things? What accounts for ownership? The first step is to take a closer look at the meaning of "ownership." The second step is to understand how it flows from productive agency.

Meaning of "one's own." The idea of "one's own" represents an affirmation of an immediate connection between unmediated individual self-reference and some particular external thing (as in the assertion that "this garden is *mine*"), and it simultaneously sets that *me-mine* dyad alongside the exclusion of another's unmediated self-reference to the same individual thing (as in the assertion that "this same garden is *not yours*"). With such a move, the prior, foundational relation of "common to all," relative to any human person, recedes into the background. A new relation is installed in the foreground: one individual person (or one determinate group of persons) asserts an exclusive tie to a por-

---

[17] Maritain, pp. 199–200 and Aquinas ST 2-2, 66, 2.

[18] Maritain, pp. 211–212: "individual ownership of material goods is based on a spiritual foundation, on the capacity of the rational being as an intellectual subject to give form to matter."

[19] In asking this question we seem to encounter a paradox: the good commonly destined for the ends or purposes of any man in general is achieved by being appropriated by one (individual or party) to the exclusion of another. In fact, holding together at this elementary conceptual level both the diffusive impulse of common destination with its universal right and the centripetal force of appropriation tending toward private dominion is just the earliest manifestation of the tension that seems inherent in our experience of property.

tion of the material things of the world. Two personal relationships now qualify external things: at the foundation lies *"... for all"* (in accordance with the principle of common destination) over which is now layered *"... for me"* ("one's own," by virtue of appropriation).

The term "one's own," is grammatically interesting. The word "own" operates semantically as an intensifier. In the fuller expression "one's own," it intensifies the subjective genitive case of "one's." The expression is not a simple redundancy: it emphatically highlights the genitive linkage of thing (possessed) to person (possessor). Absent the self-conscious, mutually opposed relation between two persons relative to the same external object, there would be no concept of ownership. It is the act of appropriation that inserts *me-mine* into our discourse and actions. And, it thereby displays the interpersonal context and the asymmetrical point of view of the first-person "me" or "I" relative to external, commonly accessible things. The principle of appropriation only makes sense within the context of a mutual recognition of two persons, one's self and another's self, together with the first person's assertion of an immediate tie of *me* to *what-is-mine* and the corresponding disassociation of *you* (or him/her/them) from the same individual thing. Ownership takes on its meaning within such an interpersonal structure.

The specifically interpersonal character of appropriation can be brought out in the following reflections. One defends one's possessions against the predations of animals and the ruin of bad weather. Their violations of my appropriations, however, stay on the non-personal, natural level. The loss one suffers through their agency is not theft. In such cases, one loses what is "one's own" by its falling back into the status of what is natural. Raccoons and tornadoes do not recognize the claims of "mine and thine." By contrast, theft and vandalism occur wholly within an acknowledged interpersonal context. They do not just take away or ruin the external things; they attack the interpersonal reality of ownership. Civil associations are, in part, structured in the shared acknowledgement and maintenance of "mine and thine" among persons and things. Victims of theft and vandalism do not just suffer loss; they are violated. The unmistakable sense of violation or personal assault makes sense in the light of the personal, and indeed, interpersonal, foundations of ownership and property.

Another interesting feature of ownership is the fact that, once established, it can be transferred. One and the same item which now belongs, say, to Martha can be transferred to Quinn. The person (owner) in the "me-mine" relationship is substitutable, while the external thing (what is owned) remains constant. Societies invent different modes of transfer, as for example, buying, inheriting, and receiving as a gift. Any instance of transfer of ownership to a new owner presumes a prior ownership, and cultures and societies devise various ways of remembering or recording title to ownership. Reflection on the process of ownership transfer presumes that the attribute "one's own" has been established in the first instance.

It is hard to imagine what meaning "one's own" could have in a solipsist's world. There would be no basis for exclusion (mine, not yours), no possibility of violation since all loss would proceed from natural causes and no interpersonal bonds would be ruptured, and no possibility for transfer of ownership to another person.

Finally, I should emphasize that the term "ownership" is used here with artificial restraints. In ordinary usage ownership carries with it notions of dominion and proprietary rights. One's property and what is one's own are commonly understood synonymously. At this stage in our inquiry, however, "one's own" is to be taken in a more elemental sense to which have not been added the notions of use and dominion, which are proper to the fuller idea of property.

Meaning of "work". Against the background of the understanding of ownership as a mutually recognized interpersonal relationship, we consider the meaning of work and how it lies at the origin of appropriation. The sort of activity that we are calling *work* is one of several broad ways that the operation of reason enters into the fabric of human affairs. Within the broad Aristotelian-Thomistic classification of specifically human activities, we distinguish production (art/*poesis*), action (ethics and politics/*praxis*), and contemplation (theoretical science and philosophy/*theoria*). Reason operates every bit as much in the fabrication of a bridge and in the performance of a just deed, as in the reflective wisdom of the sages. Our current philosophical discussion of property, for example, would represent an exercise of *contemplative* reason. By contrast, the use of property for the satisfaction of needs and interests of oneself, one's family, and the community at large would be *action* that carries us into the sphere of ethics and politics as governed by the virtues of justice and benevolence. Thought also goes into the transformation of the resources of the world into material goods, and as well into their procurement, administration, and management. In terms of its effect, productive activity communicates form to matter in ways that would not happen, or at least not dependably so, by the determinisms of natural necessity or the happenstances of chance. The formative energy in artifice derives from the independent judgment and imaginative vision which guide the laborer, worker, craftsman, or artist in the efforts he or she expends in the elaboration of the material resources found ready at hand. Judgment and vision themselves have their origins in the power of reason that belongs to the spiritual substance of the human person. Art or productive activity, therefore, is one of the distinctive ways that reason manifests itself in human affairs. [20]

Responsible agency. All three categories of rational activity – thinking, acting, making – involve responsible agency. Life in the human community is crisscrossed by all three forms. In effect, the web of human relationships is fashioned out of innumerable lines of rational activity spun out of the free and rational responses of individual persons. People are responsible for what they say, do, and make. Theoretical reason, for instance, is *immanent* activity that stays, as it were, in thought and speech, even as we share our thoughts with others. Thinkers are responsible for the truth or falsity of their predications. Contemplative reason illuminates received intelligibilities of actual things and their possibilities and thereby enriches the human community, even if it is not additive or transformative of the world in the ways that production and action are. By contrast, the modes of reason operative in production and action do enter into the external fabric of the world. In action, reason is operative in *transeunt* activity. Here we use the term in the restricted sense of moral or political action. Action involves some material performance, some rearrangement of material things, if only in a physical gesture or the whisper of a speech-act. What matters is not the product, not the reconfiguration of some material thing or condition; what matters is the new reality that this material performance has introduced into the web of interpersonal relationships. Moral and political actions either strengthen or weaken the web of human relationships that form the personal bonds of friendships, families, and civil associations. With respect to production, it is through human making that "nature alone" becomes "nature and world," with the addition of houses, factories, roads, bridges, power lines, computer chips, churches, and office buildings, along with the immense variety of human behavior at work about them. Artifice transforms significant sections of nature's landscape. Work elaborates and refigures the received forms of external things in order to satisfy human needs and interests. It is reason operative in transeunt activity that communicates new forms to external materials.

From work to "one's own". It is the personal dynamics interior to work that provides the metaphysical foundation for ownership. The original constitution of something as "one's own" arises from the maker's deployment of his reason in the creative processes of re-figuring and administering material things in the

---

[20] We have used the different terms, "art," "work," and "production," as synonyms. The differences of nuance are as follows. *Art* is an intellectual *habitus*, the acquired quality of mind, the perfected reason that artists or workers activate in producing and servicing their products. *Work* is behavior; it is personal effort guided by art. *Production* refers to activity of making or servicing somewhat more abstractly than "work." "Production" expresses the activity from the vantage point of the product made, whereas "work" expresses it more from the personal vantage point of the working agent, the worker. In actual usage, these finer distinctions are often ignored.

service of human needs and interests. It is easy to see in the fact of a house, a power line, or a harness the handiwork of some human agent. The mind leaps from artifact to artificer. What is not so easy to see is how this inference entails ownership. What claim to ownership is staked out by the imputation of responsible agency? In the act of production there occurs a transfer of identity from *maker* to *made-thing*: work brings about an identity between the person of the maker and the property of his artifact.[21] New things come from *poesis*. The communication of form from the maker's mind to the matter-at-hand in the act of production establishes the fundamental basis for the maker's claim that "this object is mine." The figuring power of mind, which is an eminently personal operation, initiates the new entity both as what it is and as ordered to the good its serves Not only does it initiate it, but the made-thing's continuance typically requires some sympathetic appropriation of the original intention of the maker as the artifact works its way into the fixings of the human world.

In this elemental understanding, work acquires a remarkable dignity. The claim might even strike one as a romantic exaggeration, given the extent that the familiar usage of the word bears connotations of drudgery, wage-earning, and proletarian meanness. Using the word in this more elemental context, however, one sees a certain splendor of reason emanating from the souls of men and women actively re-figuring the material world about them. Their actualizations of reason are free operations of human subjects. *Poesis* flows from personal freedom along two lines. First of all, the novelty of human artifacts manifests the human agent's independence from the necessities of nature and the compulsions of instinct. Secondly, work's productivity is undertaken within the context of the universal vocation of the material world to the good of all mankind, and pursued as an exercise in the providential care for the well-being of one's immediate and extended community. In both cases, productive reason extends itself into the fabric of the human community. As we noted in the introduction, to have one's nature but not be determined by it and to experience one's self in the recognition of others are intrinsic features of what it means to be a person. The notions of creativity and freedom expressed in the elemental experience of work are therefore eminently personal. In this elemental sense of work, the maker can say, "This is mine; I have made it," for the made thing is born of his envisioning of the good to be served and the form to be fashioned. The maker's assertion of ownership recognizes a communication of personal identity from maker to made-thing.

---

[21] Maritain says that "it is of the very essence of this activity to imprint on matter the mark of rational being" (ibid., p. 198).

IV. Use of Exterior Goods

At this point in our account of the genesis of the concept of property we have viewed the superimposition of the attribute "one's own" against the background of the more primordial notion the universal destination of material goods. The notions of "being one's own" and "intended for all" represent conflicting vectors. One and the same thing bears the marks, as it were, of both the particularity of personal ownership and the universal intentionality of serving anybody. It is the force of their opposition that gives rise to the two topics that remain in our account of the conceptual foundations of property. First, we must distinguish the right of use of external things from the right of their ownership. Secondly, we need to bring out the inherent legal character of the idea of property.

With respect to the *use* of external material goods, Maritain draws from Aquinas a principle to the effect that "in respect of *use* man ought to possess external things not as his own but as common."[22] If taken literally, this principle might seem to suggest, for instance, that when I pick a cayenne pepper from my kitchen garden, I harvest what is my own and not my neighbor's. But when I *use* that pepper to flavor a sauce, and thereby feed some need or interest, then I actualize a good that is there for me not by individual right of ownership but by virtue of common use. I stand in, as it were, for anyone who could benefit from the cayenne pepper. My individual act of use particularizes an achievement of a material good that is in and of itself equally destined to any *other* as to any *one*. Maritain here speaks about a "law" in the ethics of property: even when the item is expressly intended as "my own," the fruit of my work, when it is entertained from the point of view of its use as a good, then its use becomes a moral act, "and as such must somehow regard the good of all – in the first place my own good of course, but my good as a member of a community."[23]

There is nothing idiosyncratic about Maritain and Aquinas's point. It is commonly, even if only implicitly, recognized in customs and laws throughout the world. In the fuller development of social and political reality of property, the grounds of ownership are considered insufficient to establish unqualified grounds for the use of what one owns. The right of eminent domain, for instance, is a prevalent example of the broader category of legal governmental takings. In this case, civil authorities annul the rightful ownership claim of a private individual and re-appropriate the property for the purposes of the public

---

[22] Maritain, p. 205. Thomas Aquinas, *Comm. in Polit. Aristotelis*, lib. 2, lect. 4: "Unde manifestum est quod multo melius est quod sint propriae possessiones secundum dominium, sed quod fiant communes aliquo modo quantum ad usum." See also ST 2-2, 32, 5, ad 2; 2-2, 66, 2.

[23] Maritain, p. 205.

interest. More interesting are laws that do not annul claims of ownership or re-appropriate property but give use of legally held property to non-owners. In either case, the limitations on ownership respond to situations in the life of a community with the idea that the advancement of the greater good of the community trumps the rights of private ownership of individual members of that community. It indicates some measure of common claim that persists and can override the particular claims of private or personal ownership. It is instructive to look at two examples other than the more familiar right of eminent domain. In many Northern European countries, such as Scotland, Sweden, or Finland there are "right to roam" laws. The Finns, for instance, recognize in law a long established custom they call *jokamiehenoikeus*. Anyone has the right to wander through land that belongs to others; this right permits limited use of the land in activities such as camping, collecting minerals, harvesting wild berries and mushrooms, and fishing. With the right come various responsiblities to respect the property, wildlife, and the personal privacy of the entitled owners, but the key point is that one's right of ownership cannot prevent a prior right of use by non-owners. We find another interesting case of property law that separates usage from ownership in the ancient Mosaic code in what is sometimes called the "right of gleaning." "When you reap the harvest of your land, you will not reap to the very edges of the field, nor will you gather the gleanings of the harvest; nor will you strip your vineyard bare, nor pick up the fallen grapes. You will leave them for the poor and the stranger."[24] Thus when in the Book of Ruth the widowed foreigner Ruth provided for herself and her mother-in-law by gathering the gleanings from the harvest in Boaz's field, she was taking what was hers to take. Boaz the owner did not permit this because he was kind and generous man, though it seems he was such a character. The field was open to Ruth, the Moabite widow, because Boaz was a just man, rendering to her what was hers to glean by an obligation that superceded Boaz's rights of use tied to his ownership claims. The right of gleaning was not so much an individual land owner's indulgence, but the way that a righteous man in Boaz's circumstance would have followed the Mosaic law. It is important to emphasize that Finland's "right of roaming" and ancient Israel's "right of gleaning" are civil laws or customs that protect the right to the use of certain material goods and that this right cannot be superseded by the right of ownership. In asserting such rights of common use, there is no intention to deny the entitlement of private property nor to deny or dishonor the fact of landowner's work which produces and preserves the property's bounty.

Customs and laws such as eminent domain and the rights of roaming and gleaning are examples of civil accommodations to the conflicting social vectors

---

[24] Leviticus 19:9–10 (trans. New Jerusalem Bible); see also Lev 23:22; Deuteronomy 24:19–22.

built into the nature of property. Property is an object that can serve the needs or interests many (any User), but it belongs in an especial and protected way to those who are responsible for it (the Owner). In the account being developed in these reflections, both vectors need to be accommodated in an adequate account of property. To assert the common destination of the goods of the world to the exclusion of the rights of ownership dishonors the dignity of work and the meaning attained in the experience of creativity in man's manifold acts of world-making. On the other hand, to assert the rights of ownership to the exclusion of the universal destination of material goods is equally wrong, but less easy to see. It ignores the inherent sense of social responsibility built into the reality of creative reason. Not only does it show indifference to the universal vocation of the earth and its resources, but it betrays the impulse of freedom built into reason itself. Men and women are especially free in exercise of the virtues of justice and benevolence; these virtues perfect our capacities for interest in and judgment on behalf of the good of our neighbor. The sheer fact of the matter is that "this food" might well feed me and mine, but not also them and theirs, and this house might suffice to shelter me and mine, but not also them and theirs. To say, therefore, that they shall feed and shelter me and mine and not them and theirs *because I own them* is to assert that one's right of use follows from one's right of ownership. However, the nature and limits of the connection between rights of ownership and use is not immediately clear.

The hypothesis I wish to propose at this point is that the customs or civil laws[25] of one's particular community or civic association are crucial to establishing the extension of rights of ownership to rights of use. As a general matter, civil law (or custom) regulates the distribution and use of power in a civic association in accordance with some understanding of the good that pertains or ought to pertain to the community as a whole. Let us take for granted that communities or civic associations consider prosperity, peace, and justice as essential elements of the public interest or common good. As means to those dominant ends, customs and laws establish a system of property (private and public, individual and collective) to regulate the terms of ownership and use of material goods. The term "property" names the legally recognized power over the disposition of goods one owns.[26]

---

[25] See James Bernard Murphy, *The Philosophy of Positive Law: Foundations of Jurisprudence* (New Haven and London: Yale University Press, 2005) for a learned and philosophically subtle discussion of the nature of positive law and its relation to both customary and natural law.

[26] In his illuminating synthesis Anton Rauscher introduces the notion of property as the moral power of a (physical or juridical) person to dispose of the goods to which he has a right of ownership. *Private Property: Its Importance for Personal Freedom and Social Order*, trans Stephen Wentworth Arndt (publication of the German original at Paderborn: Bonifatius, 1990; English translation published in Cologne: *Ordo Socialis*,

V. From Ownership to Use

In order to bring out the importance of law and custom in the genesis of the concept of property it is important to see that the move from ownership to the right of use is not self-evident. In fact, it is precisely from and because of the gap between the two claims that *property* in the full and legal sense of the term emerges. Let me develop the notion of the gap between right of ownership and right of use. Imagine a complete stranger enters into someone's, say Arvid's, house and announces that the house suits him and his family just fine, and so he'll be moving in. Perhaps Arvid says, "You can't do that. This house is mine." The assertion of ownership, however, strikes up no resonance in the stranger. He does not deny Arvid's ownership; it just means nothing to him. There is, to his mind, no relevance of the assertion to the occasion. He simply looks about and repeats: "This house suits me just fine." And let's admit for the sake of the story that the house indeed serves quite well the stranger's needs. In this thought experiment, the stranger acts in a perfectly rational way insofar as the rationale of property is tied to the service of a (any) person's material needs. Arvid's house fits the stranger like hand to glove. Now Arvid might well block the stranger's intention to take over his house. Perhaps he threatens him with superior force. Or maybe he calls on the civil authorities who enforce the community's private property laws. The stranger understands that he is defeated by superior power. But what he does not see is the justice in the superiority of Arvid's power over the suitability of Arvid's house to his own purposes. The scenario depicted here is intended to force the question: what is the reason in the commonly accepted tie of ownership to use? What category or insight must the stranger have in order for Arvid's assertion "You can't do that; this house is mine" to count as a rational explanation?

What stands before us at this stage of our genetic account of the concept of property is what I have called the "gap" between the ownership of a thing and the right of use of that same thing. Before passing on the next section in which I shall elaborate the hypothesis that it is the civil law or the customs of a community that regulates the connection, it will be useful to draw into clearer focus the good that is at issue in regulating the operative relationships between ownership and use. The good of a thing – what needs or interests it serves – enter into consideration at the beginning, in the very making of the thing, for production requires envisioning the good at the end of the artifact's use. In productive

---

no 3), p 22. His notion of property as a recognized disposition of power over material goods by the owner is what merits attention. He calls it a *moral* power. At the very least, however, it is a legal or civic power, which is all I wish to assert at the start. As the argument develops, however, we shall see that among the more significant justifications for positive or civil laws of property are the moral and social virtues that a system of property encourages among the members of a community.

activity it is the existence of the made thing that holds pride of place; owner-ship or possession is keyed to the thing "in hand," as it were. By contrast, in the act of *using* a thing it is the good for which the thing was originally brought into existence that is actualized. What is potential in the thing *as owned* is actu-alized in the thing *as used*. Use brings a thing toward its destined purpose or end. Ownership is an expedient, however necessary, toward that end. There is a petit drama in the experience of ownership's expedient character. If what I have said is true about work's original claim to possession of a thing as "own's own," namely, that the process of transforming the raw materials at hand into an artifact involves in some sense a communication of the maker's personal identity to the made-thing, then the subsequent use of a thing can be experi-enced as a kind of loss.[27] The term "loss" is misleading if it suggests that the product ceases to exist. What it primarily intends to communicate is a kind of alienation that comes with the use of something that one owns. The act of use transports the product from the limited domain of "belonging to one (Owner)" and into the distinct and more universal sphere of "perfective of any (User)." It is the use of material goods that actualizes the universally perfective quality of the things, their promise of satisfaction to virtually any human person who is properly disposed to use or enjoy them. [28]

VI. The Legal Form of Property

It is positive law of a civic association, whether understood as its formal le-gislation or its common or customary law that mediates the gap between the af-firmation of what is one's own and the power over its use. To recall the earlier scenario, when the owner Arvid tells the stranger that he may not use his house because he owns it and that he has the right to block the stranger's entry, Arvid has reason on his side. But "reason" here is not just the assertion of authorized coercive force. His reason *is* the order of the civil or common law of the land. The term "property" in fact refers to specific socially recognized powers that one possesses over exterior things. Calling such things *one's property* signifies specific rights of power or dominion over these things. Positive laws and customs of given civic associations regulate how these exterior things stand in

---

[27] The point would be most evident in cases of the ownership of the first instance which flows directly from the work of the maker. Here the identity or personal invest-ment of the maker communicated to the made-thing would seem most acute. But it can be extended to ownership of the second instance which is had through a given culture's various mechanisms of ownership transfer, as for instance in inheritance, purchase, or receiving as a gift.

[28] This sentiment perhaps expresses something of what Maritain had in mind when he wrote that "there seems no reason ... why one person more than another should have the use of goods of this world" (Maritain, p. 206).

practical matters with respect to ownership and use. The more elemental notions of ownership and universal destination have to be lifted up into the order of
the human community through law and custom. This elevation is the final stage
in the constitution of property.[29] Texas State trespass law and the Finnish right
to roam law, for instance, represent quite different specific instances of positive
law or custom established in the concrete circumstances of distinct historical
and culture conditions. In regulating the terms of ownership and use of property, law and custom are founded upon the more elemental personal relationships
established between persons and material things that we have previously examined in terms of the principles of appropriation and universal destination.
Custom and positive law are not intended to abrogate or replace the relevance
of the universal fittingness of material wealth to humankind as a whole, nor are
they intended to annul or attenuate the identity that work establishes between
persons and the things that they fashion and administer. Law and custom ele-
vate these more fundamental personal dynamics into the order of civic associations. They should make the world of human affairs more human. Law brings
common order and public reason into community affairs. Arvid's reason was
the law (or custom) of the larger, established community. By not hearing it or
not adhering to it, the stranger stands outside of the civic order.[30]

It would be a further question to ask about the soundness of the law's reason
or the goodness of its established order. In one way or another positive and
customary law are themselves brought to judgment.[31] One ultimately wants to
believe that the law is just because it is right and not ultimately that it is right
because it is the law. In raising this issue, however, I have exceeded the limits
of this paper and crossed over to the very large question of the nature of law
and grounds of its obligatoriness. Yet, as a final contribution to these more limited reflections on the personalist foundations of property, I wish to draw at-

---

[29] Benevolence is a mode of mediating ownership and use in addition to justice. Benevolence is a human act giving what properly belongs to one's self for the use of others
in a way that stands outside or beyond the claims of justice.

[30] The stranger would either be an outlaw or the fiction of a "human being" void of
civil categories.

[31] See Alexander Passerin d'Entrèves, *Natural Law: An Introduction to Legal Phi-
losophy*, with a new introduction by Cary J. Nederman (New Brunswick and London:
Transaction, 1994), esp. pp. 163–174; Robert Sokolowski, "Knowing Natural Law," in
his *Pictures, Quotations, and Distinctions* (Notre Dame and London: University of
Notre Dame Press, 1992), pp. 277–291 and "What Is Natural Law? Human Purposes
and Natural Laws," in his *Christian Faith and Human Understanding* (Washington
D.C.: The Catholic University of America Press, 2006), pp. 214–233; and Heinrich A.
Rommen *Natural Law: A Study in Legal and Social History and Philosophy*, trans by
Thomas R. Hardy, with introduction and bibliography by Russell Hittinger (Indianapo-
lis: Liberty Fund, 1998), esp., pp. 178–233.

tention to an interesting suggestion of David Lametti. [32] Into a postmodern setting that has rejected libertarian and utilitarian theories of property, Lametti introduces the concept of moral virtues as the governing end of a viable theory of private property. He proposes to draw out of the law of property, and especially private property, what he calls the "morality of aspiration." Appealing to Aristotle and Aquinas, he proposes to recapitulate the institution of private property within a teleological vision of the common good, keyed to the service, promotion, and development of virtue. If it is the case that the social practice of private property encourages among the members of a society the cultivation of the moral virtues and intellectual gifts, and if it is the case that "the common good indicates the sum total of conditions that allow people, either as groups or as individuals, to reach their fulfillment more fully or easily,"[33] then properly regulated institutions of private property seem eminently concordant with the conditions for human flourishing. I find Lametti's proposal of the cultivation of the virtues as a justification of the institution of private property interestingly concordant with my understanding of personalist foundations of property.

VII. Property's Network of Relations

The concept of property is shaped within the broad framework of three relationships that tie material things to human persons. This set of relationships frames the way human persons provide for themselves and their communities the material wherewithal to sustain life and prosperity. Our food, clothing, land, and dwellings, the means of our transportation, communication, education, defense, entertainment and religion – these are the sorts of things that become our property. They are not persons, who are our family members, fellow citizens, friends and enemies. They are not ideas or thoughts or sentiments. Nor are they those common cosmic things such as galaxies or forces such as magnetism. When we speak of property we are interested with just those sorts of things, material non-persons, of which we can properly say that they are *one's own* and which we use in satisfaction of the needs and interests of our individual and communal lives.

The first relation in the constitution of property recognizes in material things a potentiality for satisfying some need or interest of mankind. In a broad sense,

---

[32] David Lametti, "The Objects of Virtue" in *Property and Community*, edited by Gregory S. Alexander and Eduardo M. Peñalver (Oxford and New York: Oxford University Press, 2010): pp. 1–37.

[33] *Compendium of the Social Doctrine of the Church* (Washington, D.C.: Liberia Editrice Vaticana, 2004), no. 164.

the orientation of the things of the world to the service of human life permits one to speak of the goodness of creation or the beneficence of nature. Even if the contemporary cosmologist would reject such a strong sense of purposiveness, science's own explanatory mechanisms conclude in the recognition of an equally remarkable evolutionary adaptability of human beings to the given conditions of the cosmos. In sum, the principle that has come to be called the "universal destination of material goods" rests on the fact that the non-human world provides the basic material conditions for human life. It only adds to the simple fact of the matter that it is no mere accident: one recognizes in the reality a certain fitting relationship between mankind and the world human beings inhabit. At this level of analysis there is as yet no property or ownership. We only acknowledge in a broad class of material things a universal potentiality for or orientation toward the good of mankind in general. Things are not divided into those that are mine and those that are yours. Quite the opposite: it appears that anything, seen simply as an answer to human need or interest, is equally destined to this person as to that person.

The second constitutive relation enters into our "work-up" of the concept of property due to the obvious difference between the earth's potentialities and their actualization in the satisfaction of man's particular needs and interests. Things need to be made into available and serviceable goods. Through the act of production and the arts of management and administration material things are made into serviceable and available goods. It is the genius of the laborer, the worker, and the manager that appropriates the resources of the earth. What is broadly destined for many, or any, is appropriated by this one or that one and transformed into an available good. Work introduces an essential relationship of "one's own" into the meaning of those things we shall finally call "property." Just how this is so has been a central philosophical interest of this paper, but for the moment it is enough to identify work as the original basis for the appropriation which is a further step forward in the constitution of the notion of property.

Property receives its complete identity when appropriated material goods enter into the sphere of civic life governed by law and custom. The material things around which we order our lives in civic associations are recognized as homesteads, tools, copyrights, businesses, stocks and bonds. We buy, sell, inherit, deed, loan, trade, and insure these things in mutually understood compacts of law and custom. Civic society orders particular forms for the possession and transfer of ownership. The works of fabrication, management, and administration transform material resources into serviceable goods, but it is only as these goods, their usage, and ownership are regulated by civic law and custom that they become property in the full sense of the term. If property is a form of power, it is also a power that has been ordered with regard to the integrity and common interests of a civic association. In a given civic community the relationships of ownership and the use of material things are taken up into the ties of justice and benevolence that are essential to the civic bonds of a *res publica*.

VIII. Some Practical Implications

The just appreciation of property as an essential human institution requires an array of dispositions as part of the education of a culture or society. In his *Restoration of Property* Hilarie Belloc diagnosed in Western culture a growing indifference toward ownership of private property. He thought that both capitalism and communism were symptomatic, each in its own way, of a people grown content with the wage and the entitlement. The deeper intent of his book was to re-arouse Western man to the desire for ownership and personal property. In Belloc's view the desire for ownership and property is a practical face of mankind's love of freedom.[34] He rightly understood that any restoration would have to start with a change in mentality.[35] He was little inclined to the politics of revolution, and believed that where desire is ardent and widespread, the institutions will follow. "Change the culture" would be a contemporary way to put it. A healthy civic culture would foster admiration for and participation in the creative and personal dimensions of property. Although one need not share Belloc's distributivist ideals or his nostalgia for the economy of the self-sufficient land owner, I do think there is wisdom to his understanding of the spirit of ownership and the commitment to personal property. What is needed is a restoration of a practical appreciation and effective cultivation of the dispositions and virtues that perfect the personalist foundations of property. Let me finish this paper with a short list of the sorts of disposition that I have in mind.

The importance of ownership and work. A society or legal system will find itself in some stage of immaturity or decay to the degree that it sanctions too great a separation between rights of ownership and the responsible agency of work. Recall that it is the elemental sense of work that establishes identity between the productive person and the things produced. In positive terms, work has personal meaning: one's intelligence and labor is invested in those goods and services that contribute to a society's prosperity. It is a mistake to reduce the good of work to the material goods that it puts at one's disposal for use. John Paul II and decades before him John Dewey pointed out possibilities for exercising in our work a range of human excellences.[36] There is wisdom to a culture that encourages the personalist ties of ownership and work.

---

[34] Hilaire Belloc, *Restoration of Property* (New York: Sheed & Ward, 1936), p. 64.

[35] Belloc, pp. 34–35, 105–106.

[36] John Dewey, *The School and Society and the Child and the Curriculum*, Introduction by Philip W. Jackson (Chicago and London: University of Chicago Press, 1956),

Work's creativity and subsidiarity. Genius and creativity cannot be bureaucratized. They thrive in local situations and subsidiary institutions. One can franchise their results or findings. But the findings and results come from immersion in the particular creative intuitions of the inventors and entrepreneurs. A social order that fosters prosperity will take care to protect and liberate the social and institutional spheres in which productive creativity thrives. Moreover, acknowledgement and recognition of genius and creativity will have a surer and more abiding presence in local and subsidiary communities.

Solidarity of justice and benevolence. It is a mean and meager social order, if not dangerous and repressive, that denies or practically neglects the principle of universal destination of material things. The virtues of justice and benevolence witness to the fact that men and women know a measure of personal perfection in their exercise of responsibility that extends beyond self-interest. Enjoyment of private property belongs to a pattern of conduct that bears social responsibility. Ideologies that delegitimize private property effectively authorize the social usurpation of the power of property and thereby diminish the need and occasion for the development and practice virtues of justice and benevolence among members of a community. These social virtues englobe the ethics of ownership and extend the interpersonal ties that build up the web of human relationships. They bring to perfection, through responsible conduct on the personal and civic scale, the original intention of persons and the human community flourishing in created material world.

Industriousnesss, Stewardship, Optimism. Cultivating the personal disposition of industriousness should go hand and hand with appreciating the creativity at the origin of the property that is so much a part of world that surrounds and sustains us. One should learn the arts of stewardship for both natural resources and the genius of cultures that develop them for the wellbeing of humankind. Finally, the spirit of optimism gives the confidence that it is the same powers of reason and freedom, which are released in the developing the material resource of the world, that can know and foster the good of the human community.

Summary

This essay brings out the personalist dimensions of the idea of property. What takes on the form of "property" by virtue of the law and customs of a civil society is something more primitive or foundational, namely, an external thing identified as "one's own." The idea of "one's own," for its part, rests upon or emerges from the even prior

---

pp. 23–24; John Paul II, Encyclical Letter *Laborem Exercens* December 14, 1981, esp. nos. 4, 6–7, 9.

notions of responsible agency and productive activity. These notions, in turn, originate in even more foundational notions of personal being and a meaningful cosmos.

Zusammenfassung

Der Vortrag befasst sich mit den personalen Dimensionen, die der Idee des Eigentums innewohnen. Wenn etwas zu „Eigentum" wird, wie es das Gesetz oder das Brauchtum in der Zivilgesellschaft vorsieht, dann geschieht etwas Grundlegendes: Ein äußeres Gut gehört „mir" und wird mit mir identifiziert. Dem Ausdruck „one's own" liegt der Bezug auf Verantwortung und schöpferische Aktivität zugrunde. Diese Elemente wiederum sind verankert im Bewusstsein um das Personsein und einen sinnerfüllten Kosmos.

Die universelle Bestimmung der Güter

Zur Eigentumsethik der christlichen Gesellschaftslehre

Von Manfred Spieker

I. Zwei Pfeiler der Eigentumsethik der christlichen Gesellschaftslehre

In ihrer Eigentumsethik versucht die christliche Gesellschaftslehre zwei Aussagen miteinander zu verbinden, die auf den ersten Blick nicht leicht miteinander in Einklang zu bringen sind. Die eine Aussage unterstreicht die Bedeutung des Privateigentums für die Freiheit und die personale Entfaltung des Menschen und erklärt das Recht auf persönliches Eigentum zum Naturrecht. Die andere Aussage ruft in Erinnerung, dass Gott die Güter dieser Erde zum Nutzen aller Menschen und Völker bestimmt hat und dass sie deshalb auch allen zugute kommen müssen. Wird die eine Aussage von der jeweils anderen getrennt, entstehen leicht Missverständnisse, Kontroversen oder gar Ideologien. Dies gilt für die katholische Soziallehre ebenso wie für die evangelische Sozialethik. Auch wenn die meisten der folgenden Zitate den Sozialenzykliken und anderen Dokumenten der katholischen Kirche entnommen sind, so gelten alle grundlegenden Aussagen auch für die evangelische Sozialethik in der Tradition Martin Luthers.[1] Auf Besonderheiten der Russisch-Orthodoxen Kirche ist eigens hinzuweisen.

Die erste Aussage der Eigentumsethik der christlichen Gesellschaftslehre, die Betonung des Rechts auf persönliches Eigentum, wird von Leo XIII. 1891 in der Enzyklika *Rerum novarum* (RN 4) dem Sozialismus entgegengehalten, der mit Karl Marx im Privateigentum die Quelle aller menschlichen Entfremdung und allen gesellschaftlichen Elends sah und sich – zumindest bis 1989 – von dessen Beseitigung die Aufhebung aller Entfremdung erhoffte. Diese Aus-

---

[1] Zur Eigentumsethik der Evangelischen Kirche in Deutschland vgl. die Denkschrift der EKD „Gemeinwohl und Eigennutz", Gütersloh 1991, S. 95 ff.; die Denkschrift „Eigentumsbildung in sozialer Verantwortung" von 1962, in: Die Denkschriften der EKD, hrsg. von der Kirchenkanzlei der EKD, Bd. 2, Gütersloh 1978, S. 19 ff.; den Evangelischen Erwachsenenkatechismus, 5. Aufl., Gütersloh 1989, S. 673 ff.; *Martin Honecker*, Grundriß der Sozialethik, Berlin 1995, S. 471 ff.; *Theodor Strohm*, Eigentum, II. Theologisch und sozialethisch, in: Evangelisches Staatslexikon, hrsg. von Roman Herzog u. a., 3. Aufl., Stuttgart 1987, Sp. 686 ff.

sage kann, wird sie isoliert, zu dem Missverständnis führen, die christliche Gesellschaftslehre wolle die bestehende Eigentumsordnung legitimieren. Die zweite Aussage, ebenfalls schon von Leo XIII. in *Rerum novarum* (RN 7), dann von Pius XI. 1931 in *Quadragesimo anno* (QA 45 ff.) und noch ausführlicher von Johannes Paul II. in seinen Sozialenzykliken und vom Päpstlichen Rat Justitia et Pax im Kompendium der Soziallehre der Kirche entfaltet, kann zu dem gegenteiligen Irrtum führen, die christliche Gesellschaftslehre schwäche die Bedeutung des Privateigentums ab und halte alternative Eigentumsformen bis hin zum Gemeineigentum für nicht weniger legitim. Pius XI. warnte schon in *Quadragesimo anno* vor den „zwei gefährlichen Einseitigkeiten", die sich aus der Leugnung oder Abschwächung der Sozialfunktion des Eigentums einerseits und der Individualfunktion andererseits ergäben und entweder zum Individualismus oder zum Kollektivismus führten (QA 46). Doch auch dann, wenn diese Einseitigkeiten vermieden und beide Aussagen zusammen im Auge behalten werden, ist es nicht leicht, ihr rechtes Verhältnis zu bestimmen. Dies spiegelt sich bereits in der Geschichte der Christenheit.

Im ersten Jahrtausend der Christenheit spielt die sozialethische Frage nach dem Eigentum als Ordnungsidee noch keine Rolle. Im Zentrum der Betrachtungen steht die individualethische Frage nach dem richtigen Gebrauch des Eigentums, die ihre Antwort zum einen in den Zehn Geboten und zum anderen im 1. Johannesbrief findet. Erst im 13. Jahrhundert stoßen wir bei Thomas von Aquin (1225–1274) auf sozialethische Überlegungen über das Eigentum als Ordnungsidee. Die Frage, ob es erlaubt sei, eine Sache als Eigentum zu besitzen, wird von ihm bejaht, weil erstens „ein jeder mehr Sorge darauf verwendet, etwas zu beschaffen, was ihm allein gehört, als etwas, was allen oder vielen gehört", zweitens „die menschlichen Angelegenheiten besser verwaltet werden, wenn jeder Einzelne seine eigenen Sorgen hat in der Beschaffung irgendwelcher Dinge" und drittens, „die friedliche Verfassung der Menschen besser gewahrt bleibt". Je mehr etwas allen oder vielen gehört, desto häufiger gäbe es Streit.[2] Thomas greift hier Argumente auf, mit denen Aristoteles (384–322 v. Chr.) Platons Plädoyer für eine Gütergemeinschaft kritisierte.[3] Er legitimiert das individuelle Eigentum aus pragmatischen Gründen als Ordnungsidee, weniger als subjektives Recht, und er unterscheidet zwischen dem Erwerb und dem Gebrauch des Eigentums. Der Mensch habe zwar das Recht zum Erwerb von Eigentum. Aber wie die Kirchenväter mahnte er, die äußeren Dinge nicht als Eigentum, sondern „als Gemeinbesitz" zu gebrauchen, sie also in den Dienst der Mitmenschen zu stellen. Der absolute Eigentümer aller Dinge bleibe Gott. Von Arbeit als Legitimationsgrund des individuellen Eigentums ist bei Thomas noch nicht die Rede.

---

[2] *Thomas von Aquin*, Summa theologiae II-II, 66, a. 2.

[3] *Aristoteles*, Politik 1261 a.

Der Klassiker, der das individuelle Recht auf Eigentum mit der menschlichen Arbeit begründet, ist John Locke (1632–1704). In seinem Second Treatise of Government schreibt er 1689, dass die Erde und alle niederen Lebewesen zwar allen Menschen gemeinsam gehören, dass aber „doch jeder Mensch ein Eigentum an seiner eigenen Person" habe. Deshalb seien auch „die Arbeit seines Körpers und das Werk seiner Hände ... im eigentlichen Sinne sein". Was immer der Mensch deshalb dem Naturzustand entrückt und mit seiner Arbeit gemischt hat, hat er „folglich zu seinem Eigentum gemacht"[4]. John Locke ist zwar weder Kirchenvater noch Kirchenlehrer, aber seine Begründung des Privateigentums spielte im 19. Jahrhundert, in dem die christliche Gesellschaftslehre entstand, eine erhebliche Rolle. Während sich Wilhelm Emmanuel von Ketteler (1811–1877) 1848, zwei Jahre vor seiner Ernennung zum Bischof von Mainz, in seinen berühmten Adventspredigten im Mainzer Dom, in denen er die katholische Lehre vom Eigentum gegen den Liberalismus einerseits und den Kommunismus andererseits abgrenzte, noch ganz an Thomas von Aquin orientierte[5], greifen Luigi Taparelli, Matteo Liberatore und Tommaso Zigliara, die für Papst Leo XIII. die Sozialenzyklika *Rerum novarum* vorbereiten, auch auf John Lockes Eigentumslehre zurück. Zwei Aspekte haben auf diese erste und grundlegende Enzyklika erheblichen Einfluss: Lockes Individualismus und die Arbeit als Legitimitätskriterium für das Recht auf Privateigentum.

In verschiedenen Untersuchungen zur Entwicklung der Eigentumsethik der christlichen Gesellschaftslehre, die Anfang der 1970er–Jahre erschienen, wurde der Eigentumslehre von *Rerum novarum* vorgehalten, dass sie zu individualistisch begründet werde, der universellen Bestimmung der Güter nicht den ihr angemessenen Platz lasse und den Sozialbezug des Eigentums nur über die Religion bzw. die Pflicht zum Almosengeben wieder einführe.[6] Auf Grund der Auseinandersetzung mit der marxistischen Ablehnung des Privateigentums ist das individuelle Recht auf Eigentum gewiss stark akzentuiert worden. Aber dieses individuelle Recht auf Privateigentum ist auch eine Konsequenz der personalen Anthropologie der christlichen Gesellschaftslehre und ihres Subsidiaritätsprinzips. Deshalb bleibt es ein Pfeiler der Eigentumsethik der christlichen

---

[4] *John Locke*, Über die Regierung II, 27 und 32; deutsch Reinbek 1966, S. 27 und 30.

[5] *Wilhelm Emmanuel von Ketteler*, Die katholische Lehre vom Eigentum, in: Texte zur katholischen Soziallehre, hrsg. von der Katholischen Arbeitnehmerbewegung, Bd. II, 1. Halbband, Köln 1976, S. 87 ff.

[6] *Helmut Sorgenfrei*, Die geistesgeschichtlichen Hintergründe der Sozialenzyklika Rerum Novarum, Heidelberg 1970, S. 114, 146 und 155; *Friedrich Beutter*, Die Eigentumsbegründung in der Moraltheologie des 19. Jahrhunderts, Paderborn 1971, S. 74 und passim; *Oswald von Nell-Breuning*, Soziallehre der Kirche. Erläuterungen der lehramtlichen Dokumente, 2. Aufl., Wien 1978, S. 33. Nell-Breuning spricht von einem „argen Schönheitsfehler, daß die Arbeiterenzyklika mit einer solchen Apologie des Eigentums beginnt". Vgl. auch *Martin Honecker*, a. a. O., S. 481.

Gesellschaftslehre, auch wenn es im Laufe des 20. Jahrhunderts durch die Betonung des anderen Pfeilers von der universellen Bestimmung der Güter nicht nur relativiert, sondern diesem untergeordnet wurde. Vor allem im Kompendium der Soziallehre der Kirche wird dies deutlich.[7]

II. Die Begründung des Privateigentums

Die Eigentumsethik der christlichen Gesellschaftslehre geht davon aus, dass Gott „die Erde mit allem, was sie enthält, zum Nutzen aller Menschen und Völker bestimmt" hat und dass deshalb „diese geschaffenen Güter in einem billigen Verhältnis allen zustatten kommen" müssen (*Gaudium et spes* [GS 69]).[8] Die Eigentumsethik wurzelt also in der Schöpfungslehre, und bereits die Schöpfungslehre führt zum Recht auf Privateigentum. Weil der Mensch von Gott nicht nur als Geist-, sondern auch als Leibwesen erschaffen wurde, ist er auf die äußeren Güter angewiesen. Weil er die Pflicht zur Selbsterhaltung hat, hat er auch das Recht auf die dafür notwendigen Güter, und weil ihm als Gottes Ebenbild die Herrschaft über die Erde aufgetragen wurde, ist er befugt, diese Güter in seinen Dienst zu stellen. Diese Indienststellung erfolgt in der Regel durch Arbeit. Sie führt zum Erwerb von Eigentum und damit von Verfügungsmacht über äußere Güter (*Laborem exercens* [LE 12]; *Centesimus annus* [CA 31]; Kompendium 176). Das Privateigentum vermittelt so „den unbedingt nötigen Raum für eigenverantwortliche Gestaltung des persönlichen Lebens jedes einzelnen und seiner Familie" und muss „als eine Art Verlängerung der menschlichen Freiheit betrachtet werden". Es spornt an „zur Übernahme von Aufgaben und Verantwortung" und zählt damit „zu den Voraussetzungen staatsbürgerlicher Freiheit" (GS 71; Kompendium 176).[9]

Diese positive Begründung des Privateigentums, die vor allem von Johannes XXIII. 1961 in der Enzyklika *Mater et magistra* entfaltet wird (MM 108–121), wird ergänzt durch eine Argumentation via negationis: das Fehlen des Privateigentums führe zu Trägheit, Unordnung, Bürokratie und Machtkonzentration, sozialem Unfrieden und einer Bedrohung der Freiheit und damit der Würde des Menschen (MM 109).[10] So ist das Recht auf Privateigentum – auch

---

[7] Päpstlicher Rat Justitia et Pax, Kompendium der Soziallehre der Kirche (2004), 172, 176, 282.

[8] Vgl. auch die Denkschrift der EKD „Gemeinwohl und Eigennutz", a. a. O., Ziffer 137; *Theodor Strohm*, a. a. O., S. 687.

[9] „Gemeinwohl und Eigennutz", a. a. O., Ziffer 130 und 132; „Eigentumsbildung in sozialer Verantwortung", a. a. O., S. 21.

[10] Vgl. dazu auch *Joseph Kardinal Höffner*, Christliche Gesellschaftslehre, Kevelaer 1963, S. 163 ff., und die Denkschrift der EKD „Gemeinwohl und Eigennutz", a. a. O., Ziffer 134.

an Produktionsmitteln – ein dem Menschen auf Grund seiner Natur zukommendes Recht (MM 108–112; *Pacem in terris* [PT 21]).

Eine andere Position nimmt die Russisch-Orthodoxe Kirche ein. Sie hat sich in ihrem im August 2000 verabschiedeten Sozialwort „Grundlagen der Sozialdoktrin der Russisch-Orthodoxen Kirche" zur Frage des Eigentums geäußert. Dabei sind ihre Schwierigkeiten, sich von den sowjetischen Traditionen zu lösen, unübersehbar. Sie kann sich zu keiner eindeutigen Bejahung des Privateigentums durchringen. „Die Kirche erkennt die Existenz zahlreicher Eigentumsformen an. Die staatliche, öffentliche, körperschaftliche, private und gemischte Eigentumsform sind in den einzelnen Ländern auf unterschiedliche Art und Weise im Verlauf der historischen Entwicklung verankert worden. Aus Sicht der Kirche ist keine dieser Formen zu bevorzugen."[11]

III. Die Unterordnung des Privateigentums unter die universelle Bestimmung der Güter

Das Naturrecht auf persönliches Eigentum bleibt für die christliche Gesellschaftslehre immer der universellen Bestimmung der Güter untergeordnet. Die christliche Tradition habe, so Johannes Paul II., „dieses Recht nie als absolut und unantastbar betrachtet. Ganz im Gegenteil, sie hat es immer im umfassenden Rahmen des gemeinsamen Rechtes aller auf Nutzung der Güter der Schöpfung insgesamt gesehen; m. a. W., das private Eigentumsrecht ist dem Recht auf die gemeine Nutzung, der Bestimmung der Güter für alle untergeordnet" (LE 14).[12]

In zahlreichen Begriffspaaren haben die Vertreter der christlichen Gesellschaftslehre versucht, die Beziehung zwischen den beiden Pfeilern der Eigentumsethik zu kennzeichnen. Die universelle Bestimmung der Güter wurde als „absolutes" oder „primäres" Naturrecht, das Recht auf Privateigentum als „relatives" oder „sekundäres" Naturrecht[13], erstere auch als „Gotteswerk" oder

---

[11] Die Grundlagen der Sozialdoktrin der Russisch-Orthodoxen Kirche, hrsg. von Josef Thesing und Rudolf Uertz, St. Augustin 2001, S. 61.

[12] Vgl. auch *Pius XII.*, La Solennità. Botschaft zur Fünfzigjahrfeier des Rundschreibens „Rerum novarum" vom 01.06.1941, in: Utz / Groner 506; Populorum progressio (PP 23); Libertatis conscientia (LC 87); Sollicitudo rei socialis (SRS 42); Christifideles laici (CL 43); Leitlinien der Kongregation für das Katholische Bildungswesen, 42; CA 30; Katechismus der Katholischen Kirche (KKK 2402–2404); Kompendium 177 und 282.

[13] Vgl. *Jean-Yves Calvez / Jacques Perrin*, Kirche und Wirtschaftsgesellschaft. Die Soziallehre der Päpste von Leo XIII. bis zu Johannes XXIII., Recklinghausen 1965, Bd. 2, S. 49; *Johannes Messner*, Das Naturrecht. Handbuch der Gesellschaftsethik, Staatsethik und Wirtschaftsethik, 6. Aufl., Innsbruck 1966, S. 1068; *Franz Klüber*, Eigentumstheorie und Eigentumspolitik. Begründung und Gestaltung des Privateigen-

„Grundgesetz" und letzteres als „Menschenwerk" oder „Ausführungsbestimmung" bezeichnet.[14] Schon Thomas von Aquin hatte die universelle Bestimmung der Güter auf das Naturrecht, d. h. auf die Schöpfungsordnung zurückgeführt und das Recht auf Privateigentum auf das positive Recht, das der menschlichen Vernunft entstammt und dem Naturrecht nicht entgegensteht.[15] Das Privateigentum ist „nur ein Instrument im Hinblick auf die Einhaltung des Prinzips von der allgemeinen Bestimmung der Güter und damit letztlich kein Zweck, sondern ein Mittel" (Kompendium 177). Das Prinzip von der universellen Bestimmung der Güter gilt „auch für die Völkergemeinschaft" (PP 49).[16] Gemahnt wurde immer wieder, die Eigentumsethik nicht auf eine Verteilungsethik zu beschränken, sondern auch nach der Bedeutung der Produktion und der Güterverwendung für die Realisierung des Prinzips von der universellen Bestimmung der Güter zu fragen.[17]

Das Privateigentum gilt somit als am besten geeignetes Instrument zur Verwirklichung der universellen Bestimmung der Güter. Nicht Genossenschafts- oder Gemeineigentum sind unter Berücksichtigung der conditio humana das optimale Mittel zur Realisierung dieses Prinzips, sondern das persönliche Eigentum, das in jeder Gesellschaft der Sicherung durch eine geeignete Rechts- und Verfassungsordnung bedarf. Die Sozialenzykliken, das II. Vatikanische Konzil und das Kompendium haben auf die Geschichtlichkeit und damit auf die Wandelbarkeit der Institution des Privateigentums und seiner rechtlichen Regelungen hingewiesen (RN 7; QA 49; Pius XII., La Solennità, in: Utz / Groner 506; GS 69; Kompendium 180). Sie haben die sozial- und kulturstaatliche Ausweitung des Eigentumsbegriffs rezipiert. In dieser Perspektive zählen zum Eigentum nicht nur Grund und Boden sowie veräußerbare Güter, die Konsum- oder Produktionszwecken dienen können, sondern auch Rechtsansprüche auf Leistungen staatlicher oder genossenschaftlicher Systeme der Daseinsvorsorge (GS 71; LE 19).[18] Auch eine Berufsausbildung und bestimmte handwerkliche, technische oder künstlerische Fähigkeiten, Urheberrechte, Talente oder Patente

---

tums nach katholischer Gesellschaftslehre, Osnabrück 1963, S. 81 f.; *Lothar Roos*, Ordnung und Gestaltung der Wirtschaft. Grundlagen und Grundsätze der Wirtschaftsethik nach dem II. Vatikanischen Konzil, Köln 1971, S. 104 f.

[14] *Oswald von Nell-Breuning*, Gerechtigkeit und Freiheit. Grundzüge katholischer Soziallehre, Wien 1980, S. 198.

[15] *Thomas von Aquin*, Summa theologiae II-II, 66, a. 2, ad 1.

[16] So *Joseph Kardinal Höffner*, Die Weltwirtschaft im Licht der katholischen Soziallehre, in: Lothar Roos (Hrsg.), Stimmen der Kirche zur Wirtschaft, Köln 1986, S. 37.

[17] *Oswald von Nell-Breuning*, Soziallehre der Kirche, a. a. O., S. 144; *Anton Rauscher*, Die Bestimmung der Erdengüter für alle Menschen und ihre Verwirklichung in der modernen Wirtschaft, in: ders., Kirche in der Welt. Beiträge zur christlichen Gesellschaftsverantwortung, Bd. 1, Würzburg 1988, S. 321.

[18] Vgl. auch die Denkschrift der EKD „Gemeinwohl und Eigennutz", a. a. O., Ziffer 133.

zählen als immaterielles Eigentum zum Privateigentum, das rechtlichen Schutz genießt und dem Grundsatz der universellen Bestimmung der Güter untergeordnet bleiben muss (CA 32; Kompendium 179). Der Eigentumsschutz erfordert deshalb eine „dauerhafte und verläßliche Qualifikationspolitik" für ein lebenslanges Lernen.[19]

Die Relativität des Eigentums und die staatliche Interventionsbefugnis im Hinblick auf die Eigentumsordnung bedeuten aber nicht, dass der Staat das persönliche Eigentum aufheben, durch überhöhte Besteuerung aushöhlen oder durch Gemeineigentum ersetzen darf. Das Recht auf persönliches Eigentum sowie das Erbrecht müssen in ihrer Substanz „immer unberührt und unverletzt bleiben" (QA 49). Das Recht auf Privateigentum bleibt „in sich gültig und notwendig", auch wenn es „innerhalb der Grenzen seiner sozialen Funktion umschrieben werden muß" (Leitlinien 42; CA 30). Es muss „das Recht des Menschen auf Freiheit schützen und zugleich einen unentbehrlichen Beitrag leisten zum Aufbau der rechten gesellschaftlichen Ordnung" (MM 111).

IV. Die Menschenwürde als Grenze des Privateigentums

Eigentumsansprüche können sich auf Güter und Dienstleistungen, auf Rentenanwartschaften, Urheberrechte, Patente und ähnliches, niemals aber auf Menschen richten. Einen Eigentumsanspruch auf einen Menschen zu erheben, heißt ihn versklaven. „Ein Freiheitsrecht gibt niemals Herrschaft über andere."[20] Das Recht auf freie Entfaltung der Persönlichkeit – zum Beispiel des Forschers – hat seine Grenze an den Rechten anderer (Art. 2,1 GG). „Grundrechtliche Freiheit bedeutet Selbstbestimmung, nicht aber Bestimmung über andere. Sie endet vor der grundrechtlichen Freiheit des anderen und gibt kein Recht über dessen Person."[21] Dennoch war die Sklaverei viele Jahrhunderte lang gesellschaftlich akzeptiert – auch in Völkern mit christlicher Kultur, obwohl bereits der Apostel Paulus die Axt an ihre Wurzel gelegt hatte, als er im Jahr 55 n. Chr. den Sklavenhalter Philemon bat, den Sklaven Onesimus, der Philemon entlaufen, Christ geworden und von Paulus zu ihm zurückgeschickt worden war, nicht als sein Eigentum, sondern als Bruder zu behandeln (Phlm 16). Heute scheint die Sklaverei zumindest im christlichen Kulturkreis überwunden

---

[19] Das Soziale neu denken. Für eine langfristig angelegte Reformpolitik, Erklärung der Kommission für gesellschaftliche und soziale Fragen der Deutschen Bischofskonferenz vom 12.12.2003, S. 16 f.

[20] *Paul Kirchhof*, Genforschung und die Freiheit der Wissenschaft, in: Otfried Höffe u. a. (Hrsg.), Gentechnik und Menschenwürde, Köln 2002, S. 9. Vgl. auch *Martin Honecker*, a. a. O., S. 487.

[21] *Josef Isensee*, Der grundrechtliche Status des Embryos, in: Ottfried Höffe u. a. (Hrsg.), Gentechnik und Menschenwürde, a. a. O., S. 50.

zu sein. Die Problematik des Eigentums an Menschen erhält aber über die Debatte um die Forschung an embryonalen Stammzellen eine neue Aktualität. Die Forderung, die sogenannten „verwaisten" oder „überzähligen" Embryonen für die Stammzellforschung benutzen zu können, impliziert, sie als Rohstoffressource für die Entwicklung neuer Therapien für bisher unheilbare Krankheiten zu verwenden. Sie bedeutet mithin, die Embryonen nicht als Personen und damit als Rechtssubjekte, sondern als Sachen zu betrachten. Um die Legitimität dieses Anspruchs zu begründen, wird eine Reihe von Unterscheidungen eingeführt, die den Nachweis erbringen sollen, dass der Embryo in vitro bzw. der kryokonservierte Embryo noch keine Person sei. Zu diesen Unterscheidungen zählen jene zwischen Menschen bzw. werdenden Menschen einerseits und menschlichem Leben andererseits, zwischen dem Embryo in vitro und dem Embryo in utero, zwischen dem Präembryo und dem Embryo, der abstrakten und der konkreten Möglichkeit der Menschwerdung oder zwischen Embryonen, die in kommunikativen Verhältnissen leben, Interessen besitzen und Empfindungen haben, und Embryonen, denen alle diese Merkmale abgehen. Diese Unterscheidungen dienen dem Zweck, Embryonen im jeweils minderen Status das Personsein und den Würdeschutz absprechen und Eigentumsansprüche der Gesellschaft für Forschungs- und Therapieprojekte begründen zu können.[22] Sie erinnern an die Versuche, die Legitimität der Sklaverei dadurch zu begründen, dass die Menschen in zwei Typen eingeteilt wurden, in solche, die Leitungsfunktionen wahrnehmen können, und in solche, die nur ausführende Funktionen wahrzunehmen in der Lage seien. Dieser Begründungsversuch ist vor dem Hintergrund des christlichen Menschenbildes so wenig überzeugend wie jenes Urteil des Supreme Court von North Carolina, der 1829 die Klage gegen einen Sklavenbesitzer wegen schwerer Körperverletzung seiner Sklavin – er hatte sie während eines Fluchtversuchs niedergeschossen – mit der Begründung zurückwies, die Sklavin sei sein Eigentum. Da sie damit seiner vollen Verfügungsgewalt unterstehe, könne die Tat nicht als Körperverletzung gewertet werden.[23]

Angesichts der Verfügungsansprüche der Wissenschaft und der Medizin über die sogenannten verwaisten oder die für Forschungs- und Therapiezwecke eigens erzeugten Embryonen stellt sich die Frage, ob die Gesellschaft nicht dabei ist, diese Embryonen zu den Sklaven des 21. Jahrhunderts zu machen. Eine Diskussion über das Eigentum als Ordnungsidee kann deshalb die Stammzelldebatte nicht ignorieren. Sie muss zeigen, dass es ein Eigentum an Embryonen

---

[22] Vgl. *Manfred Spieker*, Zwischen Forschungsfreiheit und Embryonenschutz. Kontroversen in der Bioethik, in: ders., Der verleugnete Rechtsstaat. Anmerkungen zur Kultur des Todes in Europa, 2. Aufl., Paderborn 2011, S. 63 ff.

[23] State vs. Mann, 13 N.C. (2 Dev) 263 (1829). Vgl. auch: Scott vs. Sandfort, 60 U.S. 393 (1857).

nicht geben kann, auch nicht an Embryonen in vitro, da sie sich nicht erst zum Menschen, sondern als Menschen entwickeln.[24] Dafür hatte Immanuel Kant (1724–1804) in seiner Metaphysik der Sitten 1798 ein entscheidendes Argument geliefert. Aus dem Akt der Zeugung gehe eine Person hervor, nicht eine Sache. Eltern könnten deshalb „ihr Kind nicht gleichsam als ihr Gemächsel und als ihr Eigentum zerstören ..."[25] Auch der Nasciturus und der Embryo in vitro sind nie Sachen, auf die Besitzansprüche erhoben werden könnten, sondern Personen mit dem Anspruch auf unbedingte Anerkennung.[26] Aus Sachen können nie Personen werden. Die Alternative Verwerten oder Verwerfen[27] ist somit eine unangemessene Alternative, weil sie den verwaisten Embryo auf eine Sache reduziert, ihn mithin einer Fremdherrschaft unterwirft. Wenn dem Embryo in vitro mit dem Uterus eine existentielle Bedingung seiner weiteren Entwicklung vorenthalten wird, bedeutet dies noch nicht, dass er in das Eigentum eines Laborchefs oder der Gesellschaft übergeht und wie eine Sache Forschungs-, Therapie- oder sonstigen Verwertungsinteressen untergeordnet werden darf. Eigentumsansprüche haben an der Menschenwürde und dem Lebensrecht eines jeden Menschen ihre unantastbare Grenze.

V. Privateigentum und Gemeinwohl

Den Beitrag zur rechten gesellschaftlichen Ordnung leistet das Privateigentum dann, wenn es sich der universellen Bestimmung der Güter unterordnet. Es hat zum Gemeinwohl beizutragen. Das Recht auf Privateigentum könne, erklärte die Glaubenskongregation, „nicht ohne die Verpflichtung für das Gemeinwohl verstanden werden" (LC 87; Kompendium 282).[28] Diese Verpflichtung bedeutet nicht, dass der Eigentümer seine Verfügungsbefugnis über das Eigentum an den Staat abzutreten hätte, wohl aber, dass das Privateigentum weit gestreut sein, und, in welcher Form auch immer, möglichst vielen Menschen zugute kommen muss. Der Eigentümer muss sich der sozialen Hypothek des Privateigentums bewusst bleiben und den Vorrang der Arbeit gegenüber dem Kapital anerkennen. Der Gesetzgeber hat dementsprechend die Pflicht, dies bei

---

[24] Vgl. auch BVerfGE 88, 203 (252).

[25] *Immanuel Kant*, Metaphysik der Sitten, § 28, in: ders., Werke, hrsg. von Wilhelm Weischedel, Bd. VIII, S. 394.

[26] Vgl. *Robert Spaemann*, Personen. Versuche über den Unterschied zwischen ‚etwas' und ‚jemand', Stuttgart 1996.

[27] *Paul Kirchhof*, a. a. O., S. 30.

[28] Vgl. auch die Denkschrift der EKD „Gemeinwohl und Eigennutz", a. a. O., Ziffer 136.

der Regelung des Eigentums-, des Steuer-, des Sozial- und des Betriebsverfassungsrechts zu beachten (MM 115; SRS 42).[29]

Problematisch erscheint dagegen die These, die Funktion des Privateigentums bestehe darin, der Verwirklichung des Gemeinwohls zu dienen.[30] Gewiss ist die gegenteilige These, das Gemeinwohl sei nur Mittel zur Sicherung des Privateigentums, falsch. Doch folgt aus dieser falschen These noch nicht, dass das Gemeinwohl „Grund, Finalität und Regulativ des Eigentumsrechts ist"[31]. Diese einseitige Indienststellung des Privateigentums für den Zweck des Gemeinwohls tendiert dazu, die anthropozentrische Orientierung des Gemeinwohls in der christlichen Gesellschaftslehre zu übersehen. Wenn das Gemeinwohl die Gesamtheit der politischen, sozialen, ökonomischen und rechtlichen Möglichkeitsbedingungen personaler Entfaltung des Menschen ist (MM 65; GS 26 und 74; CL 42), dann ist die personale Entfaltung bzw. das Gelingen des menschlichen Lebens Grund, Ziel und Grenze des Gemeinwohls und damit auch der universellen Bestimmung der Güter und des Rechts auf Privateigentum. Die katholische Eigentumsethik stellt deshalb nicht nur das Privateigentum in den Dienst des Gemeinwohls, sondern auch das Gemeinwohl in den Dienst der Person, die aber immer in Beziehungen lebt. Zu den Freiheits- und Entfaltungsbedingungen dieser Person gehört das Recht auf Privateigentum.[32] „Was für die Person getan wird, ist Dienst an der Gesellschaft, und was für die Gesellschaft getan wird, kommt der Person zugute" (CL 40).

Reflexionen über den Grundsatz von der universellen Bestimmung der Güter erwecken gelegentlich den Eindruck, der Eigentumsethik der christlichen Gesellschaftslehre ginge es nur um die Verteilung der Güter, weniger dagegen um ihre Produktion. Ein Blick in die Pastoralkonstitution *Gaudium et spes* und in die Sozialenzykliken, insbesondere in *Centesimus annus*, aber zeigt, dass dieser Eindruck nicht begründet ist. Gewiss ist es nicht Aufgabe des kirchlichen Lehramtes, wirtschaftswissenschaftliche Empfehlungen zur Produktion von Gütern und Dienstleistungen zu geben. Dies ist die Aufgabe der Christen, die sich dazu die entsprechende Sachkompetenz und Erfahrung anzueignen und die legitime Autonomie der irdischen Wirklichkeiten zu respektieren haben (PT 147–150; GS 72; CL 43). Aber das Konzil und die Päpste deuten auch an, dass es bei der Verwirklichung des Grundsatzes von der universellen Bestimmung der Güter

---

[29] Vgl. auch *Johannes Paul II.*, Ansprache auf der 3. Generalversammlung der lateinamerikanischen Bischöfe in Puebla am 28.01.1979, in: AAS, Bd. 71, S. 187–205; Libertatis conscientia (LC 84).

[30] So die Grundthese von *Franz Klüber*, a. a. O. Kritische Anmerkungen zu Klüber auch bei *Anton Rauscher*, a. a. O., S. 314.

[31] *Franz Klüber*, a. a. O., S. 107.

[32] Vgl. auch *Johannes Messner*, a. a. O., S. 1071: Das Privateigentum stehe zwar im Dienst der Gemeinwohlordnung, aber „ebenso im Dienst der Freiheitsordnung, die ja selbst fundamentaler Teil der Gemeinwohlordnung ist".

um mehr geht als um Verteilungsfragen. Es geht zunächst um Fragen der Produktion und um die vom Staat zu regelnden Produktionsbedingungen. Wenn die Güter dieser Erde allen zugute kommen sollen, dann müssen alle Zugang zum Markt haben. Jeder muss sich an der Herstellung und am Erwerb von Gütern und Dienstleistungen, d. h. am Wirtschaftsleben beteiligen können. Jeder muss die Möglichkeit haben, sein Einkommen produktiv zu verwenden, Kapital zu bilden und Eigentum auch an Produktionsmitteln erwerben zu können (RN 4). In einer dynamischen Wirtschaft führt dies zur Schaffung von Arbeitsplätzen und damit von Einkommenschancen. Der gerechte Lohn für die geleistete Arbeit ist deshalb „der konkrete Weg, auf dem die meisten Menschen zu jenen Gütern gelangen, die zur gemeinsamen Nutzung bestimmt sind" (LE 19). Die Bestimmung des gerechten Lohnes mag im Einzelfall sehr schwierig sein und aus einer ökonomischen Perspektive zu anderen Resultaten führen als aus einer sozialen Perspektive. Wenn aber Gewerkschaften, Arbeitgeberverbände und der die Rahmenbedingungen der Tarifpolitik setzende Staat am Grundsatz von der universellen Bestimmung der Güter orientiert bleiben, dann werden sie in sozialer Partnerschaft und unter Berücksichtigung der spezifischen Lage des jeweiligen Landes den monetären Lohn ergänzen um Institutionen der Vermögensbildung, der Ertragsbeteiligung und der betrieblichen Alterssicherung (LE 14). Schon Pius XI. empfahl „eine gewisse Annäherung des Lohnarbeitsverhältnisses an ein Gesellschaftsverhältnis" in der Hoffnung, dass „Arbeiter und Angestellte ... auf diese Weise zu Mitbesitz oder Mitverwaltung oder zu irgendeiner Art Gewinnbeteiligung" gelangten (QA 65; vgl. auch GS 68). Aus der christlichen Gesellschaftslehre ergeben sich zwar keine konkreten Formen der Gewinnbeteiligung. Aber Johannes Paul II. fordert die Tarifpartner auf, mit Phantasie und Sachkompetenz nach Wegen zu suchen, die die Beteiligung aller an der Herstellung und Verteilung der Güter sichern und die weite Streuung des Eigentums begünstigen (LE 14).

Darüber hinaus tragen die Mitbestimmung der Arbeitnehmer im Betrieb und der weite Bereich des Arbeitsrechts dazu bei, die Subjektstellung des Arbeitnehmers zu festigen und sein Interesse am Wirtschaftsleben zu fördern. Wenn er „Mitverantwortlicher und Mitgestalter" an seinem Arbeitsplatz ist (LE 15; CA 43), wenn er bei betrieblichen Entscheidungen Informations-, Anhörungs- und Mitbestimmungsrechte hat, wenn sein Arbeitsvertrag, seine Arbeitszeit, sein Urlaub, seine Lohnansprüche – selbst im Falle des Konkurses seines Betriebs – rechtlich geschützt sind, wenn er im Falle des Konflikts unabhängige Arbeitsgerichte anrufen kann, dann trägt dies zur Humanisierung der Arbeitswelt bei. Es erleichtert seine Integration in die Gesellschaft und seine Partizipation am ökonomischen Fortschritt.[33] So dienen Mitbestimmung und Arbeits-

---

[33] *Paul VI.*, Ansprache vor der Internationalen Arbeitsorganisation in Genf am 10.06.1969, 21; Octogesima adveniens (OA 41).

recht auch dem Grundsatz von der universellen Bestimmung der Güter (LE 15, 17, 19; Kompendium 281).

VI. Die globale Dimension der Eigentumsethik

In einer dynamischen und weltweit miteinander verflochtenen Wirtschaft kommt dem Prinzip der universellen Bestimmung der Güter eine globale Dimension zu. Wenn es auch richtig sei, so Paul VI. in *Populorum progressio*, „daß jedes Volk die Gaben, die ihm die Vorsehung als Frucht seiner Arbeit geschenkt hat, an erster Stelle genießen darf, so kann trotzdem kein Volk seinen Reichtum für sich allein beanspruchen" (PP 48). Johannes Paul II. unterstreicht in *Sollicitudo rei socialis* diese globale Dimension nicht weniger als zehn Mal (SRS 7, 9, 10, 21, 22 – zwei Mal –, 28, 39, 42, 49). Es sei unerlässlich, „jedem Volk das gleiche Recht zuzugestehen, ‚mit am Tisch des gemeinsamen Mahles zu sitzen', statt wie Lazarus draußen vor der Tür zu liegen" (SRS 33; PP 47; Kompendium 449). Deshalb seien eine Überprüfung der internationalen Handelsbeziehungen, die unter dem Protektionismus leiden, aber auch eine Stärkung internationaler Institutionen und eine internationale Sozialpolitik notwendig (SRS 43; LC 90; LE 18; Kompendium 364, 442).

Wenn die universelle Bestimmung der Güter neu und vertieft reflektiert und realisiert werden soll, dann müssen auch die verfassungsrechtlichen und politischen Rahmenbedingungen berücksichtigt werden, dann „erweist sich der Schritt von der Wirtschaft zur Politik als unerläßlich" (OA 46). Es ist zu gewährleisten, dass die innere Ordnung der Staaten das „Recht auf freie wirtschaftliche Initiative" schützt (SRS 42). Der Subjektcharakter der Gesellschaft bedarf einer möglichst engen Verbindung von Arbeit und Kapital und einer großen Vielfalt von corps intermédiaires, von Verbänden, Genossenschaften und „Körperschaften mit echter Autonomie gegenüber den öffentlichen Behörden" (LE 14; CA 49). Schließlich ist in vielen Entwicklungsländern die Ersetzung korrupter, diktatorischer und autoritärer Regime durch demokratische Ordnungen eine zentrale Entwicklungsbedingung (SRS 44; CA 20 und 48; Kompendium 411).

Die christliche Gesellschaftslehre verknüpft deshalb Reflexionen zur Eigentumsethik zunehmend mit solchen zur politischen Ethik. Die Realisierung des Prinzips von der universellen Bestimmung der Güter bedarf politischer Institutionen, die die Würde der menschlichen Person und den Primat der Eigeninitiative respektieren, die dem Bürger das Recht ökonomischer und politischer Partizipation gewährleisten, mithin demokratisch und marktwirtschaftlich verfasst sind, und die schließlich auf internationaler Ebene gleichzeitig das Selbstbestimmungsrecht der Nationen und das globale Gemeinwohl schützen (CA 15 und 48).

Zusammenfassung

Die beiden Aussagen der Eigentumsethik der christlichen Gesellschaftslehre – die universelle Bestimmung der Güter und das Naturrecht auf Privateigentum als Verlängerung der menschlichen Freiheit – sind über die menschliche Arbeit miteinander zu vermitteln. Das Recht auf Privateigentum bleibt der universellen Bestimmung der Güter untergeordnet. Aber die Funktion des Privateigentums besteht nicht allein darin, dem Gemeinwohl zu dienen. Es dient zuerst der freien Entfaltung der Person, die auch der Zweck des Gemeinwohls ist. Enteignungen können im Ausnahmefall geboten sein, Konfiskationen sind nicht zu rechtfertigen. Die Zehn Gebote und der erste Johannesbrief gelten auch im 3. Jahrtausend. Die Eigentumsethik der christlichen Gesellschaftslehre beschränkt sich aber nicht auf das Gebot „Du sollst nicht stehlen" und die Mahnung, zu besitzen als besäße man nicht. Sie schließt auch Jesu Gleichnis von den Talenten ein. Die Aufforderung, die anvertrauten Talente im Maße des eigenen Könnens zu vermehren, bezieht sich zwar auf die gesamte Person, nicht nur auf ihren Besitz. Aber letzterer ist auch nicht ausgeschlossen.

Summary

Christian social teaching makes two basic assertions about property. There is on the one hand a universal destination of material goods and on the other hand the natural right to private property as an expression of human freedom. Human work mediates both sides. The right to private property is always subordinate to the universal destination of material goods. However, the function of private property is not only to be conducive to the common good. First of all it serves the person's free development, which is also the purpose of the common good. Expropriations can be imperative, but confiscation is not justifiable. The Ten Commandments and the First Epistle of John are still valid in the third millenium. Property ethics, as Christian social teaching views them, are not limited to the commandment "You shall not steal" and the demand to possess as though one did not possess. It also includes Jesus' parable of the talents. Admittedly, the invitation to use and increase the talents God has given us refers to the person as a whole with his abilities and not only to property, but it does not exclude it either.

The Metaphysics of Property:
Relations of Ownership as Social Practices

By Robert C. Koons

I. Introduction: The Ontological Challenge
to the Liberal Theory of Property

The liberal theory dominated Western political thought from John Locke through Georg Friedrich Hegel, and it continues to have a great deal of influence, thanks to the development of "classical" liberalism and libertarianism in the twentieth century (as typified by the work of Murray Rothbard, Robert Nozick, Ludwig von Mises, Milton Friedman and many others). At the core of the liberal theory is the idea that property is a relation between an individual human thing (the owner) and some material thing (the object owned). For Locke, property consists in the unlimited right to use the "object." For Hegel, the owned object makes possible the "externalization" of the owner's will. Most liberal thinkers recognized that this theory must be adjusted to some extent to handle the case of intellectual property (and other cases of immaterial "objects"), but it is the ownership of material objects that is always the central focus and paradigm case (this can be seen clearly in as late a work as Nozick's *Anarchy, State and Utopia*).[1]

Immanuel Kant brought a Cartesian perspective to the theory of action: human action is a matter of imposing one's individual will on the phenomena of nature (including the cultural world). There is a deep dichotomy separating the interior life of the mind and will from the material processes of social life. Property is a way of bridging the gap by providing each soul with an exclusive sphere upon which its will can be fastened effectively. Hegel erases this Cartesian alienation of self from the material world, creating at least the opportunity of restoring the Aristotelian and scholastic holism of human action. But Hegel still insists on a kind of absolutizing of reason and the will that depends on liberal property as its correlative.

The liberal theory has been subject, of course, to many challenges: Marxist, progressive, neo-Thomist, and Distributist, among many others. I propose to at-

---

[1] Robert Nozick, *Anarchy, State and Utopia* (New York: Basic Books, 1977).

tack it here on a quite fundamental level, by challenging the very existence of the sort of material "objects" supposed to be the owned. If there is literally no such thing as a material object to be owned, then ownership cannot consist in absolute power over such a material object. Instead, each case of ownership must be thought of instead as a particular social practice or process. I offer strictly ontological grounds for the thesis that the only thing I could possibly own is my own rational activity or my share in a social activity.[2]

This ontological discovery leads to a very different conception of the rights of ownership from that propounded by the liberal theory in three dimensions. First, the new, process-theoretic account of ownership provides a principled basis for the respect of past tenure and occupation. Second, it also provides a natural way of finding the limits of the rights of ownership and of adjudicating conflicting rights-claims. Finally, it will make clear why the value of property can never (contrary to neo-classical theory) be purely instrumental in nature. Since property always involves a right to the perpetuation of some rational activity, and since the ultimate human good (eudaemonia) consists in such rational activity, the maintenance and use of one's property always has some intrinsic value.

II. Ontological Doubts about Artifacts and Natural Formations

In *Material Beings*,[3] Peter van Inwagen reintroduced the classical problem of material composition to the world of Anglo-American analytic philosophy. Van Inwagen argues that there are only two kinds of material things: organisms and simples. An organism is a living thing, all of whose parts participate in a continuum of life. A "simple" is a non-composite physical thing, like an ultimate particle or an indivisible "moment" of a physical field. Van Inwagen denies the existence of inorganic "heaps" (like mountains, rivers, planets) and of material artifacts (chairs, umbrellas and so on).

Like George Berkeley, van Inwagen wants to speak with the vulgar while thinking like the wise. He argues that ordinary common sense does not in fact recommend belief in the existence of natural formations and human artifacts. We are only tricked into thinking it does so by taking our ordinary language at

---

[2] One complication: I will in fact concede the existence of living organisms. Thus, I do not have ontological grounds for a liberal theory of the ownership of livestock or pets. However, this is, on independent grounds, a problematic case for the liberal, coming uncomfortably close to the case of owning other human beings. Non-human organisms do have their own desires and ends: how is the owner justified in entirely subordinating those ends to his own, simply because doing so does not infringe on the liberty of other human beings?

[3] Peter van Inwagen, *Material Beings* (Ithaca, NY: Cornell University Press, 1995).

face value. Van Inwagen proposes instead that we interpret our ordinary speech (including our internal monologues) by means of a scheme of paraphrase or translation. When someone says that he is sitting on a chair, we should (charitably) interpret him as claiming only to be sitting on some particles arranged chair-wise. We have no good reason (van Inwagen claims) for attributing to the speaker the further belief that these chair-wise arranged particles compose some further entity, to wit, the chair itself.

Van Inwagen does not propose that we apply such paraphrases to talk about persons and other living things. *We* exist in a metaphysically serious way, because we have genuinely emergent, holistic properties (like life, sensation, and rational agency) that are not wholly reducible to the nature and activities of the microphysical particles that compose them. Similarly, van Inwagen does not advocate a non-realist stance toward the world of microscopic physics with its fields, particles, quantum waves, and so on. The ontological challenge is set only against medium-sized, non-living objects, including plots of lands and products of human artifice.

Van Inwagen's challenge to artifacts and other "heaps" has a clear precedent in the Aristotelian tradition, including the views of St. Thomas Aquinas. Commenting on Aristotle's *Metaphysics*, Book Seven (Zeta), St. Thomas argues that no artificial thing is a substance. Only natural things, including homogeneous material continua and (especially) living organisms, have *substantial form* and the resulting per se unity.[4] As St. Thomas states in *The Principles of Nature*, an artifact like a statue has no substantial form "because the bronze, before it receives the shape, has existence in act and its existence does not depend upon that shape; rather it is an accidental form, because all artificial forms are accidental."[5] Coming to compose an artifact is something that happens (accidentally) to the underlying material substances, which continue to exist as independent substances after the formation of the artifact, unlike the parts of a living organism, which have only a potential and dependent existence after generation and before corruption. It is true that both Aristotle and Aquinas are willing to speak of statues as having a kind of existence, but this is only an existence *secundum quid*, after a manner of speaking, analogous to the truth of one of van Inwagen's paraphrases. Strictly speaking, only substances *exist*, since 'being' in its focal meaning applies only to them: the quasi-existence of other

---

[4] Thomas Aquinas, *In duodecim libros Metaphysicorum exposito*, VII, lect. 17, n. 1680.

[5] Thomas Aquinas, *De principiis naturae*, c. 1, n. 8, translated as *The Principles of Nature to Brother Sylvester* by R. A. Kocourek (http://josephkenny.joyeurs.com/CDtexts/DePrincNaturae.htm).

things (artifacts, accidents and privations) is ultimately to be cashed out in terms of the state and activities of substances.[6]

Even if we grant that artifacts have a kind of derived or non-fundamental existence, this is no comfort to the defender of the liberal theory of property. The liberal claims that the relation between the owner and the piece of property is an ethically fundamental one. If we take a realist stance toward ethics itself, we must suppose that fundamental ethical relations are also fundamental in terms of metaphysics. And metaphysically fundamental relations must relate metaphysically fundamental entities. Hence, if artifacts are not real substances, the relation of ownership cannot be a basic or underived principle of ethics.

1. Reasons to Reject Non-Living Composite Entities ("Heaps")

Why should we, as serious and sober ontologists, entertain doubts about such apparently ubiquitous and matter-of-fact entities as mountains and chairs? Why should we be compositional "near-nihilists" (believing only in simples and organisms, or simples and persons)? There are three general reasons for doubting the real or substantial existence of "heaps," that is, of non-living, composite material things. In addition, in the next sub-section, I will provide four reasons for doubting the existence of *artifacts* in particular.

The first reason for doubting the existence of composite material things involves an appeal to ontological economy, the principle of Ockham's razor. Other things being equal, we should prefer the ontological theory that posits the fewest ontological classes and categories. The ontological nihilist denies the existence of all material objects except for simples. To posit both simples and further entities supposedly composed by those simples is to offend against this principle, unless compelling grounds for the additional positing can be given. However, in the case of natural formations and artifacts, it is unclear that any-

---

[6] There is an exception to this principle, as Michael Rota has pointed out in his "Substance and Artifact in Aquinas," *History of Philosophy Quarterly* 21 (2004): 241–259. Aquinas supposes that a continuous mass of bread is both an artifact and a substance. Such homogeneous material continua have (in Aristotelian theory) only potential and no actual parts. Hence, a slab of bread or a quantity of wine can be one per se, while being artificial (by virtue of their chemical composition). We now know that the underlying subatomic particles survive throughout the process of creating or destroying such artificial stuffs, so we have less reason to accept such cases as exceptions to the non-substantiality of artifacts. However, it is still an open question whether some molecules might have emergent and unitary powers, in which case I would have to admit that molecules (and by extension, masses of molecules) could be both substantial and artificial. Similarly, if artificial life were created some day, the resulting organisms would be substances. However, these exceptions are too narrow to provide a basis for liberal property theory.

thing is gained by positing the existence of complex things. Can't the theoretical work of the composite things be done by the simples taken collectively, by means of van Inwagen's paraphrases? Instead of saying that Petrarch climbed a mountain, we can say that he climbed some particles arranged mountainously. Instead of saying that Michelangelo completed a statue in the form of David, we can say that he arranged some particles of a stony nature in such a way that they (collectively) resembled the form of David. Singular quantification over composite entities can be replaced by plural quantification over simples (along the lines formalized by George Boolos).[7]

Another reason for disbelieving in wholes is that the composite thing does no further *causal* work above and beyond the work done by its parts. All of the powers of the whole consist in the possession of fundamental powers by its parts. Imagine, for example, a block of stone sliding along the surface of an icy lake. The stone possesses a certain kind of causal power to move things, based in its total momentum and kinetic energy. The momentum and energy of the whole stone, however, is nothing but the sum of the momenta and energies of its constituent atoms. The whole stone as such adds nothing new. We could describe the result of the block's striking another block on the lake by referring only to the fundamental particles making up the two blocks. Their inertia and mutual interactions could fully explain the results we observe. There is no scientific reason to introduce either block as a further agent in addition to their constituent parts.

Similarly, rocks and other heaps have no essentially unitary passive powers either. Everything that can be done to a heap can always be re-described (apparently without loss of information) as something that is done to its constituent parts. Heaps can be changed in shape, scattered, or re-assembled, but each of these processes consist in nothing more than the movement of the particles. Heaps can be painted or made radioactive, but these changes also involve nothing over and above certain changes to the simplest parts. Can heaps grow or diminish in size? Yes, but only as a result of the particles being spread out or pressed together. If more particles are added to "the heap," we could always say that, strictly speaking, we have a new heap, composed of a new set of particles.

This lack of emergent and essentially unitary powers clearly distinguishes artifacts from persons and other living organisms. Organisms participate in essentially unitary processes, such as reproduction, growth, sensation and intentional action. It is the person as a whole that grows, reproduces itself, senses or acts; these processes cannot be the mere sum of the activities of the body's microphysical parts.

---

    [7] George Boolos, "To Be is to Be the Value of a Variable (or To Be Some Values of Some Variables)," *Journal of Philosophy* 81 (1984), 430–449.

This observation suggests a methodological principle: a theory should posit entities of a certain kind only if they are needed in giving a complete inventory of the world's causal powers, a principle defended by Trenton Merricks.[8] Here's a first draft of such a principle:

> *Redundancy.* Reject any theory that posits entities whose causal powers are redundant, given the other entities posited by that theory.

When do the active powers of the parts of a composite thing make the active powers of the whole redundant? What would it be for a whole to have non-redundant active powers? Some philosophers (going back to the British Emergentists of the early 20th century) have used the term 'emergent' for this case. A whole has non-redundant active powers when it has "emergent" powers.

A whole has emergent active powers when it is able to do things that could not be explained in terms of the powers of its parts. By saying that this "could not be explained" I do not mean: could not be explained *by us*, due to the complexity or other practical obstacles involved in formulating such an explanation. I mean something like: could not be explained in principle, not even by God, in terms of the powers of the parts. We are interested in *ontological* emergence, not merely some sort of human-centered epistemological emergence. When a whole has emergent powers, actions take place that are not merely the sum of the individual actions of the component parts. The whole is greater in active power than the sum of the active powers of the parts.

Could we ever be in a position to know – or at least to believe with good reason – that some whole has such emergent powers? Here is one worry: whenever we see the whole seeming to do something over and above what could be done by the parts, we could always describe what's going on as the exercise of *hidden* powers of the parts, powers that they never exercise except when they are put together in such a way as to constitute a whole of this kind. Since that always seems to be a live option, we would never be able to tell whether it is really the whole exercising some emergent power or just the parts jointly exercising some "hidden" powers. We could escape from this impasse if we could find certain powers that are *essentially unitary*, that is, powers that could only be exercised by some one, unified entity, and that could never consist in the joint possession of individual powers by the members of a plurality. Here are several possible candidates for essentially unitary powers:

(1) The power of self-reproduction, as exercised by living organisms.

(2) The power of growth, self-development and self-repair through the assimilation of new material.

(3) The power of self-determination as exercised in free, conscious choices.

---

[8] Trenton Merricks, *Objects and Persons* (Oxford, UK: Oxford University Press, 2001).

Each of these powers makes reference to the self that exercises it. This self-reference is what seems to make each essentially unitary. The particles making up an organism's body cannot exercise the power of self-replication, since it is the organism and not any of the particles that is reproduced. Similarly, the particles do not grow, either individually or collectively. If the organism contained a billion billion particles before the episode of growth, then those billion billion particles are no larger or more massive afterward than they were before. It is the organism that grows, not the particles. Finally, the particles making up person's body does not make up its mind to do one thing rather than another. The particles don't have minds to be made up – only the person does. Therefore, we will propose that a theory may reasonably posit the existence of a fundamental composite entity only if it credits that entity with powers that are essentially unitary. It seems that these essentially unitary powers will be either immanent or passive powers, not active ones. Anything that can be done to some other thing could, it seems, be done either by a single agent or by a plurality of agents acting jointly.

A passive power, in contrast, might be essentially unitary: the power of sensation, for example. Being affected with a particular sense-quality is something that can happen only to a single thing, because sensory consciousness is essentially unified. Immanent powers can also be essentially unitary, like the power of self-reproduction or organic growth. Thus, in order for a theory's postulation of composite entities to be justified, the composite entities must be assigned both emergent active powers and essentially unitary passive or immanent powers.

Def. 1. A power of a composite entity x is *emergent* if and only if the power of x is not wholly grounded in the sum of the causal powers of x's parts, together with the intrinsic qualities and mutual relations of those parts.

Def. 2. A power is *essentially unitary* if and only if it is a fundamental power that could by its very nature be possessed *only* by a single entity, not collectively possessed by a plurality of entities.

Redundancy (version 2). Reject any theory that posits any kind of composite entity without *both* emergent active powers and essentially unitary passive powers.

Heaps and other natural formations would seem to lack both emergent active powers and essentially unitary passive powers. The same thing would seem to be true of material artifacts. In fact, if artifacts had emergent powers (i.e., if they literally had a life of their own), they would be harder to make and control than they are. We can engineer inorganic artifacts precisely because the collective behavior of the particles making up the artifact is reducible to the interactions of the individual particles.

The third reason to reject "heaps" (i.e., inorganic, composite material things) concerns the problem of explaining how material things occupy space. The key question is: Why is the location of a part always part of the location of the whole? In fact, there are two facts that need explaining:

Spatial Occupation Fact 1. If x is a material part of y, then the location of x is a part of the location of y.

Spatial Occupation Fact 2. If a material body is a sum of the x's, then the location of y is a sum of the location of the x's.

There are three possible explanations of these two facts:

(1) They are metaphysically brute necessities, or necessities imposed by the laws of nature.

(2) It is only the atomic *parts* of heaps that truly exist, each having some spatial *point* as its location. The whole is nothing over and above the atomic parts, and the location of the whole is nothing but the corresponding spatial points, taken together.

(3) It is *the whole* that is real and that has an extended spatial *region* as its location (directly and fundamentally). When an extended material body has a region as its location, that body is thereby located partially in each of the parts of the region. On this view, the "parts" of an extended body are nothing over and above the whole body and its many partial locations. To say that the body has a part at some smaller region or point is to say nothing more than that the body has that spatial region or point as one of its partial locations.

The first option is unattractive from the point of view of Ockham's Razor, since it imposes a vast system of brute necessities between the locations and location-occupiers. Option 3 seems implausible if we try to apply it to heaps: how could the location of any heap be metaphysically fundamental, and the location of its parts merely derivative? The heap has no being or nature over and above the being and nature of its parts. The dependency seems to run clearly in the other direction: point-sized parts and their locations are fundamental, and the locations of heaps are dependent on them. If so, then we must embrace option 2. Given option 2, then we have a good reason to think that heaps do not really exist (metaphysically speaking). If the location of the heap is nothing over and above the point-locations of its atomic parts, then presumably the same thing is true of all the properties of heaps, including their intrinsic qualities and their material composition. If so, then the only real entities are the point-sized parts themselves, which we can identify with material simples.

2. Doubts about the Existence of Artifacts

We have looked at arguments against the existence of non-living composite material things. Now I will present four metaphysical objections to *artifacts* in particular: an appeal to the intrinsicality of existence, the possibility of non-substantial artifacts, artifacts made from living things, and the arbitrariness of the persistence conditions of artifacts.

The first argument against artifacts appeals to the principle of the Intrinsicality of Composition: Whether or not the x's compose something depends only the intrinsic nature and mutual relations of the x's, not on facts extrinsic to them.

The composition of artifacts seems to be extrinsic in two ways: first, by being dependent on the attitudes and practices of their users and maintainers, and, second, by being dependent on their physical surroundings. Whether or not some things compose an artifact seems to depend on human intentions and actions that are extrinsic to the artifact itself. For example, suppose some ancient hunters shaped and chipped some rocks in order to form some crude implements, like axes and hammers. Thousands of years later, the chipped rocks have been abandoned and their functions forgotten. Do the axes and hammers still exist? Maybe, but it also seems plausible to say that all that remains are the chipped pieces of rock, now no different from other rocks that have been chipped or shaped by purely natural, unintentional processes.

Here is another argument for the same conclusion. As we have seen, in certain cases, found objects can constitute an artifact, like a stump-chair or driftwood-art. Whether or not the wood in the stump constitutes a chair seems to depend wholly on whether or not it is used and maintained as a chair by external agents. Similarly, imagine that the exact duplicate of a watch were to form by chance in an asteroid field. The watch-duplicate wouldn't be a real watch, but the difference between it and the watch is entirely extrinsic.

The existence of artifacts is extrinsic in a second way. Consider a statue that has been cut and chipped from a natural block of marble. The existence of the statue depends entirely on the physical surroundings of the marble making up the statue. That marble existed, with the very same size and shape, before the sculptor has removed any rock. The statue comes to exist, not by virtue of what happens to its internal material parts, but by virtue of what was done to the marble surrounding it.

The second argument against artifacts appeals to *immaterial artifacts*. Let's suppose that the following sorts of things are *not* real material things: holes, shadows, and spots of light on a wall. Artifacts can be made of such immaterial entities. For example, Alexander Pruss (in conversation) has pointed out that one could make a chess set simply by forming holes in a thick, viscous mound of jelly. One moves one's queen in this set by inserting a tool into the hole in the jelly that is the queen and slowly moving the hole to a new position on the chessboard, and then removing the tool. It seems obvious that the pieces of such a chess set cannot be material entities, since their parts are not material entities. But if this holey chess set is not a material thing, then we shouldn't suppose that an ordinary chess set is, simply by virtue of its being composed of different things. Here are some more common examples of the same thing: a trench is an artifact, but a trench consists simply in a long, narrow hole that is produced by digging, and a tunnel is an artifact, but a tunnel is merely a manmade hole in a hill or mountain. In addition, there are works of art that consist of nothing but shadows or points of light.

If some artifacts are not composed of material bits, then no artifact can be composed of material bits, since any apparently material artifact can be duplicated by means of immaterial "components," like holes or images. Since artifacts are obviously not simple entities, we are forced to deny that any artifact exists at all.

A third argument concerns the possibility of artifacts made from living things. Van Inwagen asks us to imagine an artifact made entirely of a living thing. For example, we could imagine making a very long snake into a hammock by tying it together into a network of knots. Doing this to the snake would not bring into existence a new thing, nor would it destroy the snake. This isn't a case in which the living thing counts, all by itself, as a material artifact (as a bonsai tree or an artificial organism might). Since the snake hammock is neither an old nor a new material thing, it seems that it cannot be a composite material thing at all. If the snake hammock is not a composite material thing, no hammock could be a composite material thing. But if ordinary hammocks do exist, they have to be composite material things (made of bits of rope and such). Consequently, no hammock really exists.

We might suppose that turning the snake into a hammock fails to produce a new material thing precisely because the snake already existed. However, this seems an entirely ad hoc solution. How can arranging a rope in a certain way bring into existence a new material entity, if arranging the rope-like snake in precisely the same way for the same purpose fails to do so?

Finally, when we try to determine under what conditions an artifact persists or fails to persist in existence, we seem to fall into a series of insoluble paradoxes and puzzles, suggesting that artifacts are not fundamentally real.

Paradox One: the Ship of Theseus. The ship of Theseus is an ancient puzzle about the persistence of material objects through time. We are to imagine a ship whose planks of wood are taken out, one by one, placed in a warehouse, and replaced by new planks. Eventually, all of the ship's wood has been replaced, and a second ship is constructed from the planks stored in the warehouse.

Which ship is the "original"? There seems to be no clearly correct answer. If we reject the existence of artifacts and other incontinent objects, we can avoid the problem by simply denying that there ever was or is a ship at all. All we can say is that there is shipping going on here-ishly and there-ishly. The question of which ship is the "same" as the original ship of Theseus cannot be properly posed.

Paradox Two: Tab and Tab-Minus. Let's tell at story about a table that loses a corner of its top. Let's call the table before the removal of the corner Tab, and let's call the table minus the corner Tab-Minus. It seems that both Tab and Tab-Minus exist before the corner is removed. At that point in time, Tab-Minus is a proper part of the table (all of the table except for its corner). It seems clear that Tab and Tab-Minus are not identical at that time, since Tab has all four corners and Tab-Minus does not. However, after the corner is removed, the table is identical to Tab-Minus, since the table itself now lacks one of its corners. So, we seem to be saying that, at t_1 (before the leg removal) Tab and Tab-Minus were not identical, and the table and Tab were identical. At the later time t_2, the table and Tab-Minus are identical. So, the table was once not identical to Tab-Minus, and then later it is identical to Tab-Minus. But there is a strong argument (created by Saul Kripke[9]) for thinking that identity and distinctness are eternal. Once distinct, always distinct, and once identical, always identical.

This problem can also be dissolved by simply rejecting the existence of all mereologically "incontinent" objects, i.e., objects that can gain or lose parts. However, all artifacts are mereologically incontinent. Hence, artifacts do not exist.

Paradox Three: Intermittent Existence. Consider a watch that is taken to the repair shop. The watch repairman completely disassembles the watch and then re-assembles it. Does the watch exist when completely disassembled? It seems wrong to say that at that stage there is a watch on the repairman's workspace, as opposed to a complete set of watch-parts.

When a watch is re-assembled from the very same parts, is it the same watch that it was before the disassembly? Can something cease to exist and then re-sume existence at a later time? This seems impossible, so it seems that we must say that the re-assembled watch is a new entity, not identical to the original. However, there is also good reason to say that it is the same watch as the original, since it is composed of the same parts and serves the same function. In addition, it is recognized as the same by both its owner and the repairman. This paradox can be resolved by simply denying that the watch ever existed.

---

[9] Saul Kripke, "Identity and Necessity" in *Identity and Individuation*, edited by Milton K. Munitz (New York: New York University Press, 1971), pp. 135–164.

Paradox Four: Vague Identity. There once was a restaurant in Philadelphia called "Bookbinders." The restaurant is moved, changes owners and menus. Is it still the same restaurant, or a different one? There will be borderline cases in which we feel that either answer is legitimate. It is hard to believe that there is a real, fundamental fact of the matter. We can make sense of this fact if incontinent objects like restaurants are just useful fictions.

Paradox Five: Exotic Objects. Eli Hirsch asks us to imagine a community with very exotic ideas about the persistence conditions of certain objects.[10] For example, they do not believe in cars, but they do believe in "incars" and "out-cars." An incar consists in what we would call a car while and insofar as the car is inside a garage. An outcar is a car outside a garage. When we back a car out of a garage, the Hirschians would say that an incar is gradually shrinking until it vanishes, and an outcar comes into existence, first as a part of the rear bumper and gradually growing into a complete outcar. Hirschians don't believe in persisting cars. They think that the only really persisting things are incars and outcars. If you drive your outcar into a garage, you have destroyed it and replaced it with a new entity, an incar.

We find it hard to believe that incars or outcars are really there, but do we have a good reason for thinking so? Aren't the persistence conditions we assign to natural formations and artifacts just as arbitrary and conventional as the conditions used by Hirschians? A simple solution to the charge of arbitrariness is to deny the existence of *all* incontinent objects, cars and incars alike.

III. Owned Objects as Social Practices:
The Continuous History Account of Artifacts

One account of the persistence and unity of an artifact exploits certain practices of use and maintenance. For example, if a watch persists, it is because there is a certain ongoing history of use of the watch as a watch, and of maintenance of the watch as a watch. Let's suppose that these social processes or practices have a kind of unity through time, that the process as a whole is metaphysically fundamental, not the various instantaneous events that make up the process. If that is so, then the metaphysical unity of the process over time can be used to ground the persistence of the artifact. We'll call this the Continuous History theory of artifactual persistence.

Solution One: The Ship of Theseus. Let's call the ship that has been in continuous operation Theseus-A, and the ship that is reconstructed from the abandoned planks Theseus-B. The Continuous History theory entails that it is The-

---

[10] Eli Hirsch, *The Concept of Identity* (Oxford, UK: Oxford University Press, 1982).

seus-A and not Theseus-B that is identical to the ship as originally built. The-seus-A is associated with a continuous process of nautical use and maintenance, which is not the case with Theseus-B. When the abandoned planks are put to-gether into a ship, a new ship is created, because a new practice of use and maintenance is initiated.

Solution Two: Tab and Tab-Minus. Plausibly, before the corner is removed, Tab-Minus is not what is being *used* as a table. The *whole* table is used as a ta-ble. Thus, one can deny that there is any such thing as the Tab-Minus, prior to the removal of the corner. Given this, the puzzles about the identity of Tab and Tab-Minus do not arise.

Solution Three: Intermittent Existence. Consider a watch that is disassem-bled and then put back together. This looks like a case of intermittent existence. What ties the early history of the watch with the later history is again a con-tinuous process of use and maintenance, based perhaps in the intentions and practices of the watch repairman. While the watch's parts are incapable of func-tioning as a watch but still have the real potential of being re-assembled, we can plausibly say that the watch no longer exists but may exist again.

Solution Four: Vague Identity. We might here take the view that vagueness is merely a reflection of our ignorance. If we understood all there was to know about the processes of use and maintenance that are involved, we might always know the right thing to say about whether the artifact (like a restaurant) persists or not. Alternatively, we might suppose that the vagueness is ontological. Maybe restaurants are simply vague objects, sometimes indeterminate in exis-tence or in identity.

Solution Five: Exotic Objects. The artifactual objects that exist do depend on our concepts and conventions, since those concepts and conventions shape our practices, and it is our practices that are the ground of persistence for artifacts. However, there may be natural limits to the kind of social practices that can ex-ist. It is hard to imagine a set of social practices that would really die out or be-gin to exist simply by driving a car out of or into a garage. Cars just aren't the sort of things that can be built or maintained in that way.

There is an obvious objection that could be raised to such a process-of-maintenance theory of artifactual persistence: doesn't it simply push the prob-lem of persistence back a step? What is the principle that unifies the various spatial and temporal parts of a single practice of use and maintenance? Don't such practices simply correspond to myriads of overlapping microphysical processes, with no sharp boundaries in time or space?

These are deep questions, but the defenders of artifacts might well claim that social practices (including the practice of using and maintaining a particular ar-tifact, like a car or a watch) have emergent and strongly unitary powers, just as do living and sentient organisms. It certainly isn't obvious that all of the powers of such social practices are wholly grounded (without remainder) in a host of chemical and microphysical processes.

Replacing Artifacts with Social Practices. On the Continuous History view, why not take the artifacts to *be* the social practices? This would be an "error theory" about our common sense view. We ordinarily take artifacts to be ordinary material objects (with continuous locations, mass, energy and so on), when in fact they are processes, having human actions and intentions as their components. The error is explicable, since certain heaps of particles play a focal role within those processes or practices. Here is a central question that the social-practices account must answer: what gives real (ontological) unity to a process or practice, especially one involving more than one participant? Why don't we have a mere heap of micro-processes (each involving one or more simples)?

There are two cases of real unity. First, a process is *one* when it is the result of the exercise of some immanent power by a single persisting thing. To each immanent power there corresponds some final "end" or "telos," either as a target-like consequence or as a persistent pattern of activity. Second, processes are *one* when they are social practices, created and sustained by one or more intentional agents, who perform each action *as part of* a single, continuing practice. In such cases, there is a real interdependency in nature between the whole practice and its constituent actions. The actions are not wholly prior to the practice, and the practice not wholly posterior to the actions. Social practices are also unified by a single end or system of inter-connected ends. I can't think of anything else that could give an essential unity to congeries of events and micro-processes.

IV. Rights to Property are Rights to Practices, not to Things

Our tentative conclusion is that neither land nor human artifacts exist – except as quasi-permanent aspects of human social practices. My claim is not merely that legal property is itself a social practice: it is that each individual *case* of ownership is a distinct and unique practice in and of itself. If this is right, then respect for private property is nothing more than a special case of respect for rational human action. Contrary to the subjectivism of Ludwig von Mises,[11] all human action, by virtue of being human action, must have an intelligible end, one that participates in objective value by moving the agents closer

---

[11] Ludwig von Mises, *Human Action: A Treatise on Economics* (New Haven, CT: Yale University Press, 1949).

to the natural *telos* of human life. Human action can be more or less rational (objectively speaking), depending upon on how accurate a conception of that human *telos* it is predicated on. Grossly irrational practices have little or no claim on the respect of others.

Human beings are naturally social and political – that is, they are naturally cooperative and collaborative. Hence, it is irrational (other things being equal) to aim at the disruption of the rational action of others, and objectively valuable for each to respect and promote the rational action of others.

Respect for property is a case of respect for existence: what exists has, simply by virtue of its existing, some claim on our respect. This respect is a corollary of the privative theory of evil: what exist is, insofar as it exists, good. All human action, insofar as it is action, and therefore insofar as it is human and rational, is good. Each case of ownership is an instance of human action.

Ownership is not primarily a relation between a human being (the owner) and some external, typically physical, thing (the "real" property). It is instead primarily a relation between the owner and the owner's own activity, a process or practice with some intelligible relation to certain relatively stable physical things and an intelligible end. The stability or persistence of the owned "object" is entirely constituted by the owner's practices: the owned object is the "same" ontologically insofar as it is the same practically speaking. There are no autonomous, purely ontological criteria of sameness here, in contrast to the real persistence of primary substances (including human persons) and processes (including human practices).

Hence, respect for property is an essentially conservative norm, a case of natural piety. The owner has no prior right to use his property in novel or innovative ways. To do so is to initiate a new appropriation of a new "object," one that overlaps in a contingent way the material composition of the older owned object. Whether or not the new appropriation is real and binding on others depends on the usual conditions on such aboriginal appropriation: does the appropriation transgress on the prior rights of other persons, and does it leave "enough and as good" for others to appropriate?

The liberal theory of property, in contrast, is one of absolute rights over *things*, which include the right to alienate and transfer these very rights. This is plainly incoherent: rights are neither physical objects nor social practices: they are not the kind of things that can be owned. Nor can they be created, alienated or transferred. Positive laws don't create genuine rights: they recognize them. A right cannot be transferred, but an interaction can destroy one activity and create a new one (or, more precisely, alter one activity and create a new one), with the consequence that one person loses a set of rights and a second acquires an isomorphic set. Rights are corollaries of the nature of some being – either a rational substance (with its potentialities for action) or a case of concrete rational activity. For example, the right of inheritance is not absolute and is not the effect of a kind of divine fiat on the part of the testator. Family lineages are an essential component of natural human life.

The social-practices theory of property also provides a principled way of adjudicating disputed rights, including conflicts between the claims of first occupation vs. those of needy "late-comers." There is a real but not absolute condition of non-interference on rational action: as a rational social animal, my new action must not interfere with pre-existing activities of others. However, human life itself has an ontological priority, since there can be no rational activity apart from life. Consequently, the prior occupiers have the obligation to make accommodations for the basic needs of the latecomers, and this obligation corresponds to enforceable rights of those latecomers. However, the accommodation to be demanded must be the minimum one necessary for the latecomers to have an equal opportunity for eudaemonia. The latecomers have an obligation to shape their rational life-projects in such a way as to provide maximum respect for pre-existing projects.

The social-practices theory extends naturally to a theory of intellectual property. In contrast, the liberal theory cannot be so extended. Liberals must identify "ownership" with any kind of exclusive control. That is, something can be owned if and only if others can be excluded from controlling or using "it." This is too broad because it makes "ownership" co-extensive with social authority of any kind. In contrast, the social-practices theory can identify the ownership of patents, trademarks, and copyrights with the integrity of certain practices of intellectual and artistic creativity. If an idea is created with an intention to sell it, appropriation without compensation interferes with this creative process. Again, there are limits. One cannot simply exclude others arbitrarily or for no constructive purpose. In order to "own" an idea, one must be willing to accept fair compensation for its use. What about keeping patents from one's competitors? Beating one's competitors in the market place is illegitimate as a direct object of intention, because it is inherently malicious. One must always be willing to share in exchange for fair and reasonable compensation.

Moreover, since human beings are social animals, ownership is typically shared, since human activity is typically social. The liberal theory of property is paradigmatically a theory of individual rights, while the social-practice theory can encompass both individual and shared ownership with equal facility.

V. Why Property has more than Instrumental Value

We must distinguish between first-order and higher-order activities. Working a farm or building a house for one's own use and consumption are paradigms of first-order activities, whether the worker is one individual or a community (a household). Barter and producing for the sake of barter are second-order activities. The use of money and the practices of moneymaking are third-order, banking and usury fourth-order, and so on.

Contrary to a philosophical tradition dating back to Plato and Aristotle, and echoed by Cicero, Augustine, and Aquinas, first-order activities are not *uniquely* natural or noble for human beings. Commerce is as natural as farming, banking as natural as commerce. Human reason is naturally ramifying and order-raising. However, participation in higher-order activities does increase the likelihood of confusion about the nature of the human end ("the love of money is the root of all evil," as St. Paul says in the first epistle to Timothy). In seeking some tertiary good, it is easy to lose sight of the fact that the tertiary and secondary goods must be anchored in and delimited by primary goods. It is true that among the primary goods are the sort of exercises of human reason and responsibility that are found in the tertiary activities themselves, but these primary goods are also finite and in need of complementation. The pursuit of tertiary goods always threatens to become infinite and inhuman.

At the opposite extreme, utilitarians and economists instrumentalize all human action, making it all merely a means to an exogenous end (pleasure, or the satisfaction of fixed, biological desires). This ignores the fact that happiness (eudaemonia) consists in rational activity. For utilitarians, there can be no natural rights at all, and so there are no natural rights to property. Property rights are purely positive, assigned with a view to maximizing total welfare by creating optimal incentives for action.

On the social-practices theory of property, ownership is both a means and an end in itself, embodying both secondary and primary goods. The use and maintenance of property is intrinsically good, since it involves the exercise of human reason. It also possesses instrumental value as a means for meeting various human needs. Because it does embody primary and intrinsic goods, respect for property is a natural right, even though what is due respect is always a culturally conditioned activity of one or more persons and not some ahistorical power over a physical thing.

Summary

The ownership of property by a person is fundamentally a matter of that person's participation in a social practice. In fact, each "piece" of property is constituted by an individual practice involving the rational cooperation of multiple persons. For this reason, ownership is never entirely instrumental in character: the owner and the others with whom the owner cooperates are constrained by reason to treat the right use and maintenance of the property as (to some extent) an end in itself. Given the essentially social and political character of human nature, the social and political right to private property follows immediately. The result is a distinctively conservative theory of property: one that pays appropriate respect to historical facts of tenure, precedent and custom.

Zusammenfassung

Der Besitz von persönlichem Eigentum ist wesentlich Ausfluss der Teilhabe dieser Person am gesellschaftlichen Leben. In der Tat, jedes „Stück" Eigentum kommt zustande durch individuelles Handeln in vernünftiger Zusammenarbeit mit vielen Personen. Deshalb ist Besitz niemals nur von instrumenteller Art: Der Besitzer und die anderen, mit denen er zusammenarbeitet, sind gehalten, den rechten Gebrauch zu tätigen und das Eigentum zu erhalten, als ob es gewissermaßen ein Ziel in sich wäre. Da die menschliche Natur wesentlich sozial und politisch ist, ist auch das Privateigentum ein soziales und politisches Recht. Als Ergebnis kann eine eindeutig konservative Theorie des Eigentums festgehalten werden, die der geschichtlichen Entwicklung und Tradition Rechnung trägt.

"Private Ownership, Common Use"

Aquinas and Maritain on Aristotle's *Politics*

By John P. Hittinger

> In the line of moral aspirations the use of goods must be common, but in the line of production these same goods must be possessed as one's own: Saint Thomas encloses the social problem between the two branches of this antimony. – Jacques Maritain[1]

In this paper I review an argument made by Jacques Maritain, in *Freedom in the Modern World*,[2] that a right to private property derives from the rational capacity of the human person to be an "artifex" or maker. He develops the notion articulated by Aristotle, in *Politics*, that property should be a matter of private ownership and common use. Aristotle gives a political argument for private ownership, appealing above all to social harmony and efficiency and care. Aquinas repeats and develops the same argument; but he adds an additional reason for private ownership, namely, that order is established through private ownership against the confusion wrought by common ownership. He also incorporates the biblical and patristic teaching that the divine mandate for dominion over the earth is given to all; and that mankind is the ultimate beneficiary of property. This has come to be called the universal destination of goods.

Two problems emerge in this account of private ownership and common use. First, the reasons for private ownership appear to be rooted in pragmatic considerations that could change with historical conditions, and second, private ownership could be interpreted as a concession to human weakness or selfishness. The ideal perhaps remains that of a community of goods and such an arrangement would be preferable for the virtuous or righteous. Combined with the weighty demand of the universal destination of goods, the rationale for private property as a concession to human weakness leaves the institution of private ownership more vulnerable to attack. This provides the context for appreciating the significance of the argument for private ownership made by Jacques Maritain. Private ownership derives from the human capacity for making. This is a positive reason for property that highlights human excellence. I believe it is

---

[1] *Art and Scholasticism and the Frontiers of Poetry*, translated by Joseph W. Evans (Notre Dame, IN and London: University of Notre Dame Press, 1962, 1964), p. 154, n. 4.

[2] London: Sheed and Ward, 1935; republished: New York: Gordian Press, 1971.

a deepening of Aquinas's additional rationale based upon order versus confusion. Maritain uses the Thomistic account of art as an intellectual quality, or habit, to explain why private ownership is the best arrangement.

I. On Aristotle's Political Axiom,
"private possession, common use"[3]

In *Politics* Book II. 5 Aristotle sets out a critique of utopian schemes for a community of property and a defense of private property. In searching for a political solution to the problem of property, he rejects the extreme measure proposed by his friend and teacher Plato that property, along with wives and children, should be held in common. Plato's argument for common property is that the guardians, educated for a life dedicated to the good of the city as a whole, "must also have the kind of housing and other property that will neither prevent them from being the best guardians nor encourage them to do evil to the other citizens."[4] Private ownership of land, housing, money will prevent them from being the best guardians because they would need to become dedicated to household management and farming, rather than guardianship. And they would be tempted to use their power and position to expand their holdings at the expense of the citizens they are charged with defending. Plato's proposal for common property, and wives and children, applies to a very restricted class of the city. In addition, some commentators have suggested that Socrates makes the proposal in jest, or at least he does so with full awareness of its problematic character. But Aristotle rightly takes the proposal seriously because the guardians are the proto-type citizens of the best regime. For example, Aristotle says that if the farmers are not citizens, the proposal is moot. Indeed, he frames the opening question as follows: "What is the proper system of property for citizens who are to live under the best form of constitution?" (1262b40). Should property be held in common, what in fact should be held in common, is a serious issue for any constitutional arrangement of a city, which is aimed at a common good by definition.

His deepest quarrel with Plato is that the proposal violates the cardinal rule of politics – the polis is distinct from a household, and the unity of the polis must be different from the unity of a household. A city requires plurality and diversity to achieve its perfection and full functioning. Plato's community of wives, children, and property treats the city as if it was a household and this would undermine its well functioning. The inner economic and social diversity

---

[3] Aristotle, *Politics* II.5; 1263a38.

[4] Plato, *Republic*, Book III, 416c-417d; translation by G. M. A. Grube, revised by C. D. C. Reeve (Indianapolis and Cambridge: Hackett, 1992), p. 92.

and structural plurality helps the city to fulfill its function as a self-sufficient community. Aristotle's direct and immediate critique of the Socratic proposal for common property is along a more empirical or practical line. At some point the common stock must be appropriated for personal use. This will inevitably lead to difficulties and quarrels, at least over the question of merit or reward, as well as over trifles and everyday matters. He states: "In general it is a difficult business to live together and to share in any form of human activity, but it is especially difficult in such matters as property" (1263a15-16). This leads Aristotle to the first formulation of his famous axiom: "Property should be in a certain sense common, but, as a general rule, private."[5] As for the sense in which property ought to be common, he makes no account at present, and yet he gives two reasons why property as a rule ought to be private. "Men will not complain against one another [in matters of property], and they will produce more since each will be paying special attention to what he regards as being his own."[6] We could say that the two reasons are (1) an appeal to peace, or lack of quarrelling and (2) an appeal to efficiency, or greater productivity.

A deeper underlying theme pertains to an argument concerning human nature, namely that each human has a sense of "one's own." One has better care for what is one's own, and on the other hand, we observe that communal things are often neglected. This is true of property, as we all know; and it is true of children as well – Aristotle quips "it would be better to be a real cousin than a son in Plato's Republic" (1262a13). Common ownership waters down attachment and it weakens care. Aristotle speaks about the "immeasurably greater pleasure" that arises when a man "feels a thing to be his own;" love of self, he says, is "a feeling implanted by nature and not given in vain."[7] In other words, the schemes for common possession, for communist arrangements, run contrary to human nature. Communism is based upon a false premise. It wears an attractive face and claims that benevolence and fraternity will arise, and the end of the evils of selfishness will end. But evil is not simply a result of social structure; rather it is due to human wickedness. Communists still bicker, if not more.

So why does Aristotle advocate common use? It is a question of the very purpose of a political regime. Common good and common life are characteristics of the good regime. Friendship stands as an ideal for political society. And "friends will have all things in common" (1263a30). But the common use will be achieved by way of education, custom, and the inculcation of virtue. This is

---

[5] *Politics* II; 1263a25; translation by Benjamin Jowett in *The Basic Works of Aristotle*, edited and with an Introduction by Richard McKeon (New York: Random House, 1941), p. 1151.

[6] *Politics* II; 1263a26-28; translation by Hippocrates G. Apostle and Lloyd P. Gerson in *Aristotle's Politics* (Grinnell, IA: Peripatetic, 1986), p. 44.

[7] *Politics* II; 1262b40-1263a1; translation by Jowett, ibid., p. 1151.

the virtuous way to use property as a good citizen. Aristotle holds that property itself is an instrumental, enabling one to live and to live well (1253b25). The acquisition and possession of property is a limited activity. It is limited first, by natural use and secondly, by the good life. Economics arises out of needs of the body and is open to political determination. The natural use of things constitutes household management with political determination by way of judgment of what are just and noble actions. In other words, use itself is the goal of property possession, and use involves the association of the household and, beyond it, the most perfect association, the political society.

And as it turns out, other virtues simply depend upon private ownership, and we might add, particular family relationships. Natural piety, that is respect for one's parents, depends upon family. Temperance in sexual relationships, especially avoidance of adultery, depends upon private family relationships. Liberality and justice itself depend upon private ownership, and the character development, or virtue, to act according the golden mean. It is a question of disposition and virtue, not coercion. So the city must through education and custom and law develop friendship, temperance, and liberality – these restrain desire and cultivate justice and right use of property.

Some concluding points for consideration on Aristotle's treatment of property are as follows. First, property must be understood in light of the natural teleology of the cosmos. Plants and animals are ordained to human use (1256b7-8); human beings, as rational animals, have a rational capacity to develop nature and to develop themselves through production and action; the sexual attraction between male and female aims at procreation of children, and thus the maintenance and education of the young; the associations of family and extended kin, or village, are perfected in justice by political association in the common good. Second, the goal of common use finds its proper level at the polis or particular city, and not mankind at large. It is rooted more in the perfection of human being as a citizen, and not in a corresponding right of other human beings to the property or surplus of others. Third, Aristotle does not speak about a "right to private property" but rather he looks to practices and institutions that are consistent with human nature and its proper ends. Private property is an institution that shows itself to be more efficient for productivity and more peaceful for social relations. Fourth, private property is not an endorsement or a schema for unlimited acquisition of property; unlimited acquisition is judged to be an irrational mode of human life because (a) it fails to see the distinction between mere life and good life, (b) it seeks excess in pleasures of the body, that is, lust and gluttony, which originate in natural processes, ordered to the proper ends, of generation and preservation, and (c) turns to greed, with the effect that all is subjected to one aim of acquisition.

II. Thomas Aquinas on Dominion, Order, and Distribution

Thomas Aquinas incorporates the fundamental axiom of Aristotle, "private possession, common use," in his treatment of property in *Summa theologiae* 2-2, 66, 1-2. In article 2 he uses the two arguments from Aristotle that private ownership achieves greater efficiency and establishes social harmony in a way superior to common ownership. But he adds a third reason to the list; private ownership is conducive to good order, and common ownership to confusions. He says that it is "lawful for man to possess property" as "necessary to human life" for three reasons.

> First because every man is more careful to procure what is for himself alone than that which is common to many or to all: since each one would shirk the labor and leave to another that which concerns the community, as happens where there is a great number of servants. Secondly, because human affairs are conducted in more orderly fashion if each man is charged with taking care of some particular thing himself, whereas there would be confusion if everyone had to look after any one thing indeterminately. Thirdly, because a more peaceful state is ensured to man if each one is contented with his own. Hence it is to be observed that quarrels arise more frequently where there is no division of the things possessed.[8]

Although the reason of orderliness of human affairs is implied by the other two reasons, I believe that it adds a new dimension to the argument. It more firmly roots the reason for private possession in the spiritual capacities of the rational animal. Ordering of things is a function of reason and wisdom. Each human being receives the charge to fashion life in a rational way and to be provident for oneself and others. As rational animal, each man participates in divine wisdom, and eternal law, through natural law.

If we compare this argument in the *Summa* with Thomas's *Commentary on the Politics* we have an additional indication that he has added a third distinct reason. In the commentary he states that property needs to be private regarding ownership because this allows each individual to manage property and take care of his own. This has two good results, he points out, following Aristotle, namely first, there are no quarrels, or the reason of social harmony, and second, there is greater increase through attentiveness and care, or the reason of efficiency.[9] So it is clear that Thomas adds a third reason in his argument in the *Summa*. I believe that the third reason provides a greater focus upon rational capacity, and it derives from the over all account of human dominion over the earth. We must back up to article one of question 66, whether possession of ex-

---

[8] English translations of ST are by Fathers of the English Dominican Province, *The Summa Theologica of St. Thomas Aquinas*, vol. 2 (New York: Benziger, 1947), p. 1477; online edition 2008 by Kevin Knight at: http://www.newadvent.org/summa/3.htm.

[9] Aquinas, *Commentary on Aristotle's Politics*, Book II, chap. 4; translated by Richard J. Regan (Indianapolis, IN: Hackett, 2007), p. 99.

ternal goods is natural to human beings? Thomas answers in the affirmative on the grounds of God's creation of man to his own image and likeness (Gen 1:26) and the confirming position of Aristotle in *Politics* I.3:

> Man has a natural dominion over external things, because, by his reason and will, he is able to use them for his own profit, as they were made on his account: for the imperfect is always for the sake of the perfect. It is by this argument that the Philosopher proves (Polit. i, 3) that the possession of external things is natural to man. Moreover, this natural dominion of man over other creatures, which is competent to man in respect of his reason wherein God's image resides, is shown forth in man's creation (Genesis 1:26) by the words: "Let us make man to our image and likeness: and let him have dominion over the fishes of the sea," etc. (ST 2-2, 66, 1).

The reason of order, although it also has an empirical basis or pragmatic evidence in social arrangements, derives more directly or evidently from the nature of man as having spiritual capacities of intellect and will, the basis for the divine image. The reason of efficiency does derive from human nature and the love of one's own; but this trait is true of animals as well and is rooted in the material nature of man as much as the formal or rational capacity. The reason of social harmony derives from man's spiritedness and perhaps from the sinfulness of man's envy or greed. Only the third reason of orderliness connects directly to intellect and will. Man must plan his own work, and execute it accordingly, and such requires private ownership.

Thus Aquinas adds significantly to Aristotle's defense of private property and enriches the meaning of the axiom. He adds the reason of orderly achievement of planning and execution, and he provides a deeper and more exalted ground for human superiority and use of external things. Man is superior to plants and animals, and intervenes to perfect and fulfill them according to the teleology of nature; also, human beings share in the providence of God for the order of things and they serve under a divine mandate to cultivate the earth and subdue it.

As for common use, Aquinas follows Aristotle in speaking about friendship and the sharing with members of the political community. But in the *Summa* he says that the possession of external things as common means that each must be "ready to communicate them to others in their need." He cites St. Paul, the Apostle, who says (1 Tim 6:17-18): "Charge the rich of this world ... to give easily, to communicate to others" (ST 2-2, 66, 2). In replies he cites Church fathers, Basil and Ambrose concerning the obligation to assist the poor.

> Basil says (Hom. in Luc. xii, 18): "Why are you rich while another is poor, unless it be that you may have the merit of a good stewardship, and he the reward of patience?" (ST 2-2, 66, 2, ad 2)

> When Ambrose says: "Let no man call his own that which is common," he is speaking of ownership as regards use, wherefore he adds: "He who spends too much is a robber." (ST 2-2, 66, 2, ad 3)

Through alms and charity one is bound to serve the poor. There is now an eschatological dimension to property that goes well beyond the virtue of the citizen to serve the city. Bede Jarrett, O.P. explains: "Over and over again the ideal was propounded and preached that there should be individual ownership and public use – i.e., private possession concomitant with almsgiving on a very large scale."[10] The bar for "common use" is now set very high.

Bede Jarrett explains that the basic principles for understanding property derived from Aristotle and that they were repeated and copied by everyone during the middle ages. Furthermore, he claims that the idea of ownership oriented towards common use "permeated the whole system" of social organization from king to villain. Private ownership was a private "holding" of a common heritage attached to which were various social obligations. The balance of private ownership and public use was not easy to maintain. For Aquinas, "the epigram of Aristotle is the epitome of Christian teaching and economics." It was a solution that avoided the extremes of those who "would have all things in common and those who would have none." But according to Jarrett's felicitous expression, "the heretics would not have allowed private ownership and the orthodox were perhaps too chary of public use." The more things change, the more they stay the same. There is a deep tension, perhaps even an antinomy, at the heart of the Aristotle's axiom.

To conclude our overview of Aquinas's account of property, we would make the following points. First, although Aquinas draws directly upon Aristotle's *Politics*, and uses his exact formulation, private ownership and public use, he significantly develops and expands it. He expands the context of its meaning, in light of divine creation and divine providence for all of mankind. The teleology of nature is deepened by the account of creation and man as made to the image and likeness of God. The end of common use now includes civic duty but leads beyond to almsgiving and the superior ideal of voluntary, evangelical property. And Aquinas adds an additional reason for justifying the institution of private property, which is that of order versus confusion. Second, private ownership of property is said to be "lawful" and affirmed as consistent with human nature, natural law, and natural right. The detailed arrangement of private ownership is a matter for prudential decision. Private property is not obligatory, and perhaps not even necessary in some conditions. Accordingly, third, private ownership is not said to be a "right" of an individual. It is not an absolute or a primitive principle for social-political philosophy. Private ownership, although justified on the basis of the natural love of one's own, is not part of a justification of unlimited acquisition; neither does private ownership give rise to the "profit motive,"

---

[10] Bede Jarrett, O.P., *Social Theories of the Middle Ages* (Westminster, MD: Newman, 1942), p. 144.

nor is it used to explain the efficiency of the economic system, other than the care one gives to one's own. Fourth, Aquinas does open the way for a proper understanding of the natural and divine basis for private ownership. The Christian tradition tended to attribute the institution of private property to the result of original sin. Aristotle's two-fold reason of care for one's own and social harmony could be read as a necessity due to human weakness or human sin. Bede Jarrett interprets the institution of private property as a concession to sinful human nature.[11] At the very least, Jarrett sets up the fundamental tension concerning private property as a contrast between "abstract right and concrete exercise of right." Abstract right, he says, is absolute and inalienable because rooted in the nature of man as possessing intellect and will. Concrete exercise, on the other hand, depends upon discovery based on human experience and pragmatic reasons. But perhaps religious life would reveal that the necessity of private property, as an exercise of right, is no longer necessary. The two reasons of peace and love of one's own may be not operative in a religious society, but the reason of order would still seem to obtain.

Jarrett explains the medieval approach to property derived from Aristotle and the Bible, the axiom of private ownership and common use, broke down after the Black Death, for a variety of reasons. There was an increased demand for labor and the separation of wage from property. Philosophically, one or the other side of the axiom was denied or over emphasized. Wycliffe attacked begging and sought to assign property only to the righteous. The spiritual Franciscans denounced private property as pagan and urged poverty as a divine command. The general drift of the reformers detested the poor and the beggar but endorsed private property and efficiency. By the time of the Renaissance all sides merged power and wealth. With the increase of trade and the accumulation of wealth, society demanded a more absolute sense of ownership of wealth and an acknowledgement of the right of the individual to property.

III. Jacques Maritain on the Artifex and
the True Foundation of Private Ownership

Maritain approaches the problem of property after the Leonine encyclicals and the problem facing Christendom of the extremes of liberalism and communism, a variation of the denial of one or the other side of the Aristotelian axiom, private ownership, and common use. The Catholic social tradition began to use the phrasing of right to property, and civil rights across the board. But these rights are interpreted on the basis of natural law. A right is derived from natural

---

[11] "The lawfulness of private property is guaranteed by man's reason, the necessity only by his greed" (*Social Theories*, p. 127).

law. We need to understand how moral law is derived from human flourishing. And we may recall Tocqueville's notion that right is the idea of virtue applied to politics.[12] Maritain similarly said:

> There is no right unless a certain order – which can be violated in fact – is inviolably required by *what things are* in their intelligible type or their essence, or by what the nature of man is, and is cut out for: an order by virtue of which certain things like life, work, freedom are due to the human person ... Such an order ... imposes itself upon our minds to the point of binding us in conscience [and] exists in things in a certain way ... as a requirement of their essence.[13]

Maritain's grounding of rights is different from the modern nominalist and self-interested grounding; and it is not simply a theological grounding in the brotherhood of men, God's workmanship in all men, and so forth. Rights on their account are demands to establish the legal recognition of and the promotion of the good human life; they are telic, communal, and conditional. Maritain claims that all human beings possess certain rights; a minimum array of rights must be respected absolutely; but most rights are conditioned by the social and political conditions. That is, he says their exercise depends upon social conditions. He opposes the tendency to inflate and make "absolute and limitless" individual rights. Yet on the other hand, he sets a dynamic goal for human society which is properly democratic; that is, the failure to realize and have all men exercise their rights is a sign of an "inhuman element that remains in the social structure of each period."[14] Thus the metaphysical doctrine of a shared nature justifies the goal of liberal democracy. Modern democracy is the most progressive attempt to realize the latent rights of all human beings, which rights are implicit in the shared unity of human nature.

The philosophy of human rights must address the issue of the human good and human perfection. According to Maritain human rights flow from the divine order reflected in human nature. It is the "right possessed by God ... to see the order of His Wisdom in beings respected, obeyed and loved by every intelligence."[15] He does not give a Kantian type account based upon human autonomy. From a definite conception of the good life Maritain derives human rights. He defines the key modern notion of freedom in terms of virtue, which he calls "liberty of expansion and autonomy:" it is "the flowering of moral and rational life, and of those ... interior activities which are the intellectual and moral virtues."[16] But the modern philosophy of human rights "believe[s] in lib-

---

[12] See: Alexis de Tocqueville, *Democracy in America*, edited by J. P. Mayer, translated by George Lawrence (Garden City, New York: Doubleday, 1969), bk 1, ch 14.

[13] *Man and the State* (Chicago: University of Chicago Press, 1951), pp. 96–97.

[14] *Man and the State*, p. 102.

[15] *The Rights of Man and Natural Law* (London: Geoffrey Bles, 1958), p 38.

[16] *Rights of Man*, p. 27.

erty without mastery of self or moral responsibility."[17] For Maritain, therefore, the essential political task is "a task of civilization and culture."[18] The rights of man follow from this goal – they represent the conditions necessary for the full flowering of human perfection in the multitude. Maritain expounds upon personal, civic, and economic rights in light of this concrete human good. For the precise enumeration one may consult *The Rights of Man and Natural Law*, including a resume of rights provided at its end.[19] The enumerated rights protect and provide the material and legal conditions for human perfection. Suffice it to say that Maritain expects the slow but steady emancipation of man from the conditions that thwart his aspirations to truth and virtue. Liberation is for the sake of human perfection, not an end in itself, nor a freedom without terminus or measure. This account of freedom would appear to preserve what is best in a theory of rights by joining it to a notion of virtue. Rights are not a claim of subjectivity or a liberty free of obligation, but conditions for human excellence challenging political prudence in its task to achieve a common good and a decent human life for all.

Property is one such right necessary for the support of human life, human liberty, and the family. Maritain is harshly critical of the capitalist system. However he says that it should not criticized on the basis of a theory of surplus value or for the institution of private property as Marxists purport. Rather he criticizes capitalism because it breeds a culture of inverted values, placing profit as the fruit of money fed by the undertaking, not the undertaking fed by money. The cult of earthly riches is a spirit of hatred of poverty and the contempt of the poor. In an attempt to present his fair view he says: "The objective spirit of Capitalism is a spirit of bold and courageous conquest of the earth; but it is a spirit of the enslavement of all things to the endless increase of the sacred pile of material goods."[20] Now Maritain's views on capitalism, socialism, and communism have been quite controversial. I mention them only to highlight the fact that Maritain provided a very profound defense of private property, using the axiom of Aristotle and St. Thomas on private ownership and common use. His explanation and development is strikingly clear and original and provides a breakthrough, I think, to the lingering ambiguities of Aristotle's account.

In an appendix to *Freedom in the Modern World* Maritain explores the texts of St. Thomas on property. He explains that here are three phases to his account: the general principle of human appropriation and fashioning of external things of the earth; the second, why individual ownership is the typical way to

---

[17] *The Range of Reason* (New York: Scribner's, 1952), p. 167.

[18] *Rights of Man*, p. 27.

[19] *Rights of Man*, pp. 60–62.

[20] *Freedom in the Modern World*, pp. 127–131.

accomplish this goal; and third, particular kinds of ownership. Maritain is interested in the second stage in order to "determine more precisely what are the elements in human nature on which the general right to own private property is founded" (p. 195). He explains that is important to see the problem of property through the postulate undergirding man as maker, artifex, or man as an artist in the broad sense of the word.[21]

Maritain wishes to find "once and for all" the solid foundation of private ownership, that is, to find a foundation other than the contingent or pragmatic foundation of social harmony. He claims that the commentators upon St. Thomas have not elucidated the fundamental principles with sufficient care. He looks to the dynamic of human making to discover it. A fundamental distinction between doing and making is to be found in Aristotle and St. Thomas. The artist, the maker, places a focus upon the thing to be made, the *factibile*; the moral agent, the doer, must be concerned with the moral act, the *agibile*. Both are a function of rational capacity. Human action relies upon "recta ratio agibilium," prudence; making relies upon "recta ratio factibilium," art. Art is an intellectual virtue. In *Art and Scholasticism* Maritain elaborates:

> Art, first of all, is of the intellectual order, its action consists in imprinting an idea in some matter: it is therefore in the intelligence of the *artifex* that it resides, or, as is said, this intelligence is the subject in which it inheres. It is a certain *quality* of this intelligence.[22]

This imprinting of an idea upon matter entails the production of a work and "the elaboration of some material";[23] it is the good the work as such that the artifex achieves, not the good of action. Art proceeds from a habitus or quality of the soul. It achieves a rigor from the object or the work to be made. Maritain explains that art is more purely intellectual than prudence and moral action, and stands more akin to science in this riveting to the object.[24]

---

[21] Thus, see his *Art and Scholasticism*.

[22] *Art and Scholasticism*, p. 10.

[23] *Freedom in the Modern World*, p. 197.

[24] "Art does not concern itself with the proper good of the will, and with the ends that the will pursues in its own line as human appetite; and if it supposes a certain rectitude of the appetite, this is still with regard to some properly intellectual end. Like Science, it is to an *object* that Art is riveted (an object to be made, it is true, not an object to be contemplated). It uses the roundabout way of deliberation and counsel only by accident. Although it produces individual acts and effects, it does not, except secondarily, judge according to the contingencies of circumstance; thus it considers less than does Prudence the individuation of actions and the *hic et nunc*. In short, if by reason of its matter, which is contingent, Art accords more with Prudence than with Science, yet *according to its formal reason and as virtue* it accords more with Science and the *habitus* of the speculative intellect than with Prudence: *ars magis convenit cum habitibus speculativis in ratione virtutis, quam cum prudentia*. The Scientist is an Intellectual who demon-

Maritain then drives right to his conclusion: "the exercise of art or work is the *formal reason* of individual appropriation; but only because it presupposes the rational nature and personality of the artist or workman."[25] And further, "the notion of 'person' must ... be included in any complete theory of property since the *persona* is the proper subject of intellect in operation."[26] In addition, Maritain claims this is "the metaphysical element in human nature which in a general way makes personal ownership a matter of necessity and grounds proprietary right."[27] We need to fill in one more premise or step and then look at the implications and significance of Maritain's argument.

Maritain fills in the following step. It is the good of the work, attended to by the habitus of the artifex that necessitates private appropriation. He explains it in the following way:

> Now by virtue of what the work of art or work to be done demands for its proper perfection it is in the nature of things necessary that man shall have the fullest control over the material on which he has to work, that the master craftsman [artifex] shall have permanent and exclusive right of disposal of the material and of the means necessary for executing the work.[28]

We sometimes speak about artistic control or artistic liberty; these phrases acknowledge the requirement, arising from the habitus and its object, of personal ownership (in some way) of the materials and means of production or work. His main point is that that human society requires "a general system of individual ownership (whatever be the modes, more or less felicitous), in which the system takes place."[29] The important thing is to make the connection with Aquinas's phrasing in the ST 2-2, 66, 2, namely that art requires the personal power of management and use of external things (*potestas procurandi et dispensandi*). The artifex has foresight and intelligence for the good of the work; therefore, the things, materials and means of work must be the property of the artifex, "the rational being which is individual and which has an individual perfection."[30] Appropriation must be by the individual craftsman. Maritain points out that the proprietorship (*dominium*) that a person has over himself "is thus extended to the ownership of things" through the "*factibile*" and because of the intellectual quality or habitus of "art."[31]

---

strates, the Artist is an Intellectual who makes, the Prudent Man is an intelligent Man of Will who acts well." *Art and Scholasticism*, pp. 19–20.

[25] *Freedom in the Modern World*, p. 198.

[26] Ibid.

[27] *Freedom in the Modern World*, p. 197.

[28] *Freedom in the Modern World*, p. 198.

[29] *Freedom in the Modern World*, p. 199.

[30] *Freedom in the Modern World*, p. 200.

[31] *Freedom in the Modern World*, p. 198.

Some additional points will help to illustrate and explain the metaphysical foundation of private property in nature of man as maker. First, it is important to grasp the significance of the intellectual basis for individual ownership of property. Recall that Aristotle's account, by appealing to social harmony and attachment to one's own, made the foundation of private ownership a pragmatic issue. But what works under some conditions may not be necessary under others. Christian thinkers suggested that private property was by reason of sinfulness. Because of human weakness mankind has failed to achieve the ideal or true standard of communism as proposed by heretics and spirituals. Under new conditions perhaps we could do without private property. But if the reason for property is derived from art, an intellectual virtue free of the affective or volitional dimension of human action, we can say that it derives from human excellence. As we suggested above, Aquinas made such an opening when he added a third reason pertaining to the order achieved by private property. Order is caused by wisdom and intellect. Order is necessary for the good of the work itself; the confusion to be avoided is not the confusion of quarrelling or attachment to one's own, but the confusion that fails to achieve the perfection of the work.

A second aspect to appreciate in Maritain's account pertains to scope of the terms artifex and art. He means by the term "art," not specifically or exclusively the fine arts but simply the intellectual quality of making manifest throughout all productivity. The term applies to any craftsman or worker, as well as the "artist":

Not in Phidias and Praxiteles only, but in the village carpenter and blacksmith as well, they acknowledged an intrinsic development of reason, a nobility of the intellect ... It was a virtue of the intellect, and endowed the humblest artisan with a certain perfection of the spirit ... The artisan, in the normal type of human development and of truly human civilizations, represents the general run of men.[32]

Art is the standard mode of human work. "Artistic work is thus the properly human work, in contradistinction to the work of a beast or the work of a machine."[33] To perform as a beast is to be subject to drudgery which lacks all rational capacity. To work as machine is to be subject to a numbing uniformity, which lacks the dimension of spontaneity, and judgment required of human work. Thus, man as artisan as the foundation for private property provides a universal basis or justification for the practice as well as provisional standard for human flourishing.

Third, the notion of artifex could be linked to the head of household as providing for a family. The notion of rational subject also provides a basis for

---

[32] *Art and Scholasticism*, p. 20.

[33] *Art and Scholasticism*, p. 154, fn 4.

transactions throughout society and for members of intermediate groups. A free society requires private property, because a free society must be composed of persons of intelligence and foresight who provide for themselves and others.

Fourth, the foundation of private property in the artifex makes a clearer connection to the Genesis account of man made to the image and likeness of God. Human beings are given the mandate to cultivate and subdue the earth. The capacity for art is the special *munus* or gift received for such a mandate. Maritain is quick to find a passage from the *Summa contra gentiles* (1, 93, 4) that explains why art is a proper predicate of God: "Of things that come to have being from God, the proper plan of them all is in the divine understanding. But the plan of a thing to be made in the mind of the maker is Art: hence the Philosopher says that Art is 'the right notion of things to be made.' There is therefore properly Art in God, and therefore it is said: *Wisdom, artificer of all, taught me* (Wisd. vii, 21)."[34]

We have a foundation for private ownership in the intellectual virtue of art. No less crucial to the understanding of property is the demand for common use. Maritain's contribution to the notion of common use is less striking than his treatment of private ownership. In this appendix to Freedom and the Modern World, however, he does lay down the standard markers from St. Thomas to remind us again of some basics.

First of all, "use" is a special term in St. Thomas pertaining to the last moment in an act of the will, and it is defined as the application of a thing to an operation (ST 1-2, 16, 1). It pertains to moral action, to the *agibile*, as we mentioned above. Indeed, Maritain explains that use "constitutes the last moment of the will as it tends to real grasp of the means it has chosen."[35] Aquinas employs the concrete example of using a stick: "to strike is to use a stick" (ST 1-2, 16, 1).Thus, Maritain explains: "In every human act that has to do with external goods, the two aspects of *factibile* and *agibile*, appear. The one and the other, individual appropriation and common use should shine forth in every act which concerns external goods."[36]

The norm of common use refers first of all to the political common good, at least as we derive the axiom from Aristotle. The Christian theologians add the good of all mankind, as derived from the creation of all in Adam and biblical mandate of Genesis to cultivate and subdue the earth. Because of the duty to serve all mankind, the common use may initially be understood as to mean the

---

[34] *Of God and His Creatures*: An Annotated Translation (With some Abridgement) of the Summa Contra Gentiles of Saint Thos Aquinas by Joseph Rickaby (London: Burns and Oates, 1905), p. 69; available online: http://maritain.nd.edu/jmc/etext/gc1_93.htm.

[35] *Freedom in the Modern World*, p. 205; Maritain draws on ST 1-2, 16, 4.

[36] *Freedom in the Modern World*, p. 207.

donation of surplus to those in need. The citations from Ambrose and other Church Fathers imply as much. But the norm of common use, the "ordering of things to the service of all," is a universal rule. Maritain points out that any virtuous action is ordered to the common good, without necessity of conscious thought of the particular agent in the matter. Aquinas does say that we must will the universal good only formally and not materially (ST 1-2, 19, 10).[37] On the one hand, that places no special obligation on the use of property if used by a man of virtue; but on the other hand, it means that "every use of goods which is not regulated by reason is an act of avarice which deprives others of their due."[38] In fact, Maritain understands it as a sin against one's neighbor, "for I am never alone in any one of my acts."

But common use or benefit demands more than the simple virtuous act. Responsible agents "interchange goods at will by way of gift, sale, purchase, loan, hiring, deposit and so forth."[39] Or there may be social customs and organizations that facilitate common goods and sharing. As Aristotle urged, good custom and education is what works best. But Maritain argues, "The law may intervene here." After all on the Thomistic argument for authority explained in the passage cited above, the magistrate must will the common good materially. So Maritain states that we need an organization or social structure "which will ensure a certain measure of enjoyment for all and a certain administrative responsibility in all."[40]

On the question of the use of surplus for the common good Maritain agrees that this should not be a matter for legislation at all, but a matter for conscience. For sumptuary laws and taxes "make up only for deficiencies in individual virtue."[41] Modern legislation, he worries, "only secures a strict minimum by way of compensation" for the absence of spontaneous "common use." Justice secures a minimum. But the claims of common use require friendship as well as justice.

Conclusion

In this exercise of clarification of the basis for private property we did not seek concrete solutions to social and economic problems such as health care, minimum wage, or tax codes. Rather we have sought to show how Saint Tho-

---

[37] See: Yves R Simon, *Philosophy of Democratic Government* (Chicago: University of Chicago Press, 1951), pp. 40–42.

[38] *Freedom in the Modern World*, p. 208.

[39] *Freedom in the Modern World*, p. 208; Maritain draws upon ST 1-2, 105, 2.

[40] *Freedom in the Modern World*, p. 209.

[41] *Freedom in the Modern World*, p. 209.

mas "encloses the social problem between the two branches of this antimony," namely, between private ownership and common use. Maritain explains that on the one hand "human production is in its normal state an *artisan's* production, and consequently requires individual appropriation," but on the other hand, in "the line of moral aspirations the use of goods must be common." Indeed, he said that as work or art become "inhuman" so is the claim of property, and yet it corresponds to a deep human need.[42] Both claims, of ownership and of common use, are deeply human. There are no easy solutions, and yet ideologies of left and right seek to reduce the social problem to one or the other pole of the antimony. Maritain observed that moral reasons are often preferred against private ownership and intellectual or technical reasons in its favor.

As he wrote this treatise on property, in the 1920's, Maritain saw the onset of a crisis of the social economic order. He saw a failure on both fronts – namely the dwindling of private ownership and a disregard for private property, as well as the demands of the *artifex* in everyday life; but also he was concerned about the lack of a common good and devotion of individual property to common use.

Maritain called himself a man of the left, first to distinguish himself from the royalists and crypto-fascists in France, but also to urge the development of social justice in the modern liberal democracies of the West. He feared communism most of all for its suppression of private property, its spurious common good, and for the killing of true spontaneous social order. He developed his constructive political philosophy over the following decades through the notion of integral humanism, the relation of the person and common good, and the contours of a personalist democracy. He was a champion of freedom against the totalitarians and found favorable developments in the United States of America. I think his deepening of St. Thomas and Aristotle on the matter of property ownership proves to be a significant contribution to the perennial philosophy.

Summary

Central to the Aristotelian-Thomistic account of private property is an apparent antimony expressed in the formula: "private ownership, common use." This essay identifies its origins in Aristotle and then shows how Thomas Aquinas accepted the principle and in the process deepened the argument for private ownership. It goes on to show how in the 20th century Jacques Maritian recapitulates Aquinas and fashions an even more principled defense private property as an institution concordant with man's rational nature.

---

[42] *Art and Scholasticism*, p. 154, fn 4.

Zusammenfassung

Im Zentrum der aristotelisch-thomistischen Lehre über das Privateigentum findet sich eine offenkundige Antinomie in der Formulierung: „Privater Besitz, gemeinsamer Nutzen". Dieser Beitrag weist seine Herkunft bei Aristoteles und zeigt, wie Thomas von Aquin diesen Grundsatz übernommen hat und im weiteren Verlauf die Begründung für den Privatbesitz vertieft hat. Im 20. Jahrhundert greift Jacques Maritain diesen Gedanken wieder auf und entwickelt eine noch weitergehende Verteidigung des Privateigentums, weil diese Institution der Vernunft-Natur des Menschen entspricht.

II. Rechtliche und politische Aspekte
Legal and Political Aspects

Ist privates Eigentum ein Menschenrecht?
Philosophische und verfassungshistorische Überlegungen

Von Christian Hillgruber

I. Einleitung

Die Eigentumsgarantie des Art. 14 Abs. 1 GG ist kein Freiheitsgrundrecht wie jedes andere. Das Grundgesetz unterwirft das von ihm gewährleistete und geschützte Eigentum Privater einer weitreichenden Sozialbindung[1], wie sie für kein anderes Grundrecht vorgesehen ist: „Eigentum verpflichtet. Sein Gebrauch soll zugleich dem Wohle der Allgemeinheit dienen" (Art. 14 Abs. 2 GG). Mehr noch: Nicht nur die Schranken des Eigentums, sondern auch sein Inhalt werden durch die Gesetze bestimmt (Art. 14 Abs. 1 S. 2 GG). „Nur das durch die Gesetze ausgeformte Eigentum bildet den Gegenstand der Eigentumsgarantie und ist verfassungsrechtlich geschützt."[2] Es gibt danach also kein vorstaatliches „natürliches" Eigentum; Eigentum ist vielmehr ein Produkt des positiven Rechts. „Im Unterschied zu allen anderen grundrechtlichen Freiheitsgewährleistungen schützt Art. 14 GG nicht ein dem Gesetzgeber vorausliegendes Recht, sondern delegiert die Befugnis zu bestimmen, was überhaupt Eigentum ist, auf den Gesetzgeber"[3]. Erst das, was der Gesetzgeber für eigentumsfähig erklärt hat und sodann zu Eigentum erworben worden ist, wird anschließend als individuelles Recht prinzipiell vor staatlichem Zugriff geschützt. Dies macht die „Entstehungsschwäche und Bestandsstärke des verfassungsrechtlichen Eigentums"[4] aus.

Diese eigentümliche Gesetzesbestimmtheit des grundrechtlich geschützten Eigentums wirft die Frage auf, ob das Recht am Eigentum eigentlich ein Menschenrecht ist. Diese Frage hat seit jeher das sozialphilosophische Denken beschäftigt; das Eigentum Privater ist stets als begründungs- und rechtfertigungsbedürftig angesehen worden.

---

[1] Siehe hierzu *Walter Leisner*, Sozialbindung des Eigentums, Berlin 1972.

[2] BVerfGE 24, 367 (396).

[3] *Wilfried Berg*, Entwicklung und Grundstrukturen der Eigentumsgarantie, JuS 2005, 961 (962).

[4] So der Titel der Schrift von *Markus Appel*, Berlin 2004.

Das bis ins 17. Jahrhundert vorherrschende traditionelle Naturrecht verneinte ein Naturrecht auf und an Privateigentum. „Es unterstellt eine ursprüngliche Gütergemeinschaft, das Gemeineigentum als von Gott gegebenes und gebotenes Naturrecht oder wenigstens als historische Tatsache."[5] Die Anerkennung von Privateigentum an allen Gütern basiert danach auf einer Übereinkunft der Menschen wegen der mangelnden Sorge um das Gemeinsame, die das Gemeingut verkommen ließ: „Wer sich zuerst einen herrenlosen Gegenstand physisch aneignet und daraufhin einen Eigentumsanspruch geltend macht, soll als legitimer privater Eigentümer gelten. Das Privateigentum ist demnach zwar der sündhaften menschlichen Natur gemäß, aber kein wirkliches (von Gott gesetztes) Naturrecht. Es ist *lex humana*, von Menschen gemachtes Recht, aber nicht Menschenrecht! Es bleibt aufgrund seines sozialen und konventionellen Charakters [...] sozialpflichtig."[6]

II. Das Verständnis des Eigentums in der ideengeschichtlichen Entwicklung der Neuzeit – Hobbes, Rousseau, Locke

1. Hobbes:
„the introduction of propriety is an effect of Commonwealth"

In den vernunftrechtlichen Staatsvertragslehren der Neuzeit spielt die Frage des privatexklusiven Eigentums für die Herleitung politischer Herrschaft eine zentrale Rolle.

In der Widmungsepistel „To The Right Honourable William, Earle of Devonshire" seiner 1642 publizierten Abhandlung „De Cive" erklärte *Thomas Hobbes* (1588–1679) dem Leser, dass den Anfang seiner Überlegungen die Frage gebildet habe, „weshalb jemand eine Sache eher die seine als die eines anderen nennt und zu welchem Zweck und infolge welcher Nötigung die Menschen gewollt haben, dass, da eigentlich alles allen gehörte, jeder ein besonderes Eigentum haben solle"[7].

Im Naturzustand, d. h. vorstaatlich, herrscht nach *Hobbes* ein Krieg aller gegen alle: „if any two men desire the same thing, which nevertheless they cannot both enjoy, they become enemies; and in the way to their end (which is principally their own conservation, and sometimes their delectation only) endeavour

---

[5] *Ingo Elbe*, Vom Eigentümer zum Eigentum, in: Christine Zunke (Hrsg.), Oldenburger Jahrbuch für Philosophie 2010, Oldenburg 2011, S. 147–182; hier zitiert nach: http://www.staff.uni-oldenburg.de/ingo.elbe/download/%282%29_Elbe_Locke.pdf, S. 2.

[6] *Ingo Elbe*, a. a. O., S. 2 f.

[7] *Thomas Hobbes*, De Cive: the English version (The Clarendon Edition of the Philosophical Works of Thomas Hobbes, Vol. III), Oxford 1983, S. 27.

to destroy or subdue one another. And from hence it comes to pass that where an invader hath no more to fear than another man's single power, if one plant, sow, build, or possess a convenient seat, others may probably be expected to come prepared with forces united to dispossess and deprive him, not only of the fruit of his labour, but also of his life or liberty. And the invader again is in the like danger of another."[8]

Im Naturzustand gibt es keine Gerechtigkeit und folglich auch kein Eigentum, sondern nur tatsächlichen Besitz, der nur solange andauert, bis sich ein Stärkerer der Sache bemächtigt. Erst der Staat schafft Recht und Eigentum, das diesen Namen verdient: „To this war of every man against every man, this also is consequent; that nothing can be unjust. The notions of right and wrong, justice and injustice, have there no place. Where there is no common power, there is no law; where no law, no injustice. Force and fraud are in war the two cardinal virtues. Justice and injustice are none of the faculties neither of the body nor mind. If they were, they might be in a man that were alone in the world, as well as his senses and passions. They are qualities that relate to men in society, not in solitude. It is consequent also to the same condition that there be no propriety, no dominion, no mine and thine distinct; but only that to be every man's that he can get, and for so long as he can keep it."[9]

Im Naturzustand können alle Anspruch auf alles erheben, was ihrer Selbsterhaltung dienlich sein könnte. Auf diesen maßlosen Anspruch müssen die Menschen wechselseitig verzichten, wenn sie Frieden erlangen wollen. Nur durch Unterwerfung unter eine absolute Staatsgewalt können sie sich aus dem Elend des permanenten Krieges aller gegen alle befreien und in Frieden und Sicherheit leben. Dafür müssen sie allerdings all ihrer „Beherrschungsrechte" des Naturzustandes entsagen. Im Gegenzug erhalten sie Sicherheit für ihr Leben und ihre vermögenswerten Güter. Deren Zuordnung zu einer Privatperson als ihr gehörig, verbunden mit dem Recht, alle anderen Privatpersonen von deren Nutzung auszuschließen, ist allein Sache des Souveräns. „Seventhly, is annexed to the sovereignty the whole power of prescribing the rules whereby every man may know what goods he may enjoy, and what actions he may do, without being molested by any of his fellow subjects: and this is it men call propriety. For before constitution of sovereign power, as hath already been shown, all men had right to all things, which necessarily causeth war: and therefore this propriety, being necessary to peace, and depending on sovereign power, is the act of that power, in order to the public peace. These rules of propriety (or meum and tuum) and of good, evil, lawful, and unlawful in the actions of subjects are the civil laws; that is to say, the laws of each Commonwealth in particular."[10]

---

[8] *Thomas Hobbes*, Leviathan, 1660, Chapter XIII.

[9] *Thomas Hobbes*, Leviathan, 1660, Chapter XIII.

[10] *Thomas Hobbes*, Leviathan, 1660, Chapter XVIII.

Hobbes zitiert *Cicero*: „‚Take away the civil law, and no man knows what is his own, and what another man's.' Seeing therefore the introduction of propriety is an effect of Commonwealth, which can do nothing but by the person that represents it, it is the act only of the sovereign; and consisteth in the laws, which none can make that have not the sovereign power."[11] Und in der Entscheidung, in welchem Umfang Eigentum Privater anerkannt und zugewiesen wird, ist der Souverän frei: „In this distribution, the first law is for division of the land itself: wherein the sovereign assigneth to every man a portion, according as he, and not according as any subject, or any number of them, shall judge agreeable to equity and the common good. [...] For seeing the sovereign, that is to say, the Commonwealth (whose person he representeth), is understood to do nothing but in order to the common peace and security, this distribution of lands is to be understood as done in order to the same: and consequently, whatsoever distribution he shall make in prejudice thereof is contrary to the will of every subject that committed his peace and safety to his discretion and conscience, and therefore by the will of every one of them is to be reputed void. It is true that a sovereign monarch, or the greater part of a sovereign assembly, may ordain the doing of many things in pursuit of their passions, contrary to their own consciences, which is a breach of trust and of the law of nature; but this is not enough to authorize any subject, either to make war upon, or so much as to accuse of injustice, or any way to speak evil of their sovereign; because they have authorized all his actions, and, in bestowing the sovereign power, made them their own."[12] Der Souverän, der selbst keinen Rechtsbindungen gegenüber seinen Untertanen unterliegt, vielmehr „die Kräfte und das Vermögen aller nach seinem Ermessen gebrauchen kann"[13], muss auch das von ihm selbst erst geschaffene Eigentum Privater nicht unbedingt achten und schützen, sondern kann darauf aus Gründen des gemeinen Wohls nach eigenem Gutdünken zugreifen. Zwar sollen gesetzliche Einschränkungen der Freiheit, auch der Freiheit, sein Vermögen zu vermehren, nur erfolgen, sofern und soweit dies das Wohl der Bürger und des Staates erfordert. Aber dies zu beurteilen, fällt allein in die Kompetenz des Souveräns.

2. Rousseau: La propriété: „dépositaire du bien public"

Jean-Jacques Rousseau (1712–1788) teilt *Hobbes'* Ausgangspunkt: Es gibt kein natürliches Eigentum(srecht); erst der Übergang in den bürgerlichen Zustand macht Eigentum möglich. „Was der Mensch durch den Gesellschaftsver-

---

[11] *Thomas Hobbes*, Leviathan, 1660, Chapter XXIV.

[12] *Thomas Hobbes*, Leviathan, 1660, Chapter XXIV.

[13] *Thomas Hobbes*, De Cive, 1642, cap. Vi, 13.

trag verliert, ist seine natürliche Freiheit und ein unbegrenztes Recht auf alles, wonach ihn gelüstet und was er erreichen kann; was er erhält ist die bürgerliche Freiheit und das Eigentum an allem, was er besitzt."[14] Aus dem „Besitz, der nur die Folge der Stärke oder des Rechts des ersten Besitznehmers ist", wird „Eigentum, das nur auf einen ausdrücklichen Titel gestützt werden kann"[15]. Auch das Recht eines ersten Besitznehmers, obgleich mit mehr Berechtigung als das des Stärkeren, verwandelt sich erst mit Einführung des Eigentumsrechts im bürgerlichen Zustand, „durch eine vorteilhafte Abtretung an die Öffentlichkeit", in „ein wirkliches Recht"[16]. Dieses Recht ist allerdings kein privatnütziges. Die Privateigentümer besitzen als „dépositaires du bien public", d. h. als Sachwalter des Gemeinwohls, als citoyens, nicht als bourgeois.[17] Im Übrigen bleibt der Souverän übergeordnet. Es könne auch vorkommen, so *Rousseau*, dass die Menschen sich zu vereinigen beginnen, ohne irgendetwas zu besitzen und dass sie sich danach eines für alle ausreichenden Gebietes bemächtigen und es gemeinsam nutzen oder unter sich aufteilen, sei es zu gleichen, sei es zu durch den Souverän festgelegten Teilen. „Auf welche Weise dieser Erwerb auch vor sich geht, das Recht, das jeder einzelne an seinem Boden hat, ist immer dem Recht der Gemeinschaft auf alle(s) untergeordnet, sonst wäre das gesellschaftliche Band ohne Festigkeit und die Souveränität in ihrer Ausübung ohne tatsächliche Macht."[18] Der demokratische Souverän ist nach *Rousseau* po-

---

[14] *Jean-Jacques Rousseau*, Contrat Social, 1762, livre 1, chap. 8.

[15] *Jean-Jacques Rousseau*, a. a. O., livre 1, chap. 8.

[16] *Jean-Jacques Rousseau*, a. a. O., livre 1, chap. 9. Für Rousseau hat die Begründung eines „natürlichen" Rechts auf ein bestimmtes Stück Land durch Besitznahme drei Voraussetzungen: Es muss sich erstens um noch unbewohntes Land handeln, es darf zweitens nicht größer sein als zur Erwirtschaftung des eigenen Unterhalts notwendig, und drittens muss die Besitzergreifung durch Arbeit und Anbau und nicht durch bloße Erklärung erfolgt sein. Ansonsten handelt es sich um eine „widerrechtliche Besitznahme, die strafbar ist, weil sie den Rest der Menschheit um Aufenthalt und Nahrung bringt, die die Natur allen zusammen gewährt" (ebd.). Schon in seiner zweiten Preisschrift, dem Discours sur L'inégalité von 1754, hatte Rousseau die Eigentumsbegründung als Beginn der Vergesellschaftung angesehen und diesen anmaßenden Akt zugleich als Beginn menschlicher Zwietracht und Degeneration scharf kritisiert: „Der erste, der ein Stück Erde eingezäunt hatte und sich anmaßte zu sagen: ‚Dies gehört mir', und der Leute fand, die einfältig genug waren, es zu glauben, war der wahre Gründer der bürgerlichen Gesellschaft. Wieviele Verbrechen, Kriege, Morde, wieviel Elend und Schrecken hätte derjenige dem Menschengeschlecht erspart, der die Pfähle herausgerissen oder den Graben zugeschüttet und seinesgleichen zugerufen hätte: ‚Hütet Euch, diesem Betrüger zuzuhören. Ihr seid verlassen, wenn ihr vergesst, dass die Früchte allen und die Erde keinem gehört!'" (Anfang des Zweiten Teils)

[17] Vgl. *Klaus Dieter Schulz*, Rousseaus Eigentumskonzeption, Frankfurt a. M. 1980, S. 51: Der Eigentümer besitzt sein Eigentum „als einen Teil, der vollständig in den gesellschaftlichen Zusammenhang integriert ist".

[18] *Jean-Jacques Rousseau*, a. a. O., livre 1, chap. 9.

tentiell allmächtig:[19] „Wir stimmen darin überein, dass alles, was jeder einzelne durch den Gesellschaftsvertrag von seiner Macht, seinen Gütern und seiner Freiheit veräußert, nur jeweils der Teil davon ist, dessen Gebrauch für das Gemeinwesen von Bedeutung ist; aber man muss auch zugestehen, dass allein der Souverän über diese Bedeutung entscheidet.“[20] Einen hinreichenden Schutz von Freiheit und Eigentum der Einzelnen sieht *Rousseau* dadurch gewährleistet, dass die Privateigentümer als Bürger mit gleichen, wechselseitigen Rechten und Pflichten selbst darüber entscheiden, zu welchen öffentlichen Zwecken und in welchem Umfang sie für alle gleichermaßen geltende Freiheits- und Eigentumsbeschränkungen vornehmen: „Da nun der Souverän nur aus den Einzelnen besteht, aus deren er sich zusammensetzt, hat er kein und kann auch kein dem ihren widersprechendes Interesse haben. Folglich bedarf die souveräne Macht gegenüber den Untertanen keiner Bürgschaft, weil es unmöglich ist, dass die Körperschaft allen ihren Gliedern schaden will.“[21] Wenn die Bürger Belastungen, die alle treffen, zustimmen, dann sind sie im allseits anerkannten gemeinsamen Interesse notwendig.

Der Eigentumsschutz erschöpft sich bei *Rousseau* darin, dass Eigentumseingriffe nur durch allgemeine Gesetze als Ausdruck der *volonté générale* erfolgen dürfen: „Hieraus sieht man, dass die souveräne Gewalt, völlig unumschränkt, geheiligt und unverletzlich, wie sie ist, die Grenzen der allgemeinen Übereinkünfte weder überschreitet noch überschreiten kann und dass jeder voll und ganz über das verfügen kann, was ihm durch diese Übereinkünfte von seinen Gütern und seiner Freiheit gelassen wurde; dergestalt dass der Souverän niemals das Recht hat, einen Untertanen stärker zu belasten als einen anderen, weil er nicht mehr zuständig ist, sobald eine Angelegenheit eine besondere wird.“[22] Unter den Bedingungen demokratischer Mehrheitsherrschaft, der auch die Gemeinwohldefinition unterliegt, gibt es aber keine Garantie für ein alle Gesellschaftsglieder einigendes Gemeininteresse, das die gesetzlichen Beschränkungen von Freiheit und Eigentum stets aus sich heraus als im wohlverstandenen Interesse aller liegend inhaltlich zu legitimieren vermag. Die Annahme einer die volonté générale hervorbringenden objektiven Interessenidentität unter den Gesellschaftsmitgliedern erscheint fiktiv.

Die individuelle Freiheit der Privateigentümer ist nach *Rousseaus* Konzeption letztlich nicht substantiell, sondern nur prozedural geschützt. Sie steht unter dem Vorbehalt des allgemeinen, von der Einzelperson und dem Einzelbesitz abstrahierenden, dem Gemeinwohl verpflichteten Gesetzes: „Die Definition des

---

[19] *Jean-Jacques Rousseau*, a. a. O., livre 2, chap. 4, spricht von einer „allumfassenden, zwingenden Kraft“.

[20] *Jean-Jacques Rousseau*, a. a. O., livre 2, chap. 4.

[21] *Jean-Jacques Rousseau*, a. a. O., livre 1, chap. 7.

[22] *Jean-Jacques Rousseau*, a. a. O., livre 2, chap. 4.

privaten Freiheitsraums im Contrat Social enthält zwar auch eine Absage an die reglementierende Praxis der Regierungen seiner Zeit, insofern als die konkrete Begrenzung des privaten Freiheitsraumes danach für alle gleich und allgemein gesetzt werden muss, aber damit ist von Rousseau keineswegs eine Präferenz für den ‚bourgeois' ausgesprochen, sondern im Gegenteil wird der Bürger als ‚bourgeois' und sein Freiheitsraum begrenzt durch den Nutzen aller Bürger, und folglich soll die Qualität des ‚bourgeois' grundsätzlich der des ‚citoyens' vollständig untergeordnet sein."[23] Freiheit meint für *Rousseau* den „Gehorsam gegen das Gesetz, das man sich selbst vorgeschrieben hat"[24]. Privatnützige Freiheit und privatnütziges Eigentum erscheinen *Rousseau* folglich nicht schutzwürdig. „Garantiert ist nicht das Eigentum als den Gesetzen entzogenes individuelles Privileg, sondern das Eigentum als gesellschaftliche Institution; der Einzelne erhält sein Privateigentum über die Gesellschaft (die Gesamtinteressen der Eigentümer) vermittelt."[25]

Indem *Rousseau* den Eingriff in die freie Dispositionsgewalt des Privateigentümers von einer allgemeinen gesetzlichen Ermächtigung abhängig machte, stellte er sich gegen die reglementierende, individuelle und korporative Privilegien anerkennende, merkantilistische Wirtschafts- und Finanzpolitik seiner Zeit, namentlich des *ancien régime* in Frankreich. Mag seine Eigentumstheorie auch antifeudalistisch gewesen sein, so ist sie doch ihres kollektivistischen Grundzuges wegen, die den gesellschaftlichen Charakter des Eigentums stark betont sie unter den inhaltlich nicht näher bestimmten Vorbehalt ihrer Einschränkung zum öffentlichen Nutzen stellt, weit davon entfernt, bürgerlich zu sein; denn es gibt letzten Endes ein „uneingeschränktes, absolutes Zugriffsrecht der Gesamtheit der Gesellschaftsmitglieder, des Souverän, auf die Person und den Besitz jedes Gesellschaftsmitgliedes zugunsten des Gesamtinteresses"[26].

3. Locke: Die naturrechtliche Trinität von
Life, Liberty and Estate als Property Rights

Nur bei *John Locke* (1632–1704) besteht ein natürliches, vorstaatliches Eigentumsrecht, um dessen besseren Schutzes willen Menschen in den bürgerlichen Zustand überwechseln und einen politischen Körper bilden.

---

[23] *Klaus Dieter Schulz*, a. a. O., S. 38. Seines Erachtens ist „eine relativ große Homogenität der Sozialstruktur die materielle Voraussetzung zur Konstituierung eines Gemeinwillens im Sinne von Rousseaus Contrat Social" (S. 39). „Die Voraussetzung der Konsistenz des Staates ist also das Privateigentum aller" (S. 42; siehe auch S. 50).

[24] *Jean-Jacques Rousseau*, a. a. O., livre 1, chap. 8.

[25] *Klaus Dieter Schulz*, a. a. O., S. 51.

[26] *Klaus Dieter Schulz*, a. a. O., S. 50.

In dem Zustand, in welchem sich die Menschen von Natur aus befinden, genießen sie die völlige Freiheit, „innerhalb der Grenzen des Naturrechts ihre Handlungen zu regeln und über ihren Besitz und ihre Personen zu verfügen, wie sie es für am besten halten, ohne die Erlaubnis eines anderen zu fordern oder von seinem Willen abzuhängen"[27]. Es ist ebenso ein „Zustand der Gleichheit, worin alle Gewalt und Jurisdiktion"[28]. Die natürliche Freiheit des Einzelnen besteht darin, nach eigenem Gutdünken „über seine Person oder seinen Besitz zu verfügen"[29]. Bei *Locke* bildet die Trinität Leben, Freiheit und Besitz eine natürliche Einheit, die in dem Recht und in der Pflicht zur Selbsterhaltung ihre Grundlage hat: Wer das Recht und die Pflicht hat, sein Leben zu bewahren, der muss auch ein Recht auf all das haben, „was zur Erhaltung des Lebens dient, Freiheit, Gesundheit, Glieder oder Güter"[30]. Auch Freiheit und Leben werden von *Locke* eigentumsrechtlich gedeutet: Sie gehören der Person in gleicher Weise wie privates Sacheigentum als die Frucht der eigenen, in Freiheit ausgeübten Arbeitskraft. Das durch Arbeit erworbene Sacheigentum ist ebenso Teil des Menschen wie seine Freiheit und sein Leben; es verdient deshalb auch denselben Schutz wie die Person selbst.

Nun hat allerdings Gott die Erde „der Menschheit in Gemeinschaft" gegeben.[31] Es existiert folglich „kein ursprüngliches, privatexklusives Eigentumsrecht über äußere, unbearbeitete Güter"[32]. Die Erweiterung der Sphäre naturrechtlicher Rechtsgüter (Leben und Freiheit) um das Sacheigentum geschieht durch die Bearbeitung herrenloser Natur. Sie folgt aus dem Eigentum an der eigenen Person: „Obwohl die Erde und alle niedrigeren Geschöpfe den Menschen gemeinschaftlich gehören, so hat doch jeder Mensch ein Eigentum an seiner eigenen Person; auf diese hat niemand ein Recht als er selbst; die Arbeit seines Körpers und das Werk seiner Hände sind [...] im eigentlichen Sinne sein Eigentum. Alles also, was er dem Zustand, den die Natur vorgesehen und in dem sie es gelassen hat, entrückt, hat er mit seiner Arbeit gemischt und ihm etwas eigenes hinzugefügt."[33] Dies ist es, was das gemeinsame Recht der anderen Menschen ausschließt und die Sache zu einem Teil seiner selbst, zu seinem Eigentum macht.[34] Dies begründet den gleichen Rang des Eigentums unter den natürlichen Rechten wie Freiheit und Leben. Die be- oder verarbeitete Sache wird

---

[27] *John Locke*, Two Treatises of Government, 1690, II, § 4.

[28] *John Locke*, a. a. O., II, § 4.

[29] *John Locke*, a. a. O., II, § 6.

[30] *John Locke*, a. a. O., II, § 6.

[31] *John Locke*, a. a. O., II, § 25.

[32] *Ingo Elbe*, a. a. O., S. 5.

[33] *John Locke*, a. a. O., II, § 27.

[34] So auch *Patrick Horvath*, Zum Verhältnis von Eigentum und Staat bei Locke, in: Samuel Salzborn (Hrsg.), Der Staat des Liberalismus, Baden-Baden 2010, S. 133 (134).

„in den geltungslogischen Rang eines Körperteils erhoben", womit dem Privateigentum „eine außerordentliche Würde zugesprochen [wird], weil es, ebenso bedeutungsvoll wie der Leib, zum unverzichtbaren Element menschlichen Lebensvollzugs erklärt wird"[35].

So konnten Menschen schon im Naturzustand privates Sacheigentum erlangen, „und das ohne einen ausdrücklichen Vertrag mit allen anderen Menschen"[36]. „Die [...] Bedingung menschlichen Lebens, das Arbeit und Stoff, der bearbeitet werden kann, erfordert", führt „notwendigerweise zum Privatbesitz"[37], der unentziehbar ist: „Worauf er auch immer seine Arbeit richtete, war sein Eigentum, das ihm nicht genommen werden konnte."[38] Arbeit als Vermischung eigener Kräfte mit herrenloser äußerer Natur begründet somit das private Eigentumsrecht Einzelner.

Den Eigentumserwerb aufgrund Aneignung durch Arbeitsleistung sieht *Locke* durch zwei Bedingungen begrenzt: Zum einen muss „noch genug und ebenso gutes den anderen gemeinsam verbleiben"[39] (sog. sufficiency-clause), eine Voraussetzung, die wegen des von Locke angenommenen Ressourcenüberflusses[40] nicht wirklich limitierend wirkt. Zum anderen darf sich der Einzelne nur so viel durch seine Arbeit zu eigen machen, „wie irgend jemand zu irgend einem Vorteil seines Lebens gebrauchen kann, bevor es verdirbt"[41] (sog. spoilation-clause). „Sonst nahm er mehr, als ihm zustand, und beraubte andere."[42] Diese beiden Eigentumsschranken[43] werden aber durch die Erfindung des Geldes, welches den Menschen Gelegenheit gab, ihren Besitz über das zur Befriedigung des Eigenbedarfs Notwendige hinaus zu vergrößern und beständig zu machen,[44] obsolet. „Denn die Überschreitung der Grenzen seines rechtmäßigen Eigentums lag nicht in der Vergrößerung seines Besitzes, sondern darin, dass

---

[35] *Franco Zotta*, Immanuel Kant. Legitimität und Recht. Eine Kritik seiner Eigentumslehre, Staatslehre und seiner Geschichtsphilosophie, Freiburg i. Br. 2000, S. 63, 65. Siehe dazu auch *John Locke*, a. a. O., II, § 44: „Obwohl die Dinge der Natur allen zur gemeinsamen Nutzung gegeben werden, lag dennoch die große Grundlage des Eigentums tief im Wesen des Menschen (weil er der Herr seiner selbst ist und Eigentümer seiner eigenen Person und ihrer Handlungen oder Arbeit)."

[36] *John Locke*, a. a. O., II, § 25.

[37] *John Locke*, a. a. O., II, § 35.

[38] *John Locke*, a. a. O., II, § 35.

[39] *John Locke*, a. a. O., II, § 27.

[40] Vgl. *John Locke*, a. a. O., II, § 33. Siehe auch ebd., § 36: Es gebe auf der Welt „genug Land, das auch noch für die doppelte Anzahl von Bewohnern noch ausreicht".

[41] *John Locke*, a. a. O., II, § 37.

[42] *John Locke*, a. a. O., II, § 46: „Es war tatsächlich ebenso dumm wie unredlich, mehr anzuhäufen, als er gebrauchen konnte."

[43] Zur Kritik siehe *Ingo Elbe*, a. a. O., S. 7.

[44] *John Locke*, a. a. O., II, § 48.

irgend etwas ungenutzt verdarb.“[45] „Jeder kann nun über seinen Verbrauch hinaus ein unverderbliches und gegen alle anderen Güter eintauschbares Gut anhäufen.“[46]

Die Erfindung des Geldes „und die stillschweigende Übereinkunft der Menschen, ihm einen Wert beizumessen“, hat „die Bildung größerer Besitztümer und das Recht darauf mit sich gebracht“[47]. „Diese Verteilung der Dinge zu einem ungleichen Privatbesitz haben die Menschen“, so *Locke*, „außerhalb der Grenzen der Gemeinschaft und ohne Vertrag“ durch den Gebrauch des Geldes stillschweigend gebilligt. Sie sind „mit einem ungleichen und unproportionierten Bodenbesitz einverstanden gewesen“, und zwar weil auch der vereinbarte Geldwert einer Sache seinen Maßstab „zum größten Teil“ in der in sie investierten Arbeit findet.[48]

„Das Geld erlaubt eine auf den unterschiedlich großen Fleiß der Menschen begründete Eigentumsungleichheit und ist der Motor unbegrenzter Aneignung von Land und Produktion von Gütern, damit auch der Vermehrung des Gütervorrats der Menschheit.“[49] Individueller Reichtum erhöht damit zugleich das Sozialprodukt. Die damit einhergehende soziale Ungleichheit wird, weil leistungsabhängig, von den Menschen akzeptiert.

Fassen wir noch einmal die Lage der Menschen, wie sie sich im Naturzustand nach *Locke* darstellt, zusammen: Alle Menschen haben die gleichen natürlichen Rechte auf Leben, Freiheit und Eigentum, die ihnen die Selbsterhaltung ermöglichen und zu deren Verteidigung sie im eigenmächtigen Vollzug des Naturrechts Selbstjustiz üben dürfen. Der Genuss dieser Rechte ist aber „unsicher und beständig den Eingriffen anderer ausgesetzt“. Diese Unsicherheit, die Furcht hervorruft, macht die Menschen geneigt, sich mit anderen gesellschaftlich zu vereinigen, „zum gegenseitigen Schutz ihres Lebens, ihrer Freiheiten und ihres Vermögens, was ich unter der allgemeinen Bezeichnung Eigentum zusammenfasse“[50]. Von diesem Wechsel in den bürgerlichen Zustand versprechen sich die Menschen Abhilfe für die Mängel des Naturzustandes, die in der Abwesenheit eines feststehenden, publizierten und damit bekannten Rechts sowie dem Fehlen eines zur Streitentscheidung berufenen, anerkannten, unparteiischen Richters und einer Vollstreckungsgewalt bestehen.[51] Die Vorzüge der staatlichen Gemeinschaft liegen demzufolge in der Geltung positiven

---

[45] *John Locke*, a. a. O., II, § 46.
[46] *Ingo Elbe*, a. a. O., S. 9.
[47] *John Locke*, a. a. O., II, § 36.
[48] *John Locke*, a. a. O., II, § 50.
[49] *Ingo Elbe*, a. a. O., S. 8.
[50] *John Locke*, a. a. O., II, § 123.
[51] *John Locke*, a. a. O., II, §§ 124–126.

Rechts, unabhängiger rechtsprechender Gewalt sowie einer verbindlichen Rechtsdurchsetzungsinstanz, durch die der prekäre Status des Eigentums (Leben, Freiheit und Besitz) im Naturzustand überwunden werden kann. Dafür müssen die Menschen auf das Recht zur Selbstjustiz verzichten, erhalten aber im Gegenzug den sicheren Schutz der staatlichen Gewalt. Dieser Tausch ist lohnend, weil die staatlichen Gesetze ja nur das freiheitsverbürgende Naturrecht positivieren, den Menschen daher auch als Bürgern ihr Eigentum verbleibt, das sie nun umso besser in Frieden und Sicherheit genießen können. Deshalb kann auch nicht angenommen werden, „dass die Gewalt der Gesellschaft oder der durch sie eingesetzten Legislative sich weiter erstreckt als auf das gemeinsame Wohl, sondern sie ist verpflichtet, das Eigentum eines jeden [...] sicherzustellen"[52]. Obwohl die Legislative die höchste Gewalt im Staat ist, so ist sie doch „nicht eine absolute, willkürliche Gewalt über Leben und Vermögen des Volkes noch kann sie es sein. [...] Sie ist eine Gewalt, die kein anderes Ziel als Erhaltung hat, und kann deshalb nie ein Recht haben, die Untertanen zu vernichten, zu unterjochen oder mit Vorbedacht auszusaugen."[53] Den Bürgern darf ohne ihre Zustimmung ihr Eigentum weder ganz noch teilweise genommen werden.[54] Allerdings müssen sie anteilig die Kosten der Staatsgewalt tragen: „Regierungen können nicht ohne große Kosten unterhalten werden, und es ziemt sich, dass ein jeder, der seinen Teil des Schutzes genießt, aus seinem Vermögen im Verhältnis zu der Unterhaltung beitrage. Dennoch muss es unter seiner eigenen Zustimmung, d. h. der Zustimmung der Majorität, geschehen, die sie entweder selbst oder durch ihre erwählten Vertreter gibt; denn wenn jemand eine Macht in Anspruch nimmt, durch eigene Autorität, ohne Zustimmung des Volkes, Steuern aufzuerlegen und zu erheben, beeinträchtigt er das grundlegende Gesetz des Eigentums und stößt den Zweck der Regierung um."[55] Missbraucht der Staat die ihm treuhänderisch, zu keinem anderen Ziel als der Erhaltung des Eigentums verliehene Rechtsetzungs- und -durchsetzungsgewalt, verletzt er also die unveräußerlichen, weil natürlichen property rights (Leben, Freiheit und Vermögen) statt sie zu garantieren, verliert er Anspruch auf Gehorsam, und erlangen die Bürger ein Widerstandsrecht.

Man kann daher nicht behaupten, dass das Recht am Eigentum (im engeren Sinne von Besitz und Vermögen) bei *John Locke* schlechthin unantastbar wäre.[56] Aber es genießt, naturrechtlich begründet und im bürgerlichen Zustand positiviert, Schutz vor willkürlicher Entziehung. Rechtfertigender Grund dafür ist

---

[52] *John Locke*, a. a. O., II, § 131.

[53] *John Locke*, a. a. O., II, § 135.

[54] *John Locke*, a. a. O., II, § 138.

[55] *John Locke*, a. a. O., II, § 140.

[56] So aber *Walter Euchner*, Naturrecht und Politik bei John Locke, Frankfurt a. M. 1979, S. 202, 204.

der Bedingungszusammenhang mit den Rechtsgütern Leben und Freiheit. Eigentum ist materialisierter Ausdruck der freien Persönlichkeit. „Mit der in einen Gegenstand investierten Arbeit wird die Rechtsqualität der Person auf den Gegenstand übertragen. Der Gegenstand wird somit in die menschenrechtlich geschützte ursprüngliche Eigensphäre integriert und zu einem Teil der Person."[57] Wenn der Staat das Leben, die Freiheit und das Vermögen aller seiner Bürger schützt, dann ist er nicht bloße Besitzwahranstalt, sondern umfassender Garant einer als Eigentum an der eigenen Person verstandenen Freiheit.[58] Es wäre verfehlt, Lockes Freiheitsverständnis auf einen Besitzindividualismus zu verkürzen.[59]

III. Der Eigentumsschutz in
den modernen Verfassungen der Neuzeit

1. Nordamerika

Lockes Eigentumstheorie musste insbesondere bei den nordamerikanischen Siedlern, die das als herrenlos betrachtete Land, das sie in Besitz genommen hatten, kultivierten, auf fruchtbaren Boden fallen.[60] *Lockes* Eigentumstheorie war wie gemacht für die Verhältnisse in Amerika, und so überrascht es nicht, dass er zum geistigen Gründungsvater des unabhängigen Nordamerikas wurde. „Nirgendwo kamen die Prämissen des bürgerlichen Sozialmodells der Wirklichkeit so nahe wie in Amerika."[61] Hinzu kam, dass die Kolonisten die Besteu-

---

[57] *Wolfgang Kersting*, Eigentum, Vertrag und Staat bei Kant und Locke, in: Martyn P. Thompson (Hrsg.), John Locke und/and Immanuel Kant. Historische Rezeption und gegenwärtige Relevanz, Berlin 1991, S. 109–134 (123).

[58] So mit Recht *Wolfgang Kersting*, Die politische Philosophie des Gesellschaftsvertrags, Darmstadt 1994, S. 125 f. Dagegen wird teilweise aus Two Treatises of Government, 1690, II, § 139, ein Vorrang des Eigentumsschutzes vor dem Lebens- und Freiheitsschutz abgeleitet: Im Krieg könne der Bürger zwar legitimerweise zur Opferung seines eigenen Lebens, nicht aber seines Vermögens genötigt werden. Richtig verstanden dürfte danach aber nur der eigenmächtige Zugriff des militärischen Befehlshabers auf das Vermögen des unbedingt gehorsamspflichtigen Untergebenen, insbesondere die Verhängung einer gesetzlich nicht vorgesehenen Vermögensstrafe, nicht aber ein durch allgemeines Gesetz angeordnetes Vermögensopfer der Bürger zwecks Erhaltung ihrer staatlichen Gemeinschaft nach *Locke* ausgeschlossen sein.

[59] So aber insbesondere *Crawford Brough Macpherson*, Die politische Theorie des Besitzindividualismus. Von Hobbes bis Locke, Frankfurt a. M. ²1980; ihm folgend *Martin Kriele*, Einführung in die Staatslehre, Opladen ²1981, § 52, S. 202 f.

[60] Siehe dazu *Willi Paul Adams*, Republikanische Verfassung und bürgerliche Freiheit, Darmstadt u. a. 1973, S. 191–194.

[61] *Dieter Grimm*, Deutsche Verfassungsgeschichte 1776–1866, Frankfurt a. M. 1988, S. 36.

erungsversuche des Londoner Parlaments, in dem sie nicht vertreten waren, als tyrannische Eingriffe in ihr Eigentum betrachteten, in Sachen Eigentumsschutz infolgedessen besonders sensibel waren. Daher „stand die Verteidigung von ‚property rights' – jedenfalls bis zum Jahre 1774, als die sogenannten ‚Coercive Acts' zu einer Politik der unmittelbaren Repression gegen Massachusetts überging – durchaus im Mittelpunkt der gegen das Mutterland gerichteten Argumentation"[62].

„Als das Band mit dem Mutterland zerrissen wurde, mussten die von der englischen Krone den auswandernden Kolonisten verbrieften Freiheiten und Privilegien eine naturrechtliche Basis erhalten. Daher in allen Erklärungen der menschenrechtliche Introitus, dem die auf dieser Grundlage erneuerten und erweiterten alten Freiheitsrechte folgten."[63] Die Unabhängigkeitserklärung vom 4. Juli 1776 atmet unverkennbar *Lockes*chen Geist und ist von seiner naturrechtlichen Lehre maßgeblich geprägt, auch wenn dort nicht der Begriff des Eigentums fällt, sondern nur von „certain unalienable Rights" die Rede ist, und „that among these are Life, Liberty and the pursuit of Happiness". Die Trias *Life, Liberty and the pursuit of Happiness* ist eine literarisch adaptierte Version von *Lockes* Trinität der Naturrechte auf *Life, Liberty and Property*; in den ersten Entwürfen der Erklärung stand das Wort *Property*, und erst *Thomas Jefferson* ersetzte diesen Begriff später durch das weniger eindeutige *Pursuit of Happiness*.[64] Dass von der nach der Erklärung geschützten Freiheit aber auch das Recht des Eigentumserwerbs mit umfasst ist, macht die Virginia Declaration of Rights vom 12. Juni 1776 unmissverständlich klar. In Art. 1 heißt es: „That all men are by nature equally free and independent, and have certain inherent rights, of which, when they enter into a state of society, they cannot, by any compact, deprive or divest their posterity; namely, the enjoyment of life and liberty, with the means of acquiring and possessing property, and pursuing and obtaining happiness and safety."

Die anderen einzelstaatlichen Bills of Rights und Constitutions enthielten im Einzelnen durchaus unterschiedliche Grundrechtskataloge, gingen aber in gleicher Weise von gewissen natürlichen und unveräußerlichen Rechten jedes Menschen als vorgegeben aus.[65] Diese Rechte richten sich „auf Genuß und Ver-

---

[62] *Hans-Christoph Schröder*, Das Eigentumsproblem in den Auseinandersetzungen um die Verfassung von Massachusetts 1775–1787, in: Rudolf Vierhaus (Hrsg.), Eigentum und Verfassung. Zur Eigentumsdiskussion im ausgehenden 18. Jahrhundert, Göttingen 1972, S. 11–67 (14).

[63] *Gerhard Oestreich*, Geschichte der Menschenrechte und Grundfreiheiten im Umriß, Berlin 1968, S. 60.

[64] So *Willi Paul Adams*, a. a. O., S. 195 m. Fn. 13.

[65] Vgl. Art. XXV Verfassung North Carolina (1776); Art. I Verfassung Pennsylvania (1776); XLI Verfassung South Carolina (1778); Artt. I, IX, XIII Verfassung Vermont (08.07.1777); Artt. I, II, X, XII Verfassung Vermont (04.07.1786).

teidigung von Leben und Freiheit, auf Erwerb, Besitz und Schutz von Eigentum und auf Verfolg und Erhalt von Glück und Sicherheit"[66].

Dahinter stand die tiefe Überzeugung, dass Freiheit und Eigentum einen unauflöslichen Zusammenhang bildeten. „Liberty and Property", so schrieb die Boston Gazette, „are not only join'd in common discourse, but are in their own natures so nearly ally'd that we cannot possess the one without the enjoyment of the other"[67]. Zum Teil wurde das Eigentumsrecht im engeren, materiellen Sinne sogar als das grundlegendste und bedeutendste der Naturrechte angesehen, wenn dies auch nicht unbestritten blieb.[68]

Die amerikanische Bundesverfassung von 1787 enthielt gleichwohl zunächst nur einige wenige Grundrechte (Art. I Sections 9 and 10), darunter neben dem Habeas-Corpus-Prinzip das an die Einzelstaaten adressierte Verbot der Beeinträchtigung von vertraglichen Rechten. Eine Federal Bill of Rights brachten erst die 10 Amendments von 1791 mit sich. Dabei handelte es sich ganz überwiegend um die Gewährleistung persönlicher Freiheitsrechte. Das Eigentum war als solches nicht ausdrücklich geschützt, außer vor Enteignung zu öffentlichen Zwecken ohne Entschädigung: „[...] nor shall private property be taken for public use, without just compensation."[69] Damit wurde zwar einerseits implizit die grundsätzliche staatliche Befugnis zur Enteignung anerkannt, andererseits aber auch Schutz vor ungerechtfertigten, insbesondere nicht angemessen entschädigten Enteignungen geboten. „In diesem Sinn bekräftigt die Garantie klassischnaturrechtliche Postulate der Schutzwürdigkeit von Eigentum."[70]

Im Übrigen nahm nur die due process-clause des gleichen Amendments auf das Eigentum Bezug. Der unmittelbare Zusammenhang mit dem nemo-tenetur-Grundsatz (dem Recht der Verweigerung einer selbstbelastenden Aussage) macht indes deutlich, dass der Satz „[...] nor be deprived of life, liberty, or property, without due process of law"[71] lediglich das strafprozessrechtliche Verbot der Verhängung einer Todes-, Freiheits- oder Eigentums- bzw. Vermögensstrafe ohne vorangegangenes faires Strafverfahren beinhaltete.[72]

Diese due-process-clause sollte indes viel weitergehender interpretiert und angewandt und so zu einem allgemeinen Instrument des grundrechtlichen

---

[66] *Gerhard Oestreich*, a. a. O., S. 61; *Willi Paul Adams*, a. a. O., S. 195.

[67] Zitiert nach *Hans-Christoph Schröder*, a. a. O., S. 12.

[68] Siehe dazu *Hans-Christoph Schröder*, a. a. O., S. 12–14.

[69] 5. Zusatzartikel zur Verfassung der Vereinigten Staaten von 1791.

[70] Siehe *Winfried Brugger*, Einführung in das öffentliche Recht der USA, München 1993, § 10 IV, S. 100.

[71] 5. Zusatzartikel zur Verfassung der Vereinigten Staaten von 1791.

[72] Vgl. *Martin Kriele*, a. a. O., § 39, S. 159.

Schutzes des Eigentums vor staatlichem Zugriff werden.[73] Alle das Privateigentum und die Vertragsfreiheit tangierenden Gesetze wurden auf diese Weise grundrechtlich rechtfertigungsbedürftig. Das galt insbesondere auch für die von *Locke* grundsätzlich gebilligte, aber an eine gesetzliche Bewilligung gebundene Steuererhebung, ganz so wie es die amerikanischen Kolonisten dereinst gefordert hatten: „No taxation without representation"[74]. Zugleich wandelte sich das anfänglich rein prozedurale Verständnis von „due process" in ein substantielles, das der staatlichen Eingriffsmacht in Leben, Freiheit und Eigentum eine materiell-inhaltliche Grenze setzte. Diese wurde vom Supreme Court seit Beginn des 20. Jahrhunderts eng gezogen (economic due process in der sog. *Lochner*-Ära);[75] diese Rechtsprechung, die eine wirtschaftsregulierende Sozialgesetzgebung kaum zuließ, gab der Gerichtshof unter Zurücknahme seines strengen Prüfungsmaßstabs auf eine bloße Willkürkontrolle erst in den 1930er Jahren auf.

In diesem erweiterten und zeitweise auch starken Eigentumsschutz vor staatlicher Einschränkung und Belastung ist zum Teil eine der ursprünglichen Konzeption der Verfassung zuwiderlaufende Verfälschung ihres Sinns erblickt worden.[76] Näher liegt jedoch die Annahme, dass sich hierin die amerikanischem Denken eingängige *Locke*sche Überzeugung vom Eigentum als unverzichtbarem Teil persönlicher Freiheit geltend gemacht und durchgesetzt hat.[77] Sie ist nach wie vor im natürlichen Rechtsbewusstsein der Amerikaner veran-

---

[73] Siehe hierzu *Sophia Charlotte Neumann*, Verfassungsrechtlicher Eigentumsschutz in den USA, Frankfurt a. M. u. a. 2011, S. 14 ff., 42 f.

[74] Nach *David Hackett Fischer*, Albion's Seed: Four Britisch Folkways in America, Oxford u. a. 1989, S. 30, zitiert nach *Bill Bryson*, Made in America: An Informal History of the English Language in the United States, New York 1998, S. 38, hat Jonathan Mayhew in einer Predigt in der Old West Church in Boston diese Formulierung erstmalig verwandt.

[75] Siehe dazu *Winfried Brugger*, a. a. O., § 10 I–III, S. 96–100; *Sophia Charlotte Neumann*, a. a. O., S. 34 ff.; *David P. Currie*, Die Verfassung der Vereinigten Staaten von Amerika, Frankfurt a. M. 1988, S. 39 ff.

[76] Pointiert *Martin Kriele*, a. a. O., § 39, S. 158: „Die Grundrechte der amerikanischen Bundesverfassung sind in der ursprünglichen Absicht also Grundrechte der persönlichen Freiheit gegenüber staatlicher Willkür und keineswegs Grundrechte zum Schutz feudalistischer oder kapitalistischer Privilegien." Kriele kritisiert heftig die „Uminterpretation" als „Korrumpierung des Verfassungsstaates durch den Besitzindividualismus" (§ 54, S. 210 ff.). Richtig ist allerdings die Kritik (§ 54, S. 212 f.) an der die Sklaverei als verfassungsmäßig bestätigenden Rechtsprechung des Supreme Court (*Dred Scott v. Sandford*, 60 U.S. [19 How.] 393 [1857]); denn die Person ist kein veräußerliches Eigentum. Dies erkennen im Übrigen die Art. 18 der Verfassung der Französischen Republik vom 24. Juni 1793 und Art. 15 der Verfassung der Französischen Republik vom 23. September 1795 an.

[77] So soll – nach *Willi Paul Adams*, a. a. O., S. 195 m. Fn. 14 – *Jefferson* in einer von *Lafayette* entworfenen Erklärung der Menschenrechte das Wort „Eigentum" durchgestrichen und darüber geschrieben haben: „The power to dispose of his person and the fruits of his industry, and of all his faculties."

kert und lässt sie grundsätzlich ein unbefangenes Verhältnis zu privatem Reichtum haben, sofern er erarbeitet ist.

2. Frankreich

Scheinbar noch eigentumsfreundlicher als die amerikanischen Bills of Rights fielen die Garantien der französischen Menschen- und Bürgerrechtserklärung von 1789 aus, für die jene amerikanischen Bills of Rights vorbildhaftes Modell gewesen sind. Art. 2 der Erklärung bezeichnet ganz im Sinne der *Locke*schen Naturrechts- und Staatsvertragslehre als Ziel jeder politischen Vereinigung „la conservation des droits naturels et imprescriptibles de l'homme. Ces droits sont la liberté, la propriété, la sûreté et la résistance à l'oppression", und Art. 17 bestimmt: „La propriété étant un droit inviolable et sacré, nul ne peut en être privé, si ce n'est lorsque la nécessité publique, légalement constatée, l'exige évidemment, et sous la condition d'une juste et préalable indemnité."[78] Die Besteuerung wurde allerdings für mit der Garantie der Unverletzlichkeit des Eigentums vereinbar angesehen. Art. 13 erkannte dementsprechend an, dass für die Unterhaltung der öffentlichen Gewalt und für die Verwaltungsausgaben eine allgemeine Abgabe unerlässlich ist; sie müsse auf alle Bürger, nach Maßgabe ihrer Möglichkeiten, gleichmäßig verteilt werden.

Die Abschaffung der mit der naturrechtlichen Freiheit und Gleichheit unvereinbaren wirtschaftlichen und sozialen Privilegien der bevorrechtigten Stände und die Schaffung einer sich dem Erwerbsstreben hingebenden staatsbürgerlichen Eigentümergesellschaft waren das Ziel des aufgeklärten, die französische Revolution tragenden Bürgertums. Die grundrechtliche Gewährleistung der Privatautonomie und des privaten Eigentums verstand sich daher von selbst. Doch sah man „in der persönlichen Freiheit das erste unverlierbare und verletzliche Menschenrecht, die Heiligkeit des Eigentums war für [...] die Väter der französischen Deklaration eine bloße Folge des ersteren", weshalb im Konfliktsfall der zu gewährleistenden Freiheit gegenüber der Eigentumsgarantie der Vorzug zu geben war.[79]

Dass die freie wirtschaftliche Betätigung des Menschen in engem Zusammenhang mit seinen natürlichen Rechten steht, hatten die Physiokraten schon in

---

[78] Die Sprache von *Rousseaus* Contrat Social findet sich nur in Art. 6 wieder, der das Gesetz als Ausdruck der „volonté générale" definiert. Effektiver Grundrechtsschutz und Eigentumsschutz gegen die Staatsgewalt ist, wie gesehen, nicht *Rousseaus* Anliegen.

[79] *Günter Birtsch*, Freiheit und Eigentum. Zur Erörterung von Verfassungsfragen in der deutschen Publizistik im Zeichen der französischen Revolution, in: Rudolf Vierhaus (Hrsg.), Eigentum und Verfassung. Zur Eigentumsdiskussion im ausgehenden 18. Jahrhundert, Göttingen 1972, S. 179–192 (185).

der vorrevolutionären Zeit gelehrt. Sie verstanden „die lois fondamentales als die unabänderlichen Gesetze der Natur und ordneten ihnen die Rechte des Individuums propriété, liberté und sûreté [...] zu"[80]. „Die Freiheit der Person und die Unverletzlichkeit des Eigentums rechnete man seit den sechziger Jahren unter die lois fondamentales."[81] Durch seine antifeudale, gegen die exklusiven Vorrechte des Adels gerichtete, grundrechtliche Interpretation nahm das Recht auf Eigentum einen revolutionären Charakter an.[82]

Die vom besitzenden und gebildeten Bürgertum getragene Verfassung vom 3. September 1791 verbürgte in ihrem Titel I Grundeinrichtungen nochmals „die Unverletzlichkeit des Eigentums oder die gerechte und vorherige Entschädigung von dem, was die gesetzlich festgestellte, öffentliche Notwendigkeit als Opfer erfordert"[83]. Diese Verfassung wurde aber schon am 10. August 1792 nach nur knapp einjähriger Geltung suspendiert. Der Verfassung der ersten Republik vom 24. Juni 1793 war eine neue, auf 35 Artikel angewachsene Menschen- und Bürgerrechtserklärung (die Déclaration Jacobine) voran gestellt, die es zum Zweck der Einrichtung der Regierung erklärte, „[de] garantir à l'homme la puissance de ses droits naturels et imprescriptibles"[84]. „Ces droits sont l'égalité, la liberté, la sûreté, la propriété."[85] Art. 16 definierte das „droit de propriété" als dasjenige, „qui appartient à tout citoyen de jouir et de disposer à son gré de ses biens, de ses revenus, du fruit de son travail et de son industrie". Art. 122 wiederholte schließlich die allen Franzosen geltende Garantie von Gleichheit, Freiheit, Sicherheit, Eigentum. Diese Verfassung sollte allerdings nie in Kraft treten. „Die Menschenrechte blieben leere Deklamation"[86]. Es folgte die Schreckensherrschaft des Wohlfahrtsausschusses, der weder die Rechte der Persönlichkeit noch des Eigentums heilig waren, jedenfalls soweit es sich um vermeintliche Feinde der Republik handelte.

---

[80] *Gerhard Oestreich*, a. a. O., S. 66.

[81] *Gerhard Oestreich*, a. a. O., S. 67.

[82] Die überkommenen droits féodaux erwiesen sich allerdings zum Teil als ablösungs-, d. h. entschädigungsbedürftige Eigentumsrechte; siehe dazu näher *Ernst Hinrichs*, Die Ablösung von Eigentumsrechten. Zur Diskussion über die *droits féodaux* in Frankreich am Ende des Ancien Régime und in der Revolution, in: Rudolf Vierhaus (Hrsg.), Eigentum und Verfassung. Zur Eigentumsdiskussion im ausgehenden 18. Jahrhundert, Göttingen 1972, S. 112–178.

[83] „La Constitution garantit l'inviolabilité des propriétés ou la juste et préalable indemnité de celles dont la nécessité publique, légalement constatée, exigerait le sacrifice."

[84] Art. 1 der Verfassung der Französischen Republik vom 24. Juni 1793.

[85] Art. 2 der Verfassung der Französischen Republik vom 24. Juni 1793.

[86] *Martin Kriele*, a. a. O., § 41, S. 164.

3. Die verfassungsgeschichtliche Entwicklung des Eigentumsschutzes in Deutschland

a) Vom Allgemeinen Landrecht für die Preußischen Staaten bis zur Paulskirchenverfassung

In Deutschland konnte sich gegen Ende des 18. und zu Beginn des 19. Jahrhunderts die Idee naturrechtlich begründeter Menschenrechte nicht durchsetzen. Ihre Etablierung in Frankreich wurde als „metaphysisches Experiment" angesehen,[87] das, wie die Exzesse der Jakobiner zeigten, verheerende Folgen für die staatliche Ordnung wie auch die bürgerliche Freiheit haben konnten. Aus dem 1787 im Entwurf vorliegenden Allgemeinen Landrecht für die preußischen Staaten wurden nach Ausbruch der Französischen Revolution deshalb alle an die französischen Menschenrechte erinnernden, grundrechtsartigen Bestimmungen entfernt, ehe es in dieser bereinigten Form 1794 in Kraft trat.[88]

Auch die in den Verfassungen des süddeutschen Frühkonstitutionalismus enthaltenen Grundrechte waren nicht Ausdruck der Anerkennung vorstaatlicher natürlicher Rechte des Individuums, sondern einseitige, prinzipiell auch wieder rücknehmbare Gewährungen souveräner Monarchen. „Ohne die naturrechtliche Basis beanspruchten sie auch nicht wie die revolutionär erstrittenen Grundrechte den Charakter von Menschenrechten, sondern verstanden sich als Staatsbürgerrechte"[89]. Das tat ihrer Rechtsqualität keinen Abbruch, und gerade die Eigentumsgarantie unterschied sich auch in ihrer inhaltlichen Reichweite nicht wirklich von den korrespondierenden Gewährleistungen in Nordamerika und Frankreich. Sie sicherte das Eigentum als wesentliches Element und materielle Grundlage bürgerlicher Freiheit gegen staatliche Zugriffe. Enteignungen waren fortan nur noch auf gesetzlicher Grundlage und zu Gemeinwohlzwecken sowie gegen eine vorgängig zu leistende Entschädigung zulässig; die Strafe der Vermögenskonfiskation wurde abgeschafft.[90] „Dagegen fehlte eine Garantie des freien Eigentumsgebrauchs, der die Aufhebung der feudalen und korporativen Bindungen vorausgesetzt hätte, die zwar begonnen, aber nicht vollendet war."[91] Die in der sog. zweiten Verfassungswelle nach der Revolution von 1830 in Gel-

---

[87] So *Ernst Brandes*, zitiert nach *Alfred Stern*, Der Einfluß der Französischen Revolution auf das deutsche Geistesleben, Stuttgart 1928, S. 73.

[88] *Dieter Grimm*, a. a. O., S. 53. Immerhin bestimmte § 83 (Einleitung, unter II. Allgemeine Grundsätze des Rechts. Quelle des Rechts): „Die allgemeinen Rechte des Menschen gründen sich auf die natürliche Freyheit, sein eignes Wohl, ohne Kränkung der Rechte eines Andern, suchen und befördern zu können."

[89] *Dieter Grimm*, a. a. O., S. 129.

[90] *Ernst Rudolf Huber*, Deutsche Verfassungsgeschichte seit 1789, Bd. I, Stuttgart 1957, § 21 V 1, S. 359.

[91] *Dieter Grimm*, a. a. O., S. 131.

tung gesetzten Verfassungen Mittel- und Norddeutschlands wiesen – auch in Sachen Eigentumsschutz – ähnliche Grundrechte auf; im Übrigen zielten sie noch stärker auf eine wirtschaftliche Liberalisierung durch Überwindung der überkommenen feudalen und zünftischen Strukturen.

Auch die Grundrechte der Frankfurter Reichsverfassung (FRV), der sog. Paulskirchenverfassung von 1849 basierten nicht auf Naturrecht mit universellem Geltungsanspruch, sondern sollten das „geringste Maaß deutscher Volksfreiheit"[92] definieren. „Die Grundrechte des deutschen Volkes", wie sie sich nannten, waren ungeachtet ihrer liberalen, bürgerlichen Grundausrichtung auf den Individualrechtsschutz stärker gemeinschaftsbetont, ja staatszugewandt, wobei der verbreitete Genossenschaftsgedanke (*Georg Beseler*) eine Rolle spielt. Man grenzte sich durchaus bewusst von einem Liberalismus ab, der sich in der Sicherung einer staatsfreien Sphäre privater Freiheit erschöpft.[93]

Auch die Eigentumsgarantie war davon nicht ausgenommen. Zwar erklärte § 164 Abs. 1 FRV[94] das Eigentum für unverletzlich und hob tradierte Eigentumsbindungen auf (§ 165 FRV), wodurch die freie Verfügbarkeit über das Grundeigentum hergestellt wurde. Die FRV war aber weit davon entfernt, das Eigentum absolut zu schützen. Die Unverletzlichkeitsgarantie sollte nur staatliche Willkürmaßnahmen, nicht etwa jeden Eingriff in das Eigentum abwehren.[95] „Mithin waren eigentumsbestimmende und -beschränkende rechtsstaatliche Maßnahmen, soweit sie auch den §§ 165 ff. FRV entsprachen, gemäß § 164 I FRV erlaubt [...]. Im Ergebnis bot § 164 I FRV keinen unantastbaren Schutz des Eigentums, sondern ließ gesetzlichen Beschränkungen Raum, die [...] auf gewisse soziale Eigentumsschranken hinausliefen."[96] Von den vormärzlichen Eigentumsverbürgungen unterschied sich § 164 Abs. 1 FRV darüber hinaus durch die ihm zugrunde liegende Annahme, dass das Eigentum durch positives staatliches Recht ausgestaltbar sei.

Enteignungen durften nach § 164 Abs. 2 FRV „nur aus Rücksichten des gemeinen Besten, nur auf Grund eines Gesetzes und gegen gerechte Entschädigung vorgenommen werden". Allerdings galten als Enteignungen nur Zwangsabtretungen von Grundstücken an den Staat oder die diesem gegenüber

---

[92] *Dieter Grimm*, a. a. O., S. 195, Zitat nach *Jörg-Detlef Kühne*, Die Reichsverfassung der Paulskirche, Frankfurt a. M. 1985, S. 7 I. B. 1., S. 161.

[93] Siehe dazu näher mit zahlreichen Nachweisen *Jörg-Detlef Kühne*, a. a. O., S. 7 I. B. 2. b), S. 168 ff.

[94] „Das Eigentum ist unverletzlich. Eine Enteignung kann nur aus Rücksichten des gemeinen Besten, nur auf Grund eines Gesetzes und gegen gerechte Entschädigung vorgenommen werden", zitiert nach Ernst Rudolf Huber (Hrsg.), Dokumente zur Deutschen Verfassungsgeschichte, Bd. 1, Stuttgart ²1961, S. 304, 321.

[95] *Jörg-Detlef Kühne*, a. a. O., S. 9 I. A. 1. b), S. 251.

[96] *Jörg-Detlef Kühne*, a. a. O., S. 9 I. A. 1. b), S. 252.

zwangsweise erfolgte Einräumung dinglicher Dauernutzungsrechte. Unterhalb dieser Schwelle oder auf andere Eigentumsgüter bezogene Eigentumsbeschränkungen blieben auch ohne Entschädigung ohne weiteres möglich.[97] Öffentlich-rechtliche Pflichtbindungen, namentlich polizeiliche Beschränkungen, galten als unproblematisch. Feudale Besitzstände sollten keinen Bestandsschutz mehr genießen (siehe §§ 166–168 FRV).

Die Garantie der Unverletzlichkeit des Eigentums, wie sie auch Art. 9 der Revidierten Preußischen Verfassung vom 31. Januar 1850 enthielt, bedeutete daher letztlich nicht mehr und nicht weniger, als dass Eingriffe in die Eigentumssphäre einer gesetzlichen Grundlage bedurften, Enteignungen aus Gründen des Gemeinwohls darüber hinaus einer vorgängigen Entschädigung.[98]

b) Kaiserreich und Weimarer Republik

Nachdem die Paulskirchenverfassung gescheitert war, setzte das liberale Bürgertum ganz darauf, Freiheit und Eigentum gesetzlich zu garantieren, und tatsächlich sind viele grundrechtliche Forderungen spätestens im Kaiserreich durch einfache Gesetzgebung eingelöst worden. Dies führte zu der verbreiteten Ansicht, dass es „jedenfalls im Bereich der überkommenen, klassischen Grundrechte nur noch um die Gesetzmäßigkeit der Verwaltung ging"[99], eine Auffassung, die auch schon in den Beratungen der Weimarer Nationalversammlung dominierte. *Bill Drews*, Präsident des preußischen Oberverwaltungsgerichts, gab ihr mit folgender Stellungnahme Ausdruck: „Jedes Grundrecht kann vernünftigerweise nur mit einer ganzen Reihe von Ausnahmen [...] festgesetzt werden, wie sie sich in den gesetzlichen Vorschriften über Verhaftung, Beschlagnahme, Enteignung, Presserecht und Versammlungsrecht usw. finden. Die Grundrechte der persönlichen Freiheit, der Unverletzlichkeit des Eigentums usw. ohne diese Spezialbestimmungen sind ein leerer Rahmen, Form ohne Inhalt. Ich möchte vorschlagen, [...], daß in der Verfassung gesagt wird: ‚Jede Beschränkung der persönlichen Freiheit, des Privateigentums [...] usw. darf nur durch Reichsgesetz erfolgen'. Damit sind die Grundrechte an sich ausgesprochen [...]."[100]

---

[97] *Jörg-Detlef Kühne*, a. a. O., S. 9 I. B. 1. a), S. 262 f.

[98] Vor diesem Hintergrund wurde der Satz „Das Eigentum ist unverletzlich" in den Beratungen zur Preußischen Verfassung teils als „unwahr", teils als „selbstverständlich und daher überflüssig" bezeichnet; siehe die Nachweise bei *Gerhard Anschütz*, Die Verfassungsurkunde für den preußischen Staat vom 31. Januar 1850, Kommentar, Berlin 1912, Art. 9 Anm. 1, S. 154 f.

[99] *Jörg-Detlef Kühne*, a. a. O., S. 5 I. C. 1., S. 139.

[100] Zitiert nach *Jörg-Detlef Kühne*, a. a. O., S. 5 I. C. 1., S. 139.

Die Grundrechte galten nur nach Maßgabe der sie ausfüllenden und zugleich beschränkenden Gesetze. Hinsichtlich der Eigentumsgarantie bedeutete dies, dass die nähere Ausgestaltung des Eigentums, insbesondere aber Beschränkungen des Eigentumsgebrauchs dem Gesetzgeber überantwortet wurde, der insoweit Dispositionsmacht besaß.

Art. 153 der Weimarer Reichsverfassung (WRV) von 1919 schien dieser Auffassung noch stärkeren Ausdruck zu verleihen, indem er, wie Art. 14 Abs. 1 S. 2 GG, bestimmte, dass Inhalt und Schranken des verfassungsrechtlich gewährleisteten Eigentums sich aus den Gesetzen ergeben, die Sozialbindung des Eigentums ausdrücklich anordnete und die Pflicht zur Entschädigung einer Enteignung unter den Vorbehalt gegenläufiger Reichsgesetzgebung stellte. Der Schutz des Eigentums erschien prekärer denn je, die Verfügungsgewalt des Staates größer denn je.

In einer Gegenbewegung kam während der Weimarer Republik jedoch in Literatur und Rechtsprechung eine Verstärkung des verfassungsrechtlichen Eigentumsschutzes auf. Zum einen wurden dem verfassungsrechtlichen Eigentumsbegriff neben Grund und Boden nun auch Forderungsrechte unterstellt, zum anderen eine (grundsätzlich entschädigungspflichtige) Enteignung unter Umständen auch bei einer bloßen Eigentumsbeschränkung angenommen.[101] Vor allem aber wurde nun mit Verve die Auffassung vertreten, dass „ein naturrechtlich vorgegebener Kernbestand bestimmter Sachherrschaftsmöglichkeiten dem gesetzgeberischen Zugriff entzogen bleiben sollte"[102], ein Gedanke, der, wie wir gleich sehen, unter dem Grundgesetz, das sich mit Art. 14 GG weitgehend an seine Weimarer Vorgängerregelung angelehnt hat, unter dem Gesichtspunkt der sog. Institutsgarantie des Eigentums[103] der Sache nach aufgegriffen werden sollte.

Erst mit der demokratischen Neuordnung nach dem Sturz der deutschen konstitutionellen Monarchie stellt sich die Frage nach den Grenzen gesetzgeberischer Dispositionsmacht über das Eigentum in aller Schärfe. Vorher hatte das Bürgertum selbst über die von ihm dominierte Volksvertretung gegenüber der monarchischen Exekutive ihr Eigentum vor als ungebührlich angesehenen Eingriffen bewahren können. „Das bürgerliche Eigentum, das 1848 gegenüber den feudalen Besitzständen noch in der Offensive ist, sieht sich jetzt selbst gegenüber sozialegalitären Vorstellungen in die Defensive gedrängt und grenzt sich ihnen gegenüber ab."[104]

---

[101] Siehe dazu näher *Hans-Jürgen Papier*, in: Theodor Maunz / Günter Dürig, Grundgesetz, Kommentar, Art. 14 Rn. 21 f.

[102] *Jörg-Detlef Kühne*, a. a. O., S. 9 I. A. 1. b), S. 252.

[103] Siehe hierzu *Ute Mager*, Einrichtungsgarantien, Tübingen 2003, S. 175 ff.

[104] *Jörg-Detlef Kühne*, a. a. O., S. 9 I. A. 1. b), S. 252.

c) Die grundgesetzliche Eigentumsgarantie

Die in Anlehnung an Art. 153 WRV in das Grundgesetz aufgenommene Eigentumsgarantie des Art. 14 steht in einem engen Sinnzusammenhang mit der Gewährleistung individueller Freiheit. Das Eigentum ist, so das BVerfG, „ebenso wie die Freiheit ein elementares Grundrecht"[105]. Dem Eigentum kommt im Gesamtgefüge der Grundrechte die Aufgabe zu, dem Träger des Grundrechts einen Freiheitsraum im vermögensrechtlichen Bereich bereitzustellen und ihm damit eine eigenverantwortliche Gestaltung des Lebens zu ermöglichen.[106] Das verfassungsrechtlich gewährleistete Eigentum ist durch Privatnützigkeit und grundsätzliche Verfügungsbefugnis des Eigentümers über den Eigentumsgegenstand gekennzeichnet.[107] Es soll ihm als Grundlage privater Initiative und in eigenverantwortlichem privatem Interesse von Nutzen sein. Zugleich soll der Gebrauch des Eigentums dem Wohl der Allgemeinheit dienen (Art. 14 Abs. 2 GG). Hierin liegt die Absage an eine Eigentumsordnung, in der das Individualinteresse den unbedingten Vorrang vor den Interessen der Gemeinschaft hat.[108]

Der Schutz beschränkt sich nicht auf den privaten Bereich des Einzelnen, sondern erfasst auch Eigentumsgegenstände, die aus seiner wirtschaftlichen Betätigung hervorgegangen sind.[109] Er betrifft grundsätzlich alle vermögenswerten Rechte, die dem Berechtigten von der Rechtsordnung in der Weise zugeordnet sind, dass dieser die damit verbundenen Befugnisse nach eigenverantwortlicher Entscheidung zu seinem privaten Nutzen ausüben darf,[110] nicht nur das der persönlichen Lebenshaltung oder eigenen Arbeit dienende Eigentum.[111] Das „Eigentum als verdinglichte Freiheit"[112] genießt aber einen besonders ausgeprägten

---

[105] BVerfGE 14, 263 (277).

[106] St. Rspr. seit BVerfGE 24, 367 (389); zuletzt E 102, 1 (15 f.); 104, 1 (8); 115, 97 (110); 123, 186 (258).

[107] St. Rspr., siehe nur BVerfGE 31, 229 (240); 50, 29 (33); 52, 1 (30); 101, 54 (74 f.).

[108] Vgl. BVerfGE 21, 73 (83).

[109] Vgl. BVerfGE 51, 193 (218); 78, 58 (74).

[110] Vgl. BVerfGE 112, 93 (107); 115, 97 (111).

[111] So eine von der Redaktionskommission ursprünglich vorgeschlagene Fassung, die aber im Grundsatzausschuss als zu eng abgelehnt wurde; siehe *Hans-Jürgen Papier*, a. a. O., Art. 14 Rn. 2 Fn. 7.

[112] Begriff nach *Josef Isensee*, Grundrechtsvoraussetzungen und Verfassungserwartungen an die Grundrechtsausübung, in: ders. / Paul Kirchhof (Hrsg.), Handbuch des Staatsrechts der Bundesrepublik Deutschland, Bd. IX, Heidelberg ³2011, § 190 Rn. 213.

Schutz, soweit es um die Sicherung der persönlichen Freiheit des Einzelnen geht.[113]

Die Funktion der grundgesetzlichen Eigentumsgarantie besteht in erster Linie darin, den Bestand der durch die Rechtsordnung anerkannten einzelnen Vermögensrechte gegenüber Maßnahmen der öffentlichen Gewalt zu bewahren.[114] Anders als noch unter der Weimarer Reichsverfassung hat die Eigentumsgarantie unter dem Grundgesetz nicht in erster Linie die Aufgabe, die entschädigungslose Wegnahme von Eigentum zu verhindern, sondern den Bestand des Eigentums in der Hand des Eigentümers zu sichern.[115]

Die konkrete Reichweite des Schutzes durch die Eigentumsgarantie ergibt sich allerdings erst aus der Bestimmung von Inhalt und Schranken des Eigentums, die nach Art. 14 Abs. 1 S. 2 GG Sache des Gesetzgebers ist.[116] Nur das durch die Gesetze ausgeformte Eigentum bildet den Gegenstand der Eigentumsgarantie und ist verfassungsrechtlich geschützt.[117]

Bei der Inhaltsbestimmung des Eigentums ist der Gesetzgeber allerdings nicht völlig frei; er muss die in Art. 14 Abs. 1 S. 1 GG liegende „Wertentscheidung des Grundgesetzes zu Gunsten des Privateigentums"[118] beachten. Die in Art. 14 Abs. 1 GG mit enthaltene Garantie des Eigentums als Rechtseinrichtung (sog. Institutsgarantie) sichert einen Grundbestand von Normen, die als Eigentum im Sinne dieser Grundrechtsbestimmung bezeichnet werden, und verbietet es nach der Rechtsprechung des BVerfG, solche Sachbereiche der Privatrechtsordnung zu entziehen, die zum elementaren Bestand grundrechtlich geschützter Betätigung im vermögensrechtlichen Bereich gehören.[119] Privateigentum darf danach weder vollständig abgeschafft noch durch etwas ersetzt werden, was – mangels Privatnützigkeit und freier Verfügungsbefugnis – den Namen „Eigentum" nicht verdient.

Während das BVerfG jahrzehntelang die Auffassung vertrat, Art. 14 Abs. 1 GG biete keinen Schutz gegen die Auferlegung von Steuern, sofern diese keine erdrosselnde Wirkung haben, hält es nun mit Recht einen rechtfertigungsbedürftigen Eingriff in den Schutzbereich der Eigentumsgarantie für gegeben, wenn der Steuerzugriff tatbestandlich an das Innehaben von vermögenswerten

---

[113] Vgl. BVerfGE 50, 290 (340); st. Rspr. Gegen eine Überbetonung des Aspekts der Sicherung der freien Entfaltung der Persönlichkeit wegen der damit verbundenen Verkürzung des Garantiegehalts aber *Hans-Jürgen Papier*, a. a. O., Art. 14 Rn. 2.

[114] BVerfGE 72, 175 (179).

[115] St. Rspr. seit BVerfGE 24, 367 (400 f.).

[116] St. Rspr.; siehe nur BVerfGE 74, 203 (214); 122, 374 (391).

[117] BVerfGE 24, 367 (396).

[118] BVerfGE 14, 263 (278).

[119] BVerfGE 24, 367 (389).

Rechtspositionen anknüpft und so den privaten Nutzen der erworbenen Rechtspositionen zugunsten der Allgemeinheit einschränkt.[120] Insoweit vermittelt Art. 14 Abs. 1 GG ein Abwehrrecht gegen übermäßig hohe steuerliche Belastungen. Wenn auch dem Berechtigten ungeachtet der steuerlichen Gemeinlast noch ein privater Nutzen seiner Vermögensgüter verbleiben muss, so lässt sich doch eine absolute Belastungsobergrenze (die etwa im Sinne des sog. Halbteilungsgrundsatzes bei 50 % liegen würde) dem Grundgesetz nicht entnehmen.[121]

Weil und soweit Eigentum das Ergebnis und die Basis der Freiheitsausübung ist, soll dessen Beachtung auch Ausdruck der Menschenwürde sein.[122] Der so gemäß Art. 79 Abs. 3 GG auch gegenüber dem verfassungsändernden Gesetzgeber geschützte Kernbereich der Eigentumsgarantie dürfte sich allerdings auf die Vermögensgüter beschränken, deren Innehabung und Nutzung für die Sicherung der persönlichen Freiheit unverzichtbar ist. Nur insofern kann daher mit Bezug auf die Eigentumsgarantie des Grundgesetzes von einem grundrechtlich anerkannten Menschenrecht auf Eigentum gesprochen werden.

IV. Eigentumsschutz als Teil des internationalen Menschenrechtsschutzes?

Gibt es ein internationales Menschenrecht auf Eigentumsschutz? Die Allgemeine Erklärung der Menschenrechte von 1948 (AEMR) stellt kein verbindliches Völkerrecht dar, sondern eine bloße Empfehlung, die lediglich „das von allen Völkern und Nationen zu erreichende gemeinsame Ideal" formuliert. Dazu soll nach Art. 17 AEMR auch das Recht gehören, sowohl allein als auch in Gemeinschaft mit anderen Eigentum innezuhaben. Niemand darf danach willkürlich seines Eigentums beraubt werden. Der Garantiegehalt dieser Bestimmung, die auf die sozialistische Eigentumskonzeption Rücksicht nehmen musste,[123] ist eher schwach. So ist neben dem individuellen auch das kollektive Eigentum erfasst und beides nur vor willkürlichem Entzug geschützt.[124] Nur so

---

[120] BVerfGE 115, 97 (111).

[121] BVerfGE 115, 97 (113–116).

[122] *Dietrich Murswiek*, Zu den Grenzen der Abänderbarkeit von Grundrechten, in: Detlef Merten / Hans-Jürgen Papier (Hrsg.), Handbuch der Grundrechte in Deutschland und Europa, Bd. II, Heidelberg 2006, § 28 Rn. 115.

[123] Vgl. *Leopold von Carlowitz*, Das Menschenrecht auf Eigentum von Flüchtlingen und Vertriebenen, Berlin 2008, S. 65.

[124] Zur Entstehungsgeschichte der Vorschrift ausführlich *Leopold von Carlowitz*, a. a. O., S. 58–65.

ließen sich die in der Frage des Privateigentums diametral entgegengesetzten Positionen von West und Ost in einem Formelkompromiss vereinigen.[125]

Die grundlegenden ideologischen Differenzen zwischen dem Westen und den sozialistischen Ländern ließen auch keine verbindliche Kodifizierung eines allgemeinen Menschenrechts auf Eigentum in den UN-Menschenrechtspakten von 1966 zu. Zwar bestand weitgehend Konsens darüber, dass individuelles Eigentum grundsätzlich als Menschenrecht zu gelten habe. Zu unterschiedliche Vorstellungen existierten jedoch hinsichtlich seines Schutzzwecks, Regelungsumfangs und vor allem hinsichtlich seiner Beschränkungen, um zu einer präzisen Formulierung zu gelangen, welche einem verbindlichen Menschenrechtsübereinkommen angemessen gewesen wäre.[126]

„Das universelle Völkerrecht kannte und kennt eine Gewährleistung des Eigentums der eigenen Staatsangehörigen als menschenrechtlichen Schutzstandard nicht. [...] Angesichts dieses Zögerns der Internationalen Gemeinschaft, eine vertragliche Bindung einzugehen, kann von einer weltweit geltenden gewohnheitsrechtlichen Norm menschenrechtlichen Eigentumsschutzes, also zu Gunsten nicht nur fremder Staatsangehöriger, sondern auch der eigenen Bürger, nicht gesprochen werden."[127] Ungeachtet der Tatsache, dass in Mittel- und Osteuropa nach dem Zusammenbruch des Sowjetimperiums Privateigentum anerkannt und unter verfassungsrechtlichen Schutz gestellt worden ist und selbst in der Volksrepublik China seit 2004 verfassungsrechtlich Eigentum anerkannt ist und seit 2007 Privateigentum dort unter demselben gesetzlichen Schutz wie Staatsbesitz steht,[128] hat sich die Rechtsüberzeugung, dass das Eigentum Menschenrecht ist, noch nicht weltweit durchgesetzt.[129]

Trotz im Übrigen weitgehender Werthomogenität gab es in Sachen Eigentumsschutz selbst unter den westeuropäischen Staaten so erhebliche Meinungsunterschiede, dass es nicht gelang, eine Eigentumsgarantie bereits in den Rechtekatalog der Europäischen Konvention zum Schutz der Menschenrechte und Grundfreiheiten von 1950 (EMRK) aufzunehmen. Einige Staaten wollten sich in der Freiheit der Ausgestaltung ihrer Wirtschaftordnung und in der Freiheit, Sozialisierungen vorzunehmen, nicht durch eine solche internationale Garantie

---

[125] Eine ausführliche Darstellung der beiden Eigentumskonzeptionen findet sich in: *Leopold von Carlowitz*, a. a. O., S. 46 ff., 49 ff.

[126] *Leopold von Carlowitz*, a. a. O., S. 71.

[127] BVerfGE 112, 1 (34). Letztlich wohl auch *Leopold von Carlowitz*, a. a. O., S. 270–275. Nur der Schutz des Eigentums von Fremden ist völkerrechtlich geboten.

[128] Siehe: Neues Gesetz. Chinas Volkskongress billigt Eigentumsrecht, in: faz.net vom 16.03.2007, http://www.faz.net/aktuell/politik/ausland/neues-gesetz-chinas-volks kongress-billigt-eigentumsrecht-1411326.html.

[129] Gegenwärtig gibt es insbesondere in Südamerika starke, gegen den Schutz des Privateigentums gerichtete Tendenzen.

beschränken lassen.[130] So fand das Eigentumsrecht erst in das Erste Zusatzprotokoll (1. ZP) zur EMRK von 1952 Eingang.

Nach Art. 1 Abs. 1 des 1. ZP hat jede natürliche oder juristische Person ein Recht auf Achtung ihres Eigentums. Niemandem darf sein Eigentum entzogen werden, es sei denn, dass das öffentliche Interesse es verlangt. Doch selbst dann ist die Enteignung nur unter den durch Gesetz und durch die allgemeinen Grundsätze des Völkerrechts vorgesehenen Bedingungen gestattet. Bei der Bestimmung des öffentlichen Interesses in Umsetzung seiner Sozial- und Wirtschaftspolitik kommt den Konventionsstaaten ein großer Beurteilungsspielraum zu. Eine Entschädigung für Enteignungen eigener Staatsangehöriger ist regelmäßig, aber nicht unter allen Umständen zur Herstellung eines gerechten Ausgleichs geboten.[131]

Nach Abs. 2 beeinträchtigt diese Eigentumsgarantie jedoch in keiner Weise das Recht der Staaten, diejenigen Gesetze anzuwenden, die sie für die Regelung der Benutzung des Eigentums in Übereinstimmung mit dem Allgemeininteresse oder zur Sicherung der Zahlung der Steuern, sonstiger Abgaben oder von Geldstrafen für erforderlich halten. Eigentumsbeschränkungen jedweder Art sind danach unter der Voraussetzung ihrer Verhältnismäßigkeit zulässig. Eine Institutsgarantie enthält Art. 1 des 1. ZP nicht.[132]

V. Fazit

Die Frage, ob das Eigentum ein Menschenrecht ist, kann ideen- und verfassungsgeschichtlich nicht eindeutig beantwortet werden. Das Nachdenken über das Eigentum und seinen Charakter ist nicht beendet. Die Bedeutung des Eigentums für die Würde und die Freiheit des Menschen – als Bestandteil des menschenrechtlichen Mindestschutzes – ist zwar nicht, wie das BVerfG meint, erst spät erkannt worden, sondern wie wir gesehen haben, schon in einigen Naturrechtslehren des 17. Jahrhunderts verankert. Doch hat es stets auch gegentei-

---

[130] Zu den Hintergründen des Dissenses siehe näher *Wolfgang Peukert*, Der Schutz des Eigentums nach Art. 1 des Ersten Zusatzprotokolls zur Europäischen Menschenrechtskonvention, EuGRZ 1981, 97–99; *Sven Brandt*, Eigentumsschutz in europäischen Völkerrechtsvereinbarungen, Frankfurt a. M. u. a. 1995, S. 53–59; *Leopold von Carlowitz*, a. a. O., S. 153; aus den Debatten bei der Entstehung der EMRK siehe nur 2. Session der Beratenden Versammlung, Sitzung des Ausschusses für Rechts- und Verwaltungsfragen, in: Council of Europe, Collected Edition of the „Travaux Préparatoires", Vol. VI, Dordrecht 1985, S. 2–72, sowie Generalaussprache, ebd., S. 72–228.

[131] Siehe dazu *Christoph Grabenwarter / Katharina Pabel*, Europäische Menschenrechtskonvention, München ⁵2012, § 25 I 4, S. 505 ff. m. Nachw. aus der Rechtsprechung des EGMR.

[132] *Christoph Grabenwarter / Katharina Pabel*, a. a. O., § 25 I 1 Rn. 2, S. 496.

lige Auffassungen in der Sozialphilosophie gegeben. Daran hat sich bis heute nichts geändert. Dies erklärt, warum auch rechtlich der Status des Eigentums als Menschenrecht prekär geblieben ist.

Zusammenfassung

Die Frage, ob das Recht am Eigentum eigentlich ein Menschenrecht ist, wird in der neuzeitlichen Sozialphilosophie unterschiedlich beantwortet. Bei *Hobbes* ist der Souverän in der Entscheidung, in welchem Umfang er Eigentum Privater anerkennt und Individuen exklusiv zuweist, frei. Nach *Rousseau* besitzen die Privateigentümer als Sachwalter des Gemeinwohls, als citoyens, nicht als bourgeois. Allein *Locke* erkennt ein natürliches, vorstaatliches Eigentumsrecht an. Die *Locke*sche Überzeugung vom Eigentum als unverzichtbarem Teil persönlicher Freiheit hat sich im amerikanischen Denken durchgesetzt hat und ist im natürlichen Rechtsbewusstsein der Amerikaner fest verankert. In Frankreich wie in Deutschland ist dagegen stets die Sozialpflichtigkeit des Privateigentum betont worden und wird allenfalls hinsichtlich eines Grundbestands an Vermögensgütern, deren Innehabung und Nutzung in der Form exklusiver Bestimmungsmacht des Einzelnen für die Sicherung des persönlichen Freiheit unverzichtbar ist, als der staatlichen Verfügungsmacht entzogen betrachtet. Das universelle Völkerrecht kennt bis heute keine allgemeine Gewährleistung des Eigentums als Menschenrecht. So ist der Status des Eigentums als Menschenrecht insgesamt prekär geblieben.

Summary

The question whether property right should be classified as a human right has been differently answered throughout modern social philosophy. For *Hobbes* the Sovereign is free to decide to which extent he wants to accept private property and to assign it exclusively to individuals. According to *Rousseau* private property owners possess goods only as trustees of the common welfare, i.e. as citoyens and not as bourgeois. It is only *Locke* who acknowledges property is natural and anterior to the state. *Locke*'s conviction that property is an indispensable part of personal freedom has become dominant in the American thinking and is now deeply rooted in the given legal awareness of the Americans. In contrast to that the "social obligation of property" has always been stressed in France just as in Germany and only a base stock in property goods has been seen as so important as to be abstracted from state disposal under the condition that its exclusive and self-determined holding and usage is indispensable for the protection of one's personal freedom. To this day the universal international law does not know a universal guarantee of property as a human right. This is why the status of property is still precarious on the whole.

Common Law Application of the Philosophy of Property:
Where the Rubber Meets the Road

By Robert M. Duffy, Esq.

Introduction

Jeremy Bentham asserted that "property and law are born together, and die together. Before laws were made, there was no property."[1] Perhaps what Bentham meant is that property was not worth two pence absent a rule of law to enforce one's right in that property against the force or claim of another. But what is most interesting about Bentham's statement is that without a claim to private property, and the unique English/American system of creating and enforcing law, we would have no recorded common law analyzing and determining rights in property, whether absolute or relative. Cases decided at common law, arising out of a shared tradition, common sense, generally accepted moral and social principles and, perhaps most importantly, distinct and real facts, consistently and concretely test the breadth of philosophical ideals. Put another way, the razor of the common law shaves and shapes the theories of the philosopher.

There is no shortage of philosophical views on the nature of property. Some suggest that if one properly obtains it, one has a moral right to private property[2] making private ownership a cornerstone on which fundamental freedoms stand.[3] Others go so far as to suggest that the innate desire to own freely, and to the exclusion of others, is deep seated in man's nature,[4] so much so that man

---

[1] Jeremy Bentham, *Anarchical Fallacies,* republished in *Nonsense Upon Stilts: Bentham, Burke and Marx on the Rights of Man,* edited by Jeremy Waldron (New York: Methuen, 1987), pp. 46, 53.

[2] See e.g., John Locke, *Two Treatises on Government,* edited by Ian Shapiro (New Haven: Yale University Press, 2003), pp. 111–112; Robert Nozick., *Anarchy, State and Utopia* (Oxford: Basil Blackwell, 1974), pp. 150–153.

[3] D. Benjamin Barros, "Property and Freedom," *New York University Journal of Law & Liberty,* vol 4:1 (2009), pp. 36–69.

[4] Robert Ardrey, *The Territorial Imperative: A Personal Inquiry into the Animal Origins of Property and Nations* (New York: Athenaeum, 1966): "[O]ur attachment for property is of an ancient biological order," p. 103.

cannot be completely and truly human without it.[5] Most philosophers who sub-
scribe to this school of thought would likely conclude that wrapped up in property rights are the rights to privacy, security, self-sufficiency and self-
determination.

Other philosophers deny that man has a moral right to own, use or exclude
others from property, but nonetheless champion property rights for social, economic and political reasons. Most of this group would agree with Hobbes and
Bentham that there really is no natural right to private ownership *per se;* rather,
rights are created by the sovereign state and/or civil law to provide stability and
economic advantage.[6] Equal opportunity for private property encourages a po-
litically stable society and discourages upheaval and revolution because, as de
Tocqueville puts it, it constantly increases the "number of eager and restless
small property-owners ... [M]en whose comfortable existence is equally far
from wealth and poverty set immense value on their possessions. As they are
still very close to poverty, they see its privations in detail and are afraid of
them; nothing but a scanty fortune, the cynosure of all their hopes and fears,
keeps them therefrom."[7]

Still others, from Plato and extending down through Marx and his disciples
to the present day, advance the view that collective ownership and central distribution and control best promotes the common interest and inhibits social di-
visiveness. As Thomas More stated in *Utopia*, "the wise man did easily foresee
this to be the one and only way to the wealth of a commonalty, if equality of all
things should be brought in and established, which I think is not possible to be
observed where every man's goods be proper and peculiar to himself."[8] More
counseled that "no equal and just distribution of things can be made, nor that
perfect wealth shall ever be among men, unless [private ownership of things] be
exiled and banished."[9] Marx taught that society might be required to suffer
through some years of modified private ownership, but only as a step on the

---

[5] "[T]he instinct of ownership is fundamental in man's nature." William James, *The
Varieties of Religious Experience: A Study in Human Nature*, edited by Martin E. Marty
(New York and London: Penguin Books, 1982), p. 315.

[6] See e.g., M. Olson, *Power and Prosperity* (New York: Basic Books, 2000): "There
is no private property without government – individuals may have possessions, the way
a dog possesses a bone, but there is private property only if the society protects and defends a private right to that possession against other private parties and against the government as well." p. 196.

[7] Alexis de Toqueville, *Democracy in America*, edited by J. P. Mayer, translated by
George Lawrence (Garden City, New York: Doubleday, 1969), p. 636.

[8] Thomas More, *Utopia* (New York: Barnes & Noble, 2005), p. 54.

[9] Ibid., p. 55.

path to collective ownership which is the ideal to be sought and the outcome to be achieved.[10]

The ultimate point appears to be that at the bottom of any system of property is a sincere and fervent desire on the part of the philosopher to get at the essence of what it means to be human and how that is best accomplished for the individual and/or the society in which one lives. Unlike philosophy, however, the law is very little concerned with the essence of property itself and very much occupied with social order and justice; the law is constrained by practical application and this, perhaps, makes all the difference.

I. Common Law

The common law is based on judicial decisions which, in turn, are founded on social customs and traditions evolved over time as interpreted and enforced by independent judges. Common law courts typically base their decisions on prior judicial pronouncements not legislative enactments. Judges rely on decisions made in actual controversies to guide them in applying the law. The primary benefits that flow from common law are a high level of certainty, uniformity and predictability in application, combined with flexibility to deal with changes arising from unanticipated controversies.

At common law, rights accrued to those who possess or own property, whether real property which consists of land and any structures built upon the land or personal property which includes all other tangible and intangible items. These rights which run to the possessor and owner are often referred to as a "bundle of rights" because property can be used, owned, or transferred in varied ways for different purposes, many of which actions impact the rights of others. One may possess property without owning it and one may own property without possessing it. Both the possessor of property and the owner of property have rights with regard to the property and they are substantially the same.[11] Further, possession can divest ownership under certain conditions. In the law the relationships of persons to each other on the one hand, and to the particular property on the other, give rise to relative rights both between the persons themselves as well as between the individual and the property. It would be very unusual for the law to find that one has an absolute right, at all times and under all conditions, to the entire "bundle" of rights that accompany property.

---

[10] Karl Marx, *Theories of Surplus Value* (London: Lawrence and Wishart, 1972).

[11] The fact that the common law protected possession when the possessor was not also an owner greatly exercised the German philosophic mind. Oliver Wendell Holmes, Jr., *The Common Law and Other Writings* (Omaha: Legal Classics Library, 1982), pp. 206, 246.

II. Philosophical Principles and the Common Law

Let us now look at eight of the decisions of the common law in light of certain philosophical principles.

1.

> Property draws a boundary between public and private power by creating zones within which the majority has to yield to the owner.[12]

> Private property is merely a creation of the sovereign state and that it has always been that the state ultimately decides who can and who cannot exercise ownership rights with regard to property.[13]

One benefit of property, according to Charles Reich, is that it draws a boundary between public and private power and creates zones where the majority has to yield to the owner. Within these zones individuals are allowed to choose and act as they see fit regardless of how those actions may be perceived by others. Individuals may go to these zones of private property to be free from the outside world. D. Benjamin Barros sees property in this context "as giving the property owner a degree of freedom to withdraw, or exit, from the community."[14] Thomas Hobbes, on the other hand, sees no such moral right. It is the State that decides who can exercise ownership rights, and what the State decides trumps any "natural" claim. Let us consider an early American case that causes one to ponder these principles.

When the American continent was discovered by the European nations, each nation made claims to the land discovered. The nations agreed that the conquered peoples were the rightful occupants of the soil, with a legal as well as just claim to retain possession of it, and to use it according to their own discretion. Notwithstanding that, the European nations also applied the fundamental principle that discovery gave exclusive title to the discovering nation by virtue of conquest. Humanity demanded and a wise policy required, however, that the rights of the conquered to property should remain unimpaired and that the new subjects should be governed as equitably as the old. After the United States obtained by treaty and acquisition property from Great Britain and Spain it stepped into the shoes of these nations and claimed the right to the land by discov-

---

[12] Charles A. Reich, "The New Property," 73 EAL L.J. 733, 771 (1964).

[13] Thomas Hobbes, *De Cive*: *The English Version*, edited by Howard Warrender (Oxford: Clarendon Press, 1983), esp., Chap VI, no.15 (pp. 100–102) and "Epistle Dedicatory", no. 9–10 (pp. 26–27).

[14] Barros, "Property and Freedom," p. 47.

ery and, by extension, conquest. These principles greatly impacted property rights in the New World, as illustrated below.

On October 18, 1775 the Chiefs of the Piankeshaws jointly representing, acting for and duly authorized by that nation, executed a deed in favor of Thomas Johnson and others to a large tract of land primarily lying in what is now Illinois. The Piankeshaw Indians had occupied this land for many years and were recognized as its owners by the Piankeshaws and the colonists. $31,000 was paid and delivered at the time of the execution of the deed and that amount was accepted by the Piankeshaw Indians and divided among themselves. It is undisputed that the transaction was open, public, and fair, that translators were on hand and that the deed fully and accurately recorded the nature of the transaction. Johnson and the others who acquired the land, however, never took actual possession of it, initially because they were prevented by the American Revolutionary War. Following the war, they petitioned newly formed Congress continuously from 1781 to 1816 to acknowledge and confirm their title to those lands under the deeds in question, without success. On July 20, 1818 the United States conveyed by land grant the property set forth in Johnson's deed to William M'Intosh. Johnson brought an action to eject M'Intosh from the land he owned (or so he thought) and the case made its way to the United States Supreme Court.[15]

In considering the question, the Supreme Court found that the United States had an exclusive right to extinguish the Indians' right of occupancy either by purchase or by conquest. The Supreme Court acknowledged that title by conquest is normally limited by humanitarian concerns and that conquered peoples are normally assimilated into the society of the victorious nation retaining title to their property.[16] It held, however, that the Indians did not fall under the general rule, despite the fact that they occupied, possessed, and used the land for many years. It stated:

> the tribes of Indians inhabiting this country were fierce savages, whose occupation was war, and whose subsistence was drawn chiefly from the forest. To leave them in possession of their country, was to leave the country a wilderness; to govern them as a distinct people, was impossible, because they were as brave and high spirited as they were fierce ... That law which regulates, and ought to regulate in general, the relations between the conqueror and conquered, was incapable of application to a people under such circumstances. The resort to some new and different rule ... was unavoidable.[17]

---

[15] *Johnson v. M'Intosh*, 21 U.S. 543 (1823).

[16] Ibid., p. 589.

[17] Ibid., pp. 590–591.

The court was mindful how "extravagant" the pretense of converting the "discovery" of an inhabited country into conquest appeared.[18] This was particularly true given that there was never any claim of conquest made prior to the time of sale and all parties recognized the Indians as the true owners with the right to alienate the land as evidenced by the deed itself. But the court did not waiver from its holding that the Indians were merely occupants of the property and had no right to transfer title to anyone.

In *Johnson,* the state, in the form of its law court, ultimately decided that the Indians could not exercise ownership rights with regard to the property they had possessed from time immemorial, even though the law had been followed in every aspect of its transfer. Johnson's deed was worthless. This seemingly runs counter to the Lockean "first occupancy" theory of natural property rights and smacks more of Hobbes's view that we only have those rights the sovereign allows us.

2.

> Though the Earth ... be common to all Men yet every Man has a property in his own person. This nobody has any right to but himself. The labour of his body, and the work of his hands, we may say, are properly his. Whatsoever then he removes out of the State that Nature hath provided, and left it in, he hath mixed his labour with, and joyned to with something that is his own, and thereby makes it his property.[19]

In what is commonly referred to as Locke's first occupancy theory, where he combines property in the state of nature and the moral significance of man adding his labor to it, we see a moral justification for private property against all who come after.[20] For Locke, the right to private property arises in the state of nature because, although all property is initially commonly owned, an individual obtains a moral right to claim the property by mixing her labor with the object.[21] By doing so, the individual not only fulfills her fundamental duty of self preservation but also increases the value of the resources she works on for the indirect benefit of others. This classic individualism, notes Friedrich Hayek, "first fully developed during the Renaissance [and] has since grown and spread into what we know as Western civilization ... the recognition that [man's] own views and tastes are supreme in his own sphere, however narrowly that may be circumscribed, and the belief that it is desirable that men should develop their

---

[18] Ibid., p. 591.

[19] Locke, *Two Treatises,* p. 112, n.1.

[20] Ibid.

[21] Barros, p. 40, n.30.

own individual gifts and bents."[22] Locke's moral justification for property rights would appear to be the most philosophically sound[23] and one would expect the common law courts, descending from this tradition, to agree. Let us consider a few cases.

In *Ghen v. Rich*, 8 F. 159 (Mass. 1881), Mr. Ghen, an industrious whale hunter in Provincetown, shot and killed a fin back whale. Unfortunately, the whale immediately sank and was carried away by the tide leaving him without his treasure. A man named Ellis happened upon the whale washed up on shore 17 miles from where it was killed. Now at that time it was customary, upon finding a whale kill, to send notice out so that the person who actually did the deed would get the spoils. But Ellis was more enterprising. He advertised for the whale's sale and he sold it to Mr. Rich. Rich in turn sold the blubber and the oil. Eventually, Ghen heard through the grapevine that the whale had been found and he sent a boat to claim it, only to find that he was too late. Ghen sued Rich for the value of the whale. Rich did not know that Ghen had killed the whale and he had paid fair price for it. Ellis did not know Ghen killed the whale either, and worked hard to get the whale to market. Ghen, on the other hand, claimed that it was his kill and he had occupancy rights to the whale, even though he never possessed it. The court agreed with Ghen, holding that "if the fisherman does all that is possible to make the animal his own, that would seem to be sufficient."[24] Under these types of circumstances the whale became the property of the captor, not the finder. This ruling appears to be inconsistent with Locke's first occupancy theory: how could Ghen take the whale "out of nature" as his own to the exclusion of others when he never possessed it? This is, in fact, an exception in the common law.

The common law generally holds that pursuit of a wild animal does not vest any rights to the animal, even if the animal is wounded by the pursuer. One does not achieve occupancy until one achieves actual corporal possession: only when "firm possession [is] established by the taker" is the right of property clear.[25] A good illustration of this is *Pierson v. Post*.[26] There, Post and his hounds happened upon a fox in the wild, and chased the fox through the woods. Just as they were about to kill their prey, Pierson appeared, killed the fox directly in front of Post and carried it off for his own. Naturally upset, Post

---

[22] Friedrich Hayek, *The Road to Serfdom* (Chicago: The University of Chicago Press, 2007), p. 68.

[23] See: Hans-Hermann Hoppe, *The Economics and Ethics of Private Property*, 2nd ed. (Auburn, Alabama: Ludwig von Mises Institute, 2006), pp. 340–344 [http://mises.org/books/economicsethics.pdf; accessed 12 Dec 2012].

[24] *Ghen*, 8 F. at 162.

[25] *Bartlett v. Budd*, 1 Low. 223 (1868).

[26] 2 Am. Dec. 264 (N.Y. 1805).

brought suit against Pierson claiming that it was his fox. The trial court agreed with Post, as perhaps we all would. However, on appeal the verdict was reversed. However discourteous or unkind the conduct of Pierson towards Post may have been, his act produced no injury or damage for which a legal remedy could be applied. At common law, a property right in a wild animal is acquired by "occupancy only and mere pursuit of a wild animal does not vest any rights to the animal." Here is a case where Post's "first occupancy" was never achieved, despite the labor of his body. Pierson, on the other hand, did little but gained all. To show how difficult these decisions are for judges trying to balance real world problems with settled principles, one need only read Judge Livingston's colorful dissent in the case.[27]

We will consider one more case, this time involving what some would say is an interference with property rights, but whose rights?[28] Keeble owned land that included a pond. Ever enterprising, Keeble set about to lure and catch wildfowl by installing decoys in and around his pond. His neighbor Hickeringill took exception to this, apparently because wildfowl previously attracted to Hickeringill's land now preferred to visit Keeble's pond. So Hickeringill took it upon himself to discharge guns near Keeble's pond to hinder the ducks from coming to the pond. This effort proved successful, much to the dismay of Keeble who sued for damages. Keeble prevailed. The English court found that a landowner may use his pond for his trade of attracting, catching and using wildfowl and one who hinders another in his trade in a malicious manner is liable for damages. The court expressly noted that Hickeringill was certainly within his rights if he set up a competing pond or other attraction to lure and catch wildfowl himself; he apparently overstepped the line when he tried to scare the ducks away. Both men labored in nature: one to attract and the other to divert; one had the right and the other had none.

In each of the above cases, the underlying principle concerned Locke's "first occupancy" theory to some extent. Common law courts recognized the principle as the basis for initial discussion, but veered from it as needed to do justice,

---

[27] Judge Livingston ruefully noted: "who would keep a pack of hounds; or what gentleman, at the sound of the horn, and at peep of day, would mount his steed, and for hours together, 'sub jove frigido,' or a vertical sun, pursue the windings of this wily quadruped, if, just as night came on, and his stratagems and strength were nearly exhausted, a saucy intruder, who had not shared in the honours or labours of the chase, were permitted to come in at the death, and bear away in triumph the object of pursuit? Whatever *Justinian* may have thought of the matter, it must be recollected that his code was compiled many hundred years ago ... In his day, we read of no order of men who made it a business, in the language of the declaration in this cause, 'with hounds and dogs to find, start, pursue, hunt, and chase,' these animals, and that, too, without any other motive than the preservation of *Roman* poultry ..." *Pierson v. Post*, 2 Am. Dec. 264 (N.Y. 1805).

[28] *Keeble v. Hickeringill*, 103 Eng. Rep. 1127 (Q.B. 1707).

create a reliable precedent which balanced the competing interests and to promote social harmony.

3.

When private property rights are protected, people get ahead by selling productive services in exchange for income.[29]

Law ... says [to man]: Labor, and I assure to you the fruits of your labor – that natural and sufficient recompense which without me you cannot preserve; I will ensure it by arresting the hand which may seek to ravish it from you.[30]

Let us now look at a case[31] where a company spends not insubstantial sums of money to design and manufacture patterns for the fashion industry. Yet, as soon as those new designs come out its competitors copy them, undercut the manufacturer's prices and substantially hamper its sales and profitability. What would the common law say about that situation – will it ensure to the manufacturer the fruits of its labor? Will it arrest the hand that may seek to ravish it?

In 1928, Doris Silk manufactured and designed patterns for the fashion industry. The corporation spent large sums on research, design and development and made most of its profits from the relatively few designs that turned out to be popular each year. It was impractical to patent the many new designs, because it was expensive and many did not sell. The designs were impossible to copyright. Always on the lookout for an opportunity, its competitor Cheney Brothers waited to see which design was popular, copied it at the beginning of the season, undercut Doris Silk's prices and made a killing. Accordingly, it got the benefit of the ingenuity and investment of capital made by Doris Silk. Doris complained and said it wanted protection for its designs, at least during the first season in which such designs were introduced. Otherwise innovation would be hampered and people would be unwilling to invest the capital necessary to bring new items to market.

The court was very sympathetic to Doris Silk's predicament, and took a dim view of Cheney's unethical business practices. However, it found itself constrained by the common law rule which is that a person's property is limited to the chattels that embody his invention. Otherwise, intangible rights might arise and necessarily impact the rights of others in their chattels. Doris Silk found itself without any protection of any sort for its pains; at common law others may

---

[29] James Gwartney, "Private Property, Freedom and the West," *The Intercollegiate Review* 20:3 (Spring/Summer 1985), p. 43.

[30] Jeremy Bentham, *The Theory of Legislation*, translated from the French of Etienne Dumont by R. Hildreth (London: Trübner, 1871), p. 110.

[31] *Cheney Bros. v. Doris Silk Corp.*, 35 F.2d 279 (S.D.N.Y. 1929).

imitate inventions at their pleasure, and gain the benefit from the sale of the knock-offs. Cheney Brothers did not interfere with any of Doris Silk's products, it merely copied the designs, which was well within its rights. The common law, at least as applied here, did not assure to Doris Silk recompense for its labor.

Said the court in closing: "[t]rue, it would seem as though [Doris Silk] had suffered a grievance for which there should be remedy ... It seems a lame answer in such a case to turn the injured party out of court, but there are larger issues than his redress. Judges have only a limited power to amend the law ..."[32] In this case, the court showed the judicial restraint and reliance on precedent which is a hallmark of the traditional common law. Although it was faced with a clearly unjust outcome (in its view), it called out for a legislative solution not a judicial one.

Philosophy is theoretical; the common law is practical and constrained by facts of particular concrete situations. Sometimes it does not have the power to grant justice, even in a compelling case. Doris Silk created products for sale through investment of capital and ingenuity but the law was unable to protect its rights in the fruits of it labor. But as the court said, the law is concerned with issues larger than a litigant's redress, and when it involves a principle at variance with the common law, it is best done by the legislature.

4.

A person owns himself when he has control over his own body and is entitled to make use of his own body without owing any account or any contribution to anyone else and must be allowed to profit from his own mental and bodily resources.[33]

Echoing Locke, G.A. Cohen argues that a foundational element to private property is that a person owns himself and, therefore, has a right to profit from his own mental and physical processes. After all, the most fundamental of rights to property would seem to be one's right to his own body. This is consistent with the understanding of property as it developed in the common law. But is it always the case?

In *Moore v. Regents of the University of California,*[34] Moore sought treatment for leukemia at the Medical Center of UCLA owned by the Regents. Moore's condition was life threatening and his spleen was removed. What Re-

---

[32] Ibid., 35 F.2d at 281.

[33] See: G. A. Cohen, *Self-ownership, Freedom and Equality* (Cambridge: Cambridge University Press, 1995), pp. 68–71.

[34] 793 P.2d 479 (Cal. 1990), *cert denied,* 499 U.S. 936 (1991).

gents knew in advance, but did not tell Moore, was that his cells were unique and had significant scientific and commercial value. After the operation, Regents retained Moore's spleen without his permission or consent and for seven years tested, sampled, and otherwise used Moore's blood, tissue, and other fluids for research from which a cell line was established. Regents obtained a patent, the commercial value of which was estimated in the billions. Understandably upset when he found out about it, Moore sued Regents for conversion, alleging that his blood and bodily substances were his "tangible personal property." But the court disagreed. It found that Moore had neither title nor possession of the "property" and therefore could not maintain an act for conversion. We scratch our heads and wonder how this could be. After all, it was Moore's spleen that was taken out of his body and if one does not possess one's spleen, one must wonder if one possesses anything. In fact, this was the line of reasoning the dissent followed.[35] As to the patent rights, the majority found that Regents had developed a particular line of Lymphokines that are the same molecular structure in every human being and therefore they are not unique to Moore. Further, California law limited a patient's control over excised cells and restricted their use and required their eventual destruction, thus limiting many rights one might ordinarily find attached to property. The court concluded that Moore had no expectation of continued ownership in his excised cells and, at several points, it suggested that a removed body part, by its nature, may never constitute "property" for purposes of a conversion action.[36] While Moore was permitted to maintain an action for breach of fiduciary duty and informed consent, he had no action for conversion.

In *Moore,* the court, primarily for policy reasons, did not agree that a person must be allowed to profit from his own mental and bodily resources. At the same time, the court did not leave Moore without potential recovery by allowing him to proceed with other claims. This and similar cases test the principle that one has a property right in, and is free to do what one wishes with, one's body and mind, and need not account to anyone for that activity.

---

[35] The dissent stated: "it is also clear, under traditional common law principles, that this right of a patient to control the future use of his organ is protected by the law of conversion. As a general matter, the tort of conversion protects an individual not only against improper interference with the right of possession of his property but also against unauthorized use of his property or improper interference with his right to control the use of his property." 793 P.2d at 502.

[36] Ibid., pp. 489–491.

5.

The first element of property rights in particular things is that they are rights that are good against the world, wholly without the consent of any other individuals. Unless that condition were satisfied, it would not be possible to create and secure entitlements in land, structures, equipment, or indeed any form of personal property. No individual could claim to be owner of him or herself, so that no one would be in a position to bargain with everyone else to secure their own bodily protection or the ownership of external things that they acquire in all legal systems by taking first possession of otherwise unowned objects.[37]

The West has always protected possessors of property who do not own it for many different reasons. Indeed, one who possesses land he does not own has a right superior to all others except than the owner. The common law policies for this are many and include the need to maintain peace and order, to give effect to the expectations of a person who has asserted a right in a thing until another person comes along with a better right, to protect ownership, as possession makes it easier for an owner to prove title and to achieve economic efficiency in settling claims and encouraging full use of resources. How does this square with the principle that the first element of property rights is that they are good against the world? And exactly what constitutes a property right? or example, if I purchase a house and land in fee simple, do I own everything transferred within the house and on the land?

In 1938, Peel bought a large home but never moved in. In 1940 it was requisitioned by the military in England during World War II. During the war, Hannah was stationed in the house, during which time he discovered a brooch in a room being used as a sick bay. It was in an obscure place, covered with dirt and unclaimed. Ever dutiful, Hannah gave it to the police. A couple of years later, the original owner never having been found, the police gave it to Peel as owner of the property where the jewelry was found. Peel sold it for a substantial sum. Hannah found out about the sale and took objection to Peel getting the benefit of his find so he sued Peel. Hannah claimed to have a right as founder superior to Peel as owner of the freehold on which it was found. Peel scoffed at the claim; he owned the house and had possession and control of everything within it. Therefore, he argued, the brooch was his.

The court struggled with the case because the common law had a split in authority as to who had superior title: the finder or the owner of the property on which it was found (assuming the owner of the personal item did not also own

---

[37] Richard Epstein, "Property Rights and the Rule of Law, Classical Liberalism Confronts the Modern Administrative State," Hoover Institution Task Force on Property Rights, (6/29/09), p. 7 [http://www.law.nyu.edu/ecm_dlv4/groups/public/@nyu_law_website_academics_colloquia_legal_political_and_social_philosophy/documents/doc uments/ecm_pro_062726.pdf], accessed 10 Dec 2012.

the home). One line of cases found that a landowner possessed everything on the land from which he intends to exclude others while another line of cases held that a landowner possesses only those things over which he has control. The court concluded that an owner possesses everything attached to or under his land but does not necessarily possess everything that it unattached on the surface of his land.[38] Therefore, the court found that Hannah was the rightful owner of the brooch, despite the fact that Peel owned the home in which it was found.[39]

This ruling by the honorable English bench notwithstanding, let us consider the case of Mr. Ganter who purchased a dresser for $30 consigned by the Kapiloffs for sale at a used furniture store. Ganter took it home and cleaned it out and in doing so found some old magazines and newspapers as well as some old stamps. He did not pay much attention to them, thinking that they were junk; fortuitously, however, he did not throw them out. A friend urged him sometime later to have the stamps appraised, which he did in 1982 and was quite surprised at his substantial find. The stamps were consigned for sale and they were advertised for sale at a price of $150,400. Who should suddenly appear but the Kapiloffs who saw the advertisement, claimed to own the stamps and demanded their return. Somehow, the Kapiloffs had left these valuable items in the dresser when they had consigned it for sale and forgot all about them. Mr. Ganter vigorously opposed the claim. After all, it was his dresser now, he had bought it at a used furniture store, and anything in the dresser was his. He refused to return the stamps.

The common law has long held that one who finds lost personal property holds it against all the world *except* the rightful owner. Ganter had the right to exercise ownership rights in the stamps against the whole world except against the Kapiloffs, who proved themselves to be the true owners. Once the Kapiloffs made claim on the stamps, and convinced the court that they owned but lost them, Ganter's property rights in the stamps ceased. Further, once Ganter failed to return the stamps he put himself in danger of being liable for converting private property as well as larceny.[40] If the court concluded the stamps had been abandoned, the outcome would likely have been different, since one who abandons property no longer possesses an ownership interest in it.

Both of these cases test the definition of "unowned." Are the rights of a finder of lost personal property in the house of another superior to the rights of

---

[38] *Hannah v. Peel*, K.B. 509 (1945).

[39] But see, *McAvoy v. Medina*, 93 Mass. (11 Allen) 548 (1866), where in a rather obscure opinion, the Court held that as to a pocket book left on a barber's table, the barber had a better right than the finder, the distinction apparently being that the item was found in a public place of business not a private home.

[40] *Ganter v. Kapiloff*, 516 A.2d 611 (Md. 1986).

the owner of the house in objects found on his property? Apparently so, even though the property owner has superior rights to the space wherein the object was found. It seems a court could just as easily find that the object was not "unowned" precisely because it was in home of another, and the original owner of the object was nowhere to be found after a diligent search. But at common law the rights of the finder must always give way to the true owner because personal property is not "unowned" simply because it is lost and not presently possessed by the owner.

6.

The only set of rules that achieves the goal of protecting private property rights is one that requires of all persons that they forbear from interfering with the property rights of any other person.[41]

It is key, according to Richard Epstein, that the bundle of property rights which accrue to an owner be defined in ways that allow them to be known and observed by all others even where no personal communication is possible. Further, it is absolutely critical that a set of rules be developed that requires all persons to forbear from interfering with the property right of others. But is this always the way of the common law, at least insofar as it relates to real property? Let us consider adverse possession, a creature of the common law, which allows one to obtain fee simple title to property against all, including the true owner, simply by acting as if one were the true owner for a period of time. At common law, productive use and protection of private property were paramount and if an owner failed to take action to evict trespassers, it was better for the trespasser, who used the property, to own it. In short, interference by trespass is implicitly encouraged and, if unopposed over time, converts an unlawful use into fee simple ownership.

In 1946 Gorski entered land under a contract to purchase.[42] The land was conveyed to Gorski and her husband in 1952. During those six years Gorski's son improved the property. One such improvement encroached upon Mannillo's land. Over 20 years later, Mannillo filed a complaint seeking an injunction against the trespass, to which Gorski responded that he had obtained title to the property by adverse possession. Mannillo countered that Gorski could not have obtained title adversely because he (Gorski) never even knew he was trespassing and therefore did not intend to acquire title. The New Jersey Supreme Court sided with Gorski. It stressed that the very nature of the act of entry and possession is an assertion of one's title to the property and denial of title in the

---

[41] Epstein, p. 8, n.53.
[42] *Mannillo v. Gorski*, 255 A.2d 258 (N.J. 1969).

owner. It does not matter if the adverse possessor is mistaken, the result is the same: the owner is ousted from possession and if she fails to attempt to recover possession within the required time, the trespasser becomes the owner in fee simple.[43] Gorski divested Mannillo of title precisely by interfering with Mannillo's property rights for an extended period, even though he never intended to do so.

The same holds true even if the trespass only involves a limited use of another's property. Hester and Sawyers were neighbors who owned adjoining parcels of land. Sawyers used a road (the "old road") that crossed a portion of Hester's land with Hester's permission. The old road was Sawyers's only access to his property. Due to a fence later constructed on the eastern portion of the land, Sawyers could not use the old road for which he had permission from Hester. Ever enterprising, Sawyers built a new road, this one entirely on Hester's property and this time without Hester's consent. Sawyers went merrily along, maintained and used the new road for over ten years, until Hester asked Sawyers to change the road to interfere less with his property. Sawyers agreed and began grading a new road. But Hester was not happy with the second new road either and built a fence blocking all access. Upset, Sawyers tore down the fence Hester had erected. Hester went to court to get Sawyers off his property. Sawyers claimed that he had acquired the right in perpetuity to use the new road. Hester responded that he had granted permission to Sawyers so Sawyers was never trespassing on his land and could not, therefore, obtain title by adverse possession. The court sided with Sawyers holding that Sawyers had acquired title by prescription to that portion of the new road that he had used for over ten years. While Sawyers had permission to use the old road, and could never gain title by prescription once he had permission to that, he never had permission to build the new road. Sawyers kept the new road graded and in repair and used it continuously for over ten years. By doing so he obtained title to it. Once again, the common law encouraged and rewarded interference with property rights as a matter of public policy. It is more important to society that property be productively used and cared for than one's natural right to possess property be affirmed.

---

[43] This is the majority rule. A minority of courts require intent to establish adverse possession based on precedent peculiar to that jurisdiction. See e.g., *Van Valkenburgh v. Lutz*, 106 N.E.2d 28 (N.Y. 1952).

7.

Private ownership encourages individuals to develop and employ resources in a manner that is most advantageous to others.[44]

It has been suggested by many libertarian philosophers that among other things, private ownership encourages individuals to develop and employ resources in a manner most advantageous to others.[45] In free market economies, where property rights are recognized, allocation of resources is made on a decentralized basis by numerous market actors, with diversified goals and objectives yet with one common motive: to maximize profits from productive use of resources. Contrast this with a socialist market based on collective property rights and it can be readily seen that individuals acting in a socialist market have no incentive whatsoever to maximize profits or to act efficiently. Often their motivations will be completely separated from the economic question of determining the most efficient and appropriate allocation of market resources. For example, if all have equal permission to use a common piece of land, but no duty to preserve any particular piece of it, none has an incentive to plant crops or care for the land or pay for the cost to do so. Conversely, when common land is taken private, separated and distributed to individuals, each of whom has the exclusive right to use and control the activities on the land, it will likely be productively used.

But let us consider this premise a bit more closely. The common law is replete with evidence that the ownership of private property often encourages individuals to develop and employ resources in a way that is most advantageous to the owner and *not* to others. As far back as the reign of Queen Elizabeth, for example, the law recognized the natural inclination of market participants to increase profits by privately restraining trade and eliminating competition. For that reason, any contract in general restraint of trade was void as being contrary to public policy, regardless of its apparent economic benefit.[46] No shortage of fact patterns emerge in the common law illustrating man's ingenuity to use private property in a manner most advantageous to *himself* and to the detriment of others. Horizontal restraints of trade, vertical restraints of trade, price fixing, boycotts, and combinations to destroy competition, monopolize, or corner the market all increase in a free market. Any one of these is arguably economically and socially disadvantageous to others and often, if not always, deprives an-

---

[44] Gwartney, p. 43, n.45.

[45] Ibid. See also: Garrett Hardin, "The Tragedy of the Commons," *Science,* 162 (1968):1243–1248.

[46] See *Mogul Steamship Co. v. McGregor*, 23 Q.B. 598, 617.

other of his free use of private property.[47] And these were often done on a small scale among minor merchants in inconsequential towns throughout England, and not always on the scale of the Standard Oil Trust.

At common law, the general principle was that any contract that restrains trade was unlawful unless shown to have been made upon adequate consideration and upon circumstances both reasonable and useful. It was generally acknowledged in the law that the public interest is superior to private, and that all restraints on trade are injurious to the public in some degree. That did not make them any the less common.

A paradigm for this is the case of *Keeler v. Taylor*.[48] There, Keeler agreed to instruct Taylor in the art of making platform scales and to employ him in that business at a set wage. In turn, Taylor agreed that he would pay Keeler $50 for each and every scale he thereafter made for any person other than Keeler, or which should be made from information Taylor imparted to others. Keeler did not want Taylor to take the know-how imparted to him by Keeler and compete with him. This arrangement was held to be an unreasonable restriction upon Taylor's labor, and therefore void, as against the public interest. This case is but one of thousands of cases at common law illustrating this type of market action.

Another example is *Morris Run Coal Company v. Barclay Coal*.[49] In that case, certain mining companies combined by private contract to control the entire production in two large mining regions. As a result, the cartel controlled the price and supply over vast markets, causing an increase in price and decreased competition. It is fairly obvious that in cases such as this, private ownership encourages the employment of resources to benefit the owner and his confederates, and few others. Indeed, the collective activities among private market participants in the manner described above is not far different from the centralization of decision making in a communal property system because it limits the ability of individuals to freely make resource distribution and acquisition decisions.[50]

---

[47] According to Ludwig von Mises, while it is generally true that a market economy produces the highest possible standard of living, this will not happen if any firm succeeds in securing monopoly prices for its goods, and the market cannot itself produce the goods of law and order. Hoppe, *Economics and Ethics,* iPad version.

[48] *Keeler v. Taylor*, 3 P.F. Smith 467 (1866).

[49] *Morris Run Coal Co.*, 68 Pa. 173, 1871 WL 10919 (1871).

[50] While most economists hold this view, some argue that on the free market no price can be identified as monopolistic or competitive. Hoppe, *Economics and Ethics,* iPad version. Further, the state can never "correct" such perceived economic inefficiency in a free market. See, e.g., Murray Rothbard, *Man, Economy, and State* (Los Angeles: Nash, 1972), p. 887. "[T]he view [that free-market action must be brought back into optimality

8.

> The difficulties with the modern approach to the rule of law are only aggravated by the light regard paid to traditional property rights in the new legal order ... [T]he incidents of ownership were accounted for in the private law setting. Any government that respected these equally could only strip any of those rights away for some definable reason that involved either the prevention of nuisances or the provision ... of compensation.[51]

Professor Epstein rightly states that private property rights are not absolute, regardless of origin, and the common law always recognized this. The law of nuisance in particular affords no rigid rule to be applied in all instances. It is an equitable doctrine with remarkable elasticity that undertakes to require only that which is fair and reasonable under all the circumstances.[52] A good example of this in action is *Spur Industries, Inc. v. Del E. Webb Development Co.*[53] There, Spur Industries owned and operated a cattle feedlot for many years far from any housing developments. As Arizona became more populous, Del decided to develop a housing sub-division down the road from the cattle feedlot, including retirement villages. There was demand for Del's housing units and the sub-division began to spread in the direction of the feedlot. That is when the problems began. Not surprisingly, the homes closest to the feed lot enjoyed the characteristic noxious odors and flies that frequent such establishments. Del began to suffer reduced sales of those homes closest to the cattle yard, which it did not take kindly to. So it brought suit to enjoin Spur Industries from conducting its business claiming it was a public nuisance. Del argued that housing was important and persons who live in their houses should not suffer from the sights, sounds, and smell of a cattle yard. Spur argued that it owned and operated the business long before Del came to town, that it had set up far from any residential dwellings and it should be allowed to continue to own and operate its property as it always had done.

The Supreme Court of Arizona reluctantly agreed with Del. In Arizona, anything that constitutes a breeding ground for flies and is injurious to the public health is a public nuisance. The feedlot fell within this ambit. Further, a business becomes a public nuisance by being carried on at a place where the health and convenience of populous neighborhood begins to be affected. There was no

---

by corrective State action] completely misconceives the way in which economic science asserts that free-market action is *ever* optimal. It is optimal, not from the standpoint of the personal ethical view of an economist, but from the standpoint of the free, voluntary actions of all participants and in satisfying the freely expressed needs of the consumers. Government interference, therefore, will necessarily and always move *away* from such an optimum."

[51] Epstein, p. 25, n.53.

[52] *Stevens v. Rockport Granite Co.*, 216 Mass. 486, 488 (1914).

[53] 494 P.2d 700 (Ariz. 1972).

question that the owners of the homes closest to the feed lot were affected by its operation. Accordingly, Spur was required to shut down its business and move, not because of any wrongdoing on its part, but "because of a proper and legitimate regard of the courts for the rights and interests of the public."[54] Del, on the other hand, was entitled to relief, "not because it was blameless, but because of the damage to the people who have been encouraged to purchase homes in Sun City."[55] The court stressed that it did not "legally or equitably follow, however, that [Del] being entitled to the injunction, is then free of any liability to Spur."[56] Because it had brought people to the nuisance by building the homes, Del was required to indemnify Spur for the reasonable expense of moving or shutting down its business. In this case, the common law stripped away private rights to protect the public, but required just compensation in a private setting. This may not have been a philosophically sound decision but it certainly was a practical one.

Conclusion

It is plain from the above discussion that in many respects the common law shares common ground with western philosophical principles. Indeed, the basic premise of private property rights is enshrined in the common law. But such rights are not absolute and the law will not hesitate to deviate from a strictly theoretical principle when delivering justice, even when it means leaving comfortable ground and forging ahead into uncharted territory. Unlike philosophers, common law judges must adhere to tradition while ever dealing with practical contingencies and real complainants, such as Mr. Ghen who lost his whale, Mr. Post whose fox was purloined, Mr. Johnson who was divested of title to a vast tract of land and Doris Industries, whose designs were copied. Even though philosophical principles guide the application of justice in concrete cases, concrete application in the service of tangible justice proves often to be both the material out of which philosophical theories are born, and their measure. And so, while philosophical principles juxtaposed to common law decisions may be logically sound and theoretically tenable, the most pressing question should be: are they capable of practical application and, if so, to what extent? The answer to that question is best found in the common law. The common law, without a critical awareness of its philosophical mandate and thus its ideal purpose, would be left to poke haphazardly after "just" verdicts, making a farce of "rational" human society. But we have seen, on the other hand, that abstract phi-

---

[54] Ibid., p. 708.
[55] Ibid.
[56] Ibid.

losophical investigation, if it does not carefully attend to its roots in the concrete business of human society, is just as apt to render justice laughable by positing ideals which are ideally sound but quite simply foreign to human coexistence as it really is. No philosophy is prepared a priori to deal justly with ambiguously stolen foxes, stealthily pilfered whales, and reeking cattle, in the complex context of a deeply interconnected societal network.

Summary

Any system of philosophy necessarily deals with the essence of property and man's interaction with it. While there generally seems to be a sincere and fervent desire on the part of the philosopher to explore human activity vis-à-vis the material world so as to better understand who and what we are, quite often these explorations result in idealistic conclusions which are not susceptible to practical implementation. Unlike philosophy the common law is very little concerned with the ideal and very much occupied with social order and justice. Based, as it is, on judicial decisions which, in turn, are founded on social customs and traditions evolved over time as interpreted and enforced by independent judges, there is a necessary flexibility to the common law which, at times, moves away from the ideal and more toward the practical. To illustrate this phenomenon, this paper looks at certain common law decisions decided at a specific time in a specific place in light of philosophical principles which deal with the same or similar question. It becomes readily apparent that, while the common law shares common ground with western philosophical principles, private property rights are not absolute and the law will not hesitate to deviate from a strictly theoretical principle when delivering justice.

Zusammenfassung

Jedes philosophische System befasst sich notwendigerweise mit dem Wesen des Eigentums und wie der Mensch damit umgeht. Es ist verständlich, wenn vonseiten der Philosophen ein aufrichtiges und brennendes Interesse besteht, das Handeln des Menschen in die materielle Welt hinein zu erforschen, um besser zu begreifen, wer und was wir sind. Häufig verbleiben diese Überlegungen in einem idealistischen Bereich, ohne große Bedeutung für das praktische Verhalten. Anders als die Philosophie befasst sich die Rechtswissenschaft weniger mit der idealen Welt und sehr viel mehr mit dem Recht und der gesellschaftlichen Ordnung. Sie beruht auf rechtlichen Urteilen, die wiederum auf soziale Sitten und Traditionen, die sich im Lauf der Zeit entwickelt haben, zurückreichen und von unabhängigen Richtern interpretiert und angewandt werden. Das Rechtssystem erhält dadurch eine notwendige Flexibilität, die bisweilen vom Ideal abweicht und mehr den Erfordernissen der Praxis entspricht. Um dieses Phänomen zu erklären, werden Gerichtsurteile herangezogen, die unter bestimmten Voraussetzungen im Licht der philosophischen Prinzipien gefällt werden, die dieselben oder ähnliche Sachverhalte betreffen. Es wird deutlich, dass das common law eine gemeinsame Wurzel mit den philosophischen Prinzipien der westlichen Welt besitzt, dass aber die Privateigentumsrechte nicht absolut sind und deshalb die Rechtsprechung nicht zögert, von den theoretischen Prinzipien abzuweichen, wenn es die Gerechtigkeit verlangt.

Die Eigentumsfrage – Politische Entwicklungen im geteilten und wiedervereinigten Deutschland

Von Jürgen Aretz

Mehr als vierzig Jahre der Trennung und Teilung lagen hinter den Deutschen, als ihr Land am 3. Oktober 1990 wieder staatlich vereint war. Der Zusammenhalt der Menschen diesseits und jenseits der innerdeutschen Grenze war zwar im Laufe der Zeit schwächer geworden, aber keineswegs zerstört. Das galt, obwohl in den beiden Staaten in Deutschland entgegengerichtete immaterielle und materielle Entwicklungen stattfanden, die gravierende Unterschiede im Denken und Leben der Menschen zur Folge hatten. Die deutsche Teilung, so die Sozialwissenschaftlerin Renate Köcher, lasse sich „auch als ein Dokument der Prägungen von Menschen in einem unterschiedlichen politischen und wirtschaftlichen System lesen"[1]. Begriffe, die für das Gemeinwesen grundlegend sind, hatten unterschiedliche, bisweilen einander ausschließende Bedeutungen erlangt. Das führte nach 1990 zu oft belastenden Missverständnissen. In den ersten Jahren nach der Wiedervereinigung galt das unter anderem für den Begriff „Eigentum" und seine Bedeutung in der Realität des wiedervereinigten Deutschland. Die Folgen für Wirtschaft und Gesellschaft, in vielen Fällen auch für die persönliche Reaktion der Menschen auf die neue Situation, waren gravierend – auf beiden Seiten der ehemaligen innerdeutschen Grenze.

Die ersten Bilder des wiedervereinigten Deutschland lösten andere Eindrücke aus: In Ost und West brach sich am 3. Oktober 1990 ausgelassene Freude auf den Straßen und Plätzen Bahn. Diese emotionale Reaktion hatten manche Beobachter den vermeintlich unterkühlten Deutschen gar nicht zugetraut. Die Ursache der Freude war wohl weniger die Erfüllung eines nationalen Traumes als eine große Erleichterung: Die Sorge um eine unkalkulierbare Entwicklung in Deutschland hatte ebenso ein Ende gefunden wie die jahrzehntelange Furcht, das geteilte Land könnte Ausgangspunkt eines Dritten Weltkrieges werden. Nun konnten sich die Menschen in Deutschland wieder begegnen, ohne Gefahr für Leib und Leben, ohne die Risiken einer hochbefestigten Grenze, ohne Schikanen, ohne Bespitzelung durch die „Staatssicherheit", den DDR-Geheim-

---

[1] *Renate Köcher*, Die Bildung des Eigentums in der öffentlichen Meinung, in: Bitburger Gespräche, Jahrbuch 2004/I, hrsg. von der Stiftung für Rechtspolitik, Trier, und dem Institut für Rechtspolitik an der Universität Trier, München 2004, S. 111–118, hier S. 114.

dienst, so normal eben, wie das in Westeuropa seit langem der Fall war. Für einen Moment schien es, als ob eine Ära des Friedens und der Freiheit ausgebrochen sei, die weit über Deutschland hinausreichte. Den internen Problemen, die es zu lösen galt, wurde eine vergleichsweise geringe Bedeutung beigemessen angesichts dessen, was man hinter sich gelassen hatte.

Erst allmählich wurden sich die Menschen im Westen und Osten des bisher geteilten Landes bewusst, dass sie vor 1990 in weit unterschiedlicheren Realitäten gelebt hatten, als es während der Wiedervereinigungsfreude wahrgenommen worden war. Der materielle Unterschied war in Ökonomie und Ökologie mit Händen zu greifen. Die westdeutsche Bundesrepublik gehörte 1990 weit über den wirtschaftlichen Bereich hinaus zu den führenden Kräften in Europa. Die ostdeutsche DDR dagegen war mit ihrem System der, wie es offiziell hieß, „sozialistischen Planwirtschaft" am Ende. Die sozialistische Bevormundungsdiktatur hatte ihre Wohltaten nicht nach der tatsächlichen Wirtschaftskraft, sondern nach politischem Gutdünken gewährt – von der Zuteilung billiger Wohnungen bis zu der Versorgung mit Grundnahrungsmitteln, die unter den Produktionskosten abgegeben wurden. Das sind nur zwei Beispiele. Auf der Sollseite standen völlig zerrüttete Staatsfinanzen und die Notwendigkeit immer neuer Kredite. Ohne Rücksicht auf die Lebensbedingungen und die Interessen künftiger Generationen waren die Umwelt und die natürlichen Ressourcen ausgebeutet worden. Ganze Regionen der DDR waren ökologisch ruiniert. Die unterschiedlichen Ergebnisse von mehr als vierzig Jahren Marktwirtschaft auf der einen und sozialistischer Zentralverwaltungswirtschaft auf der anderen Seite konnten eindrucksvoller kaum besichtigt und konkret bilanziert werden als im Deutschland des Jahres 1990.

I. Die Teilung Deutschlands

Die vergleichende Bilanz der Systeme ist auch deswegen aussagekräftig, weil die Ausgangssituation für beide Modelle im Wesentlichen gleich bzw. vergleichbar war. Seit dem Ende des 19. Jahrhunderts war Deutschland ein einheitliches Rechts- und Wirtschaftsgebiet gewesen. Somit galten im gesamten Deutschen Reich auch dieselben Eigentumsbestimmungen, und sie galten im Grundsatz für jedermann – jedenfalls bis 1933. Das nationalsozialistische Unrechtsregime beraubte die von ihm Verfolgten, im Besonderen die jüdische Bevölkerung, auch ihrer Eigentumsrechte. Die Bundesrepublik Deutschland hat sich später zu einer materiellen Entschädigung der Opfer des Nationalsozialismus bekannt; die DDR hat dies unter Hinweis auf ihren „antifaschistischen" Ursprung abgelehnt. Zur Wiederherstellung eines einheitlichen Rechtsraumes und damit einheitlicher Eigentumsrechte kam es nach 1945 ohnehin nicht.

Nach dem Sieg der Alliierten und der bedingungslosen Kapitulation des nationalsozialistischen Deutschen Reiches sahen sich die Deutschen dramatischen Konsequenzen ausgesetzt. Mit Billigung auch der Westalliierten kam es zur faktischen Annexion des historischen Ostdeutschland (Schlesien, Pommern, Ostpreußen) durch Polen. Die neuen Machthaber vertrieben die deutsche Bevölkerung, deren gesamter immobiler und mobiler Besitz entschädigungslos enteignet wurde. Die Betroffenen mussten in der Mitte und dem Westen des weitgehend zerstörten Reiches eine neue Heimat finden. Ebenso erging es den Deutschen aus der wiederbegründeten Tschechoslowakei und den deutschen Minderheiten in anderen mitteleuropäischen Staaten. Insgesamt strandeten weit mehr als zwölf Millionen Deutsche mittellos im zerstörten Nachkriegsdeutschland. Etwa zwei Millionen Menschen, vor allem Frauen, Kinder und Alte, fielen Flucht und Vertreibung zum Opfer.

Die Alliierten teilten das verbliebene Deutschland 1945 in vier Besatzungszonen sowie die Vier-Sektorenstadt Berlin auf. An ihrer Absicht, Deutschland gemeinsam zu regieren, hielten sie jedenfalls formal zunächst fest.[2] Schon bald nach Kriegsende zeigte sich aber, dass das widersprüchliche Bündnis der westlichen Demokratien mit der stalinistischen Sowjetunion nach dem militärischen Sieg über den gemeinsamen Feind keinen dauerhaften Bestand haben würde. Die ersten Vorzeichen des späteren Kalten Krieges waren bereits im Sommer 1945 zu erkennen. Die Sowjetische Militäradministration in Deutschland (SMAD) ging daran, in ihrer Besatzungszone ein politisches System nach sowjetischem Vorbild zu errichten. Alles, was dem im Wege stand oder zu stehen schien, wurde konsequent und mit großer Härte gebrochen.

In den Besatzungszonen nahm bereits die Entnazifizierung einen unterschiedlichen Verlauf. Die SMAD entledigte sich in der Sowjetischen Besatzungszone (SBZ) zugleich vieler tausend Opponenten, die nichts mit dem Nationalsozialismus im Sinn gehabt hatten. So wurden – ohne jedes rechtsstaatliche Verfahren – u. a. im KZ Buchenwald bei Weimar nach 1945 in einem „Speziallager" selbst Personen inhaftiert, die dort schon unter den Nationalsozialisten eingesperrt gewesen waren. Die Zahl der in solchen SMAD-Lagern umgekommenen Häftlinge wird auf mindestens 65 000 geschätzt.[3] Die Lager wurden

---

[2] Vgl. dazu u. a. *Gottfried Zieger*, Vier-Mächte-Verantwortung für Deutschland als Ganzes, Berlin 1990; *Manfred Overesch*, Deutschland 1945–1949. Vorgeschichte und Gründung der Bundesrepublik, Düsseldorf 1979; Die Deutschlandfrage und die Anfänge des Ost-West-Konflikts 1945–1949 (= Studien zur Deutschlandfrage, Bd. 7), mit Beiträgen von A. Fischer, J. Foschepoth, R. Fritsch-Bournazel, D. Junker, W. Link, M. Overesch, Berlin 1984; *Hermann Graml*, Die Alliierten und die Teilung Deutschlands. Konflikte und Entscheidungen 1941–1948, Frankfurt/M. 1985.

[3] *Klaus-Eberhard Murawski*, Der andere Teil Deutschlands, München / Wien 1967, S. 40; Murawski verweist auch auf Schätzungen, dass in den Speziallagern 100 000 Menschen zu Tode gekommen seien.

erst 1950 aufgelöst. Schon die unmittelbare Nachkriegszeit belegt eindrucksvoll, dass es in der SBZ zu keinem Zeitpunkt die Möglichkeit einer demokratischen und rechtsstaatlichen Entwicklung gab. Das Ziel der SMAD war die Sowjetisierung ihres Herrschaftsbereichs unter der Camouflage einer „antifaschistisch-demokratischen Ordnung"[4].

Auf deutscher Seite wurde diese Politik getragen von der Kommunistischen Partei Deutschlands (KPD), die von der SMAD als erste Partei im Frühjahr 1945 zugelassen worden war. Aus kommunistischem Machtkalkül wurde die KPD mit der Sozialdemokratischen Partei Deutschlands (SPD) – zum Teil gegen deren Willen – 1946 zur Sozialistischen Einheitspartei Deutschlands (SED) zusammengeschlossen. Alle politisch und wirtschaftlich relevanten Positionen wurden mit Mitgliedern der neuen Staatspartei besetzt. Wer gegen die SMAD-Politik opponierte, wurde inhaftiert oder in die Sowjetunion deportiert; die Zahl der dort Hingerichteten geht in die Hunderte. Das Ziel war die Schaffung einer neuen, sozialistischen Gesellschaft, die Verwirklichung der „Volksdemokratie". An der Tautologie nahm man keinen Anstoß. Dieses Ziel setzte nach marxistisch-leninistischem Verständnis die Entmachtung der „Ausbeuterklasse" durch die Zerstörung der bisherigen Eigentumsordnung voraus. Sie war in diesem Verständnis die Grundlage der kapitalistischen Gesellschaft.[5]

Mit der Landwirtschaft und der Industrie standen die beschäftigungsintensivsten Wirtschaftsbereiche als erste im Fokus. Die Einleitung einer Bodenreform stieß durchaus auf Zustimmung von Teilen der armen ländlichen Bevölkerung. Die Propaganda knüpfte u. a. an die Bauernkriege des 16. Jahrhunderts an, die wesentlich auch ein sozialer Aufstand gewesen waren. In einer ersten Phase wurden alle landwirtschaftlichen Betriebe mit mehr als 100 Hektar (= ca. 247 acres) entschädigungslos enteignet. Die Flächen gingen an bisherige Landarbeiter, Kleinbauern und heimatvertriebene Deutsche. Sie erhielten bis zu 20 Hektar (knapp 50 acres). Angesichts der unwirtschaftlichen Betriebsgrößen, wenig ertragreicher Böden, unzureichender Ausstattung mit Vieh und Gerät und oft mangelhafter beruflicher Qualifizierung der Neubauern ging die landwirtschaftliche Produktion deutlich zurück. Das verschärfte die ohnehin schwierige Versorgungslage der unmittelbaren Nachkriegszeit, aber solche Aspekte spielten in dieser Phase des „Klassenkampfes" keine Rolle. Viele Herren-

---

[4] Ebenda, S. 38.

[5] Vgl. dazu u. a. *Helmut Leipold*, Wirtschafts- und Gesellschaftssysteme im Vergleich, 5. Aufl., Stuttgart 1988, im Bes. S. 16 ff; zum Folgenden und zur Entstehung der staatssozialistischen Wirtschaftsordnung in der SBZ bzw. DDR vgl. *Wolfgang Mühlfriedel*, Herausbildung und Entwicklungsphasen des „Volkseigentums", in: Materialien der Enquete-Kommission „Aufarbeitung von Geschichte und Folgen der SED-Diktatur in Deutschland" (12. Wahlperiode des Deutschen Bundestages), hrsg. vom Deutschen Bundestag, Bd. II/3, Machtstrukturen und Entscheidungsmechanismen im SED-Staat und die Frage der Verantwortung, Baden-Baden / Frankfurt/M. 1995, S. 2218–2286.

sitze der oft in adligem Besitz befindlichen Güter wurden ungeachtet ihrer historischen Bedeutung als „Brutstätten des Junkertums und Militarismus" niedergelegt.[6]

Im industriellen Bereich wurden alle bedeutenden Unternehmen – und keineswegs nur solche, deren Eigentümer nationalsozialistisch belastet waren – beschlagnahmt und entschädigungslos in „Volkseigentum" überführt. Betroffen waren die Grundstoff- und die Montanindustrie, alle Aktiengesellschaften sowie weitere, von der SMAD vorgegebene Unternehmen und Unternehmensbereiche.[7] Bis 1948 wurden rund 10 000 Unternehmen verstaatlicht. Damit befand sich bereits zu diesem frühen Zeitpunkt deutlich mehr als die Hälfte der Industrieproduktion in „Volkseigentum"[8]. Strategisch wichtige Unternehmen – u. a. im Uranbergbau – beanspruchte die Sowjetunion als Reparationsleistungen für sich.[9] Viele enteignete Unternehmer flohen schon in den ersten Nachkriegsjahren in den Westen und gründeten ihre Unternehmen neu. Nach der Wiedervereinigung sind sie bzw. ihre Nachfahren mit ihren Firmenzentren und Forschungsabteilungen meist nicht in den Osten zurückgekehrt. Die sozialistische Enteignungspolitik hat somit Folgen, die heute noch in der wirtschaftlichen Entwicklung der neuen Länder der Bundesrepublik nachwirken.

II. Die Abschaffung des Privateigentums in der DDR

Der Kalte Krieg zwischen Ost und West, dessen Kernursache die sowjetische Machtausdehnung in Mitteleuropa und anderen Regionen der Welt war, führte schließlich 1949 zur staatlichen Teilung Deutschlands. Auf dem Gebiet der drei Westzonen entstand die Bundesrepublik Deutschland, die verfassungsrechtlich das Weimarer Demokratiemodell weiterentwickelte. Die faktisch von der Sowjetunion etablierte DDR setzte dem ein Politikmodell entgegen, das die Verwirklichung des Sozialismus zum Ziel hatte. Aus politisch-taktischen Gründen schloss auch die erste DDR-Verfassung – es sollten bis 1974 noch zwei weitere folgen – formal an Weimar an.

Zwischen Verfassungstheorie und Verfassungswirklichkeit bestanden in der DDR von Anfang an eklatante Unterschiede. Da es eine unabhängige Justiz als gewaltenteilende Kraft nicht gab, konnte eine rechtliche Überprüfung des Re-

---

[6] Siehe Anm. 3, S. 39.

[7] Ebenda.

[8] Vgl. DDR-Handbuch, hrsg. vom Bundesministerium für innerdeutsche Beziehungen, 2 Bde., 3., überarb. Aufl., Köln 1985, hier Bd. 2, S. 1486; auch Handbuch der DDR-Wirtschaft, hrsg. vom Deutschen Institut für Wirtschaftsforschung (DIW) Berlin, 4., erweiterte und aktualisierte Aufl., Hamburg 1984, S. 32.

[9] Wie Anm. 6.

gierungshandelns bzw. der Gesetzgebung nicht stattfinden. Die Verfassung von 1968 definierte schließlich in ihrem ersten Artikel die marxistisch-leninistische SED als die politische Führungskraft auf dem Weg zum Sozialismus und den Staat DDR als Herrschaftsinstrument der Staatspartei.

Zu diesem Weg gehörte – wie von der SMAD bereits unmittelbar nach dem Krieg vorexerziert – eine neue Eigentumsordnung, die den monistischen Eigentumsbegriff des bürgerlichen Rechts ablehnte und im sozialistischen Sinne überwand.[10] Das „sozialistische Eigentum" bestand nach der DDR-Verfassung von 1968 „als gesellschaftliches Volkseigentum, als genossenschaftliches Gemeineigentum werktätiger Kollektive sowie als Eigentum gesellschaftlicher Organisationen der Bürger". Das persönliche Eigentum der Bürger war „gewährleistet"; privates Eigentum an Produktionsmitteln wurde als Übergangserscheinung zugelassen. In der politischen Wirklichkeit erwies sich die persönliche Eigentumsgarantie aber allzu oft als Makulatur. Zahllose politische Strafverfahren endeten damit, dass als Nebenstrafe das Vermögen eingezogen wurde. Auch das Steuerrecht wurde entsprechend instrumentalisiert.

Die SMAD hatte bereits weithin vollendete Tatsachen geschaffen. Die anschließenden Eigentumseingriffe der frühen DDR führten dazu, dass schon 1953 – bezogen auf die Beschäftigtenzahl – der Anteil der „Volkseigenen Betriebe (VEB)" im industriellen Bereich bei 85 % lag.[11] Eine schlagartige Verstaatlichung der noch verbliebenen, meist kleinen Privatbetriebe war im Hinblick auf die Erfüllung der DDR-Wirtschaftspläne nicht möglich. So erfolgte sie stufenweise. Durch eine erzwungene Beteiligung des Staates an Privatbetrieben, die einer Teilenteignung gleichkamen, entstanden sog. „halbstaatliche Betriebe". Damit wurde der Privatsektor Ende der 50er Jahre weiter zurückgedrängt. Lange hielt diese Lösung nicht vor. Mit den meisten Privatunternehmen wurden auch sie 1971/72 in „Volkseigentum" überführt.[12] Die bisherigen Eigentümer mussten den Betrieb vielfach als Geschäftsführer aufrechterhalten. Manche Opfer dieser letzten Enteignungswelle konnten nach der Wiedervereinigung und der Rückgabe des Eigentums ihre unternehmerische Tätigkeit wieder aufnehmen. Sie haben so an vielen Stellen wesentlich zum wirtschaftlichen Wiederaufbau der neuen Länder beigetragen, die auf dem Gebiet der ehemaligen DDR entstanden waren.

---

[10] DDR-Handbuch (s. Anm. 8), hier Bd. 1, S. 315 ff; vgl. auch *Georg Brunner*, Eigentum, in: Lexikon des DDR-Sozialismus, hrsg. von R. Eppelmann / H. Möller / G. Nooke / D. Wilms, 2., aktualisierte Aufl., Paderborn 1997, S. 226–230.

[11] *Doris Cornelsen*, Die Volkswirtschaft der DDR: Wirtschaftssystem – Entwicklung – Probleme, in: Werner Weidenfeld / Hartmut Zimmermann (Hrsg.), Deutschland-Handbuch, Bonn 1989, S. 258–275, hier S. 259.

[12] Ebenda.

Besonders hart war das Schicksal zahlloser Landwirte. Seit 1952 waren sie Kampagnen für das genossenschaftliche Eigentum – als einer Unterform des sozialistischen Eigentums – ausgesetzt, bevor schließlich 1960 die Kollektivierung der gesamten Landwirtschaft erzwungen wurde. Viele, die erst durch die Bodenreform zu Bauern mit eigenem Land geworden waren, fanden sich faktisch in ihrer alten Rolle als Landarbeiter wieder. Ganze Dorfbevölkerungen flohen vor dem Mauerbau 1961 in die Bundesrepublik. Vor dem Hintergrund wachsender ökonomischer Probleme wurden später private Initiativen u. a. im Handwerk zugelassen. Ende der 80er Jahre beschäftigte der Privatsektor etwa 2 % der „Werktätigen" in der DDR.[13]

Eine private Eigentumsbildung im westlichen Sinne war von der DDR nicht erwünscht und daher nur sehr begrenzt möglich. Der Bau eines Eigenheimes etwa erwies sich als Abenteuer, in dem zunächst politisch-bürokratische Hürden genommen werden mussten. In einem zentralverwaltungswirtschaftlich organisierten System werden Güter zugeteilt und nicht nach Angebot und Nachfrage gehandelt. Die Materialbeschaffung geriet so zu einer Herausforderung, die ohne persönliche Beziehungen und schwer zu erlangende Westdevisen nicht zu bewältigen war. Selbst der Kauf eines im Vergleich zu westlichen Modellen bescheidenen Autos war nicht ohne weiteres möglich. Der politisch festgesetzte hohe Preis diente der Kaufkraftabschöpfung. Der Erwerb forderte aber in der sozialistischen Plan- und Verteilungswirtschaft nicht nur das notwendige Geld – etwa ein durchschnittliches Jahresbruttoeinkommen –, sondern auch außerordentliche Geduld: Wartezeiten von mehr als zehn Jahren waren die Regel.

Die durchschnittlichen Einkommen aus Erwerbstätigkeit stiegen bei Arbeitern und Angestellten in der DDR zwischen 1960 und 1985 von 472 DDR-Mark auf 987 DDR-Mark monatlich.[14] Die Bandbreite zwischen den niedrigen und den höchsten Einkommen, die nur selten 3000 DDR-Mark überstiegen, war vergleichsweise gering. Grundnahrungsmittel waren hochsubventioniert, die Mieten auf niedrigem Niveau festgelegt. Sie machten einschließlich der Nebenkosten etwa 5 % des Monatseinkommens eines Durchschnittshaushaltes aus.[15] Diese politischen Mietpreise erlaubten es den noch verbliebenen privaten Hauseigentümern oft nicht, in ihren Altbauten auch nur die nötigsten Erhaltungsreparaturen durchzuführen. Der Verfall der Bausubstanz in der DDR,

---

[13] Ebenda.

[14] *Cord Schwartau / Heinz Vortmann*, Die materiellen Lebensbedingungen in der DDR, in: Deutschland-Handbuch (s. Anm. 10), S. 292–307, hier S. 294. Die Vergleichszahlen für die Bundesrepublik liegen bei ca. 515 DM (1960) bzw. ca. 2 960 DM (1985), siehe Datensammlung zur Steuerpolitik, Ausgabe 2012, hrsg. durch das Bundesministerium der Finanzen, Berlin, S. 18 f. Ein tatsächlicher Währungs- bzw. Kaufkraftvergleich ist nur sehr bedingt möglich, u. a. weil die DDR-Mark nicht konvertibel war. Der inoffizielle Umtauschkurs lag in dieser Zeit bei 4 DDR-Mark zu 1 DM.

[15] Siehe *Schwartau / Vortmann* (Anm. 14), S. 299.

nicht zuletzt in den historischen Altstädten, hat hier eine Erklärung. Die DDR-Opposition, die sich Ende der 80er Jahre artikulieren konnte, formulierte in Anlehnung an das Motto der Friedensbewegung („Frieden schaffen ohne Waffen") ihre Definition des Sozialismus: „Ruinen schaffen ohne Waffen".

Vor der offenen oder schleichenden Enteignung war allen Zusicherungen zum Trotz unterhalb der Nomenklatura kaum jemand sicher. Als die DDR in späteren Jahren unter immer größerem Devisenmangel litt, erfanden die „Staatsorgane" eine neue Einnahmequelle. Mit fragwürdigen Begründungen requirierten sie privat gesammelte oder ererbte Antiquitäten. Eine Entschädigung gab es nicht. Die Objekte wurden von der DDR im westlichen Ausland zu Geld gemacht – Staatsraub zum Wohle des Sozialismus.[16]

III. Sozialbindung des Eigentums im Westen

Nach 1945 standen die frühere Wirtschafts- und Sozialordnung und die Eigentumsverhältnisse, die daraus resultierten, auch in der grundsätzlichen Kritik vieler Westdeutscher, die sich aktiv am Aufbau einer neuen demokratischen Ordnung beteiligten. Bereits in den 20er Jahren sahen keineswegs nur Vertreter der politischen Linken, dass die eigentlichen Verlierer des Ersten Weltkrieges die Arbeiterschaft und das Bürgertum gewesen waren. Sie hatten Übermenschliches geleistet, Leib und Leben eingesetzt und als Folge der kriegsbedingten Inflation vielfach ihren Besitz verloren. Dem stand eine soziale Oberschicht gegenüber, aus der nicht wenige ihr Vermögen durch Kriegsgeschäfte gemacht oder vergrößert hatten. Dieselben Kreise trugen – wie auf der anderen Seite die verarmten Schichten – erheblich zum Aufstieg Adolf Hitlers bei. Im Gegenzug konnten sie an der militärischen Aufrüstung vor 1939 und am Kriegsgeschehen verdienen.

Schon vor 1933 hatten u. a. führende Köpfe der katholischen Sozialbewegung die Forderung nach einer „Durchleuchtung" der Wirtschaft und damit der Eigentums- und Herrschaftsstrukturen erhoben. Wirtschaftliche Ordnungsfragen wurden auch im deutschen Widerstand gegen Hitler erörtert. Nach 1945 strebten selbst Teile der westdeutschen Christlich-Demokratischen Union (CDU) eine „Vergesellschaftung" zentraler Wirtschaftsbereiche an, bevor sich unter dem maßgeblichen Einfluss von Konrad Adenauer andere Positionen durchsetzten. Die SPD, über viele Jahre die maßgebliche Oppositionskraft der jungen Bundesrepublik, ging einen anderen Weg. Für sie war die weitreichende Sozialisierung ein programmatischer Kernpunkt.

---

[16] „Maximale Gewinne erzielen" – Wie Schalck-Golodkowski mit seiner „Kunst und Antiquitäten GmbH" die DDR ausplünderte, in: Der Spiegel, 19/1991, S. 52 f; vgl. auch *Jürgen Aretz / Wolfgang Stock*, Die vergessenen Opfer der DDR, Berlin 2009, S. 84 f.

Die Diskussion schlug sich konsequenterweise in der demokratischen Neu-
gestaltung Westdeutschlands nieder. Ein ungeregelter Kapitalismus ist mit dem
1949 verabschiedeten Grundgesetz für die Bundesrepublik Deutschland nicht
vereinbar. Die Verfassung garantiert das Recht auf Eigentum (Art. 14, Abs. 1),
legt aber bereits im nächsten Absatz (Art. 14, Abs. 2) fest: „Eigentum verpflichtet. Sein Gebrauch soll zugleich dem Wohle der Allgemeinheit dienen."
Die Verfassung lässt die Möglichkeit zu, dass „Grund und Boden, Naturschätze
und Produktionsmittel" gegen Entschädigung enteignet und vergesellschaftet
werden (Art. 15). Für das politische System der Bundesrepublik Deutschland
gibt es einen zentralen Zusammenhang zwischen dem Eigentum bzw. der Eigentumsgarantie auf der einen und dem Sozialstaatlichkeitsgebot auf der anderen Seite. Die Sozialbindung des Eigentums – die nicht zuletzt auf die Christliche Gesellschaftslehre zurückgeht – gehört zu den Grundlagen des Modells, das
als „Soziale Marktwirtschaft" zu dem beispiellosen wirtschaftlichen, sozialen
und politischen Erfolg der Bundesrepublik beigetragen hat. Alfred Müller-
Armack, dem Theoretiker dieses Modells, ging es darum, die Freiheit des
Marktes mit sozialem Ausgleich zu verbinden. Heute beflügelt dieses Modell
als „Rheinischer Kapitalismus" die europäische Diskussion.[17]

Ludwig Erhard, der erste Wirtschaftsminister der Bundesrepublik, gab das
Ziel der Sozialen Marktwirtschaft vor: „Wohlstand für alle". Diese programmatische Zusage war die politische Botschaft der jungen Bundesrepublik schlechthin – jedermann sollte die reale Möglichkeit bekommen, Eigentum zu bilden
und am allgemeinen wirtschaftlichen Erfolg teilzuhaben. So konnte sich die
neue Wirtschaftsordnung gegen staatssozialistische Ideen durchsetzen und eine
hohe Akzeptanz in der Bevölkerung finden.[18]

Die 50er Jahre waren in der Bundesrepublik nicht wie in der DDR ein Jahrzehnt des ideologisch motivierten Umsturzes der Eigentumsordnung, sondern
eine Phase tiefgreifender sozialer und wirtschaftlicher Reformen. Zugunsten
der Menschen, die durch den Krieg und die Kriegsfolgen, u. a. den Bomben-
krieg und die Vertreibung, ihr Eigentum verloren hatten, wurde ein Lastenausgleich durchgeführt. Er sicherte diesem nach vielen Millionen zählenden Be-
völkerungsteil eine Grundhilfe zu. Eine vollständige Kompensation ihrer Verluste war unmöglich. Die Finanzierung erfolgte durch einen gesetzlich geregel-
ten Eingriff in das Vermögen und die Eigentumsrechte der Deutschen, die ein
vergleichbares Schicksal nicht hatten tragen müssen. Zahlreiche Sozialrefor-
men verbesserten die Situation weiter Bevölkerungskreise nachhaltig. Dazu gehörten u. a. die Einführung des Kindergeldes, der Ausbau der Arbeitslosenver-

---

[17] *Jürgen Aretz*, Zur Geschichte und Aktualität des Rheinischen Kapitalismus, in:
Michael Spangenberger (Hrsg.), Rheinischer Kapitalismus und seine Quellen in der Katholischen Soziallehre, Münster/W. 2011, S. 1–8.

[18] Wie Anm. 1, hier S. 111.

sicherung, die dynamische Rente – also die Koppelung der Renten an die Entwicklung der Löhne und Gehälter –, und der kostenlose Besuch weiterführender Schulen. Umfangreiche Programme dienten der Förderung des privaten Eigentums, im Besonderen des Wohneigentums. Es gelang, die Nachkriegsnot zu überwinden und durch einen langanhaltenden, selbsttragenden wirtschaftlichen Aufschwung eine allgemeine private und öffentliche Wohlstandsmehrung zu erreichen. Das war auch mit einer größer werdenden Spreizung der Einkommensunterschiede und Eigentumsverhältnisse verbunden.

Eine nach Branchen und Betriebsgrößen differenzierte Mitbestimmung band die Gewerkschaften stärker in das System der Sozialen Marktwirtschaft ein – und zugleich in die Erfolgsgeschichte vieler Unternehmen. Manche Unternehmer und Anteilseigner beklagen die Mitbestimmung primär als Kostenverursacher und als Eingriff in ihre Eigentumsrechte. Diese Kritik lässt außer Acht, dass die Mitbestimmung zumindest mittelbar oft zu vernünftigen Tarifabschlüssen und zu der Tatsache beigetragen hat, dass die Bundesrepublik über viele Jahre von Streikwellen wie in zahlreichen Nachbarstaaten verschont blieb.

Die Politik gerade der frühen Bundesrepublik hat die Menschen für die Idee der Freiheit und für den jungen demokratischen Staat gewonnen. Das System der Sozialen Marktwirtschaft wurde nachgerade mit der Bundesrepublik identifiziert; der Sozialstaat, so die wachsende Überzeugung, müsse garantieren, dass sich die Freiheit nicht in theoretischen Garantien erschöpfen dürfe. Von eher konservativer Seite wurde plastisch formuliert, die Handlungsfreiheit könne nicht in der Wahl bestehen, unter welcher Brücke man die nächste Nacht verbringe.[19] Freiheit muss nach dieser Überzeugung auch gelebt werden können, ohne Angst vor sozialen Lebensrisiken wie fehlender Absicherung im Alter, bei Krankheit oder Arbeitslosigkeit.

Der deutsche Reichskanzler Otto von Bismarck hatte in den 80er Jahren des 19. Jahrhunderts eine Sozialgesetzgebung durchgesetzt, die auf Versicherungsschutz zielte. Seitdem ist in breiten Bevölkerungsschichten die Überzeugung entstanden, die Absicherung solcher Risiken sei in erster Linie Aufgabe des Staates. Eine repräsentative Umfrage des Instituts für Demoskopie in Allensbach ermittelte 2009, dass 71 % der Westdeutschen und 88 % der Ostdeutschen der Meinung sind, die gesetzliche Sozialversicherung müsse die Bürger „möglichst umfassend sozial absichern"[20]. Vor dem Hintergrund des demografischen Wandels wird freilich in der nahen Zukunft der Ausbau der privaten Vorsorge weiter vorangebracht werden müssen, und es ist ebenso notwendig, eine gewis-

---

[19] *Reinhard Müller*, Freiheit – die Botschaft wird gebraucht, in: Frankfurter Allgemeine Zeitung, 10. Mai 2012.

[20] Allensbacher Jahrbuch der Demoskopie 2003–2009, Bd. 12, hrsg. von Renate Köcher, Berlin u. a. 2009, S. 141.

se „Anspruchskultur" zu überwinden. Für die Menschen, denen die Bildung eines auch für den Notfall ausreichenden Privateigentums nicht gelungen ist oder nicht gelingen konnte[21], muss weiterhin der staatliche Versicherungsschutz ein Leben in Würde und ohne materielle Existenznot gewährleisten.

Schon wenige Jahre nach der Gründung der Bundesrepublik fanden angesichts des erarbeiteten Erfolges, der sehr missverständlich auch als „Wirtschaftswunder" beschrieben wird, Utopien und Umverteilungsideologien keinen nennenswerten Rückhalt mehr. Solche Ideen sollten erst viel später in einer Zeit unvergleichlich höheren Wohlstandes wieder aufkommen. Die SPD gab 1959 ihr sozialistisches Programm auf, verzichtete auf Enteignungspläne und akzeptierte die von den demokratischen Kräften der politischen Mitte geschaffenen Grundlagen. Zu der programmatischen Neuorientierung der SPD gehörte neben der Sozialen Marktwirtschaft auch die Aufgabe neutralistischer Positionen und die Akzeptanz der Westbindung.

Die Grundvorstellung Konrad Adenauers setzte sich umfassend durch. Er wollte die Bundesrepublik unwiderruflich in die westliche Wertegemeinschaft einbinden und den Menschen eine verlässliche wirtschaftliche und soziale Perspektive bieten. Das schloss die Chance auf individuellen Wohlstand ein. Dieser Erfolg sollte auf die Menschen in der DDR eine „Sogwirkung" ausüben. In einer Situation, in der die Sowjetunion ihre politischen und im Besonderen außenpolitischen Interessen neu definieren müsste, wäre so ein friedlicher Weg zur Wiedervereinigung Deutschlands geebnet. Dieser Fall trat Ende der 80er Jahre ein. Die Menschen in der DDR konnten 1989/90 nach dem Scheitern des Sozialismus erstmals ihr Schicksal selbst in die Hand nehmen. Das haben sie in beeindruckender Weise getan.

IV. Die Probleme der Anpassung

Es wäre eine idealistische Überhöhung, wenn man annähme, „die" Menschen in der DDR hätten damals ausschließlich ihre Freiheitsrechte im Blick gehabt. Selbstverständlich hatten sie auch konkrete materielle Erwartungen. Vor dem Vertrag über eine Wirtschafts-, Währungs- und Sozialunion, der im Sommer 1990 zwischen der Bundesrepublik und der DDR geschlossen wurde, kam das in den Demonstrations-Transparenten zum Ausdruck: „Entweder die D-Mark kommt zu uns oder wir kommen zur D-Mark." Die Ostdeutschen erwarteten verständlicherweise, dass sich über die politische Situation hinaus ihre wirtschaftliche Lage verbessern würde. Auf diesem Weg standen viele vor der Notwendigkeit, geradezu ein „neues" Leben erlernen zu müssen. Die DDR war

---

[21] Siehe Anm. 18.

der Bundesrepublik beigetreten, und damit galten deren vielfältige, vor allem aber andersartige Bestimmungen sofort oder mit kurzer Übergangsfrist auch in Ostdeutschland. Hinzu kamen nicht kodifizierte gesellschaftliche Regeln. Viele Lebenserfahrungen und „Lebenstechniken" halfen nicht mehr. Nach der langjährigen Erfahrung in einem geschlossenen, aber in gewisser Weise berechenbaren sozialistischen System mussten sich die Menschen nun in einer neuen, offenen Ordnung zurechtfinden. Sie bot viele Chancen, aber bisweilen auch unerwartete Risiken und wenig persönlichen Halt.

Manches wechselseitige „Nichtverstehen" hat hier seine Ursache, denn die Westdeutschen haben keine entsprechende Erfahrung machen müssen. In ihrer Betrachtung stehen die gewaltigen Transferleistungen von West nach Ost im Vordergrund. Manche Westdeutsche halten sie inzwischen für überzogen und verstehen sie als schmerzlichen finanziellen Eingriff. Tatsächlich übertrifft diese historische Solidarleistung inzwischen den Lastenausgleich oder die Marshall-Plan-Hilfe der Nachkriegszeit um ein Vielfaches. Es ging für die Deutschen aus der DDR nach 1990 aber nicht nur darum, bisher fremde Ordnungsvorstellungen zu akzeptieren und neue „Lebenstechniken" zu erlernen. Vieles, was ihnen aus der DDR mit positiver Konnotation vertraut war, wurde im Westen anders oder gar negativ gesehen. Die neuen Bundesbürger erlebten nicht unbedingt einen persönlichen, aber einen vollständigen gesellschaftlichen Wertewandel.[22]

Zwei konkrete Beispiele dafür sind die Begriffe „Volkseigentum" und „Sozialisierung". In der Bundesrepublik des Jahres 1990 war die Sozialisierung längst kein Thema mehr. In der DDR aber war das private Eigentum an Produktionsmitteln mit Ausnahme kleiner Familienbetriebe abgeschafft worden. Eine mit Westdeutschland vergleichbare Bildung von Privateigentum hatte nicht stattfinden können. Große Einkommens- bzw. Vermögensunterschiede bestanden nicht, jedenfalls nicht offen. Abgesehen von der unzureichenden Leistungsfähigkeit der DDR-Wirtschaft war diese Nivellierung in der sozialistischen DDR politisch so gewollt. Nach vierzigjähriger Indoktrination wurde die wenig leistungsfördernde Gleichheit von vielen als „gerecht" empfunden. Auch noch 1999, also etliche Jahre nach der Wiedervereinigung, antworteten auf die Frage: „Würden Sie selbst gern in einem Land leben, in dem es keine Reichen und keine Armen gibt, sondern alle möglichst gleich viel haben?" 63 % der Ostdeutschen mit ja (47 % der Westdeutschen).[23] Schon fünf Jahre später mein-

---

[22] Vgl. dazu *Andreas Rödder*, Wertewandel im geteilten und vereinten Deutschland (= Kirche und Gesellschaft, Heft 389), Köln 2012; vgl. auch *Jürgen Aretz*, Die deutsche Einheit – ihre Voraussetzungen, die Verträge und die Perspektiven, in: Politische Studien, Heft 419, München 2008, S. 30–42, hier S. 41 f.

[23] Allensbacher Jahrbuch der Demoskopie 1998–2002, Bd. 11, hrsg. von Elisabeth Noelle-Neumann und Renate Köcher, München / Allensbach 2002, S. 635.

ten deutlich weniger Befragte, dass die Entwicklungschancen eines Landes umso besser sein würden, je geringer die Unterschiede bei Einkommen und Besitz seien.[24]

Mit der Wiedervereinigung begann die zu erwartende Auseinandersetzung darüber, wie mit den Enteignungen in der SBZ bzw. der DDR umzugehen sei. Die Kontroverse hielt über Jahre an und ist in der gesellschaftlichen Diskussion immer noch nicht vollständig abgeschlossen. Bis heute ist unter den Betroffenen umstritten, ob die Sowjetunion die Hinnahme der SMAD-Enteignungen zur Vorbedingung für ihre Zustimmung zur Wiedervereinigung gemacht hat, wie von Seiten der – im Frühjahr 1990 demokratisch gewählten – DDR-Regierung behauptet wurde. Auf allen Seiten hat die Frage der Enteignungen bzw. Rückübertragungen viel böses Blut hinterlassen. Im Mittelpunkt stand die Forderung nach Restituierung ehemals privaten, nach 1945 verstaatlichten Eigentums. Das Bundesverfassungsgericht hat letztinstanzlich entschieden, dass die von der SMAD auf besatzungsrechtlicher Grundlage vollzogenen, entschädigungslosen Enteignungen grundsätzlich hinzunehmen sind, soweit sie immobiles Vermögen betrafen. Das mobile Vermögen ist zurückzugeben. Der Deutsche Bundestag traf im sog. Entschädigungs- und Ausgleichsleistungsgesetz entsprechende Regelungen. Das bedeutet konkret, dass zum Beispiel enteignete Adelsfamilien in der Regel keinen Anspruch mehr auf ihre Schlösser und Güter erheben können, Möbel und Kunstgegenstände hingegen zurückerhalten sollen. Eine umfassende Befriedung trat nicht überall ein: Unerfüllten Entschädigungserwartungen der früheren Eigentümer standen und stehen Befürchtungen verunsicherter Bevölkerungskreise gegenüber. Sie befürchten, dass Museen nach einer Übergangsfrist, die bis 2014 reicht, wichtige Exponate an die ursprünglichen Besitzer zurückgeben müssen.

Eine andere Regelung gilt für die Enteignungen, die in die Zeit der DDR fallen. Die Betroffenen waren meist in die Bundesrepublik geflohen. Sie bzw. ihre Nachfahren beanspruchten in zehntausenden Fällen die Rückerstattung ihres Vermögens. Unter rechtsstaatlichen Gesichtspunkten schien das in den meisten Fällen selbstverständlich. In der DDR waren aber enteignete Privathäuser wieder veräußert worden oder sie wurden z. B. zu Kindergärten umgewandelt. Für die Nutzer oder die gutgläubigen Erwerber des einstmals entzogenen Eigentums stellten sich also menschlich ebenfalls nachvollziehbare Fragen. Der fragwürdige Satz „Wir wollten Gerechtigkeit und bekamen den Rechtsstaat" hat in solchen ostdeutschen Erfahrungen seine Ursache.

Aufschlussreich ist eine demoskopische Untersuchung zur Eigentumsproblematik, die unmittelbar nach der Wiedervereinigung in beiden Teilen Deutschlands durchgeführt wurde. Das Institut Allensbach bat um eine Kommentierung

---

[24] Wie Anm. 1, im Bes. S. 116 f.

des Satzes: „Wer ungerechterweise enteignet wurde, wem sein Haus oder Grundstück weggenommen wurde, dem muss man auch sein rechtmäßiges Eigentum zurückgeben." In der ausgehenden DDR fand dieser Satz im August 1990 eine Zustimmung von 35 % (Westdeutschland 50 %). Nachdem Tausende von Rückübertragungsanträgen gestellt und heftige öffentliche Diskussionen entbrannt waren, sank die Zustimmung in den neuen Ländern bis April 1992 auf 21 % (alte Länder 42 %).[25] Das Institut legte auch den Satz vor: „Ich bin für Privateigentum bei Betrieben, damit sich jemand wirklich für den Betrieb verantwortlich fühlt. Nur so kriegen wir unsere Wirtschaft in Ordnung." Dem stimmten im Juli 1990 74 % der Befragten in der DDR zu.

In den folgenden Monaten fielen erste Entscheidungen der Treuhandanstalt, die in ihren Ergebnissen nicht unumstritten war. Die noch zu DDR-Zeiten gegründete Treuhandanstalt sollte im Auftrag der Regierung fast 8000 Betriebe mit 4 Millionen Beschäftigten reprivatisieren bzw. bei fehlender wirtschaftlicher Perspektive „abwickeln", das heißt schließen. Die Entscheidungen waren mit Hunderttausenden Entlassungen verbunden. Die Treuhand wurde so „zur Projektionsfläche tiefsitzender Enttäuschungen über die Folgen der Einheit, weil die ‚blühenden Landschaften'", die Bundeskanzler Helmut Kohl vorausgesagt hatte, „nicht ohne Einschnitte und Verwerfungen entstanden, auch in den Lebensläufen der Ostdeutschen"[26]. Im September 1991, also 14 Monate später, war die Zustimmung zum Privateigentum an Betrieben aber lediglich um 14 % auf 60 % gesunken.[27] Angesichts einer langjährigen SED-Indoktrinierung und der Tatsache, dass viele Ostdeutsche die Massenentlassungen als eine ihrer ersten Erfahrungen in der Bundesrepublik erlebten, ist das ein eher positives Ergebnis. Es zeigt, dass eine große Mehrheit auch der Ostdeutschen rechtsstaatliche und klare Eigentumsverhältnisse als notwendige Grundlage für den wirtschaftlichen Wiederaufbau erkannt hatte und befürwortete.

V. Die Überwindung der Gegensätze

Euphorie ist weder eine natürliche noch eine dauerhafte Stimmungslage; die Rückkehr von der Hochstimmung zur Normalstimmung kann einen schmerzhaften Absturz bedeuten. Nach dem 3. Oktober 1990 mussten die Deutschen rasch erkennen, dass sich das politische, ökonomische und ökologische Erbe

---

[25] Allensbacher Jahrbuch der Demoskopie 1984–1992, Bd. 9, hrsg. von Elisabeth Noelle-Neumann und Renate Köcher, München u. a. 1993, S. 261.

[26] *Andreas Rödder*, Schlachthaus des Westens?, in: Frankfurter Allgemeine Zeitung, 7. September 2012; *Richard Schröder*, Ruin – lieber mit als ohne Einheit. Der Zusammenbruch der DDR-Wirtschaft war unausweichlich, in: Frankfurter Allgemeine Zeitung, 4. Februar 2013.

[27] Wie Anm. 25, S. 583.

der DDR als große Belastung erwies – weit größer als es die Menschen beiderseits der ehemaligen innerdeutschen Grenze angenommen hatten. Manche Erb-
lasten der DDR wirken bis heute nach. Die finanzielle Unterstützung für die
neuen Länder wird in den nächsten Jahren zurückgehen – auch, weil inzwischen in manchen Regionen der alten Länder ein Investitionsstau eingetreten
ist, nicht zuletzt im Bereich der Infrastruktur. Der Solidarpakt, mit dem die
neuen Länder unterstützt werden, läuft 2019 aus.

Auch mehr als zwanzig Jahre nach Wiederherstellung der staatlichen Einheit
gibt es zum Teil große Unterschiede in den grundsätzlichen Einstellungen von
West- und Ostdeutschen. Staatsgläubigkeit und Sicherheitsdenken sind im Osten deutlich ausgeprägter als im Westen, die Bedeutung der Eigenverantwortung wird geringer geschätzt.[28] Die Soziale Marktwirtschaft findet im Westen
erheblich höhere Wertschätzung als im Osten.[29] Dort wird sie vielfach für das
ökonomische und ökologische Desaster der DDR verantwortlich gemacht, das
mit ihrem Ende offen zu Tage getreten ist und dessen Folgen das wiedervereinigte Deutschland zu bewältigen hatte.

Einstellungen und Mentalitäten gleichen sich nur langsam an – auch, was
etwa die Eigentumsfrage betrifft. Dabei spielt eine Rolle, dass in Ostdeutschland noch viele Meinungsbildende anzutreffen sind, die entsprechende Funktionen schon vor 1990 in der DDR wahrnahmen und/oder sich nicht von einer
unkritischen DDR-Nostalgie lösen können.

Die Eigentumsverhältnisse erreichen im Osten noch nicht das Niveau des
Westens. Ein realistischer Ansatzpunkt zur Kritik kann das nicht wirklich sein.
Die Westdeutschen hatten vierzig Jahre länger Zeit, Eigentum und im besonderen Eigenkapital zu bilden. Durch die Weitergabe an die nächste Generation
wird sich der Abstand auch nur langsam verringern. Dass es zu einer weiteren
Annäherung kommen wird, darf längerfristig angenommen werden. Die Deutschen, die heute mit unverstelltem Blick auf die Wirklichkeit in den neuen
Ländern der Bundesrepublik Deutschland schauen, sehen unabhängig von ihrer
geographischen oder historischen Herkunft: Helmut Kohls Wort von den „blühenden Landschaften" ist, wenn auch später als erhofft, schließlich doch un-
übersehbare Realität geworden.

---

[28] Vgl. dazu die entsprechenden Allensbach-Untersuchungen, Bd. 12 (s. Anm. 20),
im Bes. S. 141.
[29] Ebenda, S. 380 ff.

Zusammenfassung

Nach mehr als 40jähriger Teilung wurde Deutschland am 3. Oktober 1990 staatlich wieder vereint. Die sozialistische DDR trat der demokratisch und marktwirtschaftlich verfassten Bundesrepublik bei. Rasch stellten sich Fragen und Herausforderungen, die auf die Unterschiedlichkeit der Systeme zurückgingen und die in dieser Form nicht erwartet worden waren. Dem Vorbild der Sowjetunion folgend hatte die SED, die Staatspartei der DDR, eine grundsätzliche Veränderung der Eigentumsverhältnisse angestrebt. Sie sah darin eine entscheidende Voraussetzung für die Verwirklichung ihres Staatszieles, die Errichtung des Sozialismus. Schon früh waren Industrie und Landwirtschaft verstaatlicht bzw. kollektiviert worden. In der Folge griff das Regime in vielfältiger Weise in die Eigentumsrechte der Menschen ein – bis tief in den privaten Bereich. Nach der Wiedervereinigung führte der Versuch, rechtsstaatliche Verhältnisse wiederherzustellen und Eigentum zurückzugeben, zu vielfältigen, nicht zuletzt politischen Problemen. Trotz jahrzehntelanger ideologischer Indoktrination und manchen für die Menschen irritierenden Erfahrungen mit dem neuen System, finden rechtsstaatliche Eigentumsvorstellungen längst aber auch große Zustimmung im Osten der Bundesrepublik. Die tatsächlichen Eigentumsverhältnisse weisen vor allem wegen der unterschiedlichen politischen und ökonomischen Vergangenheit immer noch starke Unterschiede zwischen Ost und West auf.

Summary

After more than 40 years of division, Germany was reunited as a nation on the 3rd October, 1990. The socialist German Democratic Republic (GDR) joined the Federal Republic of Germany with its democratic system, and its market economy. Very soon the Germans were confronted with questions and challenges which were rooted in the different systems, and which were unexpected in this form. Following the model of the Soviet Union, the socialist state party (SED) had aimed at a fundamental change of property rights and conditions from the very beginning. Therein they saw a decisive precondition for the realisation of their aim, the establishment of a socialist system. Industry and agriculture were nationalised, i.e. collectivised. Successively, the regime intervened in the property rights of the people in many ways, even far into their most private sphere. After reunification, the attempt to reinstate constitutional democratic conditions and to return expropriated property, led to various and not least to political problems. Despite decades of ideological indoctrination and some, for the people, irritating experiences with the new system, the notion of legally recognized property has long since been acknowledged, also in the East of the Federal Republic. Present property conditions still show large differences between East and West, especially as a result of the different political and economic past.

Quo vadis Europa?

Von Bernhard Vogel

Herzlichen Dank für die Einladung! Ich freue mich, heute wieder bei Ihnen zu sein. Ihnen, verehrter Professor Frank, und Ihnen, verehrter Pater Rauscher, herzlichen Dank dafür, dass Sie auch dieses 12. Kolloquium zustande gebracht haben! Die Konrad-Adenauer-Stiftung wird Sie gerne im Rahmen ihrer Möglichkeiten auch weiterhin unterstützen. Herr Dr. Hänsel, unser Repräsentant in Washington, ist erfreulicherweise anwesend und steht Ihnen gerne als unser Partner zur Verfügung.

„Quo vadis?" lautet der Titel eines erfolgreichen Romans vom Anfang des 20. Jahrhunderts. Sein Autor, der polnische Schriftsteller Henryk Sienkiewicz, wurde 1905 mit dem Literatur-Nobelpreis ausgezeichnet. Quo vadis? „Wohin gehst du?" Die Frage wird Petrus gestellt, als er das unter Nero 64 nach Christus brennende Rom fluchtartig verlassen will. Christus tritt ihm entgegen: Wenn es brennt, flieht man nicht, sondern man löscht.

I. Der europäische Einigungsprozess

Nun wäre es fraglos übertrieben, den Stadtbrand Roms als Metapher zu verwenden, um die aktuelle Situation in Europa zu schildern. Dennoch, wir stehen in Europa vor einer, wenn nicht der größten Herausforderung in der Geschichte des europäischen Einigungsprozesses. Wir sollten vor ihr nicht fliehen, sondern uns ans Löschen begeben. Und dabei sollten wir die Mahnung des deutschen Historikers Golo Mann bedenken: „Wer die Vergangenheit nicht kennt, wird die Zukunft nicht in den Griff bekommen."

Rufen wir uns – wenigstens in aller Kürze – die Vergangenheit in Erinnerung: Am 8. Mai 1945 endet in Europa der von Hitler mutwillig vom Zaun gebrochene Zweite Weltkrieg. Europa war zum Schlachtfeld geworden. 50 Millionen Menschen hatten ihr Leben verloren. Es herrschte Not, Leid und Elend. Und am Horizont zog ein neuer Konflikt auf: Die menschenverachtende Ideologie des Kommunismus brach sich in Europa ihre Bahn. Wie Dominosteine fielen ihr die ostmitteleuropäischen Staaten zum Opfer: Polen, die baltischen Staaten, die Tschechoslowakei, Ungarn, Jugoslawien, Albanien. Der Eiserne Vorhang senkte sich, er teilte Deutschland, Europa und die Welt in zwei Hälften. Der Kalte Krieg beherrschte für Jahrzehnte die Weltpolitik. Dort der Ostblock unter Führung der Sowjetunion; hier der Westen unter Führung der Vereinigten Staaten.

Was aus dem besiegten Deutschland werden sollte, darüber herrschte bei den Siegermächten Unklarheit und Uneinigkeit. Seine Aufteilung in Besatzungszonen war beschlossen worden. Der vereinbarte Gebietsaustausch erfolgte: die USA zogen sich aus Thüringen und Teilen Sachsens zurück. Die Westalliierten bezogen ihre Sektoren in Berlin. Während Frankreich von vornherein die Abtrennung des Saarlandes betrieb und die USA und Großbritannien unterschiedliche föderale Vorstellungen hatten, hielt die Sowjetunion zunächst an der Einheit Deutschlands fest – mit dem erklärten Ziel, Deutschland als Ganzes seinem kommunistischen Machtbereich einzuverleiben.

Dem widersetzte sich von Anfang an Konrad Adenauer mit seinem einfachen, aber weitblickenden Konzept: Freiheit vor Einheit, um am Ende die Einheit in Freiheit für alle Deutschen möglich zu machen. Entscheidend dafür war die Westintegration – die Rückkehr der Bundesrepublik Deutschland in die Wertegemeinschaft der freien Welt – und natürlich seine Vision eines vereinten Europas.

Am 9. Mai 1950 trat der französische Außenminister Robert Schuman in Paris mit einer Erklärung zur Gründung einer Europäischen Gemeinschaft für Kohle und Stahl vor die Öffentlichkeit. Der Schuman-Plan wurde zur Grundlage einer neuen Ordnung der Beziehungen der europäischen Staaten. Er markiert die Geburtsstunde eines friedlich vereinten Europas. Die Gründerväter Europas – Konrad Adenauer, Robert Schuman und Alcide de Gasperi – zogen Konsequenzen aus der blutigen Vergangenheit Europas: Sie entwickelten die Vision eines neuen europäischen Weges. Europa sollte sich über alle Gräben der Vergangenheit hinweg zusammenschließen – zunächst in den über Krieg und Frieden entscheidenden Bereichen Kohle und Stahl. Die Europäische Verteidigungsgemeinschaft (EVG) scheiterte 1954; sie erhielt in der französischen Nationalversammlung keine Mehrheit. Im Jahr darauf trat Deutschland der NATO bei.

Zwei Jahre später – im März 1957 – unterzeichneten Deutschland, Frankreich, Italien und die Benelux-Staaten die Römischen Verträge zur Gründung einer Europäischen Wirtschaftsgemeinschaft. Die Römischen Verträge wurden zur Grundlage eines immer wieder von Krisen und Rückschlägen belasteten Weges, der aber schließlich zur heutigen Europäischen Union mit inzwischen 27 Mitgliedern führte. Zunächst ging es langsam voran: Erst 16 Jahre später, 1973, schlossen sich Großbritannien, Irland und Dänemark an. 1981 trat Griechenland bei, 1986 Spanien und Portugal. Die Einbindung in ein geeintes und freies Europa ermöglichte die Wiedervereinigung Deutschlands mit Zustimmung aller seiner Nachbarn. Die Konzeption Adenauers, die Einheit Deutschlands und zugleich die europäische Einigung zu erreichen, wurde von Helmut Kohl 1990 vollendet.

Und Europa wuchs weiter: Österreich, Schweden und Finnland kamen 1995 hinzu. Am 1. Mai 2004 kam es zur Osterweiterung: Acht Staaten des früheren Warschauer Pakts sowie Malta und Zypern traten bei. Zuletzt folgten am 1. Januar 2007 Bulgarien und Rumänien. Von Anfang an war klar, dass die Europäische Union selbstverständlich eines Tages auch die Länder Osteuropas umfassen musste. Ihnen musste die Tür für den Beitritt offen gehalten werden, wenn die sowjetische Vorherrschaft überwunden sein sollte. Nur so konnte aus einer überwiegend west- und später auch nordeuropäischen Union tatsächlich eine Europäische Union werden.

Die Frage nach Krieg und Frieden stellt sich in Europa heute, Gott sei Dank, nicht mehr. Europa, das bedeutet das Ende selbstzerstörerischer Rivalitäten, das Ende autoritärer Regime, das Ende von Bruderkriegen. Friede ist in Europa selbstverständlich geworden – vielleicht zu selbstverständlich. Zum ersten Mal ist eine Generation herangewachsen, die sich um vieles Gedanken machen mag, die aber nicht fürchten muss, ihr Leben mit 22, 23 Jahren auf Schlachtfeldern in der Normandie, in der Champagne, in Flandern oder in Polen zu beenden. Europa gründet auf der Einsicht, dass Frieden, Freiheit und Wohlstand unseres Kontinents nur durch einen engen Verbund seiner Staaten dauerhaft gewährleistet werden können. In guten und erst recht in schlechten Zeiten!

Europa ist ein Wirtschaftsgebiet, ein Binnenmarkt. Ein Viertel des weltweiten Bruttoinlandsprodukts (BIP) wird von den EU-Mitgliedsstaaten erwirtschaftet. Ein Fünftel des weltweiten Warenaufkommens wird im europäischen Binnenmarkt produziert. Die gemeinsame Währung wurde am 1. Januar 1999 als Buchgeld und am 1. Januar 2002 als allgemeines Zahlungsmittel in der Eurozone eingeführt. Nicht in 27, aber immerhin in 17 Staaten. Ein mutiger Schritt, den allen voran Helmut Kohl und François Mitterrand wagten: eine Währungsunion mit einer Europäischen Zentralbank (EZB) – geschaffen nach dem Vorbild der Deutschen Bundesbank, politisch unabhängig, mit der Wahrung der Preisstabilität als oberstes Ziel – und einem Stabilitäts- und Wachstumspakt. Er fordert von den Mitgliedsländern die Begrenzung ihres Haushaltsdefizits und ihrer Verschuldung – und soll so finanzpolitische Stabilität in der Eurozone garantieren.

II. Das Problem der Staatsverschuldung

Heute wissen wir: Die Einführung des Euro wurde nicht hinreichend genug abgesichert, die Beitrittskandidaten nicht kritisch genug geprüft. 2002 überschritten ausgerechnet die damalige Bundesregierung Schröder und Frankreich

als Erste die festgeschriebenen Defizitgrenzen und verstießen somit gegen den
Stabilitäts- und Wachstumspakt. Weitere Ursachen für die gegenwärtige Krise
der Eurozone kommen hinzu. Eine Krise – dies muss in aller Deutlichkeit gesagt werden – die keine Krise des Euros ist, sondern eine Krise der Staatsschulden und der Haushalte in einigen Ländern der Eurozone: eine Staatsschulden-
krise und eine Haushaltskrise. Lassen Sie mich die Ursachen wenigstens in
Stichworten nennen: die Immobilienkrise – infolge des Platzens der Immobi-
lienblase in den USA im Jahr 2007 – und deren Ausweitung zur Weltfinanzkri-
se; in dessen Folge der Zusammenbruch des Bankhauses Lehman Brothers im
September 2008 sowie die darauffolgende Ausweitung der Weltfinanz- zur
Weltwirtschaftskrise. Regierungen und Notenbanken griffen weltweit ein, hielten die Funktionsfähigkeit des Finanzsystems aufrecht. Sie verhinderten damit
den Zusammenbruch der Weltwirtschaft.

Eine weltweite Rezession ist dagegen nicht verhindert worden. In Deutschland ging das BIP 2009 um fünf Prozent zurück, in den USA um 3,5 Prozent.
Die Bundesregierung sah sich veranlasst, die schwindende Nachfrage mit zwei
Konjunkturprogrammen in Höhe von zusammen nahezu 80 Milliarden Euro
auszugleichen. Mit Erfolg: Die deutsche Wirtschaft wuchs bereits 2010 wieder
um 3,7 Prozent und 2011 um drei Prozent. Die Folge war ein massiver Anstieg
der Verschuldung: In den fünf Jahren seit 2007 hat Deutschland mit 500 Milliarden Euro so viele Schulden aufgenommen wie in den vierzig Jahren zwischen
Gründung der Bundesrepublik und dem Mauerfall. In den USA beträgt der
Schuldenstand inzwischen annähernd hundert Prozent, in Großbritannien acht-
zig Prozent der Wirtschaftsleistung. Die Länder der Eurozone bezahlten die
Weltwirtschaftskrise mit einem deutlich erhöhten Schuldenstand: 2007 lag die
Staatsverschuldung der Eurozone bei rund 6.000 Milliarden Euro. Bis Ende
2011 stieg sie auf nahezu 8.350 Milliarden Euro.

Einer wettbewerbsfähigen Volkswirtschaft wie der deutschen traut man zu,
diese Schuldenlast langfristig tilgen zu können, anderen Ländern dagegen nicht.
Vor allem jenen nicht, die immer noch in einer wirtschaftlichen Krise stecken
oder deren Wettbewerbsfähigkeit sich bereits zuvor verschlechtert hatte. Allen
voran Griechenland: Es war Helmut Kohl, der – nicht mehr als Kanzler – die
damalige Bundesregierung Schröder warnte, Griechenland in die Eurozone aufzunehmen. Seine Warnung blieb ungehört. Mit falschen Darstellungen hat
Griechenland den wahren Zustand seiner Wirtschaft verschleiert – bis 2010, als
man das Staatsdefizit deutlich nach oben korrigierte. Daraufhin stiegen die Zinsen für griechische Staatsanleihen drastisch, die Finanzmärkte verloren das
Vertrauen in die Solidität der griechischen Staatsfinanzen. Im Mai 2010 musste
ein erstes Rettungspaket in Höhe von 110 Milliarden Euro geschnürt werden.

Heute, über zwei Jahre später, umfasst der temporäre Rettungsschirm EFSF
(Europäische Finanzstabilisierungsfazilität) 750 Milliarden Euro. Die Einrich-

tung des dauerhaften Rettungsschirms ESM (Europäischer Stabilitätsmechanismus) ist beschlossen. Inzwischen stehen auch Irland, Portugal und Zypern unter dem EFSF. Spanien hat Finanzhilfen für seinen Bankensektor beantragt. Italien kämpft mit Struktur- und Sparmaßnahmen bislang erfolgreich dagegen, Hilfen in Anspruch nehmen zu müssen. Es hat sich aber auf dem EU-Gipfel Ende Juni vorsorglich leichteren Zugang zum Euro-Rettungsschirm erstritten. Ursache der Finanzierungsschwierigkeiten dieser Staaten sind nicht allein deren übermäßige Staatsschulden. Sie haben in den vergangenen Jahren deutlich an Wettbewerbsfähigkeit eingebüßt: Anstatt mithilfe des niedrigen Zinsniveaus, das ihnen der Beitritt zur Eurozone ermöglichte, ihre Investitions- und Standortbedingungen zu verbessern, neigten sie zu einer hohen importorientierten Konsumneigung, überdurchschnittlichem schuldenfinanziertem Wachstum und mangelnden Reformanstrengungen. Nötig ist also die Bereitschaft der Krisenländer zu strukturellen Reformen zur Stärkung ihrer Wettbewerbsfähigkeit.

Vor allem aber sind solide Staatsfinanzen entscheidende Grundlage einer stabilen Währung. Die Architektur der Eurozone hat sich hier bislang nicht bewährt. Der Stabilitäts- und Wachstumspakt war wenig wirkungsvoll. Statt Verstöße zu sanktionieren, wurden seine Kriterien aufgeweicht. Es zeigt sich: Die rechtliche Ausgestaltung der Währungsunion reichte nicht aus, um sie als Stabilitätsunion zu etablieren. Alle EU-Mitgliedsstaaten müssen verpflichtet werden, eine strikte nationale Schuldenbremse einzuführen. Der „Fiskalpakt" stellt einen wichtigen Schritt innerhalb der Wirtschafts- und Währungsunion auf dem Weg zu einer Stabilitätsunion dar.

III. Solidarität setzt Solidität voraus

Nur wer den Fiskalvertrag ratifiziert und umsetzt, dem werden künftig Hilfen aus dem ESM gewährt. Es wird keine Leistung ohne Gegenleistungen geben. Solidarität setzt Solidität voraus – ein vor allem für Deutschland wichtiges und entscheidendes Prinzip. Der ESM wird 700 Milliarden Euro umfassen. Der deutsche Anteil daran wird mehr als ein Viertel betragen – knapp 190 Milliarden Euro.

Die Solidarität der Euro-Länder untereinander ist zur Bewältigung der Krise unerlässlich. Dabei muss gelten: Niemand darf übermäßig belastet werden. Wer meint, von Deutschland einen zunehmend größeren Beitrag fordern zu müssen, sei gewarnt: Man darf Deutschland nicht überfordern. Die deutsche Wirtschaft ist bemerkenswert gesund – den Menschen in Deutschland geht es gut. Aber ein überfordertes Deutschland würde die Hilfe, die von ihm erwartet wird, nicht mehr leisten können. Zu Recht lehnt Deutschland eine Vergemeinschaftung der Schulden aller Euro-Mitglieder ab. Eurobonds sind nicht das richtige Mittel zur Bekämpfung der Krise. Deutschland weiß, welche Verantwortung es bei der

Bewältigung der Krise trägt und dass es hohen Erwartungen gegenübersteht. Deutschland trägt als bevölkerungsreichstes und wirtschaftlich stärkstes Land besondere Verantwortung für Europa und den Euro. Nicht alle Deutschen sind über unsere neue Rolle glücklich. Manche empfinden sie als Last. Aber wir müssen die Realität annehmen und akzeptieren.

Deutschland spielt heute eine überaus verantwortliche Rolle in Europa, gemeinsam mit Frankreich. Daran hat der Wechsel von Nicolas Sarkozy zu François Hollande nichts geändert. Natürlich ergeben sich infolge des Regierungswechsels in Frankreich neue Herausforderungen für das deutsch-französische Gespann: Hollande hat im Wahlkampf angekündigt, den Fiskalvertrag neu verhandeln zu wollen – die Bundesregierung lehnt dies ab; Hollande setzt auf Wachstum durch Konjunkturprogramme – Angela Merkel auf Wachstum durch Strukturreformen; Frankreich sagt Ja zu Eurobonds – Deutschland sagt Nein; Frankreich will mehr Handlungsraum für die EZB – Deutschland ihre Unabhängigkeit bewahren. Nun werden in Wahlkämpfen häufig Dinge angekündigt, die nach dem Wahltag nicht mehr so heiß gegessen werden. Auch nach den Wahlen in Frankreich wissen wir: Die deutsch-französische Freundschaft ist für beide Länder Staatsräson. Beide haben sich der Rettung und der Stabilität des Euros verschrieben. Und beide müssen sich nun erst aneinander gewöhnen – so, wie sich Angela Merkel und Nicolas Sarkozy aneinander gewöhnt haben und wie sich auch Kohl und Mitterrand aneinander gewöhnen mussten.

Großbritannien dagegen fühlt sich nur bedingt als Mitglied der Europäischen Union – und rückt von ihr ab, wo und wann es nur geht; es ist der Währungsunion ferngeblieben; es ist Schengen ferngeblieben; es lehnt den Fiskalpakt ab. Es will sich nicht an der Euro-Rettung beteiligen. Schon in seiner Züricher Rede hat Winston Churchill 1946 von einem Europäischen Bundesstaat gesprochen, ohne England einzubeziehen. Schon 1930 hat er in einem Zeitungsinterview gesagt: „With Europe, not of it!" Nach wie vor ist man der Überzeugung, dass man in der globalisierten Welt auch allein bestehen könne. Eine Meinung, die ich ganz und gar nicht teile.

27 Mitglieder umfasst die Europäische Union derzeit – und eine große Zahl weiterer Staaten will Mitglied werden. Erstaunlicherweise sogar während der Krise. Mit Kroatien sind die Beitrittsverhandlungen abgeschlossen. Mit Island und Montenegro wird derzeit verhandelt. Mazedonien und Serbien sind Beitrittskandidaten. Albanien hat die Mitgliedschaft beantragt. Mit Blick auf die Staaten des ehemaligen Jugoslawiens meine ich: Wenn sie die Kriterien zum Beitritt erfüllen, dann sollen sie beitreten. Die Türkei ist Kandidat für einen Beitritt; seit 2005 wird darüber verhandelt. Aber wo sind die Grenzen Europas? Nach gegenwärtigem Stand der Verhandlungen ist die Türkei nicht beitrittsfähig; z. B. unterliegen die Meinungs- und Religionsfreiheit massiven Einschränkungen.

IV. Wie wird das Europa von morgen aussehen?

Und die Europäische Union ist gegenwärtig nicht aufnahmefähig. Wir sollten uns vor so weitgehenden, weiteren Beitrittsentscheidungen zunächst klar werden, wie das Europa von morgen aussehen soll. Welche Baupläne gibt es und was taugen sie? Quo vadis Europa? Die Lage in Europa ist ernst. Die Probleme sind noch lange nicht gelöst. Wie soll Europa morgen aussehen? Ein Staatenbund ist zu wenig. Ein Staatenbund hat keine gemeinsame Währung, schafft seine Grenzen nicht ab, hat keine gemeinsame Regierung. Ein Bundesstaat? Passt ein Bundesstaat zu Europa? Ist die Zeit dafür schon reif? Ich habe meine Zweifel, auch wenn es ein Fernziel sein mag. Die meisten EU-Mitglieder sind gegenwärtig zu einem so weitgehenden Souveränitätsverzicht nicht bereit. Sie wollen vom Nationalstaat nicht Abschied nehmen. Unsere europäische Kultur hat gemeinsame Wurzeln, die Antike, das Judentum, das Christentum, die Aufklärung; aber der Lebensvollzug der europäischen Länder ist unterschiedlich. Vereinfacht gesagt: In Nordeuropa lebt man, um zu arbeiten, in Südeuropa arbeitet man, um zu leben. Wir wollen die Nationen in Europa nicht auflösen. Europa kann die Nationen nicht ersetzen. Es soll sie befähigen, in der globalisierten Welt unsere gemeinsame Rolle wahrzunehmen. Wir brauchen eine föderale Ordnung: Europa wird föderal sein oder es wird nicht sein!

Ich meine, wir müssen etwas Neues schaffen, was es bisher so noch nicht gegeben hat. Einen Staatenverbund, in dem unter strenger Beachtung des Solidaritätsprinzips einerseits die gemeinsame Handlungs- und Entscheidungsfähigkeit der Europäischen Union in Fragen der Finanzen, der Wirtschaft, aber auch der Sicherheits- und Außenpolitik gesichert wird, in dem aber andererseits auch die bisher übertragenen Zuständigkeiten überprüft und Rückverlagerung von Kompetenzen von Brüssel an die Mitgliedsstaaten nicht ausgeschlossen wird.

Im Zuge der Notwendigkeit, Rettungsschirme gegen die Krise aufzuspannen, für die es der Zustimmung der nationalen Gesetzgeber – in Deutschland Bundestag und Bundesrat – bedarf, ist es in Deutschland zu einer Debatte über die Tragfähigkeit unseres Grundgesetzes gekommen. Der Präsident des deutschen Verfassungsgerichtes, Voßkuhle, hat angemahnt, dass bei fortschreitender europäischer Integration die Vereinbarkeit mit dem Grundgesetz „wohl weitgehend ausgeschöpft" sei. Wenn weitere Souveränitätsrechte abgegeben würden, müsse sich Deutschland eine neue Verfassung geben. Das geht über die Zuständigkeit des Bundesverfassungsgerichtes hinaus. Das Bundesverfassungsgericht ist Hüter der Verfassung, ist „Letztinterpret" unseres Grundgesetzes im Spannungsfeld zwischen Recht und Politik. Politik machen soll es nicht. Es ist eine Grenzüberschreitung, wenn dieses Gericht das Grundgesetz quasi selbst ändern will. Das darf nur der Gesetzgeber, also Bundestag und Bundesrat.

In Deutschland heute eine neue Verfassung zu schreiben, wäre ein gewaltiges Vorhaben. Es wäre viel schwerer als 1948, als 68 Mitglieder des Parlamentarischen Rates in wenigen Monaten einen so herausragenden Text zustande gebracht haben. Das liegt nicht nur an der veränderten medialen Öffentlichkeit. Es liegt insbesondere daran, dass heute die Gemeinsamkeit über den Inhalt in Frage gestellt wird, die 1948 nach der Erfahrung der Diktatur da war. Wir würden die Büchse der Pandora öffnen. Und das sollten wir auf keinen Fall tun. Ich glaube: Wo Änderungen unseres Grundgesetzes unabdingbar nötig sind, damit Europa handlungsfähig ist, sind sie möglich. Auf absehbare Zeit können wir die notwendigen Kompetenzverzichte auch auf der Basis des Grundgesetzes mit der einen oder anderen Änderung rechtlich ermöglichen.

Am Vorabend der Präsidentschaftswahl in unserem Gastland erlauben Sie mir den Blick noch kurz auf die transatlantischen Beziehungen zwischen den USA und Europa zu richten. Unverändert sind die USA der wichtigste Partner für Europa und insbesondere für Deutschland. Wir verdanken unseren Freunden diesseits des Atlantiks viel: Es waren die USA, die unter Aufbringung großer Opfer Europa zunächst von der NS-Diktatur befreiten. Mit dem Marshall-Plan haben sie dann wirtschaftliche Hilfe geleistet und politische Hilfestellung gegeben und damit zum Wiederaufbau Europas beigetragen. Ohne George Bush, ohne Michael Gorbatschow und ohne Helmut Kohl wäre es nicht zur Wiederherstellung unserer staatlichen Einheit gekommen.

Leider ist derzeit die Aufmerksamkeit gegenüber der jeweils anderen Seite rückläufig. Europa ist mit der Bewältigung der Krise in der Eurozone beschäftigt. Es wendet sich vornehmlich nach innen – und seinem südlichen Nachbarn zu, Nordafrika, den Ländern der arabischen Welt, wo die Freiheitsbewegungen nicht ohne Auswirkungen auf die EU bleiben. In den USA ist man ebenfalls sehr mit sich selbst beschäftigt. Dass beide Parteien einen Wahlkampf aus innenpolitischen Motiven gegen Europa führen, bedaure ich dabei zutiefst.

V. Zwischen den USA und Europa darf keine Kluft entstehen

Beide Seiten, USA wie Europa, müssen daran arbeiten, dass in ihren Beziehungen keine Kluft entsteht. Denn nur gemeinsam werden wir die vor uns liegenden Herausforderungen bewältigen. Es gibt genügend Gründe, dass wir uns als Amerikaner und als Europäer zusammensetzen, um über die moralischen Grundlagen und die konkreten Probleme unserer Volkswirtschaften und die gemeinsame Weltwirtschaft sprechen. Wir müssen uns auf unsere Gemeinsamkeiten besinnen. Wir können die Probleme nur gemeinsam lösen oder wir werden sie gar nicht lösen. Sie sind zahlreich: die Nachwirkungen der Weltfinanz- und Wirtschaftskrise, der Klimawandel, internationaler Terrorismus, Proliferation, die iranischen Atombestrebungen mit ihren Konsequenzen, der israelischpalästinensische Konflikt, der Wandel in der arabischen Welt. Eine lange Liste. Weiteres ließe sich hinzufügen.

Wenn in den USA im November die Entscheidung gefallen ist und wenn – hoffentlich gegen Ende des Jahres – in Europa hinsichtlich der Krise in der Eurozone ein wenig Ruhe eingekehrt ist, dann ist es Zeit, sich beiderseits des Atlantiks wieder der Vorteile unserer traditionellen Beziehungen zu besinnen. Auch bei uns stehen im Herbst nächsten Jahres Bundestagswahlen an und ihr Ausgang ist ungewiss, zumal das bei uns geltende Verhältniswahlrecht zur Folge hat, dass nicht nur zwei, sondern mehrere Parteien in den Bundestag einziehen werden. Nur eines scheint mir rebus sic stantibus sicher: Frau Merkel wird auch danach deutsche Bundeskanzlerin bleiben.

Man kann vor der Fülle der Probleme die Augen verschließen oder in Panik geraten. Die unübersichtliche Situation von heute erfordert Mut – Mut von Politikern, aber auch von den Bürgerinnen und Bürgern unserer Länder. Wir brauchen Bürger, die den Mut haben, sich zu orientieren, sich zu besinnen, anzupacken und ihre Zukunft gemeinsam zu sichern. Nicht Bürger, die nur zum Protest aufrufen und widersprechen. Mut braucht es nämlich nicht nur zum Aufbegehren gegen etwas; Mut ist vor allem erforderlich, um für das als richtig Erkannte einzustehen und zu kämpfen. Mutige Bürger braucht das Land! Mutige Bürger braucht Europa!

Um am Schluss zu Europa zurückzukehren: der Namensgeber unserer Stiftung hat einmal gesagt: „Die Einheit Europas war ein Traum von Wenigen. Sie wurde eine Hoffnung für Viele. Sie ist heute eine Notwendigkeit für uns alle. Sie ist [...] notwendig für unsere Sicherheit, für unsere Freiheit, für unser Dasein als Nation und als geistig schöpferische Völkergemeinschaft."

Zusammenfassung

Der Weg der europäischen Einigung war ein langer, steiniger und hindernisreicher, aber alles in allem sehr erfolgreicher und beispielloser Weg der Einigung eines Kontinentes, dessen Geschichte jahrhundertelang von Kriegen und Konflikten geprägt gewesen ist. Heute ist Europa ein anderes Wort für Frieden! Europa – das ist die Antwort auf Krieg und Vernichtung. In Zeiten der Krise hat Europa einen Punkt erreicht, an dem die Frage „Quo vadis Europa?" einer Antwort bedarf. Wohin soll der europäische Einigungsprozess führen: Zu einem Staatenbund? Einem Bundesstaat? Einem Staatenverbund? Die Krise ist Herausforderung und Chance zugleich: Die Herausforderung, einen Ausweg aus der Krise zu finden, der langfristig trägt und Krisen dieser Art künftig verhindert, und die Chance, Europa fortzuentwickeln; das Haus Europa vor gegenwärtigen und künftigen Bedrohungen sicher zu machen, damit das Friedenswerk Europa eine gute und erfolgreiche Zukunft hat.

Summary

The road to European integration was a long and troubled one with many obstacles.
However, it was also a successful and unprecedented road to the unification of a continent whose history for centuries had been marked by wars and conflict. Today, Europe
is another word for peace! Europe – it is the response to war and destruction. At this
time of crisis, Europe has reached a point at which the question "Quo vadis Europe?"
needs an answer. Where should the European unification process lead us: To a confederation? A federation? A union of states? The crisis is both a challenge and an opportunity: The challenge of finding a way out of the crisis which will be sustainable and will
prevent such crises in the future and the opportunity of further developing Europe; protecting the House of Europe from current and future threats and thus ensuring a positive
and successful future for the work towards peace in Europe.

Private Property:
Indispensable for Freedom and Liberty

By Bernard Dobranski

James Madison described property as, "that domination which one man claims and exercises over the external things of the world, in exclusion of every other individual."[1] You can have tyranny with private property, but you cannot have freedom and rule of law without it. Men such as Madison helped found the United States of America and believed governments are formed to secure citizens' rights, including property rights – not to create an entity to take away these rights. After all, if they believed it is wrong for individuals to take from one another, then it is equally wrong for the government to take from its citizens.

The right to private property has long been recognized as a fundamental right, not only in the United States, but throughout the course of history. This paper addresses private property rights as a necessary condition to liberty and freedom. Part I examines private property rights as inherent rights that transcend government by looking at different forms of governments from primitive society up through Marxism and into capitalism. It concludes by finding private property rights prosper most readily in a capitalist society. This is because the structure of capitalism supports competition and efficiency by turning assets into capital and allowing commerce to flow. This in turn promotes the common good and encourages private property rights.

Part II addresses the right to private property and its root in Christianity. In Christianity, to own private property is man's natural inherent right. It looks at the writings of recent scholars including Richard Pipes, Benjamin Barros, and Tom Bethell, to examine the connection between the right to private property and other fundamental rights such as the right to life, liberty, and freedom. The section two concludes by looking at Catholic teaching and doctrine that incorporates the basic Christian understanding of property rights as a natural right to man along with more recent papal encyclicals addressing property rights amidst modern day governments.

---

[1] Quoted in Ralph Ketcham, *James Madison: A Biography* (Charlottesville and London: University Press of Virginia, 1990), p. 330.

I. Private Property Rights in History and Government

Property rights have been a consistent impetus to the creation of government and law from the very beginning with edicts up through present day democratic legislation. Civilization first developed from early kingdoms and empires in order to respect an individual's right to own, trade, and devise property. Protecting property and commerce was of primary importance in these first societies. By protecting property, a society demonstrated that it valued a sense of justice.

In modern governments, protecting property is an absolute necessity to promoting the common good. Property is innately connected to a man's livelihood, and early codes and oaths were meant to preserve this livelihood in a just manner. In fact, the first governments functioned to protect property, and private property gave early legal codes their primary purpose.

Section 1 looks at property rights as rights that are inherent because they are rights that have been present irrespective of government. Section 2 traces property rights from pre-government civilizations through tribal and religious societies in an effort to demonstrate their inherency.

1. Private Property Rights are Inherent and Transcend Government

Property rights in its earliest forms came from culture and community. After all, a person living alone does not need to worry about property rights.[2] Even without detailing dominion through biblical creation, man needs property for his own self-preservation. This can be seen through the basic necessities each man needs, such as food, clothing and shelter. Individuals immediately characterize these basics as their *own* food, clothing, and shelter. If man does not hold dominion over each of these necessities he is unable to live. Essentially each person's existence implicitly affirms the necessity of private property rights, and these rights function from each person's cultivation and accumulation of private property.

Every early civilization placed property rights among cultural values that were important to them. And each civilization had methods of measuring accumulated property. Whether an individual's worth or wage was measured by salt as in Roman culture or by livestock as found in the early accounts given in the Book of Job, each early society had methods of determining and allowing the accumulation of property of one versus all others in the society.

---

[2] See generally, Max Gluckman, *Politics, Law and Ritual in Tribal Society* (New Brunswick, New Jersey: Transaction, 2012).

These property rights were implicitly assumed in early civilizations. Even though some early tribal or religious societies may not have had written or regularized law, because there were property rights, there was essentially law without government.[3] The anthropologist's idea that law is there to "curb human inclinations, passions or instinctive drives" suggests that early societies functioned on customs in a manner similar to a legal system without a state government or organized government.[4] Although early societies were able to function to a certain degree based on a common morality and the social norms of a community at large, eventually there had to be something more. Legal mechanisms needed to be implemented to enforce such grounds and prevent violation of standards of conduct.

Given that property rights are to a degree implicit, this suggests that governments are created to protect property rights, and that one of the principal purposes of government is to safeguard these rights.[5] According to Lockean theory, a government is grounded upon the principle that authority comes from the consent of the governed.[6] Thus, in a broad sense, people sustain government so that it may support the inherent rights of its citizens. If governments are formed for protecting rights, including property rights, then governments are successful when they allow for private property. In Section 2, it will be seen that while many forms of government recognize and even protect property rights to varying degrees, property rights thrive in a capitalist setting.

2. Different Societal and Governmental Recognition of Private Property Rights and its Strength in Capitalism

Property rights induce the creation of wealth and prosperity. Individual ownership provides for owners to take account of their possessions, and paves the way for law. Property rights are in many ways a prerequisite for self-government. Where property rights are respected there are better conditions,

---

[3] Bruce L. Benson, "Enforcement of Private Property Rights in Primitive Societies: Law Without Government," *Journal of Libertarian Studies* 9 (Winter 1989), p 1.

[4] Bronislaw Malinowski, *Crime and Custom in Savage Society* (London: Routledge and Kegan Paul, 1926), as quoted by Benson, ibid., p. 3.

[5] Ellen Frankel Paul, "Freedom of Contract and the 'Political Economy' of *Lochner v. New York*," 1 NYU J. L & Liberty 515, 528–530 (2005).

[6] See, John Locke, *Two Treatises of Government* (1689); see esp. 2nd Treatise (ch. 8, nos. 95, 106, 119, and 122).

and people are attracted to communities and governments where property rights are respected.[7]

Looking at property rights in Hammurabi's code, Judeo-Christian law and through Greek and Roman traditions, it is evident that property rights have had a place in government. But it is later, with the age of exploration and industrialization that modern property rights expanded and were redefined in the sense that land and a chance at private property was more readily available to the masses. Then with the rise of Marxism, property rights took a back seat to concern for equality of distribution of wealth. Finally, property rights reach a sort of zenith in capitalist society where ownership of assets is supported and encouraged allowing society to flourish and promote the common good. Hammurabi's infamous code, and his "eye for an eye" structure provided an early Babylonian legal system that functioned through civil law edicts. There were no presumed criminal law prosecutions.[8] The code was set up so that law essentially revolved around property rights. Proscribed wrongdoings, such as theft or arson, and the prosecution of these felonies, were based on the goal of trying to limit violence against individuals and their property. This structure was adopted so that the strong could not oppress the weak, and justice was in relation to wrongs against property of nobles, commoners, slaves, and particularly that of the King.[9]

Where early societies could not provide for the organization necessary for state investigations or prosecution of unjust taking of private property, civil law provided a means of justice and compensation.[10] Thus, commerce and trade necessitated the code to protect property rights of those in early civilizations.

The Hebrew people embrace the value of respecting private property in part. Property rights were addressed in the biblical Decalogue, the most well known symbol of Judeo-Christian justice. The prohibition of taking another's property is the seventh commandment. Stealing property is also the very first sin recounted in Genesis where Adam steals an apple from the tree of knowledge. Adam then lies about the theft by accusing Eve of ordering him to do so. Thus stealing and lying become the greatest indicators of man's fallen nature. Unjust taking embodies immorality to the core of Western civilization.

---

[7] Richard T. Ely, et. al., *The Foundations of National Prosperity: Studies in the Conservation of Permanent National Resources* (New York: Macmillan, 1920), pp. 313–315.

[8] Robert W. Shaffern, *Law and Justice from Antiquity to Enlightenment* (Lantham, MD: Rowman & Littlefield, 2009), p. 3. The code, which was enacted "in order that the strong might not oppress the weak that justice be given the orphan and the widow" focused its justice with regards to property of nobles, commoners, and slaves.

[9] Ibid.

[10] Ibid.

Society respecting "property in common" first arrives in Western thought and philosophy in the legal structures of society in the Greek traditions, and from early writers like Socrates and Plato.[11] Although Plato initially created a societal picture where private property is stripped and held in common, over time he developed a place for private property.[12] In *Laws*, Plato fashioned a society where there was acceptance of the existence of private property. However, for Plato's society the accumulation of property was not the focus of an ideal society.[13]

For Aristotle, property being held privately was about efficiency. Private property was valuable as the most efficient use of property within society. Property also served as a manner of maintaining and honoring the individual within the society.[14] Recognizing private property meant recognizing individuals and their rights in society. Aristotle's positions on private property were enhanced and strengthened under Christian analysis in the Middle Ages.

If private property had any insufficiencies for Aristotle, then reasonable government regulations corrected such issues.[15] While Aristotle believed government did not function to secure and protect property, he held that government's fundamental function is to protect the individual and his ability to achieve happiness and virtue.[16] And part of achieving happiness and virtue for an individual in Aristotle's society was ownership of property.

The accumulation of property and finance was particularly important to the Romans.[17] Cicero pronounced that human reason allows for the creation of government for the chief purpose of securing private property as necessary to an individual's self preservation.[18] Dignitaries were given undisputed rights and ownership in the same strict manners of contract and trade. Accumulating property provided the security that allowed individuals like Cicero to function.[19] Property meant power. The trading and accumulation of estates and pro-

---

[11] Kathy Eden, *Friends Hold All Things in Common: Tradition, Intellectual Property and the Adages of Erasmus* (New Haven, CT: Yale University Press, 2001), pp. 85–87.

[12] Ibid., p. 85.

[13] Ibid., pp. 86–87.

[14] William Mathie, "Property in the Political Science of Aristotle," in *Theories of Property: Aristotle to the Present*, edited by Anthony Parel and Thomas Flanagan (Waterloo, Ontario: Wilfrid Laurier University Press, 1979), pp. 25–27.

[15] Ibid., p. 27.

[16] Ibid., pp. 27–28.

[17] Neal Wood, *Cicero's Social and Political Thought* (Berkeley: University of California Press, 1988), pp. 105–107.

[18] Ibid., p. 105.

[19] Ibid., p. 106.

perties became more prevalent as income became tied to financing through security, as will be seen later with modern capitalist societies.[20]

Christian teachings warn against the veneration of property just as Plato did, but Christianity views private property as a vehicle for virtue through diligence and charitable giving. These concepts developed during an age of feudalism where property was held at large by kings and noblemen. There were however, subsistence property rights that were held by commoners and even servants in reward for being loyal subjects. As the middle ages came to a close, more developed trade and markets emerged in cities, and the future was filled with the discovery of seemingly endless lands in the New World. Property and its future would never be the same.

The Renaissance sparked a new age of invention, culture, growth, and expansion. The rise of a merchant class brought with it an influence on exploration and development of markets, as new lands (and hence, property) were discovered in a new world. The sixteenth-century discovery of the Americas was a stunning show of Europe's thirst to attain, explore, colonize, and claim new lands for their kingdoms and nations.

Rapid exploration and colonization was aided by additional backing from growing financial lenders and underwriters. This cooperation served as a prologue to the future use of capital for global investments to spread influence and wealth among emerging markets. What was initially marketed to investors as a means to seek treasure in the New World grew into colonies and new markets that could both provide raw materials and consume the resulting goods produced in Europe. Stock companies and king's grants provided land for anyone daring enough to find a territory they were willing to cultivate.

This abundance of property in the Americas showed the world how much could be gained through hard work and good stewardship in the New World. This ideology persists today among the ever-increasing immigrant population of the United States. In early America there was enough land to carve out some for each person willing to take charge, care for, and develop it. As colonies existed for the benefit of their mother countries, it was the taxing against colonial subjects – or really what was seen as an unjust governmental taking of private property – that led to the American Revolution. It was this revolution that sparked a new realm of thought holding that government existed to protect life, liberty, property, and the pursuit of happiness.

As the United States grew after the civil war, so did markets and industry. The ability to attain wealth in America shifted from being tied to family estates. Families such as the Vanderbilts, showed that one could amass wealth inde-

---

[20] Ibid.

pendently of lineage. Capitalism's rampant success coupled with the unchecked industrialism of nineteenth-century Europe and America permitted new perspectives of property to emerge as a growing class of factory and industrial workers saw a readily apparent difference between the compensation of management and worker classes.

The disparate difference between working classes and the growing wealth of upper-class entrepreneurs, referred to as "bourgeoisie," led to a growing outlook of economic unfairness. This accumulation of private property among the bourgeoisie led to governmental involvement in redistributing and in some cases abolishing rights to private property. It turned into an upheaval of society ruled by class struggle.

Dividing the two principal classes into an owner class and worker class, Karl Marx promoted socialism and the distribution of property. He maintained that the owner class would always take advantage of the labor provided by the worker class to make more profits unless a political revolution or upheaval through unions occurred. Then the working class "proletariat" would be brought to power and all rights to private property would be abrogated, eventually leading to a classless society.

Along Marxist lines, French anarchist Pierre-Joseph Proudhon wrote, "Property is theft!"[21] Proudhon believed the use and abuse of property was the root of societal ills in preventing a common good. Marx's only criticism of Proudhon was that his statement suggests that there is such a thing as property to begin with, which directly opposed Marx's notion that there is no such thing as property.

Still, no matter how they labeled the legitimacy of property, this perspective and view of government functioned on a view of how property should be used to properly effectuate the common good of society. In Marx's case, this was through being evenly distributed and having no individual ownership. While private property was despised, and even seen as a common theft against all mankind, it was this perspective of property that gave rise to the governmental perspective. It is no coincidence that as individual property rights would ebb within this political philosophy, the growth of government would crest at new heights that could only crash downward.

As the Soviet Union (1922–1991), rose and fell as a global political power in the twentieth-century, the difficulties of maintaining production efficiency became apparent as property owned in common was not being used efficiently. Common property was not being used to produce enough to maintain the com-

---

[21] *From Georges Sorel: Essays in Socialism and Philosophy*, edited by John L. Stanley (New Brunswick, New Jersey: Transaction, 1987), p. 18.

mon good. Further, the abolition of property unintentionally created a new class system ruled by a political class made up of government and political elites rather than the owner-based bourgeoisie. This structure failed to provide the support necessary for the society.

With the rise of modern capitalism and its system based on private ownership and grounded in acknowledging individual rights, ownership prospered. Capitalism supports ownership rights through its legal structure, and society in turn encourages private property. With capitalism, property can be turned into liquid capital either through a sale of assets or through lines of credits secured on the property. The ability to own property, while having the flexibility to liquefy it encourages ownership as a means of survival. This then promotes the common good by turning the government into a steward of the people it governs.

Property rights have consistently been a key aspect in all forms of government from early tribal societies. Property rights have held a special place in Greek and Roman times, survived Marxism and thrive under capitalism. Property rights are more than just the right to private ownership, because throughout history they have stood for the wider notion of individual rights. Protecting the right to property was a first step in securing other individual rights and in many cases the first example of justice. Governments and societies were formed to protect this fundamental right and from the right to property flows the ability to promote the common good.

II. Private Property Rights as Inherent and Christian

John Adams said, "You have rights antecedent to all earthly governments: rights that cannot be repealed or restrained by human laws; rights derived from the Great Legislator of the universe."[22] John Adams is clearly referring to God, as the Great Legislator. These rights derived from God are explicitly stated in the form of fundamental and unalienable rights in the Declaration of Independence, and the Constitution. The constitution addresses the right to property alongside the right to life and liberty in both the Fifth and the Fourteenth Amendments. Property rights are included in the God-given rights, which indicate our founders' belief that they are both inherent and fundamental. The right to private property as an inherent and fundamental right of man finds its basis

---

[22] James D. Best, *Principled Action: Lessons from the Origins of the American Republic* (Tucson, AZ: Wheatmark, 2012), p. 54.

in Christianity, which teaches private ownership is in conformity with human nature.[23]

Section 1 examines the connection between private property and the right to life, liberty and freedom through the lens of recent scholars, Richard Pipes, Benjamin Barros and Tom Bethell. Each scholar addresses the inherent nature of property rights and its link to other core God-given rights. Section 2 will examine how property rights are also inherently Christian looking at the idea behind the universal destination of goods, the virtue of charity, Pope Leo XIII's encyclical *Rerum Novarum*, and Pope John Paul II's encyclical *Centesimus Annus*.

1. Private Property Rights with Respect to Life, Liberty, and Freedom

John Adams pointed out in 1790, property rights must be secured, or liberty cannot exist.[24] Property has traditionally been seen as a safeguard to liberty, because it sets limits on the reach of a legitimate government. Property rights are a necessary component of self-government. In 1829, Justice Joseph Story noted, "[t]he government can scarcely be called free, where the rights of property are left solely dependent upon the will of a legislative body. The fundamental maxims of a free government seem to require that the rights of personal liberty and private property should be held sacred."[25]

Richard Pipes argues private property is essential for economic development, liberty, and democracy. This is because property "provides the key to the emergence of political and legal institutions that guarantee liberty."[26] Property has the ability to promote stability and constrain the power of government. By placing a restraint on the government this allows the fundamental rights to thrive which the government was created to protect.

D. Benjamin Barros, however, argues that the notion that property and freedom are conceptually connected is actually an illusion. For Barros, property and freedom are linked, but government is still free to interfere with property rights. Thus the question becomes one of degree, and to what extent does prop-

---

[23] Leo XIII, *Rerum Novarum* (1891), para. 11.

[24] John Adams, *Discourses on Davila*, in *The Works of John Adams*, vol. 6, edited by Charles Francis Adams (Boston: Little and Brown, 1851), p. 280.

[25] Wilkinson v. Leland, 27 U.S. 627, 657 (1829).

[26] Richard Pipes, *Property and Freedom* (New York: Knopf, 1999), p. xii.

erty protect freedom, and to what extent is freedom possible without private property.[27]

Barros sees property as an institution that promotes individual freedom in three ways: by creating a zone of individual autonomy and privacy; by distributing power; and by providing access to the resources that people need to be free.[28] Despite the fact Barros has broken up the effects of property on freedom into three different components, the point remains that property rights are connected and necessary for freedom.

Taking a stronger view than Barros, Tom Bethell argues that property rights and their key role in developing societies has been misunderstood for more than a century. He examines history to arrive at the conclusion that the institution of property is inextricably tied to justice and liberty. Only in allowing and supporting private property can civilization prosper.[29]

All three of these scholars demonstrate how property transcends government. In every case, property exists, rights to private property exist, and then government is formed. With a foundation of property rights, the formation of government then serves to protect other inherent individual rights such as the right to life, liberty, and freedom. Although the scholars have slightly varying notions on how, it is clear that property rights are inextricably linked to freedom. This right to property and the ensuing right to freedom that is implicated find their roots in Christianity as will be discussed below.

2. Private Property Rights and Christianity

To own goods privately is a natural right to man. Pope Leo XIII in his encyclical *Rerum Novarum*, addressed the Catholic teaching on the right to property, noting that owning property is in accord with basic human nature. It has already been seen how governments are formed to protect our natural, inherent rights including property, and now that leads to a discussion on how property rights are based in Christianity.

The first pages of the Book of Genesis make it clear that all of creation is a gift from God and meant to be bestowed as a benefit on all men.[30] "God intended the earth with everything contained in it for the use of all human beings

---

[27] D. Benjamin Barros, "Property and Freedom," 4 NYU J. L & Liberty 37–69 (2009).

[28] Ibid.

[29] Tom Bethell, *The Noblest Triumph: Property and Prosperity through the Ages* (New York: St. Martin's, 1999).

[30] *Genesis* 1:3–2:3.

and peoples. Thus, under the leadership of justice and in the company of charity, created goods should be in abundance for all in like manner."[31] This principle is what has come to be known as the universal destination of all goods. In looking at the seventh commandment, the universal destination of all goods, and Pope John Paul II's encyclical *Centesimus Annus*, it is clear that private property rights find their root in Christianity, and in particular in Catholicism.

The seventh commandment and the universal destination of goods form the basis of Catholic teaching of the natural right to private property. The seventh commandment, says "Thou shall not steal."[32] This commandment clearly forbids unjustly taking goods that belong to another. This commandment demands justice and charity in respecting what belongs to others, and it is perhaps the most basic tenet of property rights.

The seventh commandment is the foundation for other core Catholic social teachings. The principle of the universal destination of all goods is based on the belief that God entrusted the earth and all of its resources to mankind.[33] The idea is that the goods of the earth are to be used and divided among all mankind. The notion behind the universal destination of goods does not militate against personal ownership and private property as one might think. To the contrary, private ownership is essential to the ability to freely participate in the universal destination of all goods. Private property is the natural and ordinary way in which we exercise dominion over the things of the earth and provide for ourselves and others.

The key to understanding the role of private property and the universal destination of goods is that private property and individual ownership are not intended for the purpose of individual gain. The purpose of private property is to provide for the common good. Through private property, people have the opportunity to participate in God's plan, and work towards the bigger picture, and for the common good.

This is possible through property rights because it is through personal property that it can be seen that the benefits of work are ordered not to private gain but for the good of all. The universal destination of goods also serves as a reminder that governmental policies should support and encourage this natural right to private property in order to ensure liberty in the sense that each person continues to have the God-given right to private property.

The right to property has been steadfastly held to as an inherent right in Catholic teaching, despite what governments have said throughout time. As an

---

[31] Vatican II: Pastoral Constitution *Gaudium et Spes* (1965).

[32] *Deuteronomy* 5:4–21.

[33] *Catechism of the Catholic Church*, § 2402.

example, in 1891, Pope Leo XIII wrote *Rerum Novarum*, in response to the rise of industrialism that had led to a rise of socialism. Socialists were trying to do away with private property rights by asserting all private property ought to become the property of the state. By having everything become the property of the state, the state would then be able to transfer and apportion property rights to all. The entire scheme behind socialism though with respect to property rights, as Pope Leo pointed out, was that they rob the owner of his rightful possessions, distort the function of the state, and create confusion in communities over ownership.[34]

This teaching was expounded on and reaffirmed in *Centesimus Annus* by Pope John Paul II on the centenary anniversary of the publication of *Rerum Novarum*. Pope John Paul II calls on the state to be an agent of justice and to protect the rights of all citizens. He re-articulates how Catholic social teaching affirms the right to private property, limited only by the common good.[35] Private property is portrayed as an extension of the human person, stressing the inherent nature of private ownership. Pope John Paul II points out that private property is based on the fundamental recognition of human dignity. Man fulfills himself by using his freedom to take the things of the world and make them his own, which is the foundation of private property.[36]

Christianity, and in particular Catholicism, provide the basis for recognizing property as a right inherent to man. Although it has long been recognized as a fundamental right, it is in Catholicism that it can be seen this right is derived from God. It is Catholicism that teaches and explains how private ownership is in accord with human nature.

Conclusion

In this paper it has been seen how the right to property has formed the basis for government and societies throughout time. It is a right that is as fundamental as it is necessary for all other basic freedoms including liberty. They have their basis in natural law and have been established through the seventh commandment, the Catholic principle of universal destination of goods, and explained and expounded on in Pope Leo XIII's *Rerum Novarum* and Pope John Paul II's *Centesimus Annus*.

Because property rights are inherent, they transcend governments. Although property rights exist in various capacities under everything from Hammurabi's

---

[34] Leo XIII, *Rerum Novarum* (1891), para. 4.

[35] John Paul II, *Centesimus Annus* (1991), para. 30.

[36] Ibid., para. 43.

code to modern capitalist governments, they flourish best in capitalist societies where the legal structure supports competition and efficiency which in turn promote the common good. Thus, it is clear the private property rights flourish in a combination of capitalism and Christianity.[37]

Summary

An individual's right to private property has been held fundamentally throughout the ages. This paper takes the position that property rights are also an inherent right, necessarily conditioned for liberty and freedom to exist. First, looking at property rights through a historical lens, it is clear private property rights transcend government. Then, addressing property rights' roots in Christianity, it is argued that private property is an inherent right. Through the work of recent scholars, this paper examines the close connection between private property and other fundamental rights such as the right to life, liberty and freedom.

Zusammenfassung

Das individuelle Recht auf Privateigentum war zu allen Zeiten grundlegend. Dieser Beitrag geht davon aus, dass Eigentumsrechte Grundrechte sind und notwendige Bedingung für das Leben in Freiheit. Zuerst werden die Eigentumsrechte in ihrer geschichtlichen Gestalt untersucht; es ergibt sich, dass der Staat nicht über die Eigentumsrechte verfügen kann. Dann geht es um die Begründung der Eigentumsrechte in der christlichen Tradition. Unter Bezugnahme auf die moderne Forschung prüft der Beitrag die enge Verbindung des Privateigentums mit anderen Grundrechten wie dem Recht auf Leben und auf Freiheit.

[37] Particular thanks to my research assistant Erin Einhorn for her invaluable assistance in preparing this paper. Thanks also to my research assistants Mary Parent and Benjamin Bogos for their many invaluable contributions in the preparation of an earlier version of their paper which I delivered in July 2012 at the 12th German-American Colloquium in Mundelein, Illinois, and to Christopher Dobranski for his insightful and helpful comments and criticism in the shaping of this paper. The mistakes are mine.

The Old World Meets the New

The "Doctrine of Discovery" and the Origins of Property Ownership in America

By Richard J. Dougherty

A common thread running through much of the history of political thought is that private property should be protected in various ways, and that the perpetuation of a political order including the defense of legitimate property claims is beneficial to the citizens or subjects and to the larger order as well. We find notable exception to this tradition, as in the community of property proposed by Socrates in Plato's *Republic* and by Raphael Hythloday in his account of Utopia found in Thomas More's work of the same name. But these exceptions are themselves the subject of much criticism, as we find in Aristotle's critique of Socrates in Book II of the *Politics*, and the brief rejoinder to Hythloday by the character of More in *Utopia*. The defense of systems of private property is widespread, found in ancient, Christian, and modern thinkers alike.

And yet, the origins of the right to property – that is, specifically to property in land – is not entirely clear. The civil law routinely recognizes that property in land, for example, can be claimed by individuals, but where exactly that claim by any given individual originated is generally left unclear. The labor theory of property, popular with many modern economic and political thinkers, does not seem to have been decisive among early thinkers, but gained some real interest in part as a consequence of the so-called "age of discovery," and the subsequent colonization of the New World by European powers.

The question of property rights and the claims of colonizers is not an antiquated concern, but a quite real and contemporary one. For example, in the Spring 2012 the United Nations held a week-long conference devoted to the "Doctrine of Discovery," with participants from around the world testifying to the continuing negative consequences of the adoption of the principle.[1] A num-

---

[1] See, for example, the Press Release from the United Nations' Department of Public Information for the Permanent Forum for Indigenous Issues, which begins, "The Doctrine of Discovery had been used for centuries to expropriate indigenous lands and facilitate their transfer to colonizing or dominating nations, speakers in the Permanent Forum on Indigenous Issues stressed today" (May 8, 2012; accessed at: http://www.un.org/News/Press/docs//2012/hr5088.doc.htm).

ber of associations have expressed their criticism of the doctrine, and some have even called for the Pope to issue a repudiation of the doctrine, connecting it, as they do, with the early papal bulls concerning the adjudicating of rights of exploring European nations.[2] In addition, the Supreme Court has as recently as 2005 cited the "doctrine of discovery" in cases addressing Indian claims in land disputes.[3]

I. The Discovery Stage

One of the central questions that had to be addressed in the European en-counter with the Americas was precisely how the discovering or settling nations might claim the right to possession of the land in America, a right to be asserted against other European powers and also against whatever inhabitants there might be already domiciled on the land. Most of the European discoverers were in fact sanctioned or funded by sovereign authorities, and were thus empowered to make claims on behalf of the sovereign, and thus the claim to ownership over most areas was not simply a private claim but a decidedly public one. Still, that circumstance alone did not solve the difficulty of how one might account for conflicting claims between and among the various nations, or how one might establish such a claim against the native inhabitants of the land. The solution to that problem came in the adoption of what came to be called the "Doctrine of Discovery," understood to mean that the sovereign who discovered the land would have exclusive authority to settle the land or trade with whatever inhabi-tants might be found already there. The one routine limitation on that authority, as seen in papal bulls, treaties, and royal patents, was that claims could only be made to land not inhabited by people already Christian.

The difficulty in adjudicating disparate claims over new-found lands in America had a historical precedent which made the issue somewhat simpler and yet at the same time did not settle the question. Struggles between the Spanish (Castile) and Portuguese over the claims to lands in Africa and the Atlantic Is-lands in the 14th and 15th century led the kingdoms to appeal to the papacy for arbitration between them, and this resulted in the issuance of numerous adjudi-catory papal bulls. For example, in 1344, Pope Clement VI issued a bull recog-nizing France's claim to evangelize the Canary Islands, a claim that was sup-ported by Spain and Portugal, but which was never acted upon; subsequently, renewed tensions over the islands continued until Portugal gave up its claim to

---

[2] The Unitarian Universalists Association of Congregations, for example, issued a resolution at their 2012 General Assembly repudiating the Doctrine of Discovery; see: http://www.uua.org/multiculturalism/dod/index.shtml.

[3] *City of Sherrill v. Oneida Indian Nation of New York*, 544 U.S. 197 (2005).

Spain by a treaty in 1479.[4] That same 1479 treaty, though, protected the claims of the Portuguese to the lands of Guinea, the Azores, and Cape Verde islands, and to the islands from the Canaries to Guinea.[5]

But the stakes were about to get much higher, as Columbus's journeys late in the fifteenth century led to the issuance of a series of papal bulls recognizing exclusive Spanish rights to the lands discovered by Columbus. In particular, the bull *Inter Caetera*, of May 4, 1493, drew a "line of demarcation" one-hundred leagues west of the Azores or Canary Islands, granting exclusive Spanish rights to acquire territory and trade in lands to the west of the line.[6] (Though, as with earlier and later bulls, exceptions were made for those areas already in the possession of "Christian princes.") Portuguese objections to the arrangement led to the 1494 Treaty of Tordesillas, which moved the line of demarcation to 370 leagues west of the Cape Verde Islands, and protected Portugal's holding east of the line.[7] (In the event, neither nation was certain where the line actually fell, or how to measure it, with the consequence that the treaty never really settled matters completely.[8])

There are numerous interesting historical questions that arose over these disputes, but our focus is on the issue of claims to property rights in the discovered lands. Importantly, the "line of demarcation" established by the bull *Inter Caetera* in 1493 included not only a longitudinal marker but also a latitudinal one, the line running "one hundred leagues towards the west and south" of the Azores and Cape Verde.[9] The consequence of this detail, coupled with the coming Protestant Reformation in Europe, meant that subsequent discoveries and settlements in North America would be characterized by disagreements about whether to acknowledge papal authority to arbitrate disputes between nations on the continent.

---

[4] In the Treaty of Alcacovas; Frances Gardiner Davenport, *European Treaties Bearing on the History of the United States and its Dependencies to 1648* (Washington, D.C.: Carnegie Institution of Washington, 1917), pp. 9–10.

[5] Ibid., p. 34. The protection for the Portuguese claim was repeated in the bull *Aeterni Regis*, issued by Pope Sixtus IV in 1481, thus extending papal support to the treaty arrangement.

[6] Ibid., pp. 71–78.

[7] The treaty does not specify where the line will actually originate from, or exactly how long a league actually was – a matter of some dispute.

[8] Ibid., pp. 84–105. For example, disputes arose for decades over the proper claims to the Philippines and to the Moluccas, a consequence of disagreements about where to begin the base-line, and what to do when the eastern rights met the western claims.

[9] Davenport, p. 78.

II. American Colonialism

One might begin the analysis of the British colonies in America with the 1496 patent grant from King Henry VII to John Cabot. Cabot, a Venetian, was given the freedom and power to "find, discover, and investigate" lands that "were unknown to all Christians," and to "conquer, occupy, and possess" the lands.[10] (It is not known with certainty where Cabot ended up sailing, perhaps to Newfoundland, or Labrador, or Nova Scotia.) Similar arrangements were made with the companies originally authorized to settle areas on the eastern seaboard, such that the lands were held by the company but on behalf of the crown. The particular arrangements regarding property ownership within each colony were at first irregular, but in time the colonial governments became the repository for exchanges of property with the Indian tribes.[11]

The conclusion of the French and Indian War in 1763 saw the French abandon their claims to territory in most of North America, and the British thus could consolidate their holdings and reassess the terrain. This they did, through the Royal Proclamation of 1763, which limited the established colonies at their western borders, and fixed the crown as the sole negotiating authority with the Indians on the frontier.[12] Ostensibly, this was meant to encourage trust in the Indian tribes (many of whom had allied with the French in the war), who now would be protected against hostile or wily colonists intent on westward expansion. But the colonists thought the crown was acting in a heavy-handed manner, and feared that severe limitations would be placed on the freedom of the colonies, and that the British might create a joint western front with what were now more placable Indian tribes.[13] One result of the Proclamation was a greater cen-

---

[10] In the Supreme Court case to be examined below, Chief Justice John Marshall describes the Cabot charge in these terms: "In this first effort made by the English government to acquire territory on this continent, we perceive a complete recognition of the principle which has been mentioned. The right of discovery given by this commission, is confined to countries 'then unknown to all Christian people;' and of these countries Cabot was empowered to take possession in the name of the king of England. Thus asserting a right to take possession, notwithstanding the occupancy of the natives, who were heathens, and, at the same time, admitting the prior title of any Christian people who may have made a previous discovery" (*Johnson and Graham's Lessee v. M'Intosh*, 21 U.S. 543, 576–577, 1823).

[11] See, for example, William C. Canby, Jr., *American Indian Law*, 3rd Edition t. (St. Paul, MN: West Group, 1998): "In order to avoid prolonged and expensive Indian wars, and perhaps also to enforce a measure of justice, the Crown increasingly assumed the position of protector of the tribes from the excesses of the colonists" (p. 11).

[12] Stuart Banner, *How the Indians Lost Their Land: Law and Power on the Frontier* (Cambridge: Harvard University Press, 2005), pp. 85–95.

[13] This fear was borne out for the colonists, as can be seen in the charges against the King found in the Declaration of Independence in 1776: "He has excited domestic rebellion amongst us, and has endeavoured to bring on the inhabitants of our frontiers, the

tralization of relations with the tribes, such that individuals were now forbidden from engaging directly with the tribes for the acquisition of territory. This fact becomes a matter of real significance with the onset of the American Revolution, as authority over Indian affairs will be seen as passing largely to the hands of the central government, and not to the states separately or individually.

III. The American Founding and Property Rights

In the American Founding era, concerns about the protection of rights to property were ubiquitous, and there was general recognition of the importance of the right to property. The threat to property rights was seen popularly in the taxes imposed on the colonists without their consent (thus the "taxation without representation"), with the result being that most states in the aftermath of the American Revolution explicitly protected property rights through their newly-drafted state constitutions.[14]

But the continued complexity concerning the question of property can be found in various ways. For example, the language of the 1776 Declaration of Independence, which is clearly influenced by the work of John Locke, breaks somewhat from Locke's terminology in the *Second Treatise of Government*.[15] There, Locke repeatedly speaks of the purpose of government as being found in the protection of property, the possession of which is not secure in the "state of nature" that ante-dates civil society.[16] But the language of the Declaration of

---

merciless Indian savages, whose known rule of warfare, is an undistinguished destruction of all ages, sexes, and conditions."

[14] See, for example, Massachusetts Constitution of 1780, Article X: "Every individual of the society has a right to be protected by it in the enjoyment of his life, liberty, and property, according to standing laws" (Francis N. Thorpe, *The Federal and State Constitutions, Colonial Charters, and other Organic Laws of the States, Territories, and Colonies now or heretofore forming the United States of America*, Washington, D.C.: Government Printing Office, 1909, 3:1891); Pennsylvania Constitution of 1776, Article I: "That all men are born equally free and independent, and have certain natural, inherent and inalienable rights, amongst which are, the enjoying and defending life and liberty, acquiring, possessing and protecting property" (Thorpe, 5:3082); North Carolina Constitution of 1776, Section 25: "The property of the soil, in a free government, being one of the essential rights of the collective body of the people, it is necessary, in order to avoid future disputes, that the limits of the State should be ascertained with precision ..." (Thorpe, 5:2788).

[15] It should be noted that there is considerable scholarly disagreement about the extent of Locke's influence on the language of the Declaration, but that issue would have to be pursued elsewhere.

[16] See, for example, John Locke, *Two Treatises of Government* (ed. Peter Laslett, Cambridge: Cambridge University Press, 1988), *Second Treatise*, § 124; indeed, the references to this point are plentiful, e.g., § 3.3; § 85.15; § 88.8; § 91.18; § 94.22; § 95.8; § 123.17; § 124.1; § 127.9; § 131; § 134.1.

Independence alters the Lockean formula, referring to the unalienable rights of "life, liberty, and the pursuit of happiness," rather than property or estate.[17] Why this alteration of the language took place is contested among interpreters, but one reading of the assertion may be that the American founders understood that property was not a natural right in the same way that life and liberty were understood to be natural (or unalienable) rights.

In any case, the Lockean justification for the possession of property does seem to have been influential in the colonies, as claims concerning property rights were generally considered to be legitimized by the assertion that the Indians did not make their living off of the land itself, and thus those who were willing to do so, and were capable of it, had a legitimate and, indeed, more compelling claim to the land. Locke's argument to this effect can be seen in a variety of places, primarily in his *Second Treatise*, and, importantly, he there directly addresses the American Indian situation. His account of man's pre-political condition commences with the assertion that "in the beginning all the World was *America*," implying that the absence of money, commerce, and ap-propriated land was symptomatic of such orders.[18] Yet men do come to possess property, and it is acquired, in the well-known Lockean language, through la-bor:

> Whatsoever then he removes out of the State that Nature hath provided, and left it in, he hath mixed his *Labour* with, and joyned to it something that is his own, and there-by makes it his *Property*. It being by him removed from the common state Nature placed it in, it hath by this *labour* something annexed to it, that excludes the common right of other men. For this *labour* being the unquestionable Property of the La-bourer, no Man but he can have a right to what that is once joyned to, at least where there is enough, and as good left in common for others.[19]

Labor, then, is the basis of the assertion that can be made on behalf of indi-vidual property, for Locke, and the mixing of labor with something is the foun-dation of the legitimate claim to property, as long as one leaves "enough, and as good," for others.

Further, Locke argues that it is the very exertion of labor by the individual that gives something its value: "For 'tis *Labour* indeed that *puts the difference of value* on every thing; and let any one consider what the difference is between an Acre of Land planted with Tobacco, or Sugar, sown with Wheat or Barley; and an Acre of the same Land lying in common, without any Husbandry upon

---

[17] Locke, *Two Treatises of Government, Second Treatise*, § 87.3–5: man in the state of nature has the power to "preserve his property, that is, his Life, Liberty, and Estate, against the Injuries and Attempts of other Men ..." (Laslett, p. 323).

[18] Locke, *Two Treatises of Government, Second Treatise*, § 49.1 (Laslett, p. 301); emphasis in original.

[19] Ibid., 2.27 (Laslett, p. 288); emphasis in original. See also 2.33 on the appropria-tion of land being justified as long as there is "enough, and as good left."

it, and he will find, that the improvement of *labour makes* the far greater part of *the value*."[20] In Locke's analysis, then, the Indian in America, to the extent he does not mix his labor with the land, does not improve it and thus cannot assert private ownership over it. For Locke, the appropriation of land is accomplished by how much a man "Tills, Plants, Improves, Cultivates, and can use the Product of"; thus, he cannot waste it, but the clear primacy is given to the blending of labor with the land.[21] To the extent someone has acquired property through his labor, he has "inclosed" that amount of land, according to Locke, and thus set it off from any claims that might be made by others.

In addition, because America is a "state of nature" insofar as there has been no development of agriculture or civil society by the Indian nations, anyone can appropriate land in that state without relying on the consent of others, including the government (because it does not exist):

> [L]et him plant in some inland, vacant places of *America*, we shall find that the *Possessions* he could make himself upon the *measures* we have given, would not be very large, nor, even to this day, prejudice the rest of Mankind, or give them reason to complain, or think themselves injured by this Man's Incroachment, though the Race of Men have now spread themselves to all the corners of the World, and do infinitely exceed the small number [which] was at the beginning.[22]

The right to possession follows use, and when the planter mixes his labor with the land he stakes out a claim to possession over that land that the native inhabitants – who do not work the land but live off its abundance – cannot legitimately make. And while we will not pursue this question at this time, it should be noted that Locke's argument, insofar as it touches on the situation in North American, would have to acknowledge that to the extent Indian tribes were agricultural they would indeed have a legitimate claim to their land over against the colonizing powers.[23]

Locke's argument about the right to property, connected as it is with the question of discovery, echoes or is echoed in a number of other authors of the period, often in language that seems well-framed to justify the colonizing or commercial activities of the European nations. For example, Hugo Grotius's work on the *Law of Prize* was apparently written, in his own account of it, to "add courage to our countrymen not to withdraw a title from their manifest

---

[20] Ibid., 2.40 (Laslett, p. 296); emphasis in original.

[21] Ibid., 2.32 (Laslett, p. 290).

[22] Ibid., 2.36, p. 293; emphasis in original.

[23] A lengthy treatment of this issue can be found in various places; for example, see Barbara Arneil's *John Locke and America: The Defense of English Colonialism* (Oxford: Clarendon Press, 1996); Arneil treats especially Locke's keen interest in the American situation, and his selective use of historical data to buttress his philosophical and political argument (see, e.g., Chapter One, "Locke's Travel Books").

right and might find out whether it were possible to induce the Spaniards to treat the case a little more leniently."[24] Grotius is interested in defending the right of the Dutch to trade in the East Indies, a right challenged by the Spanish and Portuguese, who are operating under the arrangement articulated above, with papal approbation. But Grotius asserts that he is not trying to justify Dutch settlements or the acquisition of property, but only the right of the Dutch to employ the sea for trade. Thus his work "Freedom of the Seas," published in 1609 (*Mare Liberum* is Chapter XII from his *De Jure Pradae Commentarius*, completed in 1606), is a defense of the principle that land holdings are different in kind from movable objects, and that difference justifies a claim for freedom of the sea even in the face of a legitimate claim being made concerning property ownership in land.[25]

Grotius's argument is a matter of special interest because his defense of the freedom of the sea is predicated on the acceptance of an argument similar to the one found in Locke concerning property in land, or immovable objects. Locke had used the argument that enclosure of the land gave one a right to the land as a way of defending his labor theory. Grotius, on the other hand, uses the enclosure argument to distinguish the freedom of the sea from the freedom of the land; because the sea cannot be enclosed, it cannot be possessed in the same way. To the extent that land can be appropriated, and enclosure justifies assertions of ownership, the sea cannot be appropriated, and thus the Dutch claims to freedom of the sea justify their commercial activities.[26]

An additional authority, among others, might be cited, for the connection between the principle of discovery and the assertion of property claims. Emeric de Vattel, writing in his *The Law of Nations or the Principles of Natural Law*, in 1758, makes much the same argument in justifying the property claim of the European settlers:

> The cultivation of the soil ... is ... an obligation imposed upon man by nature. Every Nation is therefore bound by the law of nature to cultivate that land which has fallen to its share. There are others who, in order to avoid labor, seek to live upon their flocks and the fruits of the chase. Now that the human race has multiplied so greatly, it could not subsist if every people wished to live after that fashion. Those who still

---

[24] Hugo Grotius, *De Jure Pradae Commentarius*, trans. G. L. Williams (Carnegie Endowment for International Peace, 1950); in "Introduction" by J. B. Scott, p. xi (cited in: Arneil, p. 47).

[25] Much of the argument in this paragraph and the next is taken from Arneil, Chapter 2, "Colonialism and Natural Law" (pp. 45 ff). Grotius's text can be found at: http://oll.libertyfund.org/index.php?option=com_staticxt&staticfile=show.php%3Ftitle=1718&Itemid=27.

[26] Arneil also draws upon the work of Samuel Pufendorf to illuminate the influences on Locke's argument; she notes that Locke himself asserted that Pufendorf's *The Law of Nations* was the "best book of that kind" (p. 54).

pursue this idle mode of life occupy more land than they would have need of under a system of honest labor, and they may not complain if other more industrious nations, too confined at home, should come and occupy part of their lands ...[27] [W]hen the Nations of Europe come upon lands which the savages have no special need of and are making no present and continuous use of, they may lawfully take possession of them and establish colonies in them.[28]

Vattel clearly defends the right of discovering nations to appropriate the lands left uncultivated or unimproved upon by the native "savages." His assertion that the "law of nature" compels man to work the land is intended to point to the natural justice of the positive claim of the settlers both to occupy and to assert authority over the land, moved as they are by their "industry" to improve upon the earth. Locke has made a similar argument, of course, and had even connected the justification for property ownership to what he takes to be the Biblical command to till the earth.[29]

A last note on the importance of the principle of discovery might be in order here. Georg von Martens, in his 1788 work *The Law of Nations* (translated into English in 1802), states clearly the import of this principle, presumably the agreed-upon basis for European exploration:

> From the moment a nation has taken possession of a territory in right of first occupier, and with the design to establish itself there for the future, it becomes the absolute and sole proprietor of it and all that it contains; and has a right to exclude all other nations from it, to use it and dispose of it as it thinks proper; provided, however, that it did not, in any wise, encroach on the rights of other nations.[30]

Martens, a prominent figure in the development of the modern understanding of the law of nations, emphasizes the exclusivity of the right that can be claimed by the discovering power, and this is an issue that will become a matter

---

[27] Compare Thomas More's *Utopia*, where Raphael Hythloday describes the Utopian defense of the legitimacy of its colonization practice on the grounds that foreign land which they employ is not used properly or fully (left "idle and waste"); the Utopians need the land because of their population growth, which is too cumbersome to be sustained by Utopia, and thus they assert that they have a just claim to mainland territory (*More: Utopia*, ed. George M. Logan and Robert M. Adams, Cambridge: Cambridge University Press, 2002, p. 54).

[28] Emeric de Vattel, *The Law of Nations or the Principles of Natural Law*, trans. Charles G. Fenwick (Washington, D.C.: Carnegie Institute, 1902), pp. 207–210; quoted in: James Tully, "Aboriginal Property and Western Theory: Recovering a Middle Ground" (in *Property Rights*, ed. Ellen Frankel Paul, Fred D. Miller, Jr., and Jeffrey Paul, Cambridge: Cambridge University Press, 1994), pp. 165–166.

[29] See, for example, *Second Treatise*, 2.34: "God gave the World ... to the use of the Industrious and Rational, (and *Labour* was to be *his Title* to it) not to the Fancy or Covetousness of the Quarrelsome and Contentious" (p. 291).

[30] Georg von Martens, *The Law of Nations: Being the Science of National Law, Covenants, Power, & c, Founded Upon the Treaties and Customs of Modern Nations in Europe* (1788), Book III, Chapter 1, Sec. 1 (Trans. W. Cobbett. London: William Cobbett, 1802), p. 69.

of primary importance in the American context, as we shall see in the following discussion.

IV. The American Constitution and Indian Rights

The United States Constitution, drafted in 1787, sought, in part, to address a problematic aspect of the previous governing document, the Articles of Confederation, concerning the relation between the central government and the Indian nations. Under Article IX of the Articles of Confederation (ratified in 1781), the congress was granted "the sole and exclusive right and power of regulating ... the trade and managing all affairs with the Indians, not members of any of the states, provided that the legislative right of any state within its own limits be not infringed or violated ..." By the phrase "not members of any states" was meant Indians who had left the tribe and become citizens of the state within which they resided; these individuals would, it seems, be treated like any other citizen, with the same rights and obligations, though that understanding was never fully established in practice.[31] But the subsequent passage, protecting state legislative rights, led to much confusion, for it was unclear how a unified and distinct nation residing within the confines of a state might have its trade regulated by a power outside of that state.

In the *Federalist Papers*, Publius asserts that Article I, Section 8, of the 1787 Constitution clarifies the problematic aspects of the Articles of Confederation. The Constitution simply says that "Congress shall have Power ... To regulate Commerce with foreign Nations, and among the several States, and with the Indian Tribes ..."[32] This phraseology marks an advance upon the earlier language of the Articles, he argues:

> The regulation of commerce with the Indian tribes is very properly unfettered from two limitations in the Articles of Confederation, which render the provision obscure and contradictory. The power is there restrained to Indians, not members of any of the States, and is not to violate or infringe the legislative right of any State within its own limits. What description of Indians are to be deemed members of a State is not yet settled; and has been a question of frequent perplexity and contention in the federal councils. And how the trade with Indians, though not members of a State, yet re-

---

[31] The parallel passage in the 1787 Constitution, in the context of counting persons (for the sake of taxes and apportionment) excludes "Indians not taxed"; because Indians were not considered citizens, they were excluded from the enumeration. Subsequent changes in American law have made the designation moot, and the Department of the Interior in 1940 declared that no such category existed any more (Carole Goldberg-Ambrose, "American Indians and the Constitution," entry in *Encyclopedia of the American Constitution*, eds. Leonard W. Levy, Kenneth L. Karst, and Dennis J. Mahoney, New York: Macmillan Publishing Company, 1986, Vol. I, p. 51).

[32] United States Constitution, Article One, Section 8, Clause 3.

siding within its legislative jurisdiction can be regulated by an external authority, without so far intruding on the internal rights of legislation, is absolutely incomprehensible.[33]

Thus the question of how the central government was to deal with the presence of Indian tribes within the confines of the individual states was seen as problematic from the outset of the American arrangement, and the difficulties that the situation brought to the fore would only become magnified in the decades to follow.

Disputes over Indian property rights took the forefront in the early part of the nineteenth century, as states struggled to address the complexity of the presence of separated sovereignties within their borders, while at the same time the incorporation of the lands obtained through the Louisiana Purchase pushed settlers westward into greater contact with Indian nations. The troubles associated with the forced removal of Indian tribes, most notably in the "Trail of Tears", has been well-chronicled, but that development was precipitated by a series of Supreme Court decisions in the decade before, and an examination of the Court's argument in the cases reveals something of its understanding of the principles that animated the original settlements in the United States. Much has been written, appropriately, about the important 1831 case, *Cherokee Nation v. Georgia*[34], and the subsequent 1832 case of *Worcester v. Georgia*.[35] In the former case, the Marshall Court spoke of the Indian tribes as constituting "domestic dependent nations,"[36] and in *Worcester* the Court held that relations between the United States and the Cherokee nation "according to the settled principles of our constitution, are committed exclusively to the government of the union."[37] But much of what the Court addresses in these two cases draws upon a somewhat lesser-known prior decision, which is worth examining in part because it focuses specifically on the question of property claims and the discovery doctrine.[38]

In the case of *Johnson & Graham's Lessee v. M'Intosh*, decided in 1823, the Supreme Court invalidated the title claim to property purchased by individuals directly from Indian tribes, holding that title to such lands did not have to be re-

---

[33] *Federalist Paper* 42, ed. Jacob E. Cooke (Middletown, Connecticut: Wesleyan University Press, 1961), p. 284.

[34] 30 U.S. (5 Pet.) 1 (1831).

[35] 31 U.S. (6 Pet.) 515 (1832).

[36] 30 U.S. (5 Pet.) 1, at 17 (1831).

[37] 31 U.S. (6 Pet.) 515, at 561 (1832).

[38] An interesting and informative account of the *Cherokee Nation* and *Worcester* cases can be found in Gerard N. Magliocca's *Andrew Jackson and the Constitution: The Rise and Fall of Generational Regimes* (Lawrence: University Press of Kansas, 2007), pp. 34–47.

cognized by the governments operating under the United States Constitution.[39]
John Marshall penned the opinion of the Court, and set forth clearly what came
to be the legal basis for United States-Indian relations in the years to come:

> On the discovery of this immense continent, the great nations of Europe were eager
> to appropriate to themselves so much of it as they could respectively acquire ... The
> potentates of the old world found no difficulty in convincing themselves that they
> made ample compensation to the inhabitants of the new, by bestowing on them civi-
> lization and Christianity, in exchange for unlimited independence. But, as they were
> all in pursuit of nearly the same object, it was necessary, in order to avoid conflicting
> settlements, and consequent war with each other, to establish a principle which all
> should acknowledge as the law by which the right of acquisition, which they all as-
> serted, should be regulated as between themselves. This principle was that discovery
> gave title to the government by whose subjects, or by whose authority, it was made,
> against all other European governments, which title might be consummated by pos-
> session.[40]

As Marshall went on to explain, agreement to the principle of discovery
meant for the European nations that the discoverers of any land could legitimately assert the exclusive right to possession of that land, with the (potentially) important qualification that absolute title was "subject only to the Indian
right of occupancy."[41]

The fact that the right was understood to be exclusive, Marshall goes on to
show, can be seen in the historical circumstances that surrounded the transfer of
authority over lands in North America. Transfers of sovereignty from one nation to another, through pacts or war-related treaties, were acknowledged as
having taken place wholesale, with no reservation of authority over the land –
and, significantly, without taking into account the presence or absence of Indian
tribes within the borders of the transferred lands. Thus, he notes, for example,
that in the Treaty of Utrecht, in 1713, the French ceded Acadia to the British,
even though much of the territory granted was in the control of Indian inhabitants.[42] In other words, the European powers understood that their possession of
the land excluded any claims from other nations, though they would still have
to address the presence of Indian nations within the lands.

---

[39] 21 U.S. 543 (1823). Johnson and Graham (or, their families) had purchased land
from the Piankeshaw Indians prior to the American Revolution, in territory that later became the state of Illinois; M'Intosh had purchased the same land subsequently directly
from the United States government.

[40] 21 U.S. 543, 572–573.

[41] 21 U.S. 543, 584–587; I say it is a "potentially" important qualification because its
importance turns in large part on the discovering nation's willingness to recognize the
Indian claim, and to accord the tribes the freedom to maintain their occupancy of the
land.

[42] 21 U.S. 543, 581.

Yet, while Marshall understands the principle of discovery to be the basis for the legal claim of property rights by European nations, and thus to be also the root of assertions of title under subsequent American law, he is also at pains to call into question that very doctrine. Recognizing that the original claim to possession was soon converted into a claim to possession by conquest (which itself would also give simple title to the land), Marshall inquires into whether this was the "inevitable consequence" of affairs in North America. Because the land was already inhabited by peoples unlike the Europeans clashes between them produced "frequent and bloody wars, in which the whites were not always the aggressors ..."[43] What he calls the "pompous claims" of the (now) British colonists could not likely subsist alongside the Indian nations' view of their property claims. Indeed, one consequence of the white settlements was that the game which served as the provisions for the Indian population itself moved westward, leading the Indians to follow it; the unoccupied lands were then claimed as possessions by the settlers, and thus the controversy continued unabated. Over time, then, the eastern lands largely came into the hands of the settlers, either through war or through Indian abandonment.[44]

Marshall's wariness about accepting the earlier claim of possession by discovery leads him to question the principle at the heart of that claim, though in terms of the role of the Court in adjudicating claims brought before it he accepts the claim of possession by discovery as authoritative:

> However extravagant the pretension of converting the discovery of an inhabited country into conquest may appear, if the principle has been asserted in the first instance, and afterwards sustained; if a country has been acquired and held under it; if the property of the great mass of the community originates in it, it becomes the law of the land, and cannot be questioned.[45]

Here Marshall seems to be suggesting that the proper role of the judge is actually not to ascertain first principles, but only to identify the legal principle which it is then to apply to the extant case. This approach will not prevent him from contemplating fundamental principles, but will limit him in the application of such, and this we see in his subsequent comment:

> So, too, with respect to the concomitant principle, that the Indian inhabitants are to be considered merely as occupants, to be protected, indeed, while in peace, in the possession of their lands, but to be deemed incapable of transferring the absolute title to

---

[43] 21 U.S. 543, 590; Marshall's implication, of course, is that the whites were sometimes the aggressors against the Indians.

[44] Marshall suggests the complexity of analyzing the treatment of the Indians: "Although we do not mean to engage in the defense of those principles which Europeans have applied to Indian title, they may, we think, find some excuse, if not justification, in the character and habits of the people whose rights have been wrested from them" (21 U.S. 543, 589).

[45] 21 U.S. 543, 591.

others. However this restriction may be opposed to natural right, and to the usages of civilized nations, yet, if it be indispensable to that system under which the country has been settled, and be adapted to the actual condition of the two people, it may, perhaps, be supported by reason, and certainly cannot be rejected by courts of justice.[46]

As a matter of first principle Justice Marshall is willing to call into question the legitimacy of the claim of discovery to grant an exclusive right to territory, but as a matter of law it seems to be sufficiently settled such that the Court will have to accept the understanding as definitive for purposes of adjudicating claims brought before the Court.

There are a number of difficulties that the claim of "discovery" raised for the Indian tribes, but we might raise only two here. One is that enforcement of the claim of discovery severely restricted the potential market for purchasers of Indian lands, for all intents and purposes providing the colonizers the opportunity to set the monetary value for the territory. The importance of this principle is not just that it is used to invalidate the particular conveyance of property being challenged in this case, but that all subsequent potential individual buyers are now put on notice that the United States government will not recognize their property claims once the government acquires the encompassing territory from the Indians.[47] In addition, as Marshall indicates, the "concomitant principle" that the Indians were to be understood as only occupying and not possessing the land, was used as justification for the acquisition of territory that was not employed in agriculture or some similar kind of development. Indeed, this view constituted part of the argument made before the Court on behalf of M'Intosh's claims. His attorneys asserted that not only did the Indian tribes not possess the land they attempted to convey, but they could not have, for they did not employ it:

> By the law of nature, they had not acquired a fixed property capable of being transferred. The measure of property acquired by occupancy is determined, according to the law of nature, by the extent of men's wants, and their capacity of using it to supply them.[48] It is a violation of the rights of others to exclude them from the use of what we do not want, and they have an occasion for. Upon this principle the North American Indians could have acquired no proprietary interest in the vast tracts of territory which they wandered over; and their right to the lands on which they hunted,

---

[46] 21 U.S. 543, 591–592.

[47] This restriction will not necessarily prohibit all such sales by tribes to individuals, but any buyer must now recognize that his property right will only be recognized under Indian law, which will not transfer with the change of ownership of the territory as a whole.

[48] Authors cited in defense of this proposition include Hugo Grotius, Samuel Pufendorf, and John Locke.

could not be considered as superior to that which is acquired to the sea by fishing in it.[49]

Here we see the adoption of the labor theory of property, used against the Indian tribes as a way of invalidating their exchange of land to anyone other than the discovering power.

M'Intosh's argument went further, though, drawing upon the fundamental basis for claims to rights of property, theories which, we have seen, were popularized during the colonial period:

> According to every theory of property, the Indians had no individual rights to land; nor had they any collectively, or in their national capacity; for the lands occupied by each tribe were not used by them in such a manner as to prevent their being appropriated by a people of cultivators. All the proprietary rights of civilized nations on this continent are founded on this principle.[50]

The argument that the Indians had no individual rights to land was predicated on the fact that the tribes had not partitioned the territory they inhabited and granted individual title to tribe members desirous of cultivating the soil. Presuming that land was not being maximally employed, the appearance of a nation of cultivators, armed with the theory that mixing labor with the soil established proprietary rights, meant that the Indians' property claims were endangered.

The defense of the government's position, then, drew upon not only statutory law and peace treaties, but also based itself on what it took to be principles of natural law regarding property rights. And while the Supreme Court's opinion does not fully embrace this latter claim, its acceptance of the other bases for rejecting the claims of Johnson and Graham resulted in its holding in favor of the government's position on the rightful owner of the property under the law.

Conclusion

The last few decades have produced a panoply of provocative works on the rights of indigenous peoples, both around the world (as with Australian and African aborigines) and in North America in particular (as with the Canadian "First Nations"). Many interpreters have raised questions about the regular assertions that were made by the European powers concerning the justice of their discoveries of or encounters with the New World. Substantial progress in understanding the principles at stake in the conversation, though, seems in part to be held back by the absence of a common conception of property rights. To the

---

[49] 21 U.S. 543, 569–570.
[50] 21 U.S. 543, 570.

extent that defenders of the colonizing nations ground their argument in the labor theory of property, it seems as if there will be little movement on this front. Yet, given the fact that some American Indian tribes did in fact engage in agricultural pursuits, even the adoption of the labor theory might prove fruitful in some areas in serving as the basis for a deeper understanding of the competing claims.

The recognition of the tenuous character of Indian relations in America, including after the Revolution, can be seen in the analysis given by Thomas Jefferson, in a message send to Congress in 1803. In his preparations for the Lewis and Clark expedition, Jefferson reflected on the state of the Indian tribes, and what their future might hold for them.

> The Indian tribes residing within the limits of the United States have for a considerable time been growing more and more uneasy at the constant diminution of the territory they occupy, although effected by their own voluntary sales ... In order peaceably to counteract this policy of theirs, and to provide an extension of territory which the rapid increase of our numbers will call for, two measures are deemed expedient. First: to encourage them to abandon hunting, to apply to the raising stock, to agriculture and domestic manufacture, and thereby prove to themselves that less land and labor will maintain them in this, better than in their former mode of living. The extensive forests necessary in the hunting life will then become useless, and they will see advantage in exchanging them for the means of improving their farms, and of increasing their domestic comforts. Secondly: to multiply trading-houses among them, and place within their reach those things which will contribute more to their domestic comfort than the profession of extensive but uncultivated wilds. Experience and reflection will develop to them the wisdom of exchanging what they can spare and we want, for what we can spare and they want.[51]

Jefferson does not seem here to have in mind a particular form of assertion of property ownership that should guide Indian claims. Rather, his statement may be understood simply as a reflection on the most likely scenario for the American government in dealing with the tribes, and the way to produce a successful transition to domesticated relations between the two entities. Jefferson notes that the government's interest in trading directly with the Indian tribes is a way of engendering good will, by eliminating those traders who "excite in the Indian mind suspicions, fears, and irritations toward us."[52]

In practice, Jefferson sees that the future of peaceful Indian relations is likely to be found in the tribes transitioning to the way of life most common among the larger American society, away from the life of the hunt that seems to require much more territory than the Indian tribes are likely going to possess.

---

[51] Thomas Jefferson, Special Message to Congress, January 18, 1803 (*Basic Writings of Thomas Jefferson*, ed. Philip S. Foner, New York: Willey Book Company, 1944, p. 347).

[52] Ibid.

This point he makes clear in a letter to the Choctaw Nation, in December of 1803:

> I rejoice, brothers, to hear you propose to become cultivators of the earth for the maintenance of your families. Be assured you will support them better and with less labor, by raising stock and bread, and by spinning and weaving clothes, than by hunting. A little land cultivated, and a little labor, will procure more provisions than the most successful hunt; and a woman will clothe more by spinning and weaving, than a man by hunting. Compared with you, we are but as of yesterday in this land. Yet see how much more we have multiplied by industry, and the exercise of that reason which you possess in common with us.[53]

Jefferson concludes with an advisory note, that if the tribe will follow the example of the United States, then "we will aid you with great pleasure."[54]

Any attempt to reassess the earlier dominant understanding of the rights of discovering nations would have to confront the general analysis of the Indian nations as possessing no legitimate claim to landed property. For example, Alexis de Tocqueville, at the outset of his *Democracy in America*, in seeking to understand the origins of the American way of life, draws a familiar contrast between the settlers and the native inhabitants:

> Although the vast country that I have just described was inhabited by numerous tribes of natives, one can justly say that at the period of discovery it still formed only a wilderness. The Indians occupied it, but they did not possess it. It is by agriculture that man appropriates the soil, and the first inhabitants of North America lived from products of the hunt. Their implacable prejudices, their indomitable passions, their vices, and perhaps still more their savage virtues, delivered them to an inevitable destruction. The ruin of these peoples began on the day when the Europeans landed on their shores ... Providence, in placing them in the midst of the wealth of the New World, seemed to have given them only a short lease on it; they were there, in a way, only *in the meantime* ("*qu'en attendant*").[55]

Here we see the combination of the argument from nature and from providence, seemingly justifying moving the Indians off of the productive land. Yet, it should also be noted that many have argued that for all the discussion and theorizing about the claims that the law of nature justified discovering and colonizing nations in appropriating territory from the Indian inhabitants, in point of fact most land was acquired by purchase.[56]

---

[53] Thomas Jefferson, "To the Brothers of the Choctaw Nation," December 17, 1803 (New York: Library of America, pp. 559–560).

[54] Ibid.

[55] Alexis de Tocqueville, *Democracy in America*, trans. Harvey C. Mansfield and Delba Winthrop (Chicago: The University of Chicago Press, 2000), pp. 26–27; emphasis in original.

[56] See, for example, Banner *How the Indians Lost Their Land*, pp. 20–29.

Justice Joseph Story, in his 1833 *Commentary on the Constitution*, defended the wisdom of the Constitution in dealing with Indian relations in the following way: "The trade with them is, in all its forms, subject exclusively to the regulation of congress. And in this particular, also, we trace the wisdom of the constitution. The Indians, not distracted by the discordant regulations of different states, are taught to trust one great body, whose justice they respect, and whose power they fear."[57] Writing in the immediate aftermath of *Johnson* (and subsequent to *Worcester v. Georgia*[58]), Story had the opportunity to see how the Constitution's clauses would be understood, but could only make an educated guess about how exactly the Constitution and Indian treaties would be enforced. The first removal of Indians from the eastern states, the Choctaw in Mississippi and Alabama, had only begun in earnest recently, but Story later may have had reason to question to what extent the Indians respect the justice of the central government.

The analysis of the claim of discovery and its subsequent influence on considerations of the property rights of Indian nations raises a host of questions that have been left unanswered here. One further particular concern that might be raised is the question of whether alternative understandings of property rights might lead to a reconsideration of the European claim to the exclusive control over discovered lands. If, for example, one were to lend authority to the Indian claim to possess property by inhabiting it, and by owning it communally, as opposed to plowing it and parceling it out to individuals, we might be compelled to revisit the development of the historical claims.[59] Possession by discovery became the vehicle for possession by conquest over the Indian tribes, to the extent that conquest occurred, as the conquest would likely never have taken place absent the prior claim of discovery and settlement.[60]

---

[57] Joseph Story, *Commentaries on the Constitution of the United States*, Sec. 1095 (Boston, 1833).

[58] *Worcester v. Georgia*, 31 U.S. 515 (1832); the Court in *Worcester* established the principle that the Indian nations could be understood as domestic sovereign nations, not independent of the central governmental authority.

[59] This issue is at the heart of the essay by James Tully cited above, "Aboriginal Property and Western Theory."

[60] An additional principle, unremarked upon so far, is possession by abandonment; insofar as the discovered land which is inhabited gets abandoned by the inhabitants, this was used to justified ownership of the land by the discoverer. From the point of view of the Indian tribes, of course, this was seen as encouraging the settlers to push the tribes westward off the land.

Summary

The origin of the claim to property rights in North America by European colonizers is a matter still contested today in numerous courts in the United States. Still central to the American judicial system's treatment of this question is an 1823 Supreme Court case, *Johnson v. M'Intosh*, in which Chief Justice John Marshall articulates the principle behind many of the property right claims, the Doctrine of Discovery. This essay examines the historical basis of that doctrine, and considers the cogency of the doctrine as well as the aftermath of its adoption in American law.

Zusammenfassung

Um die von europäischen Einwanderern in Nordamerika geltend gemachten Eigentumsrechte gibt es heute noch zahlreiche Gerichtsverfahren in den Vereinigten Staaten. Immer noch steht im Mittelpunkt des amerikanischen Rechtssystems bei der Behandlung dieser Frage der Fall *Johnson v. M'Intosh*, wie er 1823 vor dem Obersten Gericht entschieden wurde, als der Oberste Richter John Marshall sich auf die Doktrin der Entdeckung berief, die im Hintergrund vieler Eigentumsansprüche steht. Dieser Beitrag setzt sich mit der historischen Grundlage dieser Doktrin auseinander und prüft ihre Stringenz sowie die daraus erwachsenden Folgen im amerikanischen Gesetz.

Die Eigentumsvorstellungen
der politischen Parteien in Deutschland
Eine Analyse der Grundsatzprogramme

Von Klaus Stüwe

I. Einleitung

Bereits die Klassiker der politikwissenschaftlichen Parteienforschung betrachteten das Parteiprogramm als Wesensmerkmal politischer Parteien. Robert Michels schrieb im Jahr 1911: „A party is neither a social unity or an economic unity. It is based upon its program."[1] Für Sigmund Neumann bildete bei seiner Analyse des Parteiensystems der Weimarer Republik das Programm ebenfalls ein wesentliches Bestimmungselement politischer Parteien.[2]

Auch die jüngere Parteienforschung hat immer wieder die Bedeutung des Programms für die politischen Parteien hervorgehoben. Für Angelo Panebianco etwa spielen programmatische Aspekte insbesondere in der Gründungsphase von Parteien eine Rolle („the goal is realization of the common cause"[3]), während später Organisationsmerkmale in den Vordergrund treten. Richard S. Katz und Peter Mair gewichten den Stellenwert der Programmatik politischer Parteien vor dem Hintergrund verschiedener Parteitypen. Nach ihrer Auffassung wurde der Typus der Massenpartei bzw. der Catch-All Party definiert durch ein spezifisches Interesse seiner Mitglieder, „which is articulated in the programme"[4]. Der moderne Typus der Kartellpartei werde allerdings dadurch gekennzeichnet, dass sich Parteiprogramme immer ähnlicher werden und deren Inhalt dadurch an Bedeutung verliere.[5]

---

[1] *Robert Michels*, Political Parties. A Sociological Study of the Oligarchical Tendencies of Modern Democracy, Kitchener 2001, S. 231 (1. Aufl. 1911).

[2] *Sigmund Neumann*, Das Parteiensystem der Weimarer Republik, Stuttgart 1956, S. 16.

[3] *Angelo Panebianco*, Political Parties: Organization and Power, Cambridge 1988, S. 6.

[4] *Richard S. Katz/Peter Mair*, Changing Models of Party Organization and Party Democracy, in: Party Politics 1 (1995), S. 5–28 (7).

[5] Ebd., S. 22.

Die auf Anthony Downs[6] zurückgehenden so genannten räumlichen Theo-
rien des Parteienwettbewerbs nehmen an, dass die Parteien in ihren Programmen unterschiedliche Lösungen (*policies*) für bestimmte wirtschaftliche und
gesellschaftliche Probleme anbieten und dass die Wähler – je nach ihrer eigenen politischen Position – diejenige Partei präferieren, die ihnen inhaltlich am
nächsten steht. Die mit diesem Ansatz konkurrierende Salienztheorie[7] geht hingegen davon aus, dass jede Partei ihre „eigenen" Politikfelder und Themen
aufweist, bei denen ihr die Wähler eine größere Kompetenz zuweisen als anderen *(issue-ownership)*. Aber auch dieser Ansatz beruht auf der Annahme:
„Electoral manifestos are a key instrument of democratic political parties in
their quest for popular support."[8]

Dass Parteien durch Programme definiert werden, ist freilich nicht bloß eine
These der Parteientheorie, sondern auch ein Befund der politischen Praxis. Die
Gewohnheit, dass Parteien die eigenen politischen Ziele und den sich daraus
ergebenden Handlungsplan in einem schriftlichen Programm festlegen, stammt
bereits aus dem 19. Jahrhundert. Die erste deutsche Partei mit einem festen Parteiprogramm war die 1861 gegründete liberale Deutsche Fortschrittspartei.[9] Die
bis heute existierende Sozialdemokratische Partei Deutschlands (SPD) be-
schloss ihr erstes Programm im Jahr 1875 auf dem Parteitag in Gotha.

Auch die meisten nach 1945 im damaligen Westdeutschland entstandenen
Parteien gaben sich alsbald eigene Programme. Seit dem Inkrafttreten des Par-
teiengesetzes im Jahr 1967 sind die Parteien sogar gesetzlich dazu verpflichtet,
ein schriftliches Programm vorzulegen. Das Parteiengesetz der Bundesrepublik
Deutschland schreibt ausdrücklich vor, dass Parteien ihre Ziele „in politischen
Programmen" niederlegen: „Die Partei muss eine schriftliche Satzung und ein
schriftliches Programm haben."[10] Die Parteien sind verpflichtet, ihr Programm
zu publizieren, was über § 38 PartG sogar mit Sanktionen abgesichert ist. Auch
nach der ständigen Rechtsprechung des Bundesverfassungsgerichts obliegt es
den Parteien „politische Ziele zu formulieren und diese den Bürgern zu vermit-

---

[6] *Anthony Downs*, An Economic Theory of Democracy, New York 1957.

[7] *Ian Budge*, Theory and measurement of party policy positions, in: Ian Budge et al.
(Eds.), Mapping Policy Preferences, Oxford 2001, S. 75–90.

[8] *Kaare Strøm/Jørn Y. Leipart*, Ideology, strategy and party competition in postwar
Norway, in: European Journal of Political Research 17 (1989), S. 263–288 (263).

[9] Vgl. *Manfred Görtemaker*, Deutschland im 19. Jahrhundert. Entwicklungslinien,
Bonn (4. Aufl.) 1994, S. 259.

[10] § 1 Abs. 3 PartG sowie § 6 Abs. 1 vom 31. Januar 1994 (BGBl. I S. 149), zuletzt
geändert durch Artikel 1 des Gesetzes vom 23. August 2011 (BGBl. I S. 1748).

teln"[11]. Dadurch, so das Gericht, nehmen die Parteien eine Vermittlerrolle zwischen Staat und Gesellschaft wahr.[12]

Parteiprogramme sind somit nicht nur in der Theorie, sondern auch historisch und rechtlich betrachtet ein Wesenselement politischer Parteien in Deutschland. Sie erfüllen dabei mehrere Funktionen. Heino Kaack unterschied bereits vor längerer Zeit zwischen einer Außen- und einer Binnendimension: „Die Programme der politischen Parteien haben einerseits die Aufgabe, nach außen zu wirken, andererseits die Funktion, das innere Gefüge der Partei zu gestalten."[13]

Nach innen soll ein Parteiprogramm als verbindliche Richtschnur dienen, die das politische Denken und Handeln der Parteimitglieder bestimmt. Wahlprogramme werden ja in der Regel von Parteitagen verabschiedet und können so als programmatische Festlegung zukünftiger Politik interpretiert werden. Hinzu kommen eine Integrations- und eine Legitimierungsfunktion: Parteiprogramme sollen Identität stiften und den Zusammenhalt der Parteimitglieder fördern sowie das Agieren der Parteiführung legitimieren. *Nach außen* sollen Parteiprogramme werbend wirken, indem sie neue Mitglieder ansprechen und Wähler für die Partei gewinnen. Wichtig ist zudem die Funktion der Abgrenzung gegenüber anderen Parteien, was Kaack als „Profilfunktion"[14] bezeichnete.[15] Dabei geht es nicht nur um die Wähler: „Wenn man Wahlprogramme aufmerksam durchliest, fallen einem noch weitere mögliche Adressaten auf. Das sind die Interessengruppen, vor allem diejenigen, die mit einer Partei seit langem verbunden sind. Ihnen muss die Partei signalisieren, wie sie den jeweiligen Interessenstandpunkt unter den aktuellen wirtschaftlichen und politischen Bedingungen weiterhin vertreten will."[16] Auch potentiellen Koalitionspartnern wird durch das Parteiprogramm das politische Profil der eigenen Partei deutlich gemacht.

---

[11] BVerfGE 85, 264 (285 f.); vgl. mit ähnlichen Formulierungen BVerfGE 91, 276 (286).

[12] Vgl. *Richard Stöss*, Parteienstaat oder Parteiendemokratie?, in: Oscar W. Gabriel u. a. (Hrsg.), Parteiendemokratie in Deutschland, Opladen 2002, S. 13–35.

[13] *Heino Kaack*, Geschichte und Struktur des deutschen Parteiensystems, Opladen 1971, S. 402.

[14] Ebd., S. 402.

[15] Zu den Funktionen von Parteiprogrammen vgl. auch *Michael D. McDonald/Silvia M. Mendes*, The policy space of party manifestos, in: Michael Laver (ed.), Estimating the Policy Position of Political Actors, New York/London, S. 90–114; *Andrea Volkens*, Handbuch zur Inhaltsanalyse programmatischer Dokumente von Parteien und Regierungen in der Bundesrepublik Deutschland, Berlin 1998.

[16] *Franz Urban Pappi/Susumu Shikano*, Ideologische Signale in den Wahlprogrammen der deutschen Bundestagsparteien 1980 bis 2002, in: Mannheimer Zentrum für Europäische Sozialforschung 76 (2004), S. 1.

Dass diese Funktionen von Parteiprogrammen in der Realität nicht unbedingt erfüllt werden, sondern normative Erwartungen darstellen, versteht sich von selbst. Aus diesem Grund wurde die Bedeutung von Parteiprogrammen auch aus verschiedenen Richtungen wiederholt in Frage gestellt. Für den Soziologen Max Weber, der großen Einfluss auf die moderne Parteientheorie hatte, war die Programmfunktion politischer Parteien bestenfalls zweitrangig. Für ihn stellten Parteien primär gesellschaftliche Organisationen dar, die ihrem Führungspersonal Macht verschaffen und ihren aktiven Teilnehmern dadurch die Verwirklichung ideeller oder materieller Interessen ermöglichen sollen.[17] Auch der berühmte französische Parteienforscher Maurice Duverger formulierte 1951 in seinem Buch *Les Parties Politiques*: „Die heutigen Parteien lassen sich weniger durch ihr Programm oder durch soziale Zugehörigkeit ihrer Anhänger bestimmen als durch die Art ihrer Organisation."[18]

Auch aus der Perspektive der Wähler ist die Bedeutung von Parteiprogrammen ambivalent. Zwar scheinen programmatische Aussagen der politischen Parteien nach wie vor das wichtigste Kriterium für die Wahlentscheidung zu sein: Bei einer repräsentativen Umfrage gaben Anfang 2013 71 Prozent der Befragten an, dass Parteiprogramme für sie das wichtigste Entscheidungskriterium darstellen.[19] Aber die tatsächliche Perzeption von Wahlprogrammen in der Öffentlichkeit ist höchst ungewiss.[20] Im Bundestagswahlkampf 2005 haben nur 10 Prozent der Wähler zumindest eines der Wahlprogramme der Parteien gelesen.[21] Obwohl aktuelle Daten fehlen, ist davon auszugehen, dass nur ein sehr geringer Teil der Wählerschaft eines oder mehrere Parteiprogramme im Detail kennt.[22]

Grundsatzprogramme haben somit nur eine begrenzte Reichweite. Bereits Ossip K. Flechtheim stellte fest, dass die wahre Natur einer Partei sich alleine aus der Programmatik nicht voll und ganz erschließen könne.[23] Eine Partei wird

---

[17] *Max Weber*, Begriff und Wesen der Parteien, in: Wirtschaft und Gesellschaft. Grundriss der verstehenden Soziologie, Frankfurt am Main 2005, S. 211, 212.

[18] *Maurice Duverger*, Les Parties Politiques, Paris 1951 (deutsch 1959), S. XI.

[19] TNS Emnid 2013: Entscheidungskriterium für eine Partei bei Wahlen; Deutschland, 1000 Befragte; andere Angaben: Personen, Spitzenkandidat 14 %, Image der Partei 12 %.

[20] *Daniel Rölle*, Nichts Genaues weiß man nicht!? Über die Perzeption von Wahlprogrammen in der Öffentlichkeit, in: Kölner Zeitschrift für Soziologie und Sozialpsychologie 54 (2002), S. 264–280.

[21] *Marcus Maurer*, Fakten oder Floskeln? Die Inhalte der Wahlprogramme im Bundestagswahlkampf 2005 in der Tagespresse, in: Publizistik 52 (2007), S. 174–190.

[22] Vgl. dazu *Daniel Rölle/Petra Müller/Ulrich Steinbach*, Politik und Fernsehen. Inhaltsanalytische Untersuchungen, Wiesbaden 2001, S. 31–40.

[23] *Ossip K. Flechtheim*, Parteiprogramme, in: Kurt Lenk/Franz Neumann (Hrsg.), Theorie und Soziologie der politischen Parteien, Darmstadt/Neuwied (2. Aufl.) 1974, S. 179.

heute vom Wähler in viel stärkerem Maße als früher auch über ihre Repräsentanten und ihr aktuelles politisches Handeln identifiziert. Im internationalen Vergleich differiert zudem auch der Verbindlichkeitsgrad von Parteiprogrammen erheblich. In den Vereinigten Staaten von Amerika ist die Zielfindungsfunktion der politischen Parteien bekanntlich deutlich schwächer ausgeprägt als in Europa (allerdings ist bemerkenswert, dass es in den USA seit dem Beginn der 1980er Jahre bei beiden US-amerikanischen Parteien zu einer programmatischen Profilierung und gegenseitigen Abgrenzung gekommen ist).[24]

Trotz dieser Einschränkungen gilt: Parteiprogramme lassen Rückschlüsse auf politische Positionen der jeweiligen Parteien zu. Ein empirischer Forschungszweig der Politikwissenschaft wendet deshalb bereits seit längerem inhaltsanalytische Methoden an, um die Policy-Konzeptionen (räumliche Theorie) bzw. inhaltlichen Schwerpunkte (Salienztheorie) in Parteiprogrammen zu bestimmen.[25]

In Deutschland kann man mehrere Arten von Parteiprogrammen unterscheiden:[26] Ein *Grundsatzprogramm* enthält die grundsätzlichen Forderungen, Ziele und Werte einer politischen Partei, es soll für eine längere Zeit, mitunter für mehr als ein Jahrzehnt, Gültigkeit haben und ist deshalb relativ abstrakt formuliert. Davon zu unterscheiden ist das *Wahlprogramm* einer Partei, das meist für die Dauer einer Legislaturperiode angelegt ist und Ziele beinhaltet, die innerhalb dieses Zeitraums durchgesetzt werden sollen. Wahlprogramme sind deshalb viel konkreter abgefasst als Grundsatzprogramme.[27] Ein noch engeres Themenspektrum umfasst das *Aktionsprogramm*, das meist Forderungen zu einem bestimmten Politikbereich zum Gegenstand hat. Alle Programmtypen werden in der Regel von einer eigenen Programmkommission erarbeitet und von einem Parteitag beschlossen.[28]

---

[24] Vgl. *Klaus Stüwe*, USA, Schwalbach 2013, S. 143 ff.

[25] Hervorzuheben ist hier insbesondere das Comparative Manifesto Project; vgl. Ian Budge et al. (eds.), Mapping Policy Preferences. Estimates for Parties, Electors, and Governments 1945–1998, Oxford 2001; Hans-Dieter Klingemann et al. (eds.), Mapping Policy Preferences II: Comparing 24 OECD and 24 CEE Countries, 1990–2003, Oxford 2006.

[26] Vgl. dazu *Hans Kremendahl*, Einführung. Parteiprogramme in der parlamentarischen Demokratie der Bundesrepublik Deutschland, in: Siegfried Hergt (Hrsg.), Parteiprogramme. Grundsatzprogrammatik und aktuelle politische Ziele von SPD, CDU, CSU, FDP, DKP, NPD, Opladen 1977, S. 11.

[27] Neben Grundsatz- und Wahlprogrammen sind darüber hinaus noch Aktions- und Regierungsprogramme zu nennen; vgl. *Heino Kaack*, Geschichte und Struktur des deutschen Parteiensystems, Opladen 1971, S. 402 ff.

[28] *Wulf Schönbohm*, Funktion, Entstehung und Sprache von Parteiprogrammen, in: APuZ B 34–35 (1974), S. 17.

Da es vor allem das Grundsatzprogramm ist, das die weltanschauliche Identität einer politischen Partei in Deutschland konstituiert, wird sich die folgende qualitative Analyse auf diese Programmart beschränken. Im Mittelpunkt der Untersuchung wird die Frage stehen, welchen Stellenwert das Eigentum in den Grundsatzprogrammen der politischen Parteien in Deutschland seit 1945 hat.

In einem ersten Schritt wird zunächst erläutert, welche Eigentumskonzeptionen die Programme der Parteien in der Gründungsphase der Bundesrepublik prägten. Im zweiten Schritt werden anschließend die aktuellen Grundsatzprogramme der wichtigsten politischen Parteien in Deutschland miteinander verglichen. Die Analyse wird sich auf die Parteien beschränken, die im 17. Deutschen Bundestag (2009–2013) vertreten waren: CDU und CSU, SPD, Bündnis90/Die Grünen, FDP sowie die Linke.

II. Scharfe Polarisierung: Eigentumsvorstellungen der Parteien in der Gründungsphase der Bundesrepublik

Nach dem Zweiten Weltkrieg bildeten die verschiedenen Eigentumsvorstellungen *das* zentrale Unterscheidungsmerkmal der programmatischen und ideologischen Positionen der politischen Parteien. In den westlichen Besatzungszonen Deutschlands hatten die Besatzungsbehörden durch Verordnungen vom September bis Dezember 1945 den Weg für die Bildung von Parteien frei gegeben. Vier Parteien wurden lizenziert, die sich größtenteils an der Parteienlandschaft der Weimarer Republik orientierten: SPD und KPD wurden wieder begründet, die Liberalen schlossen sich unter verschiedenen Namen (FDP, LDPD, DVP) zusammen, und als neue Volksparteien katholischer und evangelischer Christdemokraten bildeten sich die CDU und in Bayern die CSU. Ein Blick in die damaligen programmatischen Aussagen der Parteien zeigt, wie diese sich insbesondere in der Eigentumsfrage voneinander abgrenzten.

So bildete das Eigentumsrecht für die verschiedenen *liberalen Parteien*, die zwischen 1945 und 1947 in Deutschland entstanden, in der Regel ein Kernelement ihrer politischen Programmatik. Da die Vorläufer der heutigen FDP zunächst auf regionaler Ebene gegründet wurden, gab es zunächst noch verschiedene programmatische Strömungen.[29] In Niedersachsen, Nordrhein-Westfalen und Hessen setzten die liberalen Neugründungen klare wirtschaftsliberale Akzente. Für die FDP der britischen Besatzungszone z. B. bildete das Eigentumsrecht in ihrem „Wangerooger Programm" von 1948 die Grundlage ihrer wirtschaftspolitischen Vorstellungen. „Den Unternehmern", hieß es dort, „muss das

---

[29] Vgl. dazu *Peter Juling*, Programmatische Entwicklung der FDP 1946 bis 1969, Meisenheim am Glan 1977; *Jürgen Dittberner*, Die FDP: Geschichte, Personen, Organisation, Perspektiven. Eine Einführung, Wiesbaden 2010, S. 290.

Eigentum am Betriebe und die verantwortliche Geschäftsführung unter alleiniger Verfügung über die das Risiko bestimmenden Faktoren zugebilligt werden."[30] In den südwestlichen Bundesländern sowie in Hamburg und Bremen bildeten sich hingegen liberale Parteien mit eher sozialliberaler Ausrichtung.

Am 11. und 12. Dezember 1948 vereinigten sich die westdeutschen liberalen Parteien in Heppenheim zur Freien Demokratischen Partei (FDP). In der aus diesem Anlass verabschiedeten „Heppenheimer Proklamation", dem Gründungsdokument der FDP, ging es mehr um konkrete politische Fragen wie den Marshallplan und den Lastenausgleich. Das Eigentumsrecht wurde im Gegensatz zu den Programmen der lokalen Parteivorläufer nicht eigens betont, die ausdrückliche Ablehnung von Sozialisierungen konnte allenfalls als indirektes Bekenntnis zum Privateigentum interpretiert werden. Auffällig jedoch erschien eine sozialliberale Akzentuierung: „Wir bekennen uns zu dem traditionellen Ziel der deutschen Sozialpolitik, den wirtschaftlich Schwachen im Daseinskampf zu helfen."[31]

Aufgrund unterschiedlicher politischer Vorstellungen der Landesparteien gelang es der Bundes-FDP erst 1957, sich auf ein Grundsatzprogramm zu einigen, in dem wirtschaftsliberale und sozialliberale Positionen gleichermaßen bezogen wurden. Einerseits hieß es im „Berliner Programm" vom 26. Januar 1957: „Die Sozialpolitik muß gemeinsam mit der Wirtschaftspolitik die Voraussetzungen dafür schaffen, dass alle für die Wechselfälle des Lebens vorsorgen können. Sie will die Furcht vor Krankheit, Not und Alter nehmen und allen unverschuldet in Not Geratenen rasch und ausreichend helfen." Andererseits wurde betont: „Jeder soll aus eigener Kraft Eigentum bilden. (...) Die Garantie des Privateigentums schließt jedes Bekenntnis zur Sozialisierung aus."[32]

Ein Kontrastprogramm bot die *Sozialdemokratische Partei Deutschlands* (SPD), die sich auf dem Parteitag vom 9. bis 11. Mai 1946 in Hannover neubegründet hatte. Damit galt das 1925 in Heidelberg[33] beschlossene Grundsatzprogramm wieder, das – stärker noch als das gemäßigte Görlitzer Programm von 1921 – von „klassenkämpferisch-marxistischen Tönen" geprägt war: „Das Ziel

---

[30] Wangerooger Programm der Freien Demokratischen Partei, beschlossen am 03.–10.01.1948, Quelle: Archiv des Liberalismus, Bestand Liberale Parteien bis zur Gründung der FDP; Signatur 2, S. 1.

[31] Heppenheimer Proklamation der Freien Demokratischen Partei vom 12.12.1948, Quelle: Archiv des Liberalismus, Bestand Liberale Parteien bis zur Gründung der FDP, Signatur 45, S. 2.

[32] Berliner Programm der Freien Demokratischen Partei, beschlossen auf dem Bundesparteitag in Berlin am 26.01.1957, Quelle: Archiv des Liberalismus, Druckschriftenbestand, D 1–29.

[33] Vgl. *Klaus Schönhoven*, Der Heidelberger Programmparteitag von 1925: Sozialdemokratische Standortbestimmung in der Weimarer Republik, Heidelberg 1995.

der Arbeiterklasse kann nur erreicht werden durch die Verwandlung des kapitalistischen Privateigentums an den Produktionsmitteln in gesellschaftliches Eigentum. (...) Im Kampf gegen das kapitalistische System fordert die Sozialdemokratische Partei Deutschlands: Grund und Boden, Bodenschätze und natürliche Kraftquellen, die der Energieerzeugung dienen, sind der kapitalistischen Ausbeutung zu entziehen und in den Dienst der Gemeinschaft zu überführen."[34]

Diese Formulierungen müssen freilich aus dem zeitlichen Kontext des Jahres 1925 heraus betrachtet werden. Das Heidelberger Programm gilt in der Forschung als der „ideologische Preis"[35], den die Mehrheitssozialdemokratie für die Wiedervereinigung mit der weiter links stehenden USPD zu zahlen hatte. Zudem hatten sich in der Zeit der Hyperinflation die sozialen Spannungen vertieft, sodass die SPD bei den Reichstagswahlen im Mai 1924 zahlreiche Wähler an die KPD verloren hatte. Mit einem kämpferischen Programm sollten diese Wähler zurückgewonnen werden.

An dieses Heidelberger Programm, das unübersehbar von einer marxistisch gefärbten Eigentumsfeindlichkeit geprägt war, knüpfte die SPD also 1946 zunächst wieder an. Auch die im Mai 1946 beschlossenen „Politischen Leitlinien" atmeten noch einen revolutionären Geist: „Die jetzt noch herrschenden Eigentumsverhältnisse entsprechen nicht mehr den sonstigen gesellschaftlichen Zuständen und Bedürfnissen. (...) Die Sozialisierung hat zu beginnen bei den Bodenschätzen und den Grundstoffindustrien. (...) Eine grundlegende Agrar- und Bodenreform ist unter Enteignung der Großgrundbesitzer sofort einzuleiten."[36]

Doch schon bald sollte sich zeigen, dass der klassenkämpferische Ton dieser programmatischen Äußerungen nicht mehr der sozialdemokratischen Realität entsprach. Die SPD in den Westzonen begann sich in der Praxis, auch unter dem Eindruck der Zwangsvereinigung der Ost-SPD mit der KPD – von der marxistischen Wirtschaftslehre zu verabschieden. Trotzdem lehnte Kurt Schumacher, der bis zu seinem Tod im Jahr 1952 Parteivorsitzender der SPD war, jede Diskussion um ein neues Grundsatzprogramm ab. Erst 1959 sollte es auf dem Parteitag in Bad Godesberg zu einem neuen Programm kommen.

Wer nun glaubte, dass *CDU und CSU* in der frühen Nachkriegszeit ein Gegenprogramm zu den eigentumsfeindlichen Vorstellungen der SPD entwarfen,

---

[34] *Susanne Miller/Heinrich Potthoff*, Kleine Geschichte der SPD, Bonn (7. Aufl.) 1991, S. 361, 366.

[35] *Heinrich August Winkler*, Klassenbewegung oder Volkspartei? Zur sozialdemokratischen Programmdebatte 1920–1925, in: Geschichte und Gesellschaft 1 (1982), S. 9–54.

[36] Politische Leitsätze der SPD (Mai 1946), Quelle: Theo Stammen (Hrsg.), Einigkeit und Recht und Freiheit. Westdeutsche Innenpolitik 1945–1955, München 1965, S. 120–126.

der täuschte sich.[37] Die Unionsparteien waren erst auf Länder- und Zonenebene organisiert und hatten deshalb zunächst kein einheitliches Parteiprogramm. Aber nicht nur in der Sowjetzone, sondern auch bei einer Reihe westdeutscher Parteigründungen des Jahres 1945 bekannte sich die CDU zu mehr oder weniger sozialistischem Gedankengut. So war z. B. in den so genannten „Frankfurter Leitsätzen" der hessischen CDU vom September 1945 von einem „wirtschaftlichen Sozialismus" die Rede. Die Leitsätze forderten die „Überführung gewisser großer Urproduktionen, Großindustrien und Großbanken in Gemeineigentum"[38]. Die „Kölner Leitsätze" der CDU im Rheinland vom Juni 1945 prägten das Wort vom „christlichen Sozialismus"[39].

Am bekanntesten wurde das „Ahlener Programm" der CDU in Nordrhein-Westfalen vom Februar 1947, das mit dem Satz begann: „Das kapitalistische Wirtschaftssystem ist den staatlichen und sozialen Lebensinteressen des deutschen Volkes nicht gerecht geworden." Als Alternative zu „kapitalistischem Gewinn- und Machtstreben" wurde eine wirtschaftliche Ordnung entworfen, zu der u. a. gehörte: Vergesellschaftung des Kohlenbergbaus und der eisenschaffenden Industrie, verstärkte Kontrolle des Geld-, Bank- und Versicherungswesens, Kartellgesetze gegen übergroße Konzerne und monopolartige Unternehmen.

Aber es gab auch andere Akzente. In den frühen programmatischen Aussagen der Unionsparteien fanden sich auch Positionen der christlichen Sozialethik, insbesondere der katholischen Soziallehre, die im Zusammenhang mit der Enzyklika *Quadragesimo anno* Papst Pius' XI. entstanden war. Danach ist das Eigentum zwar unmittelbar in der personalen Würde des Menschen verankert, zugleich aber darf die Nutzung des Eigentums nicht egoistisch erfolgen, sondern muss stets den Mitmenschen verpflichtet sein. Aufgabe des Staates ist es nach dieser Auffassung, dafür zu sorgen, dass sich die Eigentumsverhältnisse gemeinwohlgerecht entwickeln.[40] Bereits eine der ersten programmatischen Schriften der CDU, die so genannten Kölner Leitsätze vom Juni 1945, lassen diese Eigentumsvorstellung erkennen. Dort hieß es: „Das Recht auf Eigentum wird gewährleistet." Aber zugleich: „Soziale Gerechtigkeit und soziale Liebe sollen eine neue Volksgemeinschaft beschirmen, die die gottergebene Freiheit

---

[37] Vgl. *Klaus Stüwe*, Entstehungsbedingungen wirtschaftspolitischer Aussagen des Grundgesetzes, in: Nils Goldschmidt/Klaus Stüwe/Frank Zschaler (Hrsg.), Arbeitswelt und Sozialstaat (= Kulturelle Ökonomik, Bd. 9), Münster u. a. 2009, S. 108.

[38] Frankfurter Leitsätze vom September 1945, veröffentlicht bei Ossip K. Flechtheim (Hrsg.), Dokumente zur parteipolitischen Entwicklung in Deutschland seit 1945, Bd. 2, Berlin 1963, S. 36–45.

[39] Ebd., Zitat 35.

[40] Vgl. *Anton Rauscher*, Die christliche Lehre über das Eigentum, in: ders. u. a. (Hrsg.), Handbuch der Katholischen Soziallehre, Berlin 2008, S. 511–522.

des Einzelnen und die Ansprüche der Gemeinschaft mit den Forderungen des Gemeinwohls zu verbinden weiß."[41]

Wie die katholische Soziallehre, so forderten auch die frühen Programme der CDU eine breite Eigentumsstreuung. Möglichst viele Menschen sollten persönliches Eigentum bilden. Sowohl die „Frankfurter Leitsätze" als auch die „Kölner Leitsätze" plädierten für die Schaffung von neuem Eigentum für die besitzlosen Schichten: „Durch gerechten Güterausgleich und soziale Lohngestaltung soll es dem Nichtbesitzenden ermöglicht werden, zu Eigentum zu kommen."[42] Die 1949 verabschiedeten „Düsseldorfer Leitsätze" sprachen sogar von einer „größtmöglichen Streuung des Eigentums"[43]. Die CDU war damit die erste politische Partei, die die Vermögensbildung der Arbeitnehmer als eines ihrer wichtigsten Ziele propagierte.

Die Idee einer Individual- und Sozialfunktion des Eigentums wies im Übrigen – auch wenn dies den Zeitgenossen damals nicht immer bewusst gewesen war – unverkennbar Parallelen mit dem ökonomischen Konzept der neoliberalen Freiburger Schule auf, dem Alfred Müller-Armack 1947 den Namen „Soziale Marktwirtschaft" gegeben hatte.[44] Mit Ludwig Erhard betrat wenig später ein der CDU nahe stehender Politiker die politische Bühne, der dieses Konzept als Direktor der Verwaltung für Wirtschaft der Bizone und später als erster Wirtschaftsminister der Bundesrepublik auch praktisch verwirklichen wollte.

Dass sich diese Eigentumsvorstellung auch in der politischen Programmatik der CDU durchsetzen konnte, lag freilich in erster Linie an Konrad Adenauer, der seit Februar 1946 Vorsitzender der CDU in Nordrhein-Westfalen war und 1949 zum ersten Bundeskanzler gewählt wurde. Adenauer lehnte den Begriff „christlicher Sozialismus" ebenso ab wie die Verstaatlichung der Schlüsselindustrien: „In seinen Augen war das Privateigentum der sicherste Schutz für die wirtschaftliche und damit auch für die politische Freiheit."[45] Die Grenzen des Eigentumsrechts zog Adenauer ganz im Sinne der katholischen Soziallehre

---

[41] Am Entwurf der „Kölner Leitsätze" hatten der Dominikanerprovinzial Pater Laurentius Siemer und der Professor für Sozialethik Pater Eberhard Welty mitgewirkt.

[42] Kölner Leitsätze der CDU vom Juni 1945, veröffentlicht bei http://www. grundsatzprogramm.cdu.de/doc/1945_2_Koelner-Leitsaetze.pdf.

[43] Düsseldorfer Leitsätze der CDU in der britischen Besatzungszone vom 15. Juli 1949, veröffentlicht bei: http://www.kas.de/upload/themen/programmatik_der_cdu/ programme/1949_Duesseldorfer-Leitsaetze_Kurzfassung.pdf.

[44] *Alfred Müller-Armack*, Wirtschaftslenkung und Marktwirtschaft, Hamburg 1947.

[45] *Udo Zolleis*, Die CDU. Das politische Leitbild im Wandel der Zeit, Wiesbaden 2007, S. 108.

dort, „wo höherrangige ethische Grundsätze und die Erfordernisse des allgemeinen Wohls dagegen standen"[46].

Stark von der christlichen Soziallehre geprägt war im Übrigen auch das erste Grundsatzprogramm der bayerischen CSU, das im Dezember 1946 in Eichstätt beschlossen wurde. Auch die CSU hielt am persönlichen Eigentum fest, forderte aber zugleich eine möglichst breite Eigentumsverteilung und die Sozialpflichtigkeit: „Das Recht auf Eigentum ist ein natürliches Recht, auf dessen Erfüllung alle Anspruch haben: Eigentum verpflichtet gegenüber der Gemeinschaft: Wir erwarten, dass alle Möglichkeiten geschaffen werden, um jedermann zu einem sittlich berechtigtem Eigentum kommen zu lassen. Wir treten für die Erfüllung der Gemeinschaftspflicht ein, allen jenen zu neuem Eigentum zu verhelfen, die ohne eigene Schuld ihr bisheriges Eigentum verloren haben. Wir verlangen den Schutz des rechtmäßig erworbenen Eigentums. Wir lehnen die Aufhebung des Eigentums durch Kollektivierung oder allgemeine Sozialisierung ab. Wir bekämpfen den rücksichtslosen Eigentumserwerb. Wir vertreten die Überführung von Privat- in Gemeineigentum gegen angemessene Entschädigung dann, wenn es das Gemeinwohl fordert."[47]

Zusammenfassend lässt sich festhalten: Die Eigentumsvorstellungen der politischen Parteien konnten vor der Gründung der Bundesrepublik unterschiedlicher nicht sein. Mehr noch: Sie waren das zentrale Unterscheidungsmerkmal der verschiedenen Parteien. Die Positionen reichten von einem individualistischen Eigentumsverständnis der Liberalen über den Grundsatz der sozialen Bindung des Eigentums bei CDU und CSU bis hin zur sozialistischen Auffassung, wonach erst die Abschaffung des Privateigentums die „Selbstentfremdung des Menschen" beende.

Die verschiedenen Eigentumskonzeptionen bildeten in den Jahren 1948/49 auch eine tiefe Konfliktlinie im Parlamentarischen Rat[48], der sich in Bonn mit einem Verfassungsentwurf für einen westdeutschen Staat befasste. Die Sozialisierungsermächtigung des Art. 15 GG in unmittelbarer Nachbarschaft zur Eigentumsgarantie des Art. 14 GG zeugt heute noch von der politischen Konkurrenz zweier prinzipiell konträrer und alternativer Wirtschaftsformen: „liberale,

---

[46] Ebd.

[47] Grundsatzprogramm der Christlich-Sozialen Union, beschlossen am 14./15. Dezember 1946 auf der CSU-Landesversammlung in Eichstätt, veröffentlicht bei: http://www.hss.de/fileadmin/migration/downloads/1946-Grundsatzprogramm.pdf.

[48] Nachweise der Erörterungen im Parlamentarischen Rat sind angegeben in JÖR n. F. 1 (1951), S. 144 ff.

privatkapitalistisch organisierte Marktwirtschaft einerseits und deren Überwindung durch Formen der Gemeinwirtschaft andererseits"[49].

Mit dem Sieg der CDU/CSU bei den Bundestagswahlen vom 14. August 1949, der Bildung der christlich-liberalen Koalition und der Wahl Konrad Adenauers zum Bundeskanzler fiel wenige Wochen nach der Verabschiedung des Grundgesetzes eine zentrale ordnungspolitische Richtungsentscheidung. Die ersten Bundestagswahlen brachten nicht nur eine Niederlage von KPD und SPD, sondern das Wahlergebnis konnte auch als Plebiszit gegen Planwirtschaft und Sozialisierung und für eine marktwirtschaftliche Eigentumsordnung verstanden werden.[50]

Das Privateigentum an Produktionsmitteln bildete in den folgenden Jahren eine der wesentlichen Gestaltungselemente der Sozialen Marktwirtschaft, welche die Vorteile einer freien Marktwirtschaft, insbesondere eine hohe Leistungsfähigkeit und Güterversorgung, mit dem Sozialstaat als Korrektiv verbindet.[51] Der Erfolg dieses Wirtschaftsmodells trug nicht nur zum wirtschaftlichen Aufstieg der Bundesrepublik Deutschlands bei, sondern wirkte sich zugleich auf die programmatische Entwicklung der Parteienlandschaft aus. CDU und CSU gewannen in den 1950er und 1960er Jahren eine Bundestagswahl nach der anderen und konnten sich damit in ihrer Eigentumskonzeption weitgehend bestätigt sehen. Gleiches galt für die FDP, auch wenn sie aufgrund der absoluten Mehrheit der Union im Jahr 1957 zeitweise in die Opposition gehen musste.

Die Sozialdemokraten mussten hingegen erkennen, dass ein Festhalten an sozialistischen, eigentumsfeindlichen Vorstellungen die meisten Wähler nicht überzeugen konnte. Dies führte 1959 auf dem Parteitag in Bad Godesberg zu einer programmatischen Wende, in der sich die SPD erstmals ausdrücklich zum Eigentumsrecht bekannte: „Das private Eigentum an Produktionsmitteln hat Anspruch auf Schutz und Förderung, soweit es nicht den Aufbau einer gerechten Sozialordnung hindert." Die SPD übernahm in der Folgezeit zunehmend Elemente der Sozialen Marktwirtschaft. Seit den 1990er Jahren verwendet sie den Ausdruck sogar in ihren programmatischen Schriften.[52]

---

[49] *Otto Depenheuer*, Entwicklungslinien des verfassungsrechtlichen Eigentumsschutzes, in: Thomas von Danwitz u. a. (Hrsg.), Bericht zur Lage des Eigentums, Berlin u. a. 2002, S. 115.

[50] Vgl. dazu auch *Klaus Stüwe*, Entstehungsbedingungen wirtschaftspolitischer Aussagen des Grundgesetzes, in: Nils Goldschmidt u. a. (Hrsg.), Arbeitswelt und Sozialstaat in einer globalisierten Gesellschaft, Berlin 2009, S. 95–115.

[51] *Alfred Müller-Armack*, Soziale Marktwirtschaft, in: Handwörterbuch der Sozialwissenschaften, Stuttgart u. a. 1956, S. 390 ff.

[52] *Martin Nonhoff*, Hegemonieanalyse: Theorie, Methode und Forschungspraxis, in: Reiner Keller (Hrsg.), Handbuch sozialwissenschaftliche Diskursanalyse 2: Forschungspraxis, Wiesbaden 2008.

Die Kommunistische Partei war bereits im Jahr 1956 verboten worden. In der Begründung seiner Verbotsentscheidung wies das Bundesverfassungsgericht unter anderem darauf hin, die KPD ziele auf eine gewaltsame „Veränderung der ökonomischen Eigentumsverhältnisse (...) als Voraussetzung für eine Änderung der sozialen und politischen Struktur"[53].

III. Eigentumskonzeptionen der heutigen politischen Parteien

Die nachfolgende Analyse nimmt die aktuellen Grundsatzprogramme der derzeit sechs im Deutschen Bundestag vertretenen Parteien in den Blick. Die Programme sind im Einzelnen:

– *Freiheit und Sicherheit – Grundsätze für Deutschland.* Grundsatzprogramm der CDU, beschlossen vom 21. Parteitag am 3. bis 4. Dezember 2007 in Hannover, 121 Seiten.

– *Hamburger Programm.* Das Grundsatzprogramm der Sozialdemokratischen Partei Deutschlands (SPD), beschlossen auf dem Bundesparteitag am 28. Oktober 2007 in Hamburg, 76 Seiten.

– *Chancen für alle! In Freiheit und Verantwortung gemeinsam Zukunft gestalten.* Grundsatzprogramm der CSU, beschlossen vom Parteitag am 28. September 2007 in München, 195 Seiten.

– *Die Zukunft ist grün.* Grundsatzprogramm von BÜNDNIS 90/DIE GRÜNEN, beschlossen auf der Bundesdelegiertenkonferenz am 15. bis 17. März 2002 in Berlin, 181 Seiten.

– *Verantwortung für die Freiheit. Karlsruher Freiheitsthesen der FDP für eine offene Bürgergesellschaft.* Beschluss des 63. Ordentlichen Bundesparteitages der FDP vom 22. April 2012 in Karlsruhe, 106 Seiten.

– *Programm der Partei DIE LINKE.* Beschluss des Parteitages der Partei DIE LINKE vom 21. bis 23. Oktober 2012 in Erfurt, 77 Seiten.

Die Grundsatzprogramme wurden im Hinblick auf die Eigentumsvorstellungen Rahmen inhaltsanalytisch untersucht. Schon quantitativ fielen dabei signifikante Unterschiede ins Auge:

---

[53] BverfGE 5, 85 (340).

Häufigkeit der Nennung des Begriffs „Eigentum"
in den Grundsatzprogrammen der Bundestagsparteien

Partei	Programm	In Kraft seit	Gesamtzahl der Wörter	Zita-tionen	Anteil in %
CDU	Grundsatzprogramm Freiheit und Sicherheit. Grundsätze für Deutschland	03.12.2007	27.337	9	0,033
CSU	Grundsatzprogramm Chancen für alle!	28.09.2007	30.558	12	0,039
FDP	Verantwortung für die Freiheit – Karlsruher Freiheitsthesen für eine offene Bürgergesellschaft	22.04.2012	20.152	46	0,228
Die Grünen	Grundsatzprogramm Die Zukunft ist grün	17.03.2002	43.828	7	0,015
Die Linke	Programm	23.10.2011	28.621	54	0,188
SPD	Grundsatzprogramm Hamburger Programm	28.10.2007	16.130	6	0,037

Die Tabelle zeigt die unterschiedliche Bedeutung des Begriffs „Eigentum" für die Parteien. Der höchste Wert wird in den Programmen der FDP (0,228 %) und der Linken (0,188 %) erreicht, während im Programm von Bündnis 90/ Grüne der niedrigste Wert gemessen wurde (0,015 %). In den Programmen von CDU (0,033 %), CSU (0,039 %) und SPD (0,037 %) liegen die Werte relativ dicht beieinander. Kann man aus diesem quantitativen Befund folgern, dass die Eigentumsfrage für die FDP und Linke eine größere programmatische Rolle spielt als für die anderen Parteien?

1. FDP

Eine qualitative Analyse bestätigt diese Hypothese. Im neuen Grundsatzprogramm der FDP, das im April 2012 beschlossen wurde, stellt der Eigentumsbegriff neben der „Freiheit" das zentrale Schlüsselwort dar. Ihm ist sogar ein eigener Abschnitt gewidmet, in dem es heißt: „Privates Eigentum ist notwendige Bedingung für Freiheit und Verantwortung in der Gesellschaft. (...) Ohne Eigentum sind keine Soziale Marktwirtschaft und kein Wettbewerb zum Wohle aller denkbar." Aufgabe des liberalen Rechtsstaats sei es daher, das Eigentum zu schützen: „Der Schutz privaten Eigentums ist (...) kein Grundrecht zweiter Klasse, sondern ersten Ranges."[54] Aus diesem Grund erteilt die FDP allen Umverteilungsbestrebungen z. B. durch Besteuerung von Vermögen, eine klare Absage.

Im Gegensatz zum früheren Programm, den „Wiesbadener Grundsätzen", die noch stärker von einem individualistischen Eigentumsbegriff und einem „Stakkato"[55] von Steuersenkungsversprechen geprägt waren, sind im aktuellen Programm jedoch auch deutlichere sozialliberale Zwischentöne zu erkennen. So wird „Solidarität" zu einer liberalen „Tugend" erklärt: „Die Tugend der Solidarität zeigt sich in sozialer Verantwortung." In diesem Sinn erkennt die FDP auch die Verantwortungsdimension von Eigentum an: „Eigentum stellt aber auch eine Verpflichtung zu seiner Pflege und zu einem verantwortungsbewussten Verhalten dar. Eigentum verpflichtet." Ob diese neuen Akzente eher eine Reaktion auf den Imageverfall waren, den die FDP seit 2009 erfahren hat, oder aber eine programmatische Öffnung hin zu neuen möglichen Koalitionspartnern darstellt, bleibt offen.

2. Die Linke

Den programmatischen Kontrapunkt zur FDP stellt die Linkspartei dar, deren Grundsatzprogramm von 2011 einen negativen Eigentumsbegriff aufweist. „Die Überwindung der Dominanz kapitalistischen Eigentums in der Wirtschaft" ist für die Linken eine der „wichtigsten Grundlagen". Die Linke „kämpft für die Veränderung der Eigentumsverhältnisse"[56]. Sie will mehr „öffentliches Eigentum": „Grund und Boden, Naturschätze und Produktionsmittel können zum Zwecke der Vergesellschaftung in Gemeineigentum übergeführt werden." Das ganze Programm durchzieht ein Ressentiment gegen größere Einkommen und Vermögen, allenfalls kleineres Privateigentum wird toleriert. Auch Klassenkampfrhetorik findet sich. So soll „die ökonomische Macht derer, die an Armut, Ausbeutung, Naturzerstörung, Rüstung und Kriegen verdienen, zurückgedrängt und überwunden werden". Um dies zu erreichen, erstreben die Linken „ein anderes Wirtschafts- und Gesellschaftssystem".

Auch für das Grundsatzprogramm der Linke ist der Eigentumsbegriff demnach eine zentrale Kategorie, freilich unter gänzlich anderen Vorzeichen als bei der FDP. Geplant ist der Umbau der als neoliberal und sozial ungerecht gewerteten Gesellschaft. Bei der Verabschiedung des Programms sprach Parteichef

---

[54] Verantwortung für die Freiheit. Karlsruher Freiheitsthesen der FDP für eine offene Bürgergesellschaft, beschlossen am 22.04.2012, Berlin 2012, S. 66.

[55] *Lisa Caspari*, Die FPD muss ihre Rhetorik erwärmen, Zeit Online vom 22.04.2012 (http://www.zeit.de/politik/deutschland/2012-04/fdp-programm-karlsruhe/).

[56] Programm der Partei Die Linke vom 23.10.2011, Berlin 2011, S. 27, 29.

Klaus Ernst von einem Meilenstein in der Geschichte der Linkspartei: „Unser Programm ist eine Kampfansage an die herrschenden Verhältnisse und eine Kampfansage an die Herrschenden."[57]

3. SPD

Die Sozialdemokraten hatten sich bereits 1959 auf dem Parteitag in Bad Godesberg von ihrer sozialistischen Eigentumsfeindlichkeit gelöst. Im aktuell geltenden Hamburger Programm, das im Jahr 2007 beschlossen wurde, leugnet die SPD ihre historischen wurzeln nicht. Nach wie vor bekennt sie sich zur „Idee des demokratischen Sozialismus". Ein Recht auf Eigentum wird dort ebenfalls nicht ausdrücklich formuliert. Eine Veränderung der bestehenden Eigentumsverhältnisse ist jedoch längst nicht mehr das Ziel der Sozialdemokratie. Die Begriffe „Sozialisierung" und „Verstaatlichung" sucht man vergebens. Stattdessen wird die „Soziale Marktwirtschaft" als „herausragendes Erfolgsmodell"[58] bezeichnet.

Ein Sozialdemokrat aus früheren Tagen würde sich wohl wundern, wenn er im aktuellen SPD-Programm läse: „Wir wollen die Potentiale der Kapitalmärkte für qualitatives Wachstum nutzen." Freilich wird zugleich mehrfach die Sozialpflichtigkeit von Eigentum betont. So heißt es einmal: „Eigentum verpflichtet: Wer überdurchschnittlich verdient, mehr Vermögen besitzt als andere, muss auch mehr zum Wohl der Gesellschaft beitragen", an anderer Stelle mit Verweis auf das Grundgesetz: „Eigentum verpflichtet. Sein Gebrauch soll zugleich dem Wohle der Allgemeinheit dienen." Und schließlich: „Unternehmerische Freiheit und soziale Verantwortung sind für uns zwei Seiten derselben Medaille." Mit dieser betont starken Hervorhebung der Sozialbindung des Eigentums grenzt sich die SPD von den Eigentumskonzeptionen der anderen Parteien ab. Auch einige konkretere Ziele wie eine „vorsorgende Sozialpolitik" und Mitbestimmung in den Unternehmen lassen die Unterschiede deutlich werden.

4. Bündnis 90/Die Grünen

Das Grundsatzprogramm der Partei Bündnis90/Die Grünen stammt aus dem Jahr 2002 und ist damit das älteste der untersuchten Programme. „Die Zukunft ist grün" lautet der Titel, und aus dieser Formulierung lässt sich seine Schwerpunktsetzung bereits erahnen. Nachhaltigkeit und Ökologie stehen im Zentrum der meisten Abschnitte, vom „ökologischen Zeitalter" über die „ökologische

---

[57] Zitiert nach: dpa vom 23.11.2011.

[58] Hamburger Programm der SPD vom 28.10.2007, Berlin 2007, S. 42.

Marktwirtschaft" bis hin zu einem ökologischen Europa. Andere Ziele der sozialen Bewegungen der 1970er Jahre, in denen die Grünen ihre Wurzeln haben, prägen das aktuelle grüne Programm hingegen etwas schwächer als früher, z. B. Gewaltfreiheit, Nord-Süd-Politik, Geschlechtergerechtigkeit oder das Recht auf Abtreibung.

Obwohl so genannte „Ökosozialisten", welche die Partei in den 1980er Jahren dominiert hatten, heute bei den Grünen keine große Rolle mehr spielen, lässt sich im Wirtschaftskonzept des grünen Parteiprogramms auch heute noch eine gewisse Nähe zu linken Ordnungsvorstellungen erkennen. Bezeichnenderweise fehlt im Stichwortregister der Verweis auf den Eigentumsbegriff. Auch wird an keiner Stelle des Programms auf die Bedeutung des Privateigentums hingewiesen. Stattdessen vertreten die Grünen den Ansatz einer „erweiterten Gerechtigkeit", in dem außer der Verteilungsgerechtigkeit die Geschlechter- und Generationengerechtigkeit zentrale Anliegen sind: „Die gerechte Verteilung der wichtigen gesellschaftlichen Güter ist Kernbestandteil bündnisgrüner Politik." 222 Mal ist von „gerecht" oder „Gerechtigkeit" die Rede. Und auch der Eigentumsbegriff wird fast durchgehend mit dem einschränkenden Attribut „gerecht" verbunden: „Freiheit und Selbstbestimmung brauchen eine gerechte Eigentumsordnung." Sogar eine feministische Stoßrichtung verbinden sich damit: „Die Teilhabe an (...) Eigentum muss gerecht zwischen den Geschlechtern geteilt werden." Zwar bekennen sich die Grünen zu einer „freiheitsorientierten Wirtschaftsordnung", zugleich stehen sie aber „ausdrücklich zur Sozialpflichtigkeit des Eigentums, wie sie im Grundgesetz verankert ist"[59].

5. CDU und CSU

Die größte programmatische Kontinuität des Eigentumsbegriffs findet sich ohne Zweifel bei den beiden Unionsparteien. Die CDU bezeichnet sich im Grundsatzprogramm von 2007 ausdrücklich als „Partei der Sozialen Marktwirtschaft" und lehnt sowohl sozialistische Formen des „Kollektivismus" als auch „einen ungezügelten Kapitalismus"[60] ab. Die soziale Marktwirtschaft wird als „untrennbare Verbindung von freiheitlicher Wirtschafts- und solidarischer Sozialordnung" bezeichnet. Womöglich schwächer als in früheren Programmen, aber immer noch erkennbar ist das Gedankengut der christlichen Soziallehre, etwa wenn formuliert wird: „Die Soziale Marktwirtschaft geht vom einzelnen Menschen als Geschöpf Gottes aus, dessen Würde unantastbar ist."

---

[59] Die Zukunft ist grün. Grundsatzprogramm von BÜNDNIS 90/DIE GRÜNEN vom 17.03.2002, Berlin 2002, S. 46.

[60] Freiheit und Sicherheit. Grundsätze für Deutschland. Grundsatzprogramm der CDU Deutschlands vom 04.12.2007, Berlin 2007, S. 46.

Insbesondere auch das Eigentumskonzept der CDU beruft sich auf ebendiese personale Würde des Menschen. So fordert das Grundsatzprogramm: „Leistung und Eigentum müssen geachtet und geschützt sein. (...) Der Staat hat die Pflicht, privates Eigentum zu schützen." Wie bereits in ihren ersten programmatischen Dokumenten nach dem Krieg ist für die CDU ein „möglichst breit gestreutes Privateigentum an Unternehmen und Grundstücken von zentraler Bedeutung". Und nach wie verweist die CDU auf die soziale Bindung des Eigentums: „In der Sozialen Marktwirtschaft ist der Schutz des Eigentums Voraussetzung dafür, dass es Nutzen für die Allgemeinheit stiften und damit seiner Sozialpflichtigkeit gerecht werden kann." Die CDU bekennt sich deshalb „zum freiheitlichen und sozialverantwortlichen Unternehmertum".

Etwas anders akzentuiert die bayerische Schwesterpartei ihr Eigentumskonzept. Drei Unterschiede fallen ins Auge. Auffallend ist erstens, dass der Begriff „Eigentum" im Grundsatzprogramm der CSU von 2007 erst relativ spät – auf Seite 50 – erstmals auftaucht, und zwar im Zusammenhang mit der Überschrift „Sicherheit als soziales Grundrecht"[61]. Der Staat, heißt es dort, müsse für den Schutz von Eigentum und Vermögen seiner Bürger sorgen. An anderen Stellen wird der Eigentumsbegriff im Zusammenhang mit Formulierungen wie „Durchsetzung von Recht und Gesetz" oder „Gewaltmonopol des Staates" genannt. Eigentum wird demnach zuallererst mit der Sicherheitsfunktion des Staates in Verbindung gebracht. Diese Sicht ist auch quantitativ erfassbar: Während der Eigentumsbegriff im CSU-Grundsatzprogramm zwölf Mal erwähnt wird, taucht der Begriff „Sicherheit" insgesamt 109 Mal auf. Zweitens: Anders als bei der CDU wird im Grundsatzprogramm der CSU das Recht auf Eigentum nicht ethisch begründet und aus der Personwürde des Menschen abgeleitet, sondern einfach als Grundlage der „Wirtschafts- und Gesellschaftsordnung"[62] vorausgesetzt. Da sich die CSU traditionell als Partei des Mittelstandes und der Landwirtschaft versteht, werden die Eigentumsrechte der mittelständischen Unternehmer und der Bauern besonders hervorgehoben.

Ein dritter eigenständiger Akzent des CSU-Programms ist, dass es im Vergleich mit dem CDU-Programm die Sozialbindung des Eigentums noch etwas stärker betont. Auch die CSU beruft sich auf die Idee der sozialen Marktwirtschaft, die „Eigeninteresse und Gemeinwohl bestmöglich in Übereinstimmung" bringe. Die christlich-sozialen Wurzeln der Partei sind hierbei jedoch nicht zu übersehen: „Die ethische Verantwortung der Unternehmer für die Beschäftigten, das Land und seine Menschen ist eine Grundlage der Sozialen Marktwirtschaft." Unternehmerischer Erfolg und soziale Verantwortung gehörten zu-

---

[61] Chancen für alle! In Freiheit und Verantwortung gemeinsam Zukunft gestalten. Grundsatzprogramm der CSU vom 28.09.2007, München 2007, S. 50.

[62] Ebd., S. 69.

sammen. Die „Beteiligung der Arbeitnehmer an Erfolg und Kapital" wird als „eine ethische Notwendigkeit" bezeichnet, die dem sozialen Frieden diene.

IV. Schluss

Parteiprogramme sind nicht nur ein Wesensmerkmal politischer Parteien in Deutschland, sondern sie lassen Rückschlüsse auf die Positionen der jeweiligen Partei zu. Sie stellen gewissermaßen einen Identitätskern von Parteien dar. Dies lässt sich auch im Blick auf die Eigentumsvorstellungen der Parteien in Deutschland nachweisen.

Nach dem Zweiten Weltkrieg bildeten die verschiedenen Eigentumskonzepte der politischen Parteien das zentrale Unterscheidungsmerkmal ihrer programmatischen und ideologischen Positionen. Divergierende Eigentumsvorstellungen bildeten eine tiefe Konfliktlinie[63] im politischen Prozess. Individualistisch-liberale, kollektivistisch-sozialistische und christlich-soziale bzw. ordoliberale Konzepte standen sich in Gestalt der maßgeblichen Parteien gegenüber. Die programmatische Polarisierung der Nachkriegszeit ging einher mit einer starken gesellschaftlichen Verwurzelung der politischen Parteien: Die verschiedenen Eigentumskonzeptionen der Parteien waren repräsentativ für die Interessen und Werthaltungen ganz bestimmter Bevölkerungsgruppen.[64]

Diese scharfe politische und gesellschaftliche Polarität milderte sich allmählich ab. Der ökonomische Erfolg der Bundesrepublik und der hohe Stand der sozialen Sicherheit führten zu einer gesellschaftlichen Befriedung, die auch die Parteien erfasste. Symptomatisch dafür war das Godesberger Programm der SPD von 1959, in dem die Sozialdemokraten der Beobachtung Rechnung trugen, dass in den Augen der Bevölkerung kein Bedarf mehr an systemverändernden Eigentumskonzeptionen bestand. Zugleich lösten sich seit dem Ende der 1960er Jahre im Zuge gesellschaftlichen Wandels soziale Milieus allmählich auf, sodass die politischen Parteien zunehmend um die gleichen Wählerschichten konkurrierten. In der Folge näherten sich die Grundsatzprogramme der großen Parteien einander an, sodass der Staats- und Verfassungsrechtler Otto Kirchheimer schon in den 1960er Jahren eine „Entideologisierung"[65] der Parteien voraussagte.

---

[63] Vgl. Seymour Martin Lipset/Stein Rokkan (eds.), Party Systems and Voter Alignments: Cross-National Perspectives, New York/London 1967.

[64] Vgl. *Frank Decker*, Populismus und der Gestaltwandel des demokratischen Parteienwettbewerbs, in: APuZ 5 (2012), S. 10–15 (10).

[65] *Otto Kirchheimer*, Der Wandel des westeuropäischen Parteiensystems, in: Politische Vierteljahresschrift, 6 (1965) 1, S. 27 ff.

Er hatte nur teilweise Recht: Seit den 1970er Jahren sind bekanntlich neue ideologische Konflikte entstanden. Aber in der Tat lässt sich auch und vor allem in den Eigentumsvorstellungen der politischen Parteien eine programmatische Annäherung der Parteien nachweisen. Grundsätzlich erkennen heute alle maßgeblichen Parteien der Bundesrepublik die bestehende Eigentumsordnung an (lediglich die Linkspartei hat noch immer systemverändernde Ambitionen). Auch bezüglich der Sozialpflichtigkeit des Eigentums gibt es heute ein von allen Bundestagsparteien geteiltes Einvernehmen.

Das soll keineswegs heißen, dass sich die Eigentumskonzepte der Parteien heutzutage völlig gleichen. Im Gegenteil: Zum einen lassen sich immer noch unterschiedliche Akzentsetzungen erkennen. Insbesondere zwischen den Programmen von FDP und Linken gibt es hohe inhaltliche Divergenzen, während die Positionen von SPD, CDU und CSU tendenziell näher beieinander liegen. Auch die gesellschaftlichen und weltanschaulichen Wurzeln sind bei der Eigentumsfrage nach wie vor deutlich zu erkennen.

Zum anderen aber ist daran zu erinnern, dass Grundsatzprogramme eben nur grundsätzliche Positionen formulieren und kaum konkrete politische Handlungsanweisungen geben. Klammert man die Linkspartei einmal aus, dann liegen die Unterschiede zwischen den Parteien heutzutage weniger in den grundsätzlichen Eigentumsvorstellungen als vielmehr in den konkreten Details und in den Techniken der Problemlösung.

Zusammenfassung

Parteiprogramme sind ein Wesensmerkmal der Parteien in Deutschland und lassen Rückschlüsse auf ihre politischen Positionen zu. Nach dem Zweiten Weltkrieg bildeten die verschiedenen Eigentumskonzepte der politischen Parteien *das* zentrale Unterscheidungsmerkmal ihrer programmatischen und ideologischen Ziele. KPD und SPD traten in marxistischer Tradition für eine Veränderung der Eigentumsverhältnisse ein, während die FDP im prinzipiellen Verfügungsrecht über privates Eigentum die Grundlage der Freiheit sah. CDU und CSU hingegen orientierten sich mit ihren Eigentumsvorstellungen stark an den Ideen der katholischen Soziallehre, die den gesellschaftlichen Wert des Eigentums anerkennt, aber zugleich für eine möglichst breite Eigentumsstreuung eintritt und die Sozialpflichtigkeit des Eigentums betont. Die Eigentumskonzepte der heutigen politischen Parteien unterscheiden sich hingegen nicht mehr so stark. Alle bekennen sich zum System der Sozialen Marktwirtschaft und erkennen die Bedeutung privaten Eigentums an. Lediglich das Grundsatzprogramm der Linkspartei strebt noch eine Änderung der Eigentumsverhältnisse an.

Summary

Programmatic platforms are a characteristic element of political parties in Germany. They allow an analysis of policy positions and motives of the respective party. After World War II, the programmatic and ideological positions of political parties easily could be distinguished by the different concepts of property: KPD and SPD, in a marxist tradition, called for a complete transformation of ownership structures, while the liberal FDP considered private property as the basis of freedom and economy. The property concepts of CDU and CSU were based on the ideas of the Catholic Social Teaching which recognizes the importance of private ownership and supports a broad distribution of property. According to early CDU and CSU platforms, the right to private property also brings with it social responsibilities, in particular the responsibility to care for the common good. Concerning their concepts of property, current political parties have become much closer. All party platforms make a commitment to a Social Market Economy and acknowledge the significance of private property. Only the Linkspartei still aims at altering the existing ownership structures.

Property the Basis of Freedom against the State

By Peter Simpson

The State is an invention of the modern world and specifically of what has come to be known as Liberalism. The evidence is first from the actual practice of modern states (or most of them); second from the accepted definition of the state as we now conceive of it; third from the political philosophy which created the idea of the state.

I. The Modern State

The modern state, in all its incarnations, considers that it has the right, especially in the name of security and welfare, to do anything it wants in any area it wants. True, it does allow that it should not exercise this right save in extremities. But it has the right nevertheless, and extreme situations not only permit but also require it to act on the right. No right of the people – to freedom of person, free use of property, freedom of speech, free practice of religion, free choice of education, free possession of and training in weapons, and the like – supersedes, in extremities, the right of the state to suspend or restrain these freedoms. Since the state also claims the right to decide what counts as an extremity and what measures are necessary to confront it, and to do so on the basis of evidence that it claims, in virtue of the same extremity, the right not to reveal to anyone else, the result is that the state claims and exercises the right to do whatever it wants about whatever it wants for whatever reason it wants.[1]

Confirmation of this conclusion comes from the notion of a failed state, for a failed state is precisely a state that does not have the power thus to impose its will on the people and places nominally under its control. Afghanistan is said to be such a failed state. Confirmation also comes from two characteristic institutions of the modern state, the police and the military. The police are the institu-

---

[1] George W. Bush's interpretation of the 'Commander in Chief' clause in the US Constitution is exactly of this sort. The interpretation was, however, already present, and not only in germ, in Alexander Hamilton's famous doctrine of "implied powers," or the doctrine that the US Constitution must be understood to have given the US Government all the powers necessary to carry out its functions, for if not all such powers were specifically enumerated in the Constitution they must at any rate have been implied by it.

tional locus of the state's ordinary coercive power and hold a place analogous to that held in the past by the armed guard of the tyrant. For necessity here too justifies the police in doing anything, at least for the sake of security; and it entitles them presumptively to excuse if they seem in any case to have overstepped the mark. The functions we now depute exclusively to the police were performed previously by the citizens, who relied on themselves and their relatives and friends for the enforcement of rights and for defense and protection. Second, the military today takes the form everywhere of a professional army, and a professional army is what used to be called a standing army. Standing armies also used to be considered a standing threat to peace and liberty. They constituted a permanent power of violence in the hands of the rulers that the rulers could use to impose on the people whatever they wished and whenever they wished it. Liberty and peace were to be secured, not by such permanent forces of coercion, but by occasional armies, composed of the people themselves, which rulers could only muster at such times and for such purposes as the people might approve of and willingly pay for, and which, when the time and purpose passed, naturally disbanded themselves.

The definition of the State as accepted and used by modern thinkers is still that of Max Weber:

> Today the relation between the state and violence is an especially intimate one. In the past, the most varied institutions ... have known the use of physical force as quite normal. Today, however, we have to say that a state is a human community that (successfully) claims the *monopoly of the legitimate use of physical force* within a given territory.[2]

The State, then, is that organization of political power which takes to itself a monopoly of coercion, that is, of the use of force to impose obedience. Before modern times, as Weber expressly remarks, no institutional structure had a monopoly of coercive enforcement. The power to coerce was not concentrated at any one point but suffused through the mass of the population. The nearest approach to the state in pre-modern times (though Weber does not mention the fact) was what the ancients called tyranny, where one man did possess something close to a monopoly of coercion over everyone in a given area. They called it tyranny for precisely this reason: instead of all the citizens sharing control, only one or a very few did.

---

[2] Max Weber, *Politics as a Vocation*, trans. H. H. Gerth & C. Wright Mills (Philadelphia: Fortress Press, 1965), p. 2. *Politik als Beruf* (Duncker und Humblot, 1919): „Gerade heute ist die Beziehung des Staates zur Gewaltsamkeit besonders intim. In der Vergangenheit haben die verschiedensten Verbände ... physische Gewaltsamkeit als ganz normales Mittel gekannt. Heute dagegen werden wir sagen müssen: Staat ist diejenige menschliche Gemeinschaft, welche innerhalb eines bestimmten Gebietes ... das *Monopol legitimer physischer Gewaltsamkeit* für sich (mit Erfolg) beansprucht."

The idea of the state derives from the state of nature doctrine invented by Thomas Hobbes (though with heavy debts to Machiavelli)[3]. This doctrine has two features that deserve special notice: it treats human beings as equal anti-social units, and it treats political power as indivisibly single.

In the state of nature people are thought of as individuals moved by individual goods. Now such individuals could happily unite if the individual goods they pursued were also joint goods that required joint pursuit and joint possession. They would, on the other hand, not unite, but they would still live in peace, if the goods they pursued were not mutually exclusive. By contrast, they would unavoidably come into conflict if one individual cannot pursue his goods without preventing other individuals pursuing theirs. Human goods would, in this case, divide and set at odds; they would not unite.[4] By nature, on this view, individuals are anti-social units. They are also equal anti-social units. That all human beings, *qua* human, are equal is an old idea. What is new in the state of nature doctrine is that the desires of all human beings are equal too. Earlier doctrines taught that some goods were intrinsically superior and that those who pursued these goods were superior in character (though not in nature) to those who did not. This inequality of character naturally carried over into inequality of social and political status. Such inequality can find no justification in the state of nature doctrine. It is replaced by what we misleadingly call liberalism. For first, if goods do not unite but divide people, and second, if all desires are equal, then the solution for keeping a peace that is equal for all is that each only pursue his goods to the extent and in the way that all others can also pursue theirs.

There is another way of keeping peace. One individual could dominate everyone else and pursue his goods at their expense. This solution is the very unequal peace of the tyrant. In practice there can be no such tyrant; he is only possible in idea. No mere man could manage to be sufficiently strong and clever to keep everyone else in subjection. But while an all-powerful tyrant is impossible, an all-powerful tyranny is not. In fact, as Hobbes saw, such a tyranny is necessary. For liberalism is intrinsically unstable. It requires people to refrain from doing what, according to the theory, they naturally most want to do, namely pursue to the full their individual goods. Admittedly anyone who at-

---

[3] Machiavelli's *Prince* is the classic text, but his *Discourses* carry the same message, if less on the surface; Simpson, *Goodness and Nature, with a Supplement on Historical Origins: A Defense of Ethical Naturalism and a Critique of Its Opponents* (New York: Occasio Press, 2011): chs. Suppl. 1 and Suppl. 3.

[4] Such is what happens in the state of nature, whether immediately, as in Hobbes's version, or progressively, as in Locke's and Rousseau's, or by idealized construction, as in Kant's and Rawls's. The sources are Hobbes's *Leviathan*, Locke's *Second Treatise of Government*, Rousseau's *Social Contract*, Kant's *Universal History* and *Perpetual Peace*, and Rawls's *Theory of Justice*.

tempted this pursuit would come into conflict with those around him and frustrate himself as much as them. But the temptation to do what one by nature really wants must always be strong, and so, since the fear of Hobbes's war of all against all in the state of nature is not enough to deter everyone all the time (or to deter the strong and clever much of the time), it needs to be backed up by the fear of the state. The state fulfills the role of the all-powerful tyrant and imposes, by brute force, liberal tolerance on chronically intolerant individuals.

The state as so conceived is the state of Weber's definition. No state could do the job required if there were other powers of coercion around that could rightly oppose it, for then the war of nature, which the state was set up to stop, would just be continued. The state must, by necessity as well as by the right of liberal doctrine, be a single, comprehensive power that brooks no rival.

II. The Freedom that is Property

1. Sociality

The first desideratum to escape the tyranny of the state is to deny the liberalism that, in practice and in idea, lies at its root. The individual should not be conceived of as anti-social, or equal, or a unit. This claim may seem paradoxical, for it is the equal rights of equal individuals that are the basis of freedom and that the modern world was the first to realize and put into practice. The equal individual is considered to be the source and measure of government authority, since the state's right of coercion arises from individuals and is for the sake of individuals, and is limited by both. But, as just indicated, the coercion arises from and is measured by individuals against and not in accord with their nature. The individual is not naturally social and not naturally peaceful, and the state imposes social peace by fighting against nature. Its idea, as stated by Weber, is total and undivided coercion because its function is total and undivided coercion. But if, in contrast, the individual is by nature social and by nature peaceful, while there may be need of government (for guidance rather than compulsion), there will be no need of the state, because there will be no need of total and undivided coercion.

That the individual, however, is by nature social and by nature peaceful is a matter of daily experience. Neither society nor the state could survive otherwise, because not even today's states exercise so direct and minute a control over individuals as to monitor and coerce their every move. Propagandists and apologists for the state are, to be sure, striving to get as close to such a control as they can, but even they admit to being a long way off. Antichrist may be close but not, I think, as close as such propagandists wish. When individuals behave anti-socially they are going against what is natural and against what is normal. They need to be resisted, no doubt, but the resistance will come naturally from naturally social and peaceful individuals. There will be no need for a state with a monopoly of coercion to do the job. The state, in fact, if it exists, will intervene to prevent this resistance by naturally social and peaceful individuals. It will view such resistance as a threat to its own monopoly of coercion and therefore, necessarily, as a threat to its own existence (for monopoly of coercion *is* its existence).

2. Property

Unfortunately the state does now exist, and all forms of government, even those which have no connection in fact or in idea with the state, are said to be governments only insofar as they are states. The first way to resist the state and the statist propaganda of the state is, as just said, the repudiation of liberalism. But this first way, while the most important for beings that live most by ideas, is not the most immediately necessary way for beings that also have material bodies and are coerced by the state through their material bodies. The second way, then, is property, which may be divided into material and spiritual, or property relative to the needs of the body and property relative to the needs of the soul.

As to material property, or to property ordinarily understood, we can say that food, clothing, and shelter are the most obvious such needs, and because of these there is also need of land to provide the food and the materials for clothing and the places for shelter. But before all these there is the need for parents. No human body comes to be or continues to be without parents. The family, as composed first of parents and children, is the first expression of natural sociality and natural peace. It is the first origin of the need for property, and it entails that property too is first a social thing, not an individual thing. It also entails that property is not a thing of the state, but exists prior to and independently of any state or any apparatus of the state. It therefore also entails that the preservation and protection of property is not a thing of the state. Means of self-defense, and nowadays primarily guns, belong naturally to the family. By nature guns exist for hunting and defense. By nature the first defense is against wild beasts and human attackers. By the situation of present times the first defense is against the state. If land naturally belongs to property, guns for defense also naturally belong to it.

Therefore, by the same token, separate police forces do not naturally belong to property. Separate or professional police forces, as we call them, are creatures of the state, brought into being, sustained, directed, and exploited by the state so as to be the visible form of its self-serving propaganda that it alone can and should coerce. Standing armies are creatures of the state in the same way.

Both are a direct attack on natural property, the natural property of families to possess their own means of coercion and to determine the correct use of them. Even if families naturally combine into larger associations which may, eventually, reach the size of states, they never lose their natural property or their natural right to natural property. Police forces and standing armies are a direct denial of nature and right. They should be abolished. All policing and military functions belong directly to the people and always remain directly the property of the people. Delegation may be necessary and desirable; but alienation is intrinsically unjust and conceptually impossible. Lest these ideas seem utopian, consider only the case of Switzerland which, despite slippage in recent years, has held closest to the natural vision of natural defense by natural society.

Material property has two natural uses, consumption and exchange. Exchange is the natural way to secure a sufficiency of what is needed for consumption, since by nature not all property or the produce of property exists equally in all places and at all times. The exchange of property naturally belongs to natural society. Therefore the means of exchange do as well. The chief such means is money. Therefore money belongs to natural society. It does not belong to the state, which, as said, is unnatural and repudiates natural society. All modern money does belong to the state because all modern money is paper sanctioned by the state. Without the state's sanction all modern money would be worthless. In fact all modern money is worthless in its intrinsic nature because it only has the worth that the issuing state says it has. The state, because it claims a monopoly of coercion, has to claim a monopoly of money, because money, as the means of exchange for property, is the means of exchange for the means of coercion (especially weapons). To control all the money is ultimately, therefore, to control all the property. State money is an all-out assault on natural property and the natural right to natural property. It should be abolished, and the money needed for exchange, as well its creation as its control, should be entirely in the hands of natural society.

3. Teaching

The body is for the soul, and the property of the body therefore is also for the soul. The soul's chief functions in man are thought and will and feeling. Man's natural sociality and peacefulness naturally express themselves in naturally social and peaceful thoughts, choices, and feelings. But as the body, when immediately born, is dependent on mature bodies to grow and flourish, so also is the soul. The soul's food and clothing are education. These are, as it were, the natural property of the soul, and they belong as naturally to natural society as any other property does. They do not belong to the state. But the state seizes on them all, and necessarily so.

The state's monopoly of coercion exists only in idea because the means to make it exist in practice are lacking and will always be lacking (even if the lack asymptotically declines). The state's existence, thus, depends far more on teaching than on force. If it does not control teaching it cannot preserve its own existence. The state's control of teaching is first unnatural, because contrary to the natural property in teaching that belongs to natural society, and second it is perverse, because all it teaches, and all it wants to teach, is its own preservation. It has no interest in the natural development of the mind, or the will, or the feelings; for if these develop naturally, they will develop against the state. They will develop in, through, and to the natural sociality and peacefulness that man is. Therefore the state uses its coercion in education too and arrogates all of education, directly or indirectly, to itself.

Accordingly, just as man has a natural right to material weapons, that is, guns, against the state, so he has a natural right to spiritual weapons, that is, education, against the state. No education, therefore, of any sort, from cradle to grave, should be in the hands or in any way under the control of the state. It should all belong to natural society. But, in order to be done well, it will have to belong, ultimately, to some organ or institution that has a special concern with education. Such organ or institution, in order to be true to its function, will itself have to possess, and by nature, a fundamental orientation to truth. Therefore, again, such organ or institution cannot be the state or any part of the state or in any subordinate relation to the state. For the state, as already remarked, has no fundamental orientation to truth. It has a fundamental orientation to its own extension and self-promotion, and it will use lies as much as truth for this purpose. Science, as it describes a natural human endeavor, has an orientation to truth, but science as subordinate to the state is not seldom perverted, not just to promoting means of coercion and surveillance, but also to promoting lies in the service of the state.

4. Truth

Now there is in human life, and naturally in human life, one institution whose whole being is orientation to truth. I mean religion. For man has natural property rights in religion as he has natural property rights in anything else necessary for his being. By religion I mean in the first instance the natural desire for truth about the ultimate meaning and end of human existence. This desire is nevertheless peculiar in a special way. It is a natural desire for what, as far as we naturally know, is not naturally attainable. If there is a God or gods, they are not subject to us but we to them. Consequently we cannot have property rights in them but they could have property rights in us. For the truth about God or the gods is naturally known only to God or the gods, and to man only to the extent that God or the gods are naturally known through things naturally known to man. But there is no reason to think that what is naturally known to man about God is all or the most important of what can and needs to be known to man about God. The natural desire for religion is thus also, and necessarily, a natural desire for revelation, a revelation that will depend on the will of God and not on the will of man. To the extent that there is a revelation, since it will be made to man as he naturally is and since man is social as he naturally is, revelation too will be social. It will throw itself into some social form, or some more or less organized institution within society.

Historically there are only three organized revealed religions in the world: Judaism, Christianity, and Islam. Abstracting for the moment from the truth or adequacy of these religions, we can say that all of them are and must be independent of the state and of all functions and coercion of the state. Indeed, if there is any power of coercion here, it must be all from religion against the state and not from the state against religion. The state, therefore, will necessarily be hostile to revealed religion, or to any religion that is or claims to be above the state. Such a religion is necessarily hostile to the state, certainly in idea if not also often in practice. The so-called separation of state and church is not enough to capture the true relation between state and church. These two things may be separate in their ordinary spheres, to the extent at least that the state concerns itself with man's temporal needs and religion with his spiritual needs. But they cannot be wholly separate, as if religion could never have the right, or the duty, to teach, discipline, correct, and coerce the state to treat religion as religion deserves. In this respect the role played by Islam in, say, Iran, or by the Church in medieval Christendom is superior, in nature and in truth, to the role played by religion, of any sort, in the secular West. The property of religion, its property in truth as much as in the material substructure that it needs to function as a social organ, does and should altogether escape the authority and control of the state. The state, by natural right not to mention divine right, can have no authority over any of the property of religion and, by the same right, can exercise no coercive power over it.[5] The state will of course want to exercise such power, for such power is its very essence. But any such exercise will be unjust and a further instance of the state's intrinsic tyranny and passion for tyranny.[6]

The claim, of course, is made that sometimes the common good may require the state to intervene in any area of property, as above all by what is called "eminent domain," in order to preserve and promote that common good. Hence

---

[5] See the long and very instructive discussion by Suarez on this question in book 4 of his *Defense of the Catholic and Apostolic Faith*, English translation at: http://aristotelophile.com/current.htm.

[6] Cf. the recent statement of the US Catholic Bishops on some aspects of President Obama's health bill.

the claim is further made that religion cannot have ultimate or absolute rights against the authority of the state. These claims are false because the basis on which they are made is false. The common good is not the exclusive preserve of the state, either as to its protection or, more importantly, as to its meaning. The state's authority, even by the right of nature, extends only to the part of the common good which is temporal and not also to the part which is spiritual. Neither does the state's authority extend to ultimate determination of where and how and when these parts overlap. Such determination must belong to religion, which, because it deals with what is intrinsically superior (the spiritual property of man), is itself intrinsically superior. The spiritual part of the common good can only be determined by religion, so that, if the state were to try to determine this part where it overlaps with the temporal part, the common good would not be secured but defeated.

The right of religion, therefore, especially revealed religion, to be superior to and independent of the state is a natural right inherent in man's natural right to spiritual property, above all his natural right to property in truth. It is thus an indispensable element of his freedom. To the extent religion in Iran has and exercises this right, to that extent Iran is freer than any country in the secular West. We should, therefore, be finding ways to admire Iran, not ways to attack it.

5. Freedom

One might say, and opponents of religion in the secular West do say, that religion, especially organized religion, would be a threat to liberty if it had over the state the authority that it had in medieval Christendom or has now in Iran. The charge is self-serving and hypocritical. The modern state is a far greater threat to freedom than religion ever has been or ever could be. Man's freedom consists in his right to pursue his good through his natural property. The chief such good is truth. The state does not care for truth as such. It spreads error indifferently and systematically whenever such error will serve its purpose. The state does not deny its essence when it spreads error. Religion, by contrast, always does, for it claims authority in virtue of the truth it teaches about God. A challenge to religion in the name of truth is a threat that religion ultimately cannot resist. And the human mind, being itself naturally oriented to truth, would eventually issue such an irresistible challenge. Any religion, therefore, that has survived for any considerable length of time among any considerable body of people must have truth at its core. The state, by contrast, can always resist truth, and has no intrinsic need to welcome it. The survival of the state depends, not on truth, but on power.

From the point of view of freedom, religion, even organized religion, is always superior to the state, and indeed all religions, where they exist in any numbers, operate as superior to the state. A religion, whether natural or revealed, that is not superior to the state and is not capable of laying down limits to the state in the name of truth, is confessing that it has no divine authority, because it is confessing that it has no authority superior to man. So it is confessing that it is not a religion, or not a doctrine and worship directed to what is higher than man. Even the old pagan religions never made so self-negating a claim.

These considerations about religion lead to the conclusion that freedom cannot be preserved in or by the state but can be preserved if the state is prevented from pursuing its idea and is subordinated instead, at least in all matters that concern man's interest and property in truth, to some religion, revealed or natural or both. Without such subordination, in fact if not also in idea, there can be no freedom, because there can be no property. All property instead becomes the plaything of the state and stands at the disposal of the state. The superiority of religion to the state, or rather, if possible, the abolition of the state and a return to natural forms of social life, is alone the path of freedom.

Summary

The paper is divided into two parts. The first part argues that the modern state is a form of tyranny. Three proofs are given, from the actual practice of modern states, from Weber's classic definition of the state, and from the doctrine of liberalism. The second part argues that freedom is to be secured by property, material and spiritual. Material property includes land and weapons and requires the abolition of police forces, professional armies, and state-sanctioned paper money. Spiritual property is primarily education and requires the abolition of state-run schools. Its best guarantee is religion, for truth is the professed object of religion but power, regardless of truth, is the professed object of the state.

Zusammenfassung

Der Vortrag umfasst zwei Teile: Der erste Teil zeigt, dass der moderne Staat tyrannische Züge hat. Dafür gibt es drei Hinweise: einmal die politische Praxis, zum andern die klassische Definition des Staates von Max Weber, schließlich die Auffassung des Liberalismus. Der zweite Teil legt dar, dass das Eigentum, sowohl das materielle als auch das geistige, die Freiheit schützt. Das materielle Eigentum umfasst den Boden und die Waffen und verlangt die Abschaffung der Polizei, der Berufsarmee und des staatlichen Papiergeldes. Das geistige Eigentum besteht vor allem in der Erziehung und verlangt die Zurücknahme der staatlichen Schulen. Der beste Garant der Freiheit ist die Religion, weil es ihr um die Wahrheit geht und nicht, wie dem Staat, um die Macht.

III. Wirtschaftliche Aspekte
Economic Aspects

Property, Freedom, Prosperity, and the Multinational Corporation

By Nicholas T. Pinchuk

I. Overview

The quality of life created by the axis of property, freedom, and prosperity is determined primarily by enlightened judgment and the difficult choices inherent in its application. A fulfilling and successful society is rooted not in the presence of property or freedom, but rather is created by judicious choice on the individual range of action allowed.

Some may believe property is necessary for freedom. Today, this appears to be borne out by everyday practice. It has become clear that responsibility, like that associated with ownership, must be present before freedom, i.e., discretion in discharging that duty can have significant meaning. But, it's not the presence of ownership or freedom which defines a quality life. The primary temporal goal of individuals or organizations is to achieve prosperity i.e., a fulfilling existence. In this regard, prosperity is enabled by property and freedom, but only if that freedom is provided in the appropriate measure. And, this balance is only achieved by judgment and choice.

The relationship among property, freedom, and prosperity is not easily definable. It varies depending on a particular situation and a specific set of conditions. Prosperity and fulfillment are clearly the primary goals of both individuals and of organizations. It, however, cannot be guaranteed simply by the ownership of property or by the granting of freedom. The effective pursuit of prosperity depends on the imprecise characteristics of judgment and choice. Success of the property, freedom, prosperity axis depends on striking the correct balance among them and determining the range of action or amount of freedom to be granted in wielding responsibility.

Much can be learned from observing the examples demonstrated by multinational corporations. It can be seen from those commercial organisms that the value of perceived ownership and shared benefit is broadly recognized and documented. It can also be seen that only when individuals or organizations are endowed with the freedom to use property appropriately can prosperity and fulfillment be attained. The challenge, however, is in granting just the right amount of freedom that matches the situation. This conclusion is evident from examples at Ford, Carrier and Snap-on, in which it becomes clear that too much latitude can destroy value and too little range of action will equally restrict prosperity. In fact, judgment on the amount of freedom to be granted is the crucial ingredient in creating fulfilling lives. This assertion is further confirmed when examining the role and effect of property, freedom, and prosperity in various nations from China to India to Singapore to the United States. In the end, it is the application of freedom in proper measure, guided by judgment, that creates a satisfying society. The observations also show that these judgments cannot be made without also making tough choices that require a strong understanding of both the situation and the human condition.

The pages that follow include my attempt to define the concepts of property, freedom, and prosperity as they commonly function in today's world of human endeavor. I also offer an explanation of my view on the relationship among property, freedom, and prosperity and on the issues raised in utilizing those characteristics in constructing an effective community. It's based on my experience in various multinational corporations and my direct participation in balancing the sense of ownership and range of action in pursuit of prosperity over a broad reach of geographies and in a variety of cultural and economic situations. My thoughts also reflect direct observation of various national governments and their efforts to create fulfilling societies. In so doing, I have tried to accurately describe events that I have witnessed and the related episodes that have been passed on to me by credible sources. I have mixed these anecdotes with analyses of the various situations and set forth conclusions based on these experiences and observations. There are, of course, alternate views of the evidence. I can only offer my own interpretations in the hope that they are both persuasive and helpful.

II. Property: A Concept not a Physical Object

The English dictionary definition of property is "something to which a person or business has legal title." It's something owned or possessed. This is the classical meaning of the word. But, as James W. Ely indicates in his book on the constitutional history of property, "property is a dynamic concept, property now takes different forms."[1] For the purpose of the relationship to freedom and prosperity, it appears that contemporary property is not limited to a physical object and clearly not necessarily to real estate, land, or buildings. In this linkage, property is best represented as a combination of responsibility and a clear con-

---

[1] T James W. Ely, Jr., *The Guardian of Every Other Right, A Constitutional History of Property Rights*, 2nd ed. (New York: Oxford University Press, 1998), p. 6.

viction that one will share in the results created by the discharge of that duty. As demonstration of the broad nature of property, consider the classic case where an individual owns a home and land on which it sits. The owner would, in-fact, be responsible for that real estate, and would realize the benefit of that ownership, including ongoing use of the building and land and would be entitled to the financial proceeds should the assets be sold. On the other hand, an individual e.g., a teacher, could be responsible for the educational well-being of students and would reap the benefits in terms of satisfaction, reputation and, perhaps, financial rewards, if the students performed well. Both the real estate and the responsibility for the students fill the role of property/ownership in the construct linking property to freedom and prosperity.

III. Freedom: The Eye of the Beholder

The standard meaning of freedom is "the absence of necessity, coercion, or constraint in choice or action." The root of this definition is the array of choices an individual wishes to exercise and or the actions that are seen as being in his or her interest. This appropriate range of action is highly dependent on many conditions for the individuals: the norms of the society which they inhabit, the outlook for their future, their sense of satisfaction with their current situation, and multiple other factors. These conditions can vary widely from country to country, from nationality to nationality, from business situation to business situation.

It's clear, based on observation that range of action or opportunity for self-actualization is an essential component of the human condition. Everyone has a need to be in control of their own situation, their own destiny. It's that sense of responsibility which generates the energy that moves society forward both individually and collectively. Put in very basic terms, everyone wants to choose the color of the walls within which they live. Such responsibility generates effort and progress. It's been proven time and time again from the collective forms of the Soviet to the iron rice bowl of mid-twentieth century China. Lack of freedom and absence of responsibility weakens effort and constrains progress. The presence of freedom energizes it, as is confirmed by the long standing experience of the Western democracies and more recently by the rise of capitalist Asia.

Having recognized that freedom is a positive and necessary condition, it then, however, is not so clear what range of action is required for the sense of responsibility to be strong and effective. This range varies from place to place. One group may thrive, feeling quite free, under conditions that would seem restrictive and disheartening to another group. For example, the people of Sweden feel quite free under their social democracy, while an American in that situation may feel somewhat restricted. Freedom is clearly essential for a ful-filling life. The definition of that condition, however, can change significantly from community to community. This paper will provide examples highlighting the difficult, but crucial, task of deciding a level of freedom that is appropriate to the situation.

IV. Prosperity: A Goal for all Seasons

Prosperity is defined as "the condition of being successful or being able to describe oneself as thriving." It's often associated with economic well-being. It is, however, a much broader concept than simple financial strength. Prosperity is best described by having the capability to engage in a satisfactory life on a continuous basis. Even those with substantial economic wherewithal will gen-erally attest that fulfillment is the most important component of one's life. To deserve and receive the respect of those who know, to leave the world a better place – these are the most important achievements, far greater than the accumu-lation of assets. Further, these goals are quite personal. One person's satisfac-tion might have little value for another. Blessed Mother Teresa of Calcutta once told me that "poverty is liberating." She and her congregation obviously viewed their "property" as their collective responsibility for the poor of India. She found her prosperity in the satisfaction and fulfillment she gained from serving the very disadvantaged, even as she had little in the way of comforts or assets. In the end, farmers, auto mechanics, doctors, philosophers, professors, and presidents all find fulfillment. Each, however, find it doing different things, ap-plying different skills, affecting different groups of humans, and with different levels of urgency. But each can find their own special brand of fulfillment. This is why prosperity can be considered a goal for all, in many different situations, in multiple cultures.

This leads to the second facet of prosperity: the concept of growth and the feeling of improvement. It appears clear that part of the human condition is a need for advancement, day-to-day, year-to-year, decade to decade. It may be one of the qualities that separates us from other sentient beings. In effect, what might have been viewed as a thriving condition 10 years ago, may not be seen as prosperity today. The average Chinese citizen of 2012 has a very different view of a minimum economic standard than just 20 years ago. I dare say that even Americans have a very different view of minimum existence today, than they had in the late 1950's. Americans of that era, generally took buses, en-dured the summer's heat, and lived in compact dwellings similar to the Chinese of 1995. They had much different lives than those they enjoy in the 21st cen-tury. In fact, prosperity is not an absolute condition so much as a relative feel-ing, a sense of moving forward. Americans today feel unsatisfied because they have not progressed; Indonesians, despite having a more frugal lifestyle, have a different view because they see the forward movement.

Having highlighted the flexible nature of prosperity, we also must recognize that there is a required minimum economic condition that is the substrate for satisfaction and a reasonable existence. Humans must have food, clothing, shelter, and in turn, the financial wherewithal or support to provide them. Without such conditions, satisfaction and fulfillment are not possible. Mother Teresa, required support for herself and her congregation even while adhering to the vows of poverty. Of course, even this substrate can be flexible; it can be relative to the surroundings and can change. So prosperity is a multi-faceted characteristic of the human condition. It has an intangible component associated with fulfillment, respect, and making a difference. It has a base component reflecting the minimum financial wherewithal to maintain oneself. Finally, it has a growth component, responding to the human need for advancement over time.

V. Property, Freedom, and Prosperity: Building Blocks of a Satisfying Life

Property has sometimes been characterized as a condition necessary to achieve freedom. And, so it is. Property, or as we more broadly characterized it, responsibility, is indeed the underpinning of freedom. Freedom, however, does not appear to be the end point in the human condition. Prosperity/fulfillment is in fact, the primary goal as people strive against the tides of life.

Freedom can be present without responsibility, but prosperity in the individual or collective sense seldom follows. It's freedom combined with responsibility that can generate the fulfillment of a successful existence. The relationship among these conditions is circular and their role in the human condition are intertwined. Richard Pipes says, "Property is an indispensable ingredient of both prosperity and freedom ... prosperity and fulfillment is the essence of liberty."[2]

In fact, however, the presence of property and freedom does not always guarantee prosperity. These two characteristics simply provide the opportunity for success. There are instances and individuals where people or organizations enabled by both property and freedom do not find satisfaction, either because of weak motivation, confusion, or some mismatch of conditions. Equally, however, property with the addition of freedom in proper measure, does clearly enable prosperity for those so inclined.

---

[2] Richard Pipes, *Property and Freedom*, (New York: Knopf, 2000), p. 286.

The concepts of property, freedom, and prosperity do build one upon the other to provide individuals, organizations, or communities with a meaningful existence. In fact, without these characteristics in balance, the human condition can suffer and wither. Property, as defined previously, goes beyond a physical asset. In fact, it is the responsibility which is crucial and which creates the motivation. This feeling of ownership can be established either through legal possession or simply by being perceived as the primary actor in determining outcomes. When an individual feels this responsibility, he or she becomes active in controlling the way forward, against any eventuality, to ensure that the path leads to positive results. They must, of course, be convinced that their actions will heavily influence, if not fully determine, the outcome. They must also clearly be confident that the fruits of that labor, financial or otherwise, will at least in part accrue to their benefit. The key point is that responsibility rather than direct ownership is the essential nature of the term property as we use it here. In addition, physical assets are not necessarily required to feel responsible. One can feel as responsible for a brand name or other intangibles, as they do for a parcel of real estate.

Once having responsibility, one must be able to take action. This is the role of freedom as an energizer. It must, however, be granted in just the proper measure. If individuals feel constrained, they will not develop the energy necessary to be successful. If a central or higher authority restricts excessively, individuals will respond by abdicating their responsibility. Of course, every environment, no matter how free, must be restricted within the envelope of natural law. "Thou shalt not kill" and "Thou shalt not steal" must be operative for all individuals, organizations, and communities. It is a responsibility of central authority, corporate headquarters, community leadership, or churches, to establish, nurture and maintain this envelope of moral behavior. Beyond these collective and moral restrictions, however, it's clear that individuals are most effective when endowed with the proper range of action we call freedom, and when they possess the ability to discharge their responsibilities as they see fit.

Property and freedom, therefore, are the building blocks of the satisfying life, which we call prosperity. People of all backgrounds, of varied economic levels, of multiple cultures, all across the world seek that condition of thriving. This fulfillment is one of the major goals of human life. It's the primary reason for which property and freedom are brought together.

Property, freedom, and prosperity form a social, psychological, and economic axis, which underpin the fulfilling modern life. This can be seen across the various communities that overlap around the world. It can be observed in corporations where responsibility, range of actions, and success are demonstrated on a daily basis. It's observable in the nations of our world where the situations develop over decades and the benefits of success are broad and the consequences of failure are devastating. The relationship can be demonstrated by positive examples, where property and freedom combine to yield fulfilling or prosperous lives. It can also be confirmed by considering those situations where either property or freedom is missing and the result is not positive.

VI. Multinational Corporations: Templates for Behavior

Multinationals as social laboratories can provide useful insights into the relational and physical issues which can be applied with efficacy to larger entities. A company is, after all, a community, a grouping of people coming together to achieve growth and prosperity. Corporations are social organisms where the members coordinate effort to optimize the use of capital and to amplify the positive effects of their collective energy.

Governments, at all levels, cities, states, and countries, are also communities of individuals which come together for a common purpose. Churches, universities, and social societies, can also be included in this general framework. These organizations share many things, but first and foremost they share a primary nature, i.e., the goal of organizing human beings to achieve a collective positive result.

One of the major differences among these organizations is that the time constants by which companies proceed are much shorter than those for countries or religions. The requirements of investors and the cadence of the competitive marketplace create a great urgency that inhabits the corporate environment. Multinational corporations, therefore, act to match these rapid realities. If a company does not change quickly, it cannot compete with its rivals. Its management teams will be disenfranchised and its stakeholders disadvantaged. As it is, the average tenure of a Chief Executive is three to four years. Those who do not change successfully have even shorter careers. On the other hand, countries and churches change much more slowly. Absent crises, the time constraints in these communities are much longer than those seen in corporations. The difficulties of creating reasonable consensus among the independent interests which comprise a country and the general preference of the broad population for certainty combine to make national change a very extended process. The same is true of other major institutions. Churches, if anything, change over even longer periods than countries, and religious orders of magnitude move more slowly than multinationals.

In general, therefore, corporate trends can be observed in quarters of a year while those in other major social organisms are only detectable over many years, if not multiple decades. Because of the shorter time constraints, a multinational can be an effective laboratory in which to determine the likely implication for broader society. This paper, therefore, will use corporations as a template for understanding the relationship among Property, Freedom, and Prosperity.

VII. Multinational Corporations: Centripetal Tendencies Resisted

Multinational corporations do regularly joust with the difficulties of balancing property and freedom in pursuit of prosperity. In most hierarchical organization, like businesses, there is a natural tension between the center where strategy and policy are generally determined and the periphery, where the primary daily value is created.

Ownership of assets is communal in multinationals. All businesses know, however, that ownership of outcome must be borne by the members of the organization at the periphery, by the people who design, manufacture, sell, and service the company's product. Volumes have been written on performance measurement and companies have spent countless hours to ensure that individual results are recognized and evaluated. Equally, multinationals dedicate great attention to ensuring that its employees see as much linkage as possible between their personal welfare and the outcome of their efforts on behalf of the organization. After all, as David Landes says in *The Wealth and Poverty of Nations*. "Why should anyone invest capital or labor in the creation of wealth that he may not be allowed to keep."[3] Corporations, therefore, work hard to ensure its associates perceive a clear relationship between their performance and their own compensation, benefits, and job stability. A stroll through the business section of any airport bookstore will confirm that assertion. Even a casual inspection on such a visit will reveal a great deal of literature dedicated to establishing the linkage between performance and benefit. Assigning responsibility, assessing performance, and establishing compensation are among more studied aspects of organizational structure for a multinational.

In the parlance of this paper, there has been much consideration on how to imbue the associates of a corporation with a feeling of property, of ownership, of responsibility. It's clear that every business leader takes great pain to remind his extended team of their individual and collective responsibilities. Considerable time is dedicated to measuring performance both quantitatively and judgmentally. Further, there is an equal amount of effort directed at ensuring all stakeholders of a corporation – shareholders, employees, communities, custom-

---

[3] David S. Landes, *The Wealth and Poverty of Nations: Why Some Are So Rich and Some So Poor* (New York: W. W. Norton, 1998), p. 32.

ers – enjoy the fruits of organizational success in appropriate proportion to their contribution.

The more difficult task, however, is not assigning responsibility or allocating benefits. Rather, it is determining what range of action, what freedom, the center should grant to the various elements of responsibility in the enterprise. CEO's, presidents, managing directors, almost every node of corporate authority must deal with this question. It often is a natural tendency to control decision making at the center. But, to be successful, the organization must resist these centripetal proclivities. The most successful multinationals recruit and deploy people that clearly have capabilities matching their responsibilities and tasks. The healthy organization then builds trust in those capable individuals deployed to the periphery. Because of that trust, little oversight is required to assure the center that all is well on the commercial front lines. Then, the successful organization pushes decision making as close as possible to where the actual value is created: in the design lab, on the factory floor, at the point of sale, i.e., away from the center toward the periphery. Having said that, there are, of course, some decisions that do require either a perspective that can only be seen from the center, or from a level of experience only present in the senior players. But, in general, most decisions require neither extraordinary experience, nor the broad view, and are best handled at the periphery. There are, of course, also instances where an associate is not up to the task and is struggling in his role. In those situations, the center must "ride to the sound of guns" temporarily reduce the freedom of the periphery, and take direct charge of the situation, lending its significant capabilities to the problem. In prosperous multinationals, however, these situations are few and far between. If not, something is gravely wrong. Most CEO's recognize that if the corporation is running properly creating appropriate prosperity, he or she should only be making those decisions that cannot be made on the facts, but must be based primarily on judgment, born of experience and perspective. The associates of a functioning organization should have clear ownership, and the range of action or freedom to exercise their capabilities in their area of responsibility. That combination will create prosperity, which in turn, will author more resources, providing the opportunity to gain additional responsibility. The additional responsibility offers the possibility for even more prosperity, and on it goes in the circular relationship among property, freedom, prosperity. This dynamic, however, represents a balance which is not always easy to strike. It's not always clear just how much range of action should be granted to the periphery.

The issues surrounding responsibility and freedom become especially challenging when the corporation spreads across national boundaries. It becomes vividly clear that local people in places like China, India, Russia, France, et.al., must be primary actors in creating their own prosperity and in bearing their own responsibility. Once again, setting the appropriate range of action for the local organization is the most difficult question. On one hand, each country is different: maturity of the industry, local practices, and capabilities of the in-country team all lead to the fact that a tailored approach will best match the specific situation. Local business operations must be given the latitude to accommodate those differences. On the other hand, a corporation, even a multinational, has certain characteristics which it considers essential in defining itself and its activity across the entire organization. The Snap-on Corporation, the U.S. based tool maker, does business in 130 countries and adjusts its activity to each of those unique environments. The Company however, does define itself as serving professionals. Even though the "Do-It-Yourself" retail market may be bigger in France than the professional market in that country, Snap-on will not allow its French subsidiary to target local DIY customers. "Thou shalt not sell to DIY" is a kind of natural law in Snap-on and a restriction on the freedom of its many subsidiaries. In this case, the restriction seems well founded and effective as the corporation's many international subsidiaries are creating considerable prosperity focusing on solely professionals and ignoring the DIY segment.

There is also the question of cost inherent in freeing the subsidiaries to act independently. It's very tempting to constrain freedom across countries, to adopt a common solution, and to monetize the economics of scale inherent in that commonization. Centralization is a popular corporate concept that has broad seductive appeal reflecting cost efficiency. However, as will be demonstrated in the following pages, sometimes it works, sometimes it doesn't.

In the late 70's and early 80's, the Ford Motor Company attempted to become more efficient by the developing a world car, the "Escort" which would sell around the globe using essentially the same design. The idea was to accommodate local flavor only with non-essential, non-core aspects of the vehicle. The effort failed. The corporate center could not overcome the periphery's desire for freedom of action and its need to sell a customized local offering. In the end, despite the much publicized globalization effort, the Escorts offered in Germany were quite different than the ones sold in the U.S. In fact, during that period, there was a meeting at Ford Engineering in which an executive brought the "World" car into the room, in his suitcase, holding inside the one or two parts that the American and European Escorts had in common. Those owners at the periphery had retained the freedom to customize their vehicles and address the preferences of their domestic customers. But, it restricted prosperity and damaged the overall enterprise, creating substantial hardship. Ford struggled for some time managing this complexity born of freedom to customize. Following the recession of 2009, however, Ford did create common world cars, acting like an empire, restricting the freedom of its subsidiaries to drive customized product completely. The result was quite positive and Ford found a collective prosperity that it hadn't seen in years. Given the massive economics of scale available, the center should have acted earlier. Opportunities were missed, jobs lost, and lives compromised, in part because freedom to act was granted.

To illustrate the difficulty in making these judgments around freedom in pursuit of prosperity, it might be useful to consider another corporate example involving the Carrier Corporation. Carrier in Asia, and, in fact, around the world, was best characterized as a federation of commercial national companies held together in a commonality based on only a few central principles and a common technology. Local customers were served with products designed specifically for their particular needs and preferences. The Carrier companies were so focused on the local markets that the Prime Minister of Singapore once remarked that he thought Carrier was a Singapore-based entity as opposed to a large American multinational. This approach worked well. The enterprise and the stakeholders prospered, and, the circle of property, freedom and prosperity was in balance. Then, corporate headquarters, the center, attempted to prescribe a global, common product that would tap substantial scale economics, reduce costs, and drive increased prosperity. Of course, use of the global product would restrict some of the freedom that responsible local management exercised with regard to product choice. Customer preferences would be compromised, but the common product would be more sophisticated in its design and more extensive in its features. It was a well intentioned and strategically sound initiative. Unfortunately, this time the shift from federal to a more imperial approach did not work. The product was acceptable everywhere, but not particularly attractive anywhere. It was viewed as only average. And, so it was. The average of the preferences across the world's varied markets. Customers did not embrace the new offering. Sales decreased; operations shrunk, people lost jobs, and prosperity decreased. This time restricting freedom, pursuing scale, and driving the apparent common good, led to a loss of prosperity.

These two corporate examples show the real difficulty in pursuing prosperity. Responsibility must be created. Those responsible must see themselves sharing in the benefits achieved in discharging that responsibility. These, however, are the easier steps. The primary challenge is setting the right range of motion, the correct amount of freedom: too much freedom and the associated dispersion may be debilitating; restrict too much and the lack of freedom may equally wound the enterprise. Further, the examples demonstrate the crucial role of choice and judgment. In Ford, the solution was less freedom. For Carrier, the best approach was for more freedom. It's a choice based on informed judgment of what is best in a particular situation.

In these examples, we can see that the range of action can impact effectiveness in pursuing prosperity. In the next, we shall see that range of action also must consider motivation. Freedom not only allows latitude to find just the right solution, it also motivates the party involved to dedicate considerable energy toward the task. It still, however, remains a challenge to find just the appropriate range to allow.

VIII. Snap-on: The Captain of His Ship

Snap-on has thousands of mobile tool vans that sell its products across North America. The vast majority of these trucks are driven by owner operators under a franchise agreement. As is common for franchisors, however, the corporation itself also owns and operates a small number of these mobile outlets in order to have first-hand understanding of the operating challenge across the network. The franchised vans are run by self-motivated entrepreneurs who own the enterprise, receive the benefits of success, and have freedom, within the envelope of the franchise specifications, to pursue his or her individual prosperity. The Company-owned vans, on the other hand, are run by capable people who are company employees. They do not have legal ownership of the vans. Much effort, however, is focused on ensuring that the Company drivers feel ownership for the performance of their truck and that they clearly share in the prosperity that their particular outlet generates. The corporation also ensures that they all can clearly see a significant linkage between their personal prosperity and their results. They're given a substantial range of responsibility to make choices in product stocked on the truck, in discounts given to customers, and in the use of their own time. It's this range of action that enables them to pursue their success. And, it works quite well. The company vans are a strong contributor to the corporation's success and they make clear the important relationship between freedom and motivation. Given the proper freedom and the ability to personalize their van, the Company employee feels like the "captain of his ship," and his role as the person responsible for any prosperity created comes into clear focus. His feeling of ownership, his pride, and his satisfaction all intensify even though he does not hold legal title to the assets. Being free to drive results creates a strong feeling of ownership and responsibility for his individual and for the corporation's collective success. This is another vivid example of the value and satisfaction that the relationship among responsibility, freedom, and prosperity can create if it is balanced correctly.

The Snap-on franchisees, on the other hand, offer an example of the perils in granting too much latitude and the possibilities in using judgment to restore the balance. The franchisees are each focused on a list of repair shops clustered around a relatively narrow area. The van drivers encounter different preferences and problems from shop to shop and from customer to customer. This is to say nothing of the variation that can be seen moving from franchisee to franchisee or region to region across the North American continent. Over the years, the franchisees were allowed to customize their trucks, to find their own selling styles, and to meet the specific preferences and tendencies of their mechanic customers. A particular van might market product, promote sales, process payments, and manage inventory in a very different way than the franchisee immediately adjacent to his or her location. The corporation allowed this, granting a broad range of action to the franchisee in pursuit of his prosperity. What it meant, however, is that corporate support: computer systems, promotional programs, point of sale materials, and sales training had to encompass very large variety. The economies of scale that might otherwise have been an advantage were not available. Support, while broad based and accommodating of variety, might have traded depth for breadth. Snap-on judged that this was not the optimal situation in which to pursue franchisee prosperity. The Corporation moved to a more common model, restricting some freedom to customize, but trading that restriction for strong support with more depth. Vans now employed similar collection structures, common stocking protocols and congruent product setups. The franchisees were also given more in-depth training in common approaches to optimize their business. The focus paid off handsomely: productivity increased; van sales rose; and individual franchisees became much more prosperous. Satisfaction and fulfillment for both the franchisees as individuals, and the Corporation collectively, soared to new heights.

IX. Multinationals: The Lessons Learned

The corporate examples discussed are a demonstration of the delicate relationship among property, freedom, and prosperity. Each characteristic is essential to the other. Without the burden of responsibility or feeling of ownership, there is no sense of freedom and, as documented in numerous texts on the subject, prosperity will not flow. But, that ownership is only valuable if it leads to a sharing of the value and prosperity created by its use. Corporations work hard to ensure that this linkage is both real and perceived. We also see that ownership and responsibility cannot lead to prosperity if freedom, and a range of action, is not granted. It's clear, in the examples presented, that from Ford to Carrier to Snap-on, indeed, for all corporations, that determining the freedom, i.e., the appropriate range of action, is central to efficacy. It is, however, a quite difficult balance to achieve. Too much range and individuality will defeat the pursuit of prosperity and negate the value of ownership. Control too tightly, restrict freedom, and motivation will plummet. Prosperity will be stunted and the value of ownership and responsibility will also be negated. Multinationals show us that freedom is essential, but the range of action is a difficult choice that like many thorny decisions can only be made guided by judgment.

Countries around the world joust with many of the same issues surrounding property, freedom, and prosperity that challenge corporations. A country, like a corporation, is a social organism formed to achieve prosperity and fulfillment for its citizens through collective action. The range of national activity can extend from simply providing the substrate of services that are necessary to pursue prosperity, all the way to direct action that will attempt to assure redistribution of prosperity across the population to all citizens. In the discussion that follows, we will attempt to confirm the relationship among property, freedom, and prosperity observed in multinationals by examining the role of these characteristics in various important nations.

It's likely that China is not the first country that comes to mind when seeking to observe an effective balance among property, freedom, and prosperity. In my opinion, however, it is a very clear example of this axis at work. Much could be written regarding China's favorable journey from the disastrous periods marked by phrases such as "The Great Leap Forward," and the "Cultural Revolution" to the impressive skyscrapers of today's Shanghai and Beijing. The people of China, although not as free or as prosperous or fulfilled as citizens of some other nations, have certainly seen rare progress in gaining individual ownership, in receiving a broader range of action, and in enjoying the associated prosperity. The improvement in Chinese life has shown a steeper positive trend than that demonstrated by any other country in today's world, possibly faster gains than any other nation in history.

One of the middle kingdom's clearest examples of ownership, freedom, and prosperity is in the relationship between the Chinese central government in Beijing and the governments of the various provinces and major cities. The Beijing government, instead of controlling China centrally, has given substantial ownership of outcome to municipal and provincial leaders. These leadership groups are charged with the responsibility for the prosperity and satisfaction of their local citizens. This is especially important in China because economic progress has become one of the government's key factors in establishing and maintaining its legitimacy. In addition to the responsibility of the local economy, the central government has also granted the freedom or range of action in deciding whether to proceed on commercial projects either locally-funded or using direct foreign investments. This delegation has been one of the key factors in attracting foreign capital to China. The local governments have a direct and active interest in the prosperity of the population in their regions. They are, therefore, quite motivated to seek and aide investment that would drive focused progress. They appear in this area to have been granted free range of action for all possible business activities up to a relatively large threshold after which the project must receive Beijing's imprimatur. This policy drives the decision down closer to the population, which will actually receive the benefit in the form of jobs or general economic stimulation. It also generally frees all but the largest commercial decisions from ideological considerations. For example, if China and the U.S. are embroiled in a war of words over Taiwan, which happens from time to time, Beijing tends to get icy with all things American. If a central government approval was required, it could be much delayed in order for the Chinese to appear tough and ideologically pure. Local governments, however, don't have such a sensitive interest in ideological disputes. Their prime goal, on which they are measured, is local prosperity. In these circumstances, they're motivated to move ahead without disruption regardless of the international political climate. This policy has been at the core of much economic development and increased prosperity for the Chinese people. And, at its base, it's rooted in the freedom or range of action granted by Beijing to other localities.

X. India: The Tyranny of Freedom

India is another nation that provides a useful example in examining the balance among property, freedom, and prosperity. The nation represents the world's second largest population and the largest democratic society on the globe. Property ownership, though modest, is reasonably spread across the country. Freedom through both robust democratic institutions and individual range of action is an integral part of the nation's social landscape. Despite the presence of property and freedom, broad prosperity remains quite elusive with many of India's citizens living with struggle. Minimal education, illiteracy, limited comfort, and difficult living conditions are common in most of India's almost 650,000 villages. To be sure, there has been considerable progress in the last 20 years, but much of that improvement has been narrowly focused. For most of India's population, the march of prosperity has been slow and meager. Certainly, in comparison to other emerging markets, such as China, India has trailed both in overall development and in the distribution of gain across the population. From close observation over almost 25 years, it appears that India has failed to find the correct balance between responsibility and freedom. It may be that the general population has too large a range of action. Bernard H. Siegow, in *Property and Freedom, The Courts and Land-Use Regulation*, recognizes that "freedom's unlimited exercise may be harmful to both an individual and society."[4] India may have entered that territory. In fact, in India effective collective action is now made difficult by the need to accommodate so many freely individual interests. Indeed, the current government is a coalition in which the Prime Minister, though superbly capable, is constrained by the competing interests within his cabinet. This is in a country which already is in sore need of central commonality, with multiple major alphabets in regular use, and many, many dialects spoken. In addition, the concepts on which India was

---

[4] Bernard H. Siegaw, *Property and Freedom, The Constitution, The Courts and Land-Use Regulation* (New York: W.W. Norton, 1998), p. 157.

founded, including civil disobedience, make marshaling the country in a disciplined pursuit of common prosperity doubly difficult. The citizens of India are blessed with extensive freedom, but it is a freedom to pursue the specific interest of the minority, the varying perspectives of the 650,000 individual villages. The government, legitimized by the support of these individual interests, caters to each of them, in effect making collective progress difficult. So, India is an example where the people are endowed with both property and freedom, but their prospects for prosperity is limited by incoherent interest. It appears to be a nation that has not yet determined the proper balance among ownership, freedom and prosperity. In India, the need for proper judgment in the axis of property, freedom, prosperity appears clear. The large range of freedom, person by person, village by village, actually compromises the value of property and constricts the pursuit of prosperity. In turn, the resulting minimal economic condition, serves to mute the value of freedom. A solution for India might be to find a better balance between freedom and direction. A path forward might offer less room for individuality, energize more collective action, drive prosperity and, in so doing, make lives more fulfilling. This, however, would take the application of clever judgment and a courageous confidence in the choices implied in that commonality; both are difficult but perhaps necessary measures in the current environment.

XI. Singapore: The Disciplined Dragon

The Lion City is an example of effective balance among property, freedom, and prosperity. The leadership of that island nation understands the importance of each element of the axis. They clearly recognize the delicate nature of the difficult balance. The story of Singapore begins in 1965 when the nation seceded from the Malaysian Federation. In that period, the city was a fairly underdeveloped port for transshipment at the straits of Malacca. The newly-minted nation suffered from a significant problem regarding the supply and quality of housing. Low construction rates dating back to before the Second World War coupled with massive war damage had created a substantial housing shortage. A major portion of the population, 300,000 people lived in squatter settlements. Indeed, the British Housing Committee described post-war Singapore as "one of the world's worst slums."[5] By the 1960's, the situation had not much changed, beside the squatters, there were 250,000 people living in squalid shop houses. This meant that, at the time of independence, about 30% of the Singapore population was living in extremely difficult, substandard conditions.

---

[5] Belinda Yuen, "Squatters No More: Singapore's Social Housing," *Global Urban Development*, Vol. 3, Issue 1 (November 2007), p. 3 (http://www.globalurban.org/ GUDMag07Vol3Iss1/Yuen%20PDF).

Recognizing the central importance of ownership, the associated sense of responsibility, and the favorable effect on the population, the government commissioned a robust Housing Development Board which sought to build modern apartment blocks and to set Singaporeans on the path to ownership. Today, almost 90% of Singaporeans own a modern house, with the overwhelming majority of these being Housing Development Board apartments. So, citizens now enjoy the benefits of property and regularly deploy the energy associated with that responsibility.

Singaporeans enjoyed a sense of freedom even as British colonial subjects and, indeed, they were quite free under democratic self-rule after their independence. This freedom, however, did not automatically enable prosperity. But, from the beginning, the new independent government struck an effective balance between the citizens' new responsibility and an appropriate range of action. Democracy was established, but with clear norms. A forced savings/retirement program was established, creating capital formation to fuel growth. Drug trafficking was severely punished, establishing a level of safety above most other nations of the world. And, strong education was mandated including a study of common language to focus the culture. Singaporeans were free to act individually. They clearly were given the democratic right to life, liberty, and the pursuit of happiness, but within the boundaries that the government deemed best for collective progress. It has worked well. Singapore has progressed from one of the "world's worst slums" to one of the most advanced countries on the planet. It's among the world's leaders in infrastructure, safety, per capita income and broad prosperity. It has risen from a third world slum to having an enviable quality of life for its people. And, it all emanates from the ability to strike an effective balance among property, freedom, and prosperity.

XII. The United States: Balance Lost

The United States has been a fine example of a strong balance among property, freedom, and prosperity. The Northwest Ordinance, signed by George Washington in 1789, sought to promote the common good by ensuring the availability and distribution of land to the general population willing to occupy and farm their assigned parcels. This established broad property ownership and the attendant responsibility as a cornerstone of the newly-born republic. Freedom, as set forth in the U.S. Constitution and its Bill of Rights, was also part of this birth. As decades became centuries, the United States has passed through multiple crises. Through it, however, it always engendered a sense of responsibility in its citizens, creating a range of action rooted in individuality and authoring ample progress and relative prosperity. The conditions of citizenship were always reasonably clear. Wave after wave of immigrants entering the "melting pot" were expected to adopt American culture, eventually standing shoulder to shoulder with all others, becoming indistinct from those who came before. The government was active in providing for the common defense and in engaging the big issues like infrastructure, slavery, and education. The axis of property, freedom, and prosperity was in balance generating consistent progress and prosperity.

As the years have passed, however, the balance between ownership and freedom of action has become harder to strike as the Americans have urbanized, living closer together, and naturally needing more collective rules to avoid the conflicts formerly avoided by the insulating spread of the American land-scape. In the 21st century, the United States is now struggling greatly to reignite its prosperity and restore the balance between ownership and freedom. The centrifugal forces of individualism have driven even more conflict among competing interest groups. Every constituency seems to have very focused perspectives, which they want supported by government intervention. They do not, however, readily enlist in or support other causes for individual or collective good. This plethora of interests makes it difficult to create effective collective action, to pursue broad common prosperity, and to solve the issues of the day, because any effective proposal cannot satisfy enough of these individual interests.

In effect, America has lost some of the plot for the collective melting that reasonably aligned Americans in the past. The culture of freedom has morphed into one of extreme individuality. It appears that, like businesses that grant too much range of action and eliminate the advantages of scale economies, the United States has drifted to become a nation of isolated groups that view their interests as paramount and are encouraged by modern American culture to pursue those very narrow goals. At the same time, the American majority confused by the rising culture of non-judgmentalism and perhaps by an oversize devotion to range of action, lacks the will to constrain these centrifugal interests. The result is collective action which serves individual interests regardless of their value in enabling the broad collective good and without concern for its effect on prosperity. In the end, this loss of balance has lead to a Babel-like dysfunction in the United States where the central authority serves often to cater to disparate constituent interests: supporting abortion, saving the environment, amending health care, redefining marriages, driving broad university education – but without common purpose. These may or may not be meritorious actions. The common denominator is that they all serve to support specific interest groups of Americans who vote and empower the political leadership. In effect, the United States appears to have become ruled by vocal minorities.

To restore balance, Americans must focus on the virtuous cycle of characteristics with which we started this paper: property/ responsibility; freedom, and prosperity. The American majority must regain the will to meld its citizens in a common purpose, the pursuit of prosperity. If anything is to be learned from the examples set forth above, it's that property and freedom are useful only in the pursuit of prosperity and fulfillment. America and its leaders should return to coherence of objective. They should create effective collective actions, but only those that clearly will be in pursuit of prosperity for all. This will require that the county cast off the culture of non-judgmentalism and make decisions that will discard actions that may be good for individual interests, but in fact, do not serve the advancement of collective American prosperity. In short, it will require judgment, difficult choice, and a balance among property, freedom, and prosperity.

XIII. The Church: Identity Challenged

The balance of property, freedom, and prosperity has a place in religions as well as in corporations and countries. The Catholic Church encourages ownership including responsibility for one's spiritual health, for the well-being of the parish, and for the provision of charity to others. Equally, the Church endorses a freedom and range of action to pursue the prosperity of fulfillment and satisfaction. The Church, like other institutions, must find limits for that freedom. Like corporations and countries, it must determine the boundaries within which its communicants can have a range of action. The right to life, the definition of marriage, and the message of the Gospels are among the elements defining the Church beyond which individuals cannot stray, even in the pursuit of fulfillment and prosperity. It appears that drawing these lines has become challenging and problematic in this era of non-judgmentalism. Despite the difficulties, the Church, like other collective entities, must make these distinctions and maintain the courage of choice to restrict freedom. It must ensure that those people committed to its guidance will pursue and find a positive quality of life, but always consistent with its essential beliefs.

XIV. Conclusion

The observation of multinational corporations and selected countries demonstrates that the effectiveness of the Property, Freedom, Prosperity axis depends greatly on judgment and difficult choice. This is a common phenomenon among the algorithms that govern social interactions of our time.

Freedom and property are not goals in themselves. They are, however, essential ingredients in structuring prosperous and satisfying lives for both individuals and communities. In the end, it is prosperity, broadly defined, that is the primary temporal objective of all contemporary social organisms.

It also appears from a consideration of various nations and cultures that private ownership and individual responsibility are today widely accepted as necessary building blocks for a positive society. In fact, in the current world, it is not so much that ownership guarantees freedom. Rather, it is that freedom and the range of action enables the prosperity creating power of individual ownership. This linkage is generally recognized throughout the world of the 21st century. But, the presence of property and freedom does not in itself guarantee prosperity. The primary ingredient in creating prosperity in today's world, is deciding the appropriate range of action, without violating the natural limits of common restraint.

Further, it's clear from corporations and countries, that judgment and choice are required to determine the appropriate range of action in any situation. But, as demonstrated in examples from Ford to Carrier to Snap-on, extensive freedom is not always the answer. Equally, it is evident, that broad restriction can just as easily lead to difficulty and block the pursuit of prosperity. There is, therefore, no clearly defined path through property and freedom to prosperity, fulfillment, and a positive quality of life.

These lessons apply to larger communities, such as, nations or religions as surely as they apply to multinational corporations. Singapore, for example, appears to have found the proper balance. While recently, nations like the United States seem to struggle in marshaling property and freedom to effectively deliver consistent and broad prosperity. For communities such as these that are having difficulty in creating fulfillment, it will take informed judgments, resolve, and courage of conviction in making difficult choices to restore the prosperity and continuing progress for which we all strive.

Summary

Property, freedom, and prosperity are essential to contemporary communities but, it's striking the appropriate balance among those characteristics that creates the fulfilling society.

From the experiences of multinationals and their relatively compact time horizons, it can be determined that property/responsibility and freedom are necessary, but not sufficient, conditions to achieve prosperity. Corporate examples show fulfillment follows only when freedom or range of action is granted in just the appropriate measure. This, however, is a challenging task: grant too little freedom and attenuate the value-creating energy of property; grant too broad a range of action and the power of the collective in generating prosperity is diluted. It's a balance which, whether applied to corporations, nations, or churches, requires judgment and difficult choice.

Zusammenfassung

Eigentum, Freiheit und Wohlstand sind Kennzeichen der modernen Gesellschaft; aber es ist nicht einfach, das richtige Gleichgewicht zwischen ihnen zu finden, das eine gute Gesellschaft bewirkt. Aus den Erfahrungen mit multinationalen Unternehmen und ihres überschaubaren Zeithorizonts kann man erkennen, dass Eigentum/Verantwortung und Freiheit notwendige, aber nicht hinreichende Bedingungen sind, um Wohlstand zu schaffen. Die Beispiele zeigen, dass dies nur gelingt, wenn die Freiheit oder der Handlungsspielraum richtig bemessen ist. Dies jedoch ist eine schwierige Aufgabe: Zu wenig Freiheit wirkt sich auf die Werte schaffende Energie des Eigentums aus; ein zu großer Spielraum schwächt die Kraft der Gemeinschaft, Wohlstand zu schaffen. Es kommt auf die Balance an, ob es sich um Unternehmen, Nationen oder Kirchen handelt, die ein klares Urteil und eine oft schwierige Entscheidung verlangt.

Freiheit als Fassade, Eigentum als Negativum?

Wie der Staat die Entmündigung und Enteignung seiner Bürger vorantreibt

Von Michael Eilfort

I. Freiheit und Eigentum

Freiheit! Das Recht, selbst zu entscheiden, auszuwählen und, in der Formulierung aus der amerikanischen Verfassung, nach Glück zu streben. Die Chance, sich einzubringen, im demokratischen Rechtsstaat teilzuhaben am gesellschaftlichen Leben und Wohlstand, Leistung erbringen und aufsteigen zu können. Die Pflicht, Verantwortung für das eigene Handeln zu tragen, im Sinne des Kant´schen kategorischen Imperativs die Grenzen der eigenen Freiheit und jenseits des Ich den Anderen und die Gemeinschaft zu sehen.

Und Eigentum? Kann es eine wichtige Facette, wenn nicht Ergänzung der Freiheit sein? Was hat „schnöder" Besitz, meist Materielles, mit dem so hochstehenden Ideal der Freiheit zu tun? Ist Eigentum gleichfalls ein Menschen- oder Bürgerrecht? Im Rahmen des großen europäischen Freiheitsstrebens der französischen Revolution wurde dies so gesehen, der Schutz des Eigentums in Artikel 17 der Erklärung der Menschen- und Bürgerrechte an herausgehobener Stelle kodifiziert – und damit ein innerer Zusammenhang von Freiheit und Eigentum dokumentiert. Dies ist unverändert gültiges französisches Verfassungsrecht: „Da das Eigentum ein unverletzliches und heiliges Recht ist, kann es niemandem genommen werden, wenn es nicht die gesetzlich festgelegte, öffentliche Notwendigkeit augenscheinlich erfordert und unter der Bedingung einer gerechten und vorherigen Entschädigung."[1]

Kurz zuvor war 1787 in einem Zusatz zur Verfassung der Vereinigten Staaten von Amerika der Schutz des Eigentums als Grundrecht und vor allem Schutz vor staatlichem Zugriff in der Verfassung der Vereinigten Staaten von Amerika verankert worden, stark beeinflusst vom Gedankengut des im 17. Jahrhundert wirkenden britischen Liberalen John Locke: Er hatte das Naturrecht des Menschen auf Freiheit und Individualität in den Mittelpunkt seiner Ausführungen gerückt und einen engen Bezug zum Eigentum hergestellt. Der

---

[1] Nach *Günther Franz*, Staatsverfassungen, Darmstadt 1964.

Staat basiert bei Locke auf einem Gesellschaftsvertrag zwischen freien Individuen und ist für den Schutz ihrer Freiheitsrechte, insbesondere des Privateigentums, zuständig. Am Ende stand in der „neuen Welt" die „Überzeugung vom Eigentum als unverzichtbarem Teil persönlicher Freiheit ... Sie ist nach wie vor im natürlichen Rechtsbewusstsein der Amerikaner verankert und lässt sie grundsätzlich ein unbefangenes Verhältnis zu privatem Reichtum haben, sofern er erarbeitet ist."[2]

Von einem eher befangeneren Verhältnis zum Eigentum dagegen kann man beim Frühsozialisten Pierre Proudhon („Eigentum ist Diebstahl") und Karl Marx, Friedrich Engels und all ihren Anhängern sprechen, die im 19. Jahrhundert im Privateigentum die Ursache von Entfremdung und Ausbeutung sahen. Folgerichtig erhofften sie sich vom Kommunismus und all seinen Spielarten die Überwindung des Privateigentums. Letzteres ist in allen später real existierenden Ausprägungen der sozialistischen Gesellschaftsordnung weitgehend gelungen. Aber um welchen Preis? Kaum zu bestreiten ist, dass die Menschen, ob im ehemaligen Ostblock, in Kuba oder Nordkorea, nicht nur materiell schlechter gestellt waren als die jeweiligen Zeitgenossen in freiheitlichen Demokratien und Rechtsstaaten mit Schutz privaten Eigentums. Vor allem aber war die Freiheit abhanden gekommen. Es gibt in modernen Zeiten und entwickelten Industriegesellschaften keinen Beleg dafür, dass die Abwesenheit von geschütztem privaten Eigentum und Gewinnstreben auf der einen und die Anwesenheit von persönlicher Freiheit auf der anderen zusammenkommen können. Der Verfügung des Staates über „Produktionsmittel" und Eigentum, der Vergemeinschaftung von Grund und Gütern wohnt keine freiheitliche, sondern eine totalitäre Neigung inne.

Wo Eigentum nicht geschützt, Wettbewerb unterdrückt und Kreativität sowie Eigenverantwortung behindert werden, kommt es auf niedrigem und, wie die Erfahrung mit der DDR zeigte, gleichwohl nicht nachhaltigem Niveau zur gelegentlich als totale Gerechtigkeit verklärten Gleichheit der Grautöne: Die Antriebskräfte des Menschen erlahmen und auch der allmächtige Staat ist alles andere als effizient. Der Grund wurde schon von Thomas von Aquin im 13. Jahrhundert formuliert: Er bejahte das Eigentum an Sachen, weil „ein jeder mehr Sorge darauf verwendet, etwas zu beschaffen, was ihm allein gehört, als etwas, was allen oder vielen gehört". Zudem betonte er, dass „die menschlichen Angelegenheiten besser verwaltet werden, wenn jeder Einzelne seine eigenen Sorgen hat in der Beschaffung irgendwelcher Dinge"[3]. Adam Smith als spiritus rector der Marktwirtschaft hat das in seinem Hauptwerk „Der Wohlstand der

---

[2] *Christian Hillgruber*, Ist privates Eigentum ein Menschenrecht?, in diesem Band, S. 125 f.

[3] Zitiert nach *Manfred Spieker*, Die universelle Bestimmung der Güter, in diesem Band, S. 60.

Nationen" später mit der „unsichtbaren Hand" beschrieben: Von ihr gesteuert, stelle sich durch richtig verstandenes Eigeninteresse im freien Wettbewerb ein Gleichgewicht von Produktion, Verbrauch, Lohn und Preis sowie vor allem das Gemeinwohl ein. Wirtschaftspolitisches Handeln des Staates lehnte Smith nicht ab, dessen zentrale Aufgabe sah er allerdings in der Sicherung von Eigentum – und dabei einen angelegten Gegensatz klar voraus: „Es gibt keine Kunst, welche eine Regierung schneller von der andern lernt, als die, dem Volke Geld aus der Tasche zu locken."[4] Smith sah auch, dass „keine Gesellschaft gedeihen und glücklich sein kann, in der der weitaus größte Teil ihrer Mitglieder arm und elend ist". Abhilfe lag für ihn aber eben nicht in staatlichem, sondern in der Summe privaten Handelns, auf der Basis funktionierender Anreize bei gegebenem Schutz des Eigentums: „Ein Mensch, der sich kein Eigentum erwerben kann, hat kein anderes Interesse, als so viel zu essen und so wenig zu arbeiten, als möglich."[5]

Freiheit ohne Eigentum und dessen Schutz gibt es nicht. Privates Eigentum mit all seinen positiven Anreizwirkungen und seinem Wachstumspotential scheint es dagegen zumindest eine gewisse Zeit ohne oder in sehr eingeschränkter Freiheit und bei nur mäßig verlässlicher Rechtssicherheit geben zu können. Ein entsprechender Versuch mit ungewissem Ausgang findet in der Volksrepublik China statt. Die enorme Entwicklung im „Reich der Mitte" widerspricht nicht dem Ergebnis zahlreicher Studien, die zeigen, dass im internationalen Vergleich mindestens ökonomische Freiheit und Wohlstand positiv korreliert sind. Freiere Gesellschaften sind also tatsächlich gleichzeitig reicher. Teilbereiche der ökonomischen Freiheit hängen dabei besonders eng mit dem Wohlstand einer Gesellschaft zusammen. So scheinen die Sicherstellung von privaten Eigentums- und Verfügungsrechten ebenso wie eine stabile Währung und die wirtschaftliche Offenheit eines Landes einen noch positiveren Einfluss auf das Bruttoinlandsprodukt pro Kopf und die Wachstumsrate des Bruttoinlandsprodukts auszuüben als die politische Freiheit mit ihren demokratischen Strukturen. Wie lange indes „wirtschaftliche Offenheit" mit politischer Beschränkung vereinbar ist, wird sich zeigen.

II. Die Soziale Marktwirtschaft

Als eine Art dritten Weg zwischen linken bis sozialistisch-kommunistischen Gesellschaftsentwürfen auf der einen Seite und dem in Kontinentaleuropa als „Marktradikalismus" verunglimpften Kapitalismus angelsächsischer Prägung

---

[4] *Adam Smith*, The Wealth of Nations, Book V, Chapter 2, Part 2: Of Taxes.

[5] Ebenda, Book III, Chapter 2: Of the Discouragement of Agriculture in the Ancient State of Europe after the Fall of the Roman Empire.

auf der anderen Seite sehen viele die Soziale Marktwirtschaft. Nach der Fi-
nanzmarkt- und der folgenden schweren Wirtschaftskrise mit allen Verwerfungen wird sie noch mehr als zuvor schon fast weltweit als Vorbild gesehen. In
vielen Ländern besteht ein überaus großes Interesse am „deutschen Weg". Aus
ausländischer Perspektive wird dabei oft und mit gewisser Faszination eine
scheinbar mühelos gelingende Verbindung von großer Wirtschaftskraft und
Wohlstand auf der einen sowie einem hohen Maß an Ausgleich und sozialem
Frieden auf der anderen Seite gesehen. Dass beides in Deutschland seit 1948 im
Westen und seit 1990 in Gesamtdeutschland weitgehend zusammenfällt, ist tatsächlich ein unschätzbarer Erfolg der Sozialen Marktwirtschaft. Wahrscheinlich hat sie mehr zur Festigung und Festigkeit der zweiten deutschen Demokratie beigetragen als umgekehrt das demokratische politische System der Bestän-
digkeit der Grundlagen der Sozialen Marktwirtschaft zuträglich war – und damit der Nachhaltigkeit von beidem, der wirtschaftlichen wie vor allem der demokratischen Ordnung.

Schon die Bezeichnung „dritter Weg" ist eigentlich eine Irreführung, eine
Art gerösteter Schneeball. Es gibt keinen Mittelweg zwischen Freiheit und Un-
freiheit, zwischen Schutz privaten Eigentums und Vergemeinschaftung, zwischen individuellem Streben und Zwang zum Kollektiv. Aber es gibt sehr wohl
eine Möglichkeit, im Rahmen einer kapitalistischen Wirtschaftsordnung die
Kräfte des Marktes für einen sehr breiten Teil der Bevölkerung nutzbar zu machen, dem Markt den von einem handlungsfähigen Staat gesetzten Rahmen
überzuordnen, Ergebnisse des Marktgeschehens auszubalancieren sowie über
das Verständnis von Maß und Mitte immer wieder neu demokratisch zu ringen.
Schon der Neoliberalismus[6] der 1930er Jahre hatte den Markt nicht als selbst-
regulierenden Automatismus, sondern als durch einen starken Staat und eine
entsprechende Wettbewerbskontrolle zu gewährleistenden gesehen. Vorgesehen war auch schon eine gewisse soziale Grundsicherung, wenngleich Arbeit
für die beste Form sozialer Gerechtigkeit gehalten wurde. Einer der deutschen
neoliberalen Vordenker, steter Mahner zu „Maß und Mitte", war Wilhelm Röpke. Freiheit und Verantwortung gehörten für ihn untrennbar zusammen, und
ebenso war Eigentum aus seiner Sicht logisch mit Verantwortung verbunden.

Auf dieser Grundlage bewegte sich einer der Gründerväter der Sozialen
Marktwirtschaft, Alfred Müller-Armack, als er wegweisend davon sprach, „das
Prinzip der Freiheit auf dem Markte mit dem des sozialen Ausgleichs zu ver-

---

[6] Nicht zu verwechseln mit dem Zerrbild, das Ahnungslosen und Ideologen im 21.
Jahrhundert, unter irreführender Berufung auf Ronald Reagan und Margaret Thatcher,
als Begründung für den Ruf nach immer mehr Staat und Umverteilung dient. Vgl. Stiftung Marktwirtschaft, Soziale Marktwirtschaft – Auslauf- oder Zukunftsmodell?, Berlin
2013; ebenso: *Karen Horn*, Die Soziale Marktwirtschaft. Alles, was Sie über den Neoliberalismus wissen sollten, Frankfurt am Main 2010.

binden"[7]. Dieses Prinzip der Freiheit wird innerhalb des demokratischen Systems der Bundesrepublik Deutschland ökonomisch umgesetzt als Gewährleistung der Berufs-, Gewerbe- und Unternehmerfreiheit sowie als Recht der freien Wahl des Arbeitsplatzes, der Ausbildungsstätte (Art. 12 GG) und als Vertragsfreiheit (Art. 2 GG). Vor allem jedoch die staatliche Garantie des Privateigentums (Art. 14 GG) stellt einen entscheidenden Anreiz für Unternehmer und abhängig Beschäftigte dar, Leistungen zu erbringen.

Wörtlich heißt es im Artikel 14 des Grundgesetzes:

(1) Das Eigentum und das Erbrecht werden gewährleistet. Inhalt und Schranken werden durch die Gesetze bestimmt.

(2) Eigentum verpflichtet. Sein Gebrauch soll zugleich dem Wohle der Allgemeinheit dienen.

(3) Eine Enteignung ist nur zum Wohle der Allgemeinheit zulässig. Sie darf nur durch Gesetz oder auf Grund eines Gesetzes erfolgen, das Art und Ausmaß der Entschädigung regelt. Die Entschädigung ist unter gerechter Abwägung der Interessen der Allgemeinheit und der Beteiligten zu bestimmen. Wegen der Höhe der Entschädigung steht im Streitfalle der Rechtsweg vor den ordentlichen Gerichten offen.

Auch in der Europäischen Union gehört das Recht auf Privateigentum zu den wichtigsten Grundrechten, dort allerdings ohne den ausdrücklichen Hinweis auf die Verpflichtung zur Beachtung des Gemeinwohls. In Artikel 17 der Charta der Grundrechte der Europäischen Union steht im Wortlaut:

(1) Jede Person hat das Recht, ihr rechtmäßig erworbenes Eigentum zu besitzen, zu nutzen, darüber zu verfügen und es zu vererben. Niemandem darf sein Eigentum entzogen werden, es sei denn aus Gründen des öffentlichen Interesses in den Fällen und unter den Bedingungen, die in einem Gesetz vorgesehen sind, sowie gegen eine rechtzeitige angemessene Entschädigung für den Verlust des Eigentums. Die Nutzung des Eigentums kann gesetzlich geregelt werden, soweit dies für das Wohl der Allgemeinheit erforderlich ist.

(2) Geistiges Eigentum wird geschützt.

Für Walter Eucken, einen weiteren Begründer der Sozialen Marktwirtschaft, zählt das Privateigentum insbesondere an Produktionsmitteln zu den konstituierenden Prinzipien der Wettbewerbsordnung „Soziale Marktwirtschaft"[8]. Die vermeintliche Alternative zum Privateigentum – das Kollektiveigentum – ist Eucken zufolge aus mehreren Gründen nicht mit einer freiheitlichen Wettbewerbsordnung vereinbar: Zum einen würde der Staat wohl kaum die Lenkung des Kollektiveigentums aus der Hand geben, das Eucken als Machtinstrument der politischen Führungsschicht sah: „Die Machtposition provoziert die Machtausübung."[9] Aber selbst wenn der Staat auf seine Lenkungsmacht verzichten

---

[7] *Alfred Müller-Armack*, Wirtschaftslenkung und Marktwirtschaft, Hamburg 1947.

[8] *Walter Eucken*, Grundsätze der Wirtschaftspolitik, Tübingen 1952, S. 270–275.

[9] Ebenda, S. 136.

würde, ließe sich die effizienzfördernde Wirkung des Wettbewerbs bzw. des Preismechanismus nicht durch die Hintertür implementieren. Denn die Entscheidungsträger wären keine Unternehmer, sondern „Beamte", welche die Produktionsmittel lediglich „bürokratisch" verwalteten, so dass am Ende doch nur eine Art zentralistische Planwirtschaft stehen würde.

Zwei weitere Aspekte des Privateigentums werden von Eucken betont: Zum einen hält er es aus Sicht der Wettbewerbsordnung für unschädlich, wenn sich einzelne Betriebe in der Hand des Staates befinden, solange sich diese in Wettbewerbsmärkte einordnen, in Konkurrenz zu privaten Unternehmen stehen und der Preismechanismus nicht durch staatliche Subventionen gestört wird. Zum anderen – und wichtiger noch – weist Eucken darauf hin, dass Privateigentum zwar eine notwendige, aber keine hinreichende Bedingung für die Durchführung einer Wettbewerbsordnung ist. So argumentiert Eucken, dass Privateigentum in monopolistischen Marktformen aufgrund der damit verbundenen Machtpositionen – z. B. gegenüber Arbeitnehmern, Kunden, Konkurrenten – zu schweren Schäden führt, und daher die im 19. und beginnenden 20. Jahrhundert teilweise geäußerte Kritik am Privateigentum an Produktionsmitteln oft im Recht war.

Nach Eucken kann Privateigentum nur in einer Wettbewerbsordnung auch für die Nicht-Eigentümer positive Effekte entfalten, etwa in Form ökonomisch effizienter Produktionsprozesse oder Wahlmöglichkeiten beim Konsum oder auf dem Arbeitsmarkt: *„Wie also Privateigentum an Produktionsmitteln eine Voraussetzung der Wettbewerbsordnung ist, so ist die Wettbewerbsordnung eine Voraussetzung dafür, dass das Privateigentum an Produktionsmitteln nicht zu wirtschaftlichen und sozialen Missständen führt."*[10]

Die Soziale Marktwirtschaft und ihre Wettbewerbsordnung haben sich in der Folge sehr weitgehend bewährt, im Prozess wie im Ergebnis: Der von Ludwig Erhard postulierte „Wohlstand für alle" wurde vom Buchtitel zur Realität. Das deutsche Wirtschaftswunder vornehmlich der 1950er Jahre beruht neben dem Fleiß, dem Wohlstandshunger und millionenfachem Willen zum Aufstieg eben darauf, dass die genannten Prinzipien weitgehend Beachtung fanden: Rendite und Risiko, Gewinn und Haftung gehörten zusammen, Maß und Mitte wurden dank verbreiteter Wertvorstellungen und internalisiertem Konsens eher beachtet, bedurften nur weniger gesetzlicher Festlegungen und kaum des sich später verbreitenden Paternalismus. Das galt übrigens auch für Spitzengehälter im Verhältnis sowohl zur jeweiligen Leistung wie auch zu den durchschnittlichen Löhnen z. B. in einem Unternehmen – niemand glaubte in den ersten Jahrzehnten der Sozialen Marktwirtschaft, entgegen dem Prinzip der Vertragsfreiheit die Höhe z. B. von Managergehältern gesetzlich begrenzen zu müssen. Stark ver-

---

[10] Ebenda, S. 275.

ankert waren auf der anderen Seite das Bestreben, durch Arbeit voranzukommen und nicht von anderen abhängig zu sein: Staatliche „Stütze", z. B. Sozialhilfe, war selbst in vielen Fällen echter Not verpönt und wurde oft nicht beantragt. Zudem war das soziale Netz noch grobmaschiger, auch weil der Staat damals in größerem Maß auf Wettbewerbsaufsicht und klassische politische Aufgaben fokussiert war – und der zur Sozialen Marktwirtschaft zwingend gehörenden, ausgleichenden Tätigkeit nur in vergleichsweise bescheidenem Umfang nachging.

Der zentrale Umverteilungshebel liegt seit Bestehen der Bundesrepublik im Steuersystem, vornehmlich bei der Einkommensteuer. Besteuerung nach der Leistungsfähigkeit und Steuerprogression sorgen dafür, dass die Unterschiede zwischen nach Einkommen differenzierten Bevölkerungsgruppen durch den Abzug von Steuern und Sozialabgaben auf der einen und durch Transferleistungen auf der anderen Seite deutlich nivelliert werden. Die Darstellung verdeutlicht, dass das im Marktgeschehen erzielte Einkommen bei den am besten gestellten 10 Prozent der Bevölkerung nach staatlicher Korrektur deutlich gemindert, auf der anderen Seite die Lebenssituation deutlich verbessert wurde: Breite Schultern tragen in Deutschland seit Jahrzehnten mehr als Schwache – 10 Prozent der Einkommensteuerzahler beispielsweise trugen 2012 fast 55 % des gesamten Einkommensteueraufkommens. Auch bei der als „Steuer des kleinen Mannes" geltenden Mehrwertsteuer tragen die anteilig am Einkommen weniger, aber in absoluten Zahlen mehr konsumierenden Besserverdienenden das Hauptaufkommen. Der soziale Ausgleich funktioniert also – und das ist richtig. Wirtschaftlicher Erfolg ermöglicht den Sozialstaat, die Leistungsträger sind solidarisch. Die Steuerprogression als solche trägt das Adjektiv in der Sozialen Marktwirtschaft in starkem Maße, sie ruht auf einem breiten gesellschaftlichen Konsens. Wer mehr verdient, zahlt absolut und relativ mehr. Dies in Frage zu stellen, ist politisch aussichtslos und in der Sache falsch bzw. der Preis zu hoch: Eine Flat Tax könnte durchaus steuervereinfachend wirken, würde aber bei einem Großteil der Bevölkerung die ohnehin zunehmenden Zweifel an der Sozialen Marktwirtschaft exponentiell wachsen lassen (siehe Abbildung 1).

III. Die eingebaute Expansion des Wohlfahrtsstaates

Irgendwann begann der Staat, sich neue, zusätzliche Aufgaben zu suchen – irgendjemand ruft immer und sieht wahlweise eine „Gerechtigkeitslücke" oder „Handlungsbedarf". Irgendwann wollte Politik nicht mehr nur Rahmengeber und Kontrolleur, sondern tatkräftiger, prägender Akteur und Beglücker sein. Irgendwann fanden einige heraus, dass man mit etwas weniger bis gar keinem Fleiß, aber umso mehr Gewitztheit, Chuzpe und effizientem öffentlichen Klappern gut „durchkommt" – was sich im Lauf von Jahrzehnten herumsprach. Ir-

gendwann wurde die Nivellierung durch den Staat als wichtiger angesehen als
der durch Unterschiede erst entstehende Anreiz für den Einzelnen, sich zu verbessern. Eines Tages begann so der allseits bejahte und beliebte Begriff der
„Gerechtigkeit", vorwiegend als Verteilungs- und weniger als Leistungsgerech-
tigkeit verstanden zu werden. Gleichheit wurde, gemessen in vielen Langzeit-
studien, wichtiger, Freiheit dagegen war nicht mehr so wichtig oder galt als
selbstverständlich, wie Wohlstand und der Strom aus der Steckdose.

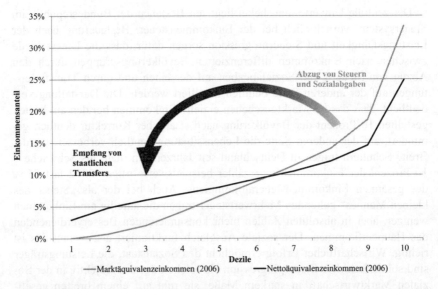

Datenquelle: SOEP.

Quelle: Hauser, R. / Becker, I. / DIW / ZEW: Integrierte Analyse der Einkommens- und Vermögensvertei-
lung, Bonn 2007.

Abbildung 1: Umverteilung vom Markt- zum Nettoäquivalenzeinkommen

Die veränderte Nachfrageorientierung in höchster Professionalität und mit
durchaus basisdemokratischem Impetus abdeckend, richteten die Parteien sich
darauf ein, tendenziell weniger den demokratischen Souverän zu fordern – was
zugegebenermaßen in Form von Aufnahme und Bündelung von Interessen und
Vermittlung von Kompromissen oder unangenehmen Wahrheiten anstrengend
ist. Sie gingen häufiger dazu über, eher den wählenden Konsumenten zu fördern bzw. zu ködern, mit simplen und auf kürzeste Sicht angelegten Mitteln.
Statt der verbal beschworenen „Richtungsentscheidungen" waren Wahlen in
wachsendem Maß auch Überbietungswettbewerbe.

Ist es ein Zufall, dass CDU und CSU die einzige absolute Mehrheit der bun-
desrepublikanischen Geschichte 1957 erzielten, dem Jahr, in dem die umlagefi-

nanzierte staatliche Rente eingeführt wurde – mit Millionen von Einführungsgewinnern, die Auszahlungen erhielten, ohne selbst Beiträge geleistet zu haben? Die ungedeckten Schecks auf der anderen Seite – bei Adenauer hieß es „Kinder kriegen die Leute immer" – waren jedenfalls erst später einzulösen. Nach dem gleichen Muster mag die Einführung der Sozialen Pflegeversicherung 1994 zum Sieg Helmut Kohls bei einer eigentlich schon verloren geglaubten Bundestagswahl beigetragen haben. Wie hieß es so schön beim „Kanzler der Einheit": Er wolle Wahlen gewinnen, nicht den Ludwig-Erhard-Preis. Auch die SPD ließ sich in den 1970ern nicht lumpen: Ein zweistelliger Gehaltssprung im Öffentlichen Dienst sowie dessen massive Ausweitung, Beschäftigungsprogramme und der Aufbau einer flächendeckenden und machtvollen „Sozialindustrie" erbrachten durchaus den erhofften Zuspruch. Auf der anderen Seite, der des Erwirtschaftens und Steuerzahlens, lösten sie noch keine Widerstände aus, es gab ja die Möglichkeit der Schuldenaufnahme. Erste steuergestaltende Reaktionen auf wachsende Belastungen und Intransparenz waren indes schon erkennbar. Zudem konnte man häufiger dem Eindruck begegnen, mit dem eigenen Steuerbeitrag den Bereich „gesellschaftliche Verantwortung" abgegolten zu haben und sich selbst nicht mehr für andere engagieren zu brauchen. Dadurch wiederum war neue Staatsaktivität oder halbstaatliche Wohlfahrt gefragt, mit neuer Steuerbelastung. Keineswegs nur in Deutschland war der Teufelskreis der Sozialstaatsexpansion geschlossen.

Ludwig Erhard hatte die dem demokratischen Wohlfahrtsstaat inhärente Expansion und ihre Gefahren früh erkannt[11]:

> „Ich bin in der letzten Zeit (1957, Anm. d. Verf.) allenthalben erschrocken, wie übermächtig der Ruf nach kollektiver Sicherheit im sozialen Bereich erschallte. Wo aber sollen wir hinkommen und wie wollen wir den Fortschritt aufrechterhalten, wenn wir uns immer mehr in eine Form des Zusammenlebens von Menschen begeben, in der niemand mehr die Verantwortung für sich selbst zu übernehmen bereit ist und jedermann Sicherheit im Kollektiv gewinnen möchte ..., wir in eine gesellschaftliche Ordnung schlittern, in der jeder die Hand in der Tasche des anderen hat ... Die Blindheit und intellektuelle Fahrlässigkeit, mit der wir dem Versorgungs- und Wohlfahrtsstaat zusteuern, ... ist mehr als alles andere geeignet, die echten menschlichen Tugenden: Verantwortungsfreudigkeit, Nächsten- und Menschenliebe, das Verlangen nach Bewährung, die Bereitschaft zur Selbstvorsorge ... allmählich aber sicher absterben zu lassen – und am Ende steht vielleicht nicht die klassenlose, wohl aber die seelenlos mechanisierte Gesellschaft. Besonders unverständlich erscheint dieser Prozeß, weil in dem gleichen Maße, in dem sich der Wohlstand ausbreitet und die wirtschaftliche Sicherheit wächst, dazu unsere wirtschaftlichen Grundlagen sich festigen, das Verlangen, das so Erreichte gegen alle Fährnisse der Zukunft absichern zu wollen, alle anderen Bedenken überschattet. Hier liegt ein wahrlich tragischer Irrtum vor, denn man will offenbar nicht erkennen, daß wirtschaftlicher Fortschritt und leistungsmäßig fundierter Wohlstand mit einem System kollektiver Sicherheit unvereinbar sind.

---

[11] *Ludwig Erhard*, Wohlstand für alle, Düsseldorf 1957, S. 260–263.

Ebensowenig wie ein Volk mehr verzehren kann, als es als Volk an Werten geschaffen hat, sowenig kann auch der einzelne mehr an echter Sicherheit erringen, als wir uns im ganzen durch Leistung Sicherheit erworben haben ... Das mir vorschwebende Ideal beruht auf der Stärke, daß der einzelne sagen kann: ‚Ich will mich aus eigener Kraft bewähren, ich will das Risiko des Lebens selbst tragen, will für mein Schicksal selbst verantwortlich sein. Sorge du, Staat, dafür, daß ich dazu in der Lage bin.‟

Manche Wortwahl mag nicht mehr ganz zeitgemäß klingen – die hellsichtige Beschreibung dagegen auch das Jahr 2013 in besonderer Weise treffen. Erhard, der gegen das Umlageverfahren bei der Rente argumentiert hatte, sollte mindestens mit seiner Warnung Recht behalten, dass im demokratischen Staat eine stete Ausweitung der Versprechen eingebaut sei. So kam es: Eben die staatliche Rentenversicherung, deren Umlageverfahren schon durch die demographische Entwicklung gefährdet war und ist, wurde zusätzlich mit versicherungsfremden Leistungen belastet, die zum Zeitpunkt des Beschlusses viel Zustimmung brachten, denen aber keine Einzahlungen gegenüberstanden und die damit die Nachhaltigkeit der Rente in Gefahr bringen: Die erstmalige Anerkennung von Kindererziehungszeiten kurz vor der Bundestagswahl 1987 war ebenso gut gemeint wie die Verheißung von DM-Rentenauszahlungen für ältere Ostdeutsche vor der Bundestagswahl 1990. Politisch nachvollziehbar, systematisch aber falsch, ökonomisch auch und nachhaltig auf keinen Fall. Auch 2013 ist ein Bundestagswahljahr. Und worin sind sich die meisten Wahlkämpfer einig? In der Unterstützung für die Ausweitung von Leistungen, ohne dass dem neue Einzahlungen gegenüberstünden: Beifall im Hier und Jetzt, Verschiebung der Lasten in die Zukunft.

Adenauers Umlagerente 1957 war der Vorbote, besonders vorangetrieben wurde die Expansion des Wohlfahrtsstaates in der Zeit der Großen Koalition Ende der 1960er Jahre, mit dem von einem einseitig interpretierten Keynes inspirierten Glauben an „Globalsteuerung". In den 1970er, 1980er und 1990er Jahren, dann für das wiedervereinigte Land, wurde das soziale Netz fast unabhängig von parteipolitischen Mehrheiten relativ kontinuierlich enger geknüpft, der Sozialstaat ausgebaut, die Leistungen erhöht. Der Staat wurde zum immer mehr Menschen umsorgenden „Wohltäter". Abhängigkeiten vielfältiger Natur entstanden und eine zumindest gerne hingenommene Intransparenz sorgte im Laufe der Jahre dafür, insbesondere in der Steuer- und Familienpolitik, dass niemand mehr so genau wusste, was er unter dem Strich bekam ... oder gab: Finanzpolitik wurde, wie es der frühere Stuttgarter Oberbürgermeister Manfred Rommel formulierte, zur „Kunst, dem Bürger möglichst unauffällig sein Geld abzunehmen und es nach Abzug steigender Verwaltungskosten in einem feierlichen Zeremoniell so zu verteilen, dass sich jeder noch für beschenkt hält".

Der von Erhard formulierte Begriff der „mechanisierten Gesellschaft" scheint im 21. Jahrhundert jedenfalls durchaus geeignet zur Beschreibung mancher deutschen Realität. Allzu oft wurden aus Menschen Sozial„fälle", aus Zuwendung und persönlicher Hilfsbereitschaft anonyme Geldtransfers und gutes Gewissen via Steuerzahlung, aus persönlicher Verantwortung für andere in einem überschaubaren Umfeld sozialstaatlich-bürokratische Betreuung. Statt Bedürftigkeit in Notfällen gibt es „grundlegende Bedarfe", statt Hilfe zur Selbsthilfe dauerhaften Transfer. Vielfach wurde aus dem Anliegen, der Gemeinschaft nicht auf der Tasche zu liegen, das Pochen auf Ansprüche.

Auch Politik wandelte sich, wurde in vielen Fällen von der Berufung zum Beruf. Offen bleibt, inwieweit das Ursache oder Folge veränderter gesellschaftlicher Gegebenheiten ist. Überzeugungstäter – positiver ausgedrückt „Wertegebundene" – wurden weniger, Sozial-Ingenieure mehr: Sie drehen innerhalb eines kaum überschaubaren Be- bzw. Getriebes je nach Tagesopportunität mal an diesem, mal an jenem Rädchen – und je nach Bedarf auch in unterschiedliche Richtungen. Was am Ende herauskommen mag oder die Frage, ob womöglich die gesamte Maschinerie falsch konstruiert sein könnte, treibt sie nur begrenzt um – Hauptsache, das Räderwerk läuft in der Gegenwart halbwegs störungsfrei.

Die Ursachen oft ignorierende, an Folgen aber einzelfallperfekt laborierende Mechanisierung hängt auch mit denen zusammen, die an der Dauerhaftigkeit tatsächlicher oder vermeintlicher Not durchaus ein persönliches Interesse haben, oft, weil ihr Arbeitsplatz, ihre Medienpräsenz und ihr Einfluss daran hängen: Die Wohlfahrtsverbände als Teil eines beeindruckenden sozial-industriellen Komplexes. Sie sind die arbeitsplatzintensivsten deutschen Arbeitgeber nach Bund und Ländern: Arbeiterwohlfahrt, Caritas, Rotes Kreuz, Diakonie und Paritätischer Wohlfahrtsverband beschäftigen allein hauptamtlich rund anderthalb Millionen Menschen, zwischen 1970 und 2010 hat sich die Zahl vervierfacht. Ein lukratives Geschäftsmodell, basierend auf öffentlicher Förderung, einem erstaunlichen Maß an auch auf Intransparenz basierender Narrenfreiheit und einem Blanko-Scheck für eingebaut gute Gesinnung: Die Wohlfahrtsverbände werden dem Non-Profit-Sektor zugeordnet und erbringen anerkannt vielerlei Leistungen für viele Menschen – jedes Hinterfragen ihrer Strukturen, Undurchsichtigkeit, Effizienz und der Sinnhaftigkeit des einen oder anderen Bereiches wird sofort als kalter, marktradikaler, unmenschlicher Sozialabbau gegeißelt und damit meist erfolgreich verhindert. Selbst offensichtlicher Missbrauch von öffentlichen Mitteln durch Sozialunternehmer und Betreuer wird relativ lässig abgewettert: Der frühere Chef der staatlich alimentierten Berliner Treberhilfe ließ sich im Dienstmaserati vom Chauffeur zu betreuten Obdachlosen fahren und in der Dienstvilla von Gärtner und Haushälterin umsorgen. Er ist nicht mehr im Amt und 2013 mit der letzten Wiedereinstellungsklage gescheitert. Öffentliche Folgedebatten hielten sich aber in engen Grenzen: Wenn „Gute" Schlechtes tun, führt das in Deutschland zu weniger Verdrossenheit als vermeintlich „Schlechte", z. B. Unternehmer und Manager, sie auch dann erregen, wenn sie durch wirtschaftlichen Erfolg viel Gutes tun.

Natürlich wird bei dem Geschäftsmodell im Regelfall kein Geschäft im Sinne von Gewinn gemacht – der Gewinn ist der Fortbestand zahlreicher Arbeitsplätze und, im Bereich der Funktionärsebenen, zum Teil unethisch ansehnliche Einkommen und ein überhoher und demokratisch in keiner Weise legitimierter gesellschaftlicher Einfluss. Eine Studie spricht von „Firmen mit dem Siegel der Barmherzigkeit", „Wohlfahrtsimperien" und, wegen Tausender unabhängiger Trägergesellschaften, Landes- und Kreisverbänden, einer „einzigartigen Form des Franchisings im Namen der Nächstenliebe"[12]. Große Teile der Branche wachsen selbst in guten Zeiten, denn „im vorsorgenden Sozialstaat wird die Daseinsfürsorge präventiv: Es wird geholfen, obwohl es noch gar keinen Bedarf gibt. Konkret funktioniert das so, dass die Betreuer den Fürsorgebedarf durch die Erfindung von Defiziten erzeugen. Der Wohlfahrtsstaat fördert also nicht die Bedürftigen, sondern die Sozialarbeiter."[13]

Die wichtigste Grundlage für Mittel und Einfluss der Sozial-Industrie ist ein „korrektes" politisches Bewusstsein der Öffentlichkeit, also eine verbreitete Betroffenheit und negativ-nörgelnde Verlustangst anstelle von Aufstiegsoptimismus und Chancenzuversicht. Genau dazu tragen als institutionalisiertes Depressivum die methodisch-statistisch fragwürdigen Armutsberichte[14] vor allem aufgrund ihrer einseitigen Aufnahme und medialen Zuspitzung bei: Je schauderhafter die Zahlen über angebliche Armut in einem der reichsten Länder der Welt, je mehr angeblich Abhängige, zu Betreuende und Versorgende, desto mehr Forschungsaufträge, Aufmerksamkeit und Talkshow-Auftritte für universitäre „Armutsforscher", desto mehr Ausschreibungen für Lehrstühle im Bereich der „sozialen Arbeit", desto üppiger das Gehalt des Hauptgeschäftsführers des Paritätischen Wohlfahrtsverbandes, desto mehr Spenden an Hilfsorganisationen und Tafeln, desto mehr öffentliche Förderung für die Sozialindustrie. Desto mehr Einfluss und Macht auch für Organisationen, die sich an der Seite der Schwachen, Beladenen und Chancenlosen sehen und denen hohe Verdienste für den Zusammenhalt der Gesellschaft gebühren – die aber auch einen gerüttelten Anteil am Schuldenstaat als Versündigung an kommenden Generationen tragen und für ihre Zielgruppe oft gut Gemeintes statt Gutes erreichen. Wird nicht zuweilen z. B. in Kirchen und Gewerkschaften der „Gutmensch" etwas zu sehr zu Lasten Dritter – der Steuerzahler – und zum Wohle auch des eigenen Einflusses gegeben? Geht es bei Forderungen nach einem flächendeckenden gesetzlichen Mindestlohn um die, die schlechter entlohnte, aber

---

[12] Institut der Deutschen Wirtschaft, Wohlfahrtsverbände in Deutschland. Auf den Schultern der Schwachen, Köln 2004, S. 8/9.

[13] *Norbert Bolz*, Diskurs über die Ungleichheit: Der Anti-Rousseau, München 2009.

[14] *Philip Plickert*, Armut und Reichtum in Deutschland: das Elend des Sozialstaats, in: Ludwig-Erhard-Stiftung (Hrsg.), Orientierungen zur Wirtschafts- und Gesellschaftspolitik, Heft 134 (4/2012).

doch Arbeit haben – und eben vielleicht eine Zuzahlung des Staats? Oder um gewerkschaftliche Macht, als Großorganisation für alle und alles zu sprechen? Und was ist in der Evangelischen Kirche Deutschlands aus calvinistisch geprägten Traditionen der Ermutigung und des Fleißes und den in der katholischen Soziallehre formulierten Verpflichtungen für den Einzelnen in der Praxis geworden, jenseits einer bemerkenswerten Schrift der deutschen Bischöfe zur „Chancengerechten Gesellschaft – Leitbild für eine freiheitliche Ordnung"[15]? Vielleicht agieren die beiden Kirchen zu sehr im Sinne des Erhalts kirchennaher Dienstleister und kooperieren mit dem Staat im Hinblick auf Ruhigstellung und Dauerbetreuung in der Unmündigkeit Verbleibender?

Vielsagend waren erste deutsche Reaktionen auf Wahl, Namensgebung und erste Worte des Papstes Franziskus, den manche sofort als spirituelle Untermauerung von Forderungen nach Einkommensteuererhöhungen und weiter steigenden Transfers begriffen. Das entspricht dem obrigkeitsstaatlichen Verständnis von „Barmherzigkeit": Die etatistisch geprägte, flächendeckend ausgerollte und von Dritten finanzierte Administrierung von subjektiver wie objektiver Beschwernis durch Transfers. Und wenn der Papst unter „Barmherzigkeit" eher subsidiäre Hilfe, Engagement von Menschen für andere, individuelle Verantwortung und Kümmern im Umfeld verstünde? Belege z. B. für die Forderung nach einem bedingungslosen Grundeinkommen, das den Sozialstaat tatsächlich abrunden würde – allerdings im Sinne des dann vollendeten Ruins – sind jedenfalls bei Franziskus von Assisi nicht zu finden.

Gleichwohl: Der soziale Frieden, zu dem Kirchen, Gewerkschaften und Staat zentrale Beiträge leisten, ist und bleibt ein hohes Gut und ein zentraler Pfeiler der Sozialen Marktwirtschaft. Darüber kann man bei gegebenem sozialem Frieden durchaus auch von einem Standortvorteil sprechen, sieht man die Folgen häufiger Streiks, Unruhen oder Ausschreitungen in anderen europäischen Ländern. Der aufopferungsvolle ehrenamtliche wie der meist – auch an der Basis der Wohlfahrtsverbände – alles andere als gut bezahlte berufliche Einsatz von Millionen Menschen für andere ist Grundlage einer humanen Gesellschaft. Nicht zu bestreiten ist auch, dass Bindungen zurückgehen oder z. B. von vielen gewünschte, zusätzliche Frauenerwerbstätigkeit Spielräume verringert , wo früher subsidiär Hilfe geleistet wurde, unter anderem in Familien bei dauerhaft zu Pflegenden. Und doch muss zumindest in manchen Bereichen die Frage gestellt werden, inwieweit das Angebot auch Nachfrage schafft, Mitnahmeeffekte provoziert und Fehlanreize darstellt. Beispielhaft sei hier die mögliche kumulative Wirkung politisch gewollter und im Einzelnen vielleicht durchaus nachvollziehbarer Umverteilung genannt.

---

[15] Sekretariat der Deutschen Bischofskonferenz (Hrsg.), Chancengerechte Gesellschaft. Leitbild für eine freiheitliche Ordnung, Bonn 2011.

Die folgende Übersicht, errechnet für den Fall eines Ehepaars mit zwei Kindern, verstärkt den Eindruck, dass im deutschen Wohlfahrtsstaat die Umverteilung zuweilen zu gut funktioniert und Eigeninitiative und Arbeitsanreize nicht ausreichend fördert. Mit einem Bruttogesamteinkommen von 2500 Euro steht die Familie jedenfalls netto am Ende aller Abzüge oder Transfers nur unwesentlich besser da als mit einem halb so großen Bruttoeinkommen, und auch der Abstand zum „Nulleinkommen" sollte beim Ergebnis nach Staat größer sein (siehe Abbildung 2).[16]

Die Kurzformel lautet: Je mehr Kinder, desto geringer der Anreiz zur Arbeit. Nur zu einem Teil hängt das nur begrenzt sinnvolle Gesamtresultat mit der in der Sache richtigen, im Verlauf aber schon lange nicht mehr gut ausgestalteten Steuerprogression zusammen. Andere Einflüsse kommen dazu: Systematisch wesentlich fragwürdiger ist schon, dass im Rahmen der Gesetzlichen Krankenversicherung ebenfalls massiv umverteilt wird. Die monatlichen Beiträge von Arbeitgebern wie Arbeitnehmern zu den Krankenkassen lagen im Jahr 2012 bei 15,5 % des Bruttoeinkommens. Sie steigen nicht progressiv, aber absolut mit der Höhe des Einkommens, 2013 zumindest bis zu einer Gehaltsgrenze von 47250 Euro im Jahr, der sogenannten Beitragsbemessungsgrenze. Besserverdienende zahlen im gesetzlichen System höhere Beiträge für gleiche Leistungen. Eine unangenehme Begleiterscheinung dieses sachlich weitgehend sinnfreien, aber fiskalisch sehr nützlichen Abkassierens sind hohe Lohnzusatzkosten, die reguläre Arbeitsverhältnisse vor allem im besser bezahlten Bereich nicht eben fördern.

Ein weiteres Element des insbesondere in seiner kumulativen Wirkung höchst fragwürdigen deutschen Umverteilungssystems sind in mehreren Bundesländern nach Einkommen gestaffelte Beiträge pro Kind für Kindergärten und Kindertagesstätten. Dazu kommen, meist auf Antrag, Fördermöglichkeiten für Geringverdiener oder Bezieher von SGB II (Hartz-IV-Empfänger). Das beginnt bei Zuschüssen für Kleidung und Schulausflüge der Kinder, geht weiter über das Bafög durch den Bund, Leistungen der Länder und kommunale Unterstützung zum Beispiel beim Wohnen. Alles natürlich gut gemeint. Da ist es auch keine Überraschung mehr, dass Hartz-IV-Empfänger auch von der im Januar 2013 eingeführten Haushaltsgebühr für die Segnungen des öffentlichrechtlichen Rundfunks befreit sind.

Auch ohne detaillierte Kenntnis sozialstaatlicher Förderinstrumente: Die Gesamtwirkung all der beschriebenen Umverteilungen lässt sich schon durch einen genaueren Blick auf die Darstellung erahnen, die manche der beschriebe-

---

[16] *Wolfgang Meister*, Neuerungen bei Hartz IV, beim Wohngeld und bei den Lohnabzügen seit Januar 2011: Auswirkungen auf das Einkommen einzelner Haushaltstypen, ifo-Schnelldienst 9/2011.

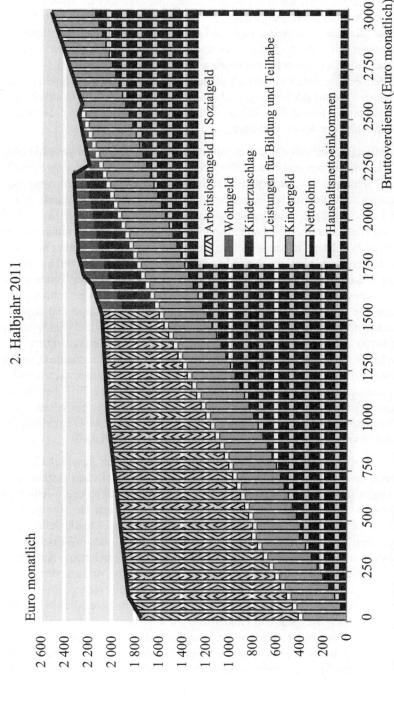

2. Halbjahr 2011

Euro monatlich

Arbeitslosengeld II, Sozialgeld
Wohngeld
Kinderzuschlag
Leistungen für Bildung und Teilhabe
Kindergeld
Nettolohn
Haushaltsnettoeinkommen

Bruttoverdienst (Euro monatlich)

Ehepaar mit zwei Kindern (eines unter 6 Jahren, eines mit 6 bis unter 14 Jahren).
Quelle: Berechnungen des ifo Instituts.

Abbildung 2: Komponenten des Haushaltsnettoeinkommens

nen Tatbestände noch gar nicht berücksichtigt hat und höhere Bruttoeinkommen ganz ausklammert. Angesichts der Höhe der sogenannten „Transferentzugsrate", de facto eine Bestrafung von Leistung und Arbeit und angesichts der kumulativen Wirkung mehrerer Umverteilungssysteme ist man fast geneigt, Millionen von Deutschen für ein überaus hohes Maß an intrinsischer Motivation zu danken: Sie stehen täglich um 6h auf, obwohl sich das nur begrenzt rechnet. Würden sie auf der jeweiligen Mikroebene rein betriebswirtschaftlich denken, „maximaler Ertrag für minimalen Aufwand", müssten sie logischerweise die Nichtarbeit der Arbeit vorziehen.

Intrinsische Motivation und durchaus noch vorhandene Pflichtwerte hin oder her: Wie ein langsam wirkendes Gift entfalten derartige Fehlanreize ihre zerstörerische Wirkung. Mit einem jüdischen Sprichwort: „Die Guten lernen von den Schlechten mehr als die Schlechten von den Guten." Eine Gesellschaft, in der mehr als die Hälfte der Bürger Transfers erhalten und ein überwiegender Teil ausschließlich oder überwiegend davon lebt, kann nicht dauerhaft funktionieren oder ihren Wohlstand halten – auch wenn zu den Transferempfängern natürlich auch die Rentner zählen, die zumindest größtenteils in früheren Jahren entsprechende Leistungen erbracht haben. Ein Land, das bei steigender Tendenz die Hälfte seines (Bundes-)Haushalts für soziale Zwecke und Tageskonsum ausgibt, für die unterfinanzierte Rentenversicherung, für Nachsorge und Reparaturbetrieb, für sich widersprechende Familiensubventionen und vieles mehr, das anteilig die Zukunftsinvestitionen immer weiter herunterfährt, dürfte das Beste hinter, nicht vor sich haben. Das Resultat der Wohlfahrtsstaatsexpansion ist jedenfalls unter anderem an der sich verändernden Zusammensetzung des Bundeshaushalts gut abzulesen. Der leichte Rückgang 2012/2013 beruht nur auf einem konjunkturellen Hoch, strukturell kommen weitere Soziallasten auf den Bundeshaushalt zu, z. B. durch die absehbar vollständige Übernahme der Grundsicherung im Alter von den Kommunen (siehe Abbildung 3).

Gewiss spiegelt all dies einen auf Ausgleich bedachten gesellschaftlichen Grundkonsens wider. In ähnlicher Weise hat sich auch zwischen Institutionen und Organisationen über Jahrzehnte hinweg eine hochkomplexe Vielfalt an Ausgleichssystemen und -mechanismen entwickelt: So, um nur wenige Beispiele zu nennen, zwischen Bundesländern, Kommunen, Rundfunkanstalten, gesetzlichen Krankenversicherungen. Die Effizienz des Wirtschaftens, Wachstum und Wohlstand, das Zusammenfallen von Einnahmen-, Aufgaben- und Ausgabenverantwortung, Transparenz und ehrliches, offenes demokratisches Ringen um den besten Weg wurden dadurch nicht befördert. So gesehen kann man die Tatsache, dass Deutschland und seine Soziale Marktwirtschaft trotz allzu vieler Bremsen und Hindernisse im internationalen Vergleich 2013 jenseits der Konjunktur überaus gut dastehen, als zweites deutsches Wirtschaftswunder bezeichnen. Die wirtschaftliche Ordnung, die Wirtschaftsstruktur mit starkem Anteil an industrieller Fertigung und mittelständischen, innova-

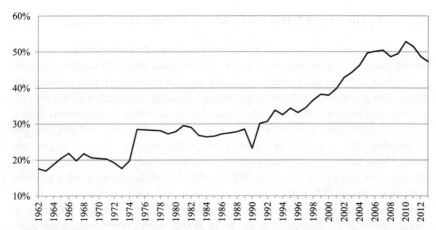

Sozialausgaben ohne soziale Leistungen für Folgen von Krieg und politischen Ereignissen; 2012 Haushalts-
entwurf inkl. Nachtrag; 2013 Regierungsentwurf.
Datenquelle: BMF (2012), Finanzbericht 2013.

Abbildung 3: Anteil der Sozialausgaben am Bundeshaushalt (1962 – 2013)

tiven Unternehmen, maßvolle Gewerkschaften und nicht zuletzt Millionen gut
qualifizierter und engagierter Arbeitnehmer stehen dafür.

Wachstum und Wohlstand sind aber keine Selbstverständlichkeit. Sie basierten jahrzehntelang auf freiheitlich-marktwirtschaftlichen Anreizen und An-
triebskräften. Diese werden schwächer, wenn den einen zu viel vom Erarbeiteten genommen und manchen anderen zu viel ohne entsprechende Leistung gegeben wird: Schon entstehen erste Schlagzeilen zum „Mythos vom fleißigen
Deutschen": Wie im Frühjahr 2013 ein Vergleich von Eurostat[17] zu 14 EU-
Staaten ergab, wird Deutschland bei der geleisteten Jahresarbeitszeit nur von
Dänemark und Frankreich unterboten und bei den Urlaubs- und Feiertagen von
keinem übertroffen.

Und sie basieren auf dem Wettbewerb als Entdeckungsverfahren und tief
demokratischem Element, weil er, in einem fairen Rahmen, immer wieder neue
Chancen, Bewegung ermöglicht und alles und jeden immer wieder auf den
Prüfstand stellt, auch und gerade die „Etablierten". Von zentraler Bedeutung
bleibt der Schutz des Eigentums, der in all den Jahren wohlfahrtsstaatlicher Expansion weiter hochgehalten wurde, in Sonntagsreden kraftvoll, in der politischen Realität mit ersten Einschränkungen. Sie ließen schon das Grundmuster
der schwieriger werdenden Finanzierung des alle und alles erfassenden Wohlfahrtsstaates der 2010er Jahre erahnen.

---

[17] Eurostat, Eurofound, WKO: Daten für Vollzeitbeschäftigte aus 2011, zu Urlaubs-
und Feiertagen aus 2010.

IV. Gier nach frischem Geld – der Staat als Abhängiger

Die einmal in Gang gesetzte Wohlfahrtsstaatsspirale und einen der teuersten Sozialstaaten der Welt trüge man gerne – sofern zum einen die Generationengerechtigkeit nicht aus den Augen verloren werden würde und zum anderen die Menschen glücklich, vielleicht sogar einmal dankbar wären. Beides hat sich allerdings ein großes Stück weit als Illusion erwiesen. Von Zufriedenheit damit, in einer schwierigen Lebenssituation von der Solidargemeinschaft aufgefangen zu werden, ist in vielen, vor allem in den wahrnehmbaren Fällen, kaum eine Rede. Dank hat noch kaum ein Politiker oder Steuerzahler gehört, eher die Forderung nach mehr Grundleistung, höheren Sonderzahlungen, Erfüllung weiterer Anliegen. Das Problem und auch die Ursache für Diskussionen über Transferkarrieren über Generationen hinweg dürfte zumindest in einigen Fällen darin liegen, dass die Lebenssituation gar nicht als schwierig empfunden wird, dank des Transfers und möglicherweise individueller Kombilohnmodelle à la „Hartz und schwarz". Menschen haben sich eingerichtet in dem, was, in den Worten Helmut Schmidts, heute offiziell Armut genannt wird, in den 1950er Jahren aber als bescheidener Wohlstand bezeichnet worden wäre.

Glücklich scheinen die Menschen dabei aber nur begrenzt, unabhängig von der an ein chinesisches Sprichwort angelehnten Interessenaustragungserfahrung, dass nur die Tür geölt wird, die quietscht, Jammern also Geschäftsgrundlage ist. Es bleibt das Paradoxon, dass Deutschland, auf der Basis von Marktwirtschaft, für das Adjektiv „sozial" so viel ausgibt wie nie zuvor, die in Umfragen gemessene Zustimmung zur „Sozialen Marktwirtschaft" als Wirtschaftsordnung und auch die Zufriedenheit mit unserem demokratischen System aber zugleich Tiefstände erreichen. Aufwand und Ergebnis stehen in einem miserablen Verhältnis zueinander. Macht der selbstverdiente Euro nicht doch in jedem Fall zufriedener als der transferierte? Sollte Hilfe wieder mehr Hilfe zur Selbsthilfe sein?

Um zumindest ungewollten Missverständnissen vorzubeugen: Der Sozialstaat ist eine großartige Errungenschaft und gehört unverzichtbar zur Sozialen Marktwirtschaft. Er bzw. die, die ihn tragen, sorgen für Ausgleich und sozialen Frieden. In Berlin z. B., wo es einzelne Stadtquartiere mit weit über 50 % Hartz-IV-Empfängern unter den Bewohnern gibt, sind Unruhen, Krawalle und Anarchie, wie man sie aus Vorstädten von Paris oder Lyon, aus Teilen amerikanischer oder englischer Städte kennt, nicht zu beobachten. Die Transferleistungen funktionieren insoweit: Vielleicht zu oft als Ruhigstellung und Schweigeprämie, vielleicht zu selten als Anreiz oder Ermutigung, aus einer schlechten Lage herauszufinden. Aber sie funktionieren.

Der Sozialstaat soll also keineswegs als Ganzes in Frage gestellt bzw. „abgebaut" werden – eine Prüfung und Korrektur mancher Strukturen und Anreize ist allerdings unvermeidlich. Erstens im Hinblick darauf, ob Menschen in Not oder Schwierigkeiten nicht auf anderen Wegen genauso gut oder vielleicht besser und nachhaltiger geholfen werden könnte. Und, zweitens, damit zusammenhängend: Die Kosten wird die Gesellschaft in Zeiten knapperer Spielräume und versperrter Fluchtwege in die jährliche Neuverschuldung so nicht mehr stemmen können. Dies umso mehr, als sie bei unveränderter politisch-gesellschaftlicher Praxis angesichts der zuweilen irreführenden Versuchungen – die Ökonomen sprechen von „moral hazard" – eher noch steigen.

Der Druck ist schon 2013 gewaltig, die Unmöglichkeit des „Weiter so" offensichtlich: Die europäische Schuldenkrise und die bislang vorwiegend südeuropäischen Beispiele belegen, dass die über Jahrzehnte auch in Deutschland kaum hinterfragte Teilfinanzierung eines stetig expandierenden Wohlfahrtsstaates durch jährliche Neuverschuldungsroutine an ihre Grenze stößt. Die Schuldenlogik ist gebrochen, auch Deutschland wird als Einäugiger unter Blinden in Europa auf der Basis bisheriger Politikpraxis nicht ewig Kredite zu guten Konditionen bekommen.

Das Land steht nur relativ besser da, seine Glaubwürdigkeit steht ebenfalls in Zweifel: Seit Ende der 1960er Jahre hat keine Bundesregierung einen ausgeglichenen Haushalt erreicht, völlig unabhängig von Konjunktur und der Entwicklung auf der Einnahmeseite. Das Haushaltsjahr 2013 ist ein weiteres Beispiel für die sich langsam und sicher erschöpfende Gefälligkeitsdemokratie: Rekordeinnahmen in allen Steuerbereichen und eine gute Konjunktur, gleichwohl kein Haushaltsausgleich, statt ernsthafter Anstrengung sogar noch Festlegungen auf neue, dauerhafte Ausgaben – fast ausschließlich im Sozialbereich. Je mehr Geld die Politik hat, desto mehr hat sie zu wenig. „Nur noch ein allerletztes Mal", heißt es, wenn die echte Konsolidierung wieder einmal auf eine mittelferne Zukunft verschoben oder mit hübschem Wortgeklingel als schon erreicht gefeiert wird (siehe Abbildung 4).

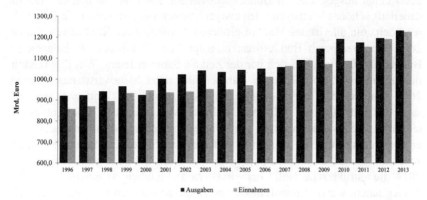

Quelle: AMECO Datenbank, 2013 Prognose.

Abbildung 4: Die deutschen Staatsfinanzen im Verlauf: Entwicklung
der Staatsausgaben und -einnahmen in Deutschland 1996 bis 2013

Die Ausgaben des Staates – Bund, Länder, Kommunen, Sozialversicherungen – steigen mit erschreckender Zwangsläufigkeit als Folge der beschriebenen Wohlfahrtsstaatsexpansion. Während in manchen Bereichen Ausgaben sogar in absoluten Zahlen rückläufig waren, z. B. bei der Verteidigung, in anderen relativ, liegt der Gesamtanstieg in erster Linie im jeweils größten Einzeltitel der öffentlichen Haushalte, dem Sozialhaushalt, begründet. Verblüffend ist unter anderem, wie wenig und wie langsam die Neigung zur Ausgabensteigerung auf in schlechteren Jahren geringere Einnahmen reagiert. Der Sozialstaat als Summe von Einzelansprüchen, Einzelforderungen und Besitzständen hat seine ganz eigene Dynamik – auch jenseits der Tatsache, dass naturgemäß in wirtschaftlich schwierigeren Zeiten höhere Sozialausgaben anfallen.

Nur in der Höhe abhängig von der Konjunktur, aber auf dem falschen Weg kontinuierlich haben z. B. Bund und fast alle Länder seit Ende der 1960er Jahre mit frappierender Selbstverständlichkeit Jahr für Jahr neue Schulden aufgenommen. Schon vor der Finanzmarkt- und Schuldenkrise verbreitete sich erste Einsicht in die Endlichkeit solchen Tuns wie in die Ungerechtigkeit gegenüber zukünftigen Generationen. Das Wort „Konsolidierung" gehört seitdem zur verbalen Grundausstattung jedes Finanzpolitikers. Meistens bleibt es auch beim Wort oder beschränken sich die Taten auf Verbesserungen auf der Einnahmeseite: Der Staat ist wie ein Drogenabhängiger auf Entzug – ständig braucht er frischen Stoff, in dem Fall frisches Geld. Hat er es dann, kommen sofort neue Ideen für neue Ausgaben auf – vor allem in konjunkturell guten Zeiten legt man sich gern strukturell auf neue Leistungen fest, die dann in der folgenden Krise für umso größere Verheerungen in den öffentlichen Haushalten sorgen.

Bundesfinanzminister und „Sparminator" Hans Eichel versprach im Jahr 2000 einen ausgeglichenen Bundeshaushalt für 2006 und wollte nur, um für dauerhaft schönes Wetter und den ewigen Aufschwung zu sorgen, in Folgejahren noch „ein allerletztes Mal" in größerem Umfang neue Kredite aufnehmen. 2006 dann versprach Bundesfinanzminister Peer Steinbrück ein balanciertes Budget für 2010 und ließ sich vor der Zeit als Sanierer feiern. Was ihm tatsächlich gelang, war, trotz Rekordeinnahmen und satter Mehrwertsteuererhöhung, 2007 neue Kredite zu benötigen. Bundesfinanzminister Wolfgang Schäuble sagte 2010 für 2014 die „schwarze Null" zu. Weil zumindest Teilöffentlichkeiten inzwischen wachsamer sind, ein Kollateralnutzen der Schuldenkrise, konnte er aber nicht wie seine Vorgänger auf die Vergesslichkeit hoffen. So wurde schon 2013 regierungsoffiziell die „schwarze Null" auf 2015 geschoben und für 2014 die „strukturelle Null" herbeirelativiert: Plötzlich ist ein Budget schon ausgeglichen, wenn „Einmaleffekte" herausgerechnet werden. Aber wann gibt es die nicht?

Entscheidend ist der Blick auf das Muster der Finanzpolitik zwischen 1967 und 2013: Der geeignete Zeitpunkt zum Sparen ist nie da. Solides Wirtschaften hatte über Jahrzehnte keine Lobby. Zukünftige Generationen und die Steuerzahler als Gesamtheit sind nicht vernehmbar. Alle versammelten Besitzstandswahrer, Wohlfahrtsverbände, andere Interessengruppen und gierige Trittbrettfahrer staatlicher Verschuldung im Hier und Jetzt schon – sie wissen Lärm zu machen und interessante Koalitionen zu schmieden, „Win-win-Situationen" zu kreieren zu Lasten Dritter. Ein Held der kürzestmöglichen (Spekulations-)Frist wie Großinvestor George Soros betreibt auf kapitalistisch-nehmender Seite und mit effektiver Hebelwirkung das, was die Wohlfahrtsverbände auf vermeintlicher Geberseite praktizieren – ein solides, attraktives und berechenbares Geschäftsmodell. Soros fördert Stiftungen und gibt Interviews, deren Tenor immer auf das eine hinausläuft: Staatliche Neuverschuldung in der Gegenwart für selbstverständlich immer „gute" Zwecke – Staatenrettung, Währungsrettung, Bankenrettung, Wohlfahrtsrettung, Konjunkturrettung. Und bei all dieser Retterei steigen wie von Zauberhand die Kurse seiner Investments ...

Intellektuell garniert wird das Ganze von Ökonomen wie Nobelpreisträger Paul Krugman. Nach seiner Vorstellung stellt sich staatliche Konjunkturförderung bzw. der Ablauf der Jahreszeiten so dar: Im Winter müsse der Staat anheizen und allen Wärme spenden – das leuchtet durchaus noch ein. Im Frühjahr dürfe, es könnte ja noch ein Kälteeinbruch kommen, man die zarten Pflänzchen nicht zertreten. Im Sommer, wenn alles blüht, treibt, zur Reife kommt, heißt es, man müsse jetzt an diejenigen denken, die sich noch zu kurz gekommen fühlen, Einlagern könne man später noch. Im Herbst schließlich solle man den Sommer nicht vorzeitig abwürgen. Keynes als Einbahnstraße – die sich über die Jahre als Sackgasse erwies.

Die Ausflüchte sind schwieriger geworden, die Schlupflöcher enger: In den Vereinigten Staaten werden die Zeiträume zwischen den Haushaltskrisen immer kürzer und das Umschiffen der fiskalischen Kliffe immer dramatischer. In Deutschland erreicht die Schuldenbremse im Grundgesetz – allein ihre Einführung kündet von enormem, positiven Bewusstseinswandel – bis 2020 mindestens psychologisch ihre volle Wirkung, dazu kommt der Fiskalpakt auf europäischer Ebene. Nicht zu vergessen absehbare Mehrbelastungen aufgrund der Euro-Rettungsbemühungen wie, noch unvermeidlicher, der Demographie: Weniger zahlen ein, mehr machen Ansprüche geltend. Der Politik dürfte es in Zukunft schwerer fallen als bislang, nur Prioritäten zu benennen – und alles und jeden als solche und damit als förderungswürdig zu bezeichnen. Es wird nun auch Posterioritäten geben müssen. Der Wohlfahrtsstaat auf Pump ist am Ende, in Deutschland nach 45 Jahren der Schuldenaufnahme nun Demokratie ohne Geschenke gefragt.

Dies umso mehr, als sich langsam herumspricht, dass das Schuldenproblem weitaus größer ist, als es den Anschein hat. Denn die offiziellen Schuldenstatistiken machen in der Regel nur einen eher kleineren Teil der gesamten Staatsverschuldung aus. Der Grund ist einfach: Betrachtet werden ausschließlich das aktuelle Haushaltsdefizit sowie die in der Vergangenheit bereits entstandenen Schulden. Dabei wird außer Acht gelassen, dass der Staat jedes Jahr neben seinen laufenden Ausgaben rechtswirksame Verpflichtungen eingeht, ohne entsprechende Rückstellungen zu bilden. Diese werden in zukünftigen Jahren zu beträchtlichen Staatsausgaben führen – beispielsweise in Form gewährter Renten- und Pensionszusagen oder Gesundheits- und Pflegeleistungen.

Zum einen werden durch die Bevölkerungsalterung große staatliche Ausgabenposten mit altersabhängigen Leistungen wie beispielsweise die Gesetzliche Renten-, Kranken- und Pflegeversicherung in den kommenden Jahrzehnten erheblich anwachsen. Zum anderen sinkt gleichzeitig der Anteil der Menschen im erwerbsfähigen Alter, die den Großteil der Sozialversicherungsbeiträge wie auch der Lohnsteuer tragen. Beides führt dazu, dass die staatlichen Einnahmen deutlich hinter den staatlichen Ausgaben zurückbleiben werden, wenn man auf Reformen verzichtet und den gesetzlichen Status quo fortführt. Diese impliziten, zukünftigen Staatsschulden sind bis heute in offiziellen Statistiken nicht enthalten, obwohl sie das direkte Ergebnis schon getroffener Politikentscheidungen sind. Jedes Unternehmen dagegen, das z. B. rechtlich bindende Zusagen im Hinblick auf die Altersversorgung macht, muss sofort entsprechende Rückstellungen bilden und ausweisen (siehe Abbildung 5).

Abbildung 5: Staatsschulden: Nur die Spitze des Schuldenbergs ist sichtbar.

Die Stiftung Marktwirtschaft veröffentlicht jährlich die Höhe der tatsächlichen Staatsverschuldung[18]. In Deutschland waren es Stand 2012 ca. 3,5 statt der offiziell genannten 2 Billionen Euro. Damit wies das im europäischen Vergleich noch relativ besser dastehende Land einen Konsolidierungsbedarf von jährlich 75 Milliarden Euro bzw. 2,9 % des BIP auf! Das ist die Summe, um die

---

[18] *Bernd Raffelhüschen/Stefan Moog*, Ehrbare Staaten? Staatsverschuldung in Europa im Vergleich, hrsg. von der Stiftung Marktwirtschaft, Berlin 2013. Berechnungen durch das Forschungszentrum Generationenverträge der Albert-Ludwigs-Universität Freiburg.

die Staatsausgaben dauerhaft gesenkt – oder alternativ die Staatseinnahmen dauerhaft erhöht – werden müssten, um zu einem nachhaltigen Staatshaushalt zu kommen. Klar festzuhalten ist bezüglich des Vergleichs der ehrlich gerechneten Schulden der 27 EU-Staaten auch: Es handelt sich nicht um Schwarzmalerei! Erstens sind Rechenmethodik und Ergebnisse nicht umstritten, zweitens beruhen die Resultate auf positiven Wachstumsannahmen der Europäischen Kommission, erscheinen also eher positiver als die Realität ausfallen dürfte (siehe Abbildung 6).

	in Prozent des BIP	Implizite Schuld	Explizite Schuld	Nachhaltigkeitslücke
1	Italien	-123	121	-2
2	Lettland	-42	43	0
3	Estland	75	6	81
4	Polen	74	52	126
5	Deutschland	55	81	136
6	Bulgarien	160	16	176
7	Schweden	138	39	177
8	Portugal	73	108	181
9	Ungarn	109	72	181
10	Rumänien	234	33	267
11	Litauen	264	38	303
12	Österreich	242	72	315
13	Malta	253	71	324
14	Tschechien	379	39	418
15	Frankreich	356	86	442
16	Dänemark	396	47	442
17	Finnland	420	49	469
18	Slowakei	506	43	549
19	Niederlande	499	65	565
20	Großbritannien	550	88	639
21	Belgien	558	98	655
22	Slowenien	620	47	667
23	Zypern	764	71	835
24	Spanien	735	69	805
25	Griechenland	720	171	891
26	Luxemburg	1209	18	1228
27	Irland	1271	106	1378

Abbildung 6: Ehrliche Schuldenrechnung im Vergleich:
EU-27-Nachhaltigkeitsranking

Wie auch immer die EU-Staaten und nicht minder die Vereinigten Staaten, die mit einer Nachhaltigkeitslücke von 1337 Prozent des BIP zwischen Luxemburg und Irland platziert wären, mit den „Daumenschrauben" umgehen, die sie sich aus gutem Grund zum Teil ja selbst auferlegt haben: An einer kritischen Revision der Struktur und Höhe der Staatsausgaben wird jedenfalls kein Weg vorbeiführen. Damit rücken vor allem in Deutschland die dominierenden Sozialausgaben in den Blickpunkt: Die Herausforderung schlechthin für die Politik dürfte es sein, hier Ergebnisse, also Einsparungen zu erzielen, ohne das hohe Gut des sozialen Friedens zu gefährden. Das dürfte auch erreichbar sein, umso mehr, als viele Transfers nicht bei wirklich Bedürftigen landen oder zu Mitnahmeeffekten führen. Ein Beispiel dafür ist der angeblich so soziale ermäßigte Mehrwertsteuersatz, im Ergebnis eher eine Branchensubvention.

Natürlich gibt es, wenn man jenseits der unmittelbar drängenden Frage nach ausgeglichenen aktuellen Haushalten auch über den Abbau von Altschulden nachdenken will und darf, durchaus einen sanften Weg: Ohne je explizit zu tilgen, woran ohnehin niemand glaubt, könnte man aus den Altschulden über mehrere Jahrzehnte „herauswachsen", würde beispielsweise ein reales Wachstum von jeweils 1,5 % bei einer maßvollen Inflation von 2 % im Jahr erreicht und, natürliche Voraussetzung der relativen Entschuldung, eine ausgeglichene Haushaltsführung. Wollte man so die in 45 Jahren angehäuften Schulden ohne Tilgung und ohne drakonische Maßnahmen wie einen Schulden- oder gar Währungsschnitt hinter sich lassen, bedürfte es eines deutlich längeren Zeitraums (siehe Abbildung 7).

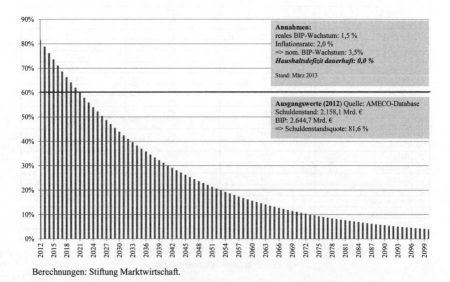

Berechnungen: Stiftung Marktwirtschaft.

Abbildung 7: Schulden„abbau" ohne Tilgung –
Projizierte Schuldenstandsquote (in % des BIP) – Modellrechnung

Nun hat der Staat auch kraft seiner starken Rolle im System der Sozialen Marktwirtschaft in den letzten Jahrzehnten vieles erreicht und zur guten Entwicklung unseres Landes wesentlich beigetragen. Er wird sich aber konzentrieren müssen. Der Staat kann nicht alles. Er kann uns nicht vor allen Fährnissen des Lebens schützen. Schon gar nicht ist der Staat, wie unter anderem die Landesbanken belegen, der bessere Unternehmer. Auch soziale Bindungen, Nestwärme, Werte vermag der Staat mit noch so viel Mitteleinsatz nicht zu schaffen. Und allzu oft kommt die Politik kaum den von ihr selbst geschaffenen und herbeigeredeten Ansprüchen hinterher. Oder weitet sein Tätigkeitsfeld noch sprunghaft aus, z. B. durch die vom Land Nordrhein-Westfalen angestrebte „präventive Sozialpolitik", die, als Höhepunkt der Selbsttäuschung, sogar konsumtive Staatsausgaben zu Zukunftsinvestitionen in sozialen Frieden verklärt.

Dazu schreibt ein bekanntes Magazin[19]:

> „Über die gigantische Umwälzpumpe der Finanzen will der Staat gleichzeitig den eigenen Apparat finanzieren und die öffentliche Infrastruktur, er will Konjunkturpolitik, Arbeitsmarktpolitik, Familienpolitik und Sozialpolitik betreiben, durch Umverteilung für mehr soziale Gerechtigkeit sorgen. Was unter Reichskanzler Otto von Bismarck als Sozialstaat für Alte und Kranke entwickelt wurde, ist im Laufe der Jahrzehnte ... zu einem umsorgenden Wohlfahrtsstaat geworden, der nicht mehr nur Not lindern, sondern das Entstehen von Not verhindern soll ...
>
> Indem der Staat sich immer tiefer einmischt in die Gesellschaft und Ungerechtigkeiten zu beseitigen versucht, schafft er neue Ungerechtigkeiten, die wiederum neue Regelungen erfordern. Das Hauptproblem des Sozialstaats ist inzwischen das Geld, das er braucht, um den von ihm selbst geschaffenen Ansprüchen gerecht zu werden. Trotz der höchsten Steuereinnahmen der Geschichte ist die Staatsverschuldung so hoch wie nie ...“

Der im Regelfall mit ausgeglichenem Haushalt wirkende, generationengerechte Staat der Zukunft wird Politikern wie Bürgern also viel abverlangen: Die einen werden mehr erklären, die anderen mehr verstehen müssen. Zu beneiden sind Politiker nicht, sie dürften es schwerer haben als ihre Vorgänger in den Anfängen der Republik. 1948, als die Soziale Marktwirtschaft mit der Währungsreform ausgerufen wurde, lagen Städte und Betriebe noch in Trümmern und Menschen hungerten. Das Wort „Reform" wurde mit Chance übersetzt – es konnte ja nur besser werden. In der saturierten Wohlstandsgesellschaft des frühen 21. Jahrhunderts geht die Veränderungsbereitschaft eher gegen Null. Angesichts des auch in den Mittelschichten verbreiteten Unkens, das Land habe seinen Zenit womöglich überschritten und die guten Jahre seien vorbei, erscheint der Begriff „Reform" als Bedrohung, als Synonym für Kürzung, Abbau, Streichung, Flexibilisierung alias Unsicherheit.

Vergegenwärtigt man sich die zu beobachtende Schwierigkeit, wenn nicht Unmöglichkeit, auf der Ausgabenseite an noch so offensichtliche unsinnige und/oder ineffiziente Programme bzw. Leistungen zu gehen, ist die Herkulesaufgabe leicht zu ermessen. Politiker können nicht mehr den Nikolaus geben, und riskieren dazu überschaubare „Popularität" als Knecht Ruprecht. Davor mögen sie sich im Wahljahr 2013 noch einmal drücken. Gleichwohl sind Geschenke durch zusätzliche Leistungen aus der Rentenkasse oder das Betreuungsgeld mindestens vorletzte Relikte einer zu Ende gehenden Zeit. Das muss

---

[19] Der Spiegel, 18. März 2013, S. 56.

kein Drama sein und wird neue oder verschüttete Kräfte wecken. Vor allem dann, wenn Veränderungen umsichtig, balanciert und mit entsprechenden Bremswegen, also Übergangszeiten erfolgen: So wie die Rente mit 67, eine angesichts der Bevölkerungsalterung unabweisbare, völlig schlüssige und erst 2030 zu voller Wirkung gelangende Reform. Auch dieser, mit breiter Mehrheit im Deutschen Bundestag beschlossene, in der Sache eher noch zu kurze Schritt wird trotzdem unablässig in Frage gestellt. Und dies meist von Bürgern höheren Alters, die selbst gar nicht betroffen sind. Aber er wird bleiben. Eher kommt die Rente mit 70 als die mit 65 zurück – so wie 2 plus 2 eben 4 ergibt. Wie bei so vielem, wird der „gefühlte Einschnitt" im öffentlichen Diskurs lange intensiv wahrgenommen, die Fakten weniger. In Deutschland wird seit 2003 über „Sozialabbau" geklagt, obwohl die realen Ausgaben in fast allen entsprechenden Bereichen gestiegen sind. Manchmal benötigen Wahrheiten etwas mehr Zeit – und nutzt sich auf der anderen Seite interessengeleitete Panikmache ab.

Die feststehende demographische Entwicklung der kommenden Jahrzehnte wird, das ist ein positiver Aspekt, die unmittelbaren Soziallasten etwas absinken lassen: Jeder wird gebraucht werden, Arbeitslosigkeit weiter absinken. Das Fehlen von Arbeitskräften und möglicherweise in Zukunft vor allem von gut Qualifizierten dürfte allerdings auch zu einer Wachstumsbremse und damit zu einem Wohlstandsrisiko werden. Noch bedeutsamer könnten im ungünstigen Fall indes die politisch-psychologischen Nebenwirkungen einer alternden Bevölkerung sein: Gerade diejenigen, die sich nach seit Jahrzehnten gleichem Muster am ehesten an Wahlen beteiligen, nämlich die über 60jährigen[20], zeichnen sich tendenziell weniger durch Offenheit für Neues, Mut zu Veränderungen, Kreativität und Innovation aus. Meist sind in entsprechenden Altersgruppen im Durchschnitt – nicht bei jedem! – eher Risikoaversion und Besitzstandswahrungsmentalität angesiedelt. Das Schlüsselwort ist Sicherheit, nicht Dynamik. Da also diese engagiertesten Wähler an Zahl noch deutlich zunehmen, werden Wahlen in Deutschland auf Jahrzehnte in noch wesentlich stärkerem Maß von Älteren entschieden als schon in den 1990er und 2000er-Jahren. Für Veränderungen, neues Gestalten und Investitionen in die Zukunft ist das kein gutes Vorzeichen – wovon nicht nur Widerstände gegen Hauptbahnhöfe und Flughäfen künden, sondern auch die deutsche „Energiewende": Widerstand von neuen NIMBY-Wutbürgern – „not in my backyard!" – gleichzeitig gegen Kernkraft-, Kohle- und Gaskraftwerke, gegen Pumpspeicher, CO_2 im Boden, Fracking, Oberlandleitungen und Erdleitungen. Nur Steckdosen sind willkommen in der vergreisenden Republik.

---

[20] *Michael Eilfort*, Die Nichtwähler. Wahlenthaltung als Form des Wahlverhaltens, Paderborn 1994.

Dennoch: Veränderung ist möglich, auch in Deutschland. Zehn Jahre nach der Agenda 2010, bei der nicht alles gelungen aber doch Wegweisendes in Gang gesetzt wurde, zeigt sich besonders im europäischen Vergleich, wie sehr Reformschritte das Land gestärkt, Wachstum ermöglicht, Arbeitsplätze und Wohlstand, damit auch Wohlfahrt, gesichert haben. Unter dem Strich haben die Menschen profitiert, so wie durch wesentlich weitergehendes Reformwerk in den skandinavischen Staaten, insbesondere Schweden in den 1990er Jahren. Dort folgte auf Übertreibung nicht Abschaffung oder Abbau, sondern Justierung.

Nicht verschwiegen werden soll, dass auch in Deutschland seit langen Jahren schon einige Korrekturen erfolgten – ohne den sozialen Frieden zu beeinträchtigen oder die Republik zu erschüttern. Neben den Arbeitsmarktreformen 2003 die schon genannte Rente mit 67 sowie in früheren Jahren die Absenkung des Rentenniveaus u. a. durch einen Demographiefaktor, Änderungen an der Rentenformel und die Einführung von Abschlägen. Nach 1960 Geborene haben

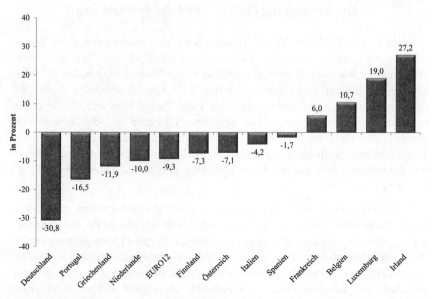

Berechnung: Forschungszentrum Generationenverträge der Albert-Ludwigs-Universität Freiburg, basierend auf Daten der Europäischen Kommission.

Abbildung 8: Die demographische Wachstums- und Reformbremse:
Veränderungen des Erwerbspersonenpotentials 2010–2060

es verkraftet, nicht mehr von Staats wegen gegen Berufsunfähigkeit versichert zu sein. Zahlreiche Kostendämpfungsgesetze, u. a. Zuzahlungen und Leistungseinschränkungen haben die Volksgesundheit nicht gefährdet, die Krankenversicherung aber bei aller Unvollkommenheit jeweils ein kleines Stück zukunftssicherer gemacht. Der schrittweise Rückzug des Staates aus der Eigenheimförderung war bzw. ist in seiner hoffentlich letzten Phase für die öffentlichen Haushalte wichtig, ordnungspolitisch richtig und hat weniger das Bauen für den Bürger verteuert als die Gewinnmargen der Bauwirtschaft gesenkt. Der frühere Bundeskanzler Gerhard Schröder ist übrigens nicht nur für die Agenda zu loben und diese nicht allein für den folgenden Aufschwung des Wirtschaftsstandorts verantwortlich: Die Absenkung des Spitzensteuersatzes 2000 mitsamt einer gewissen Bereinigung bzw. Verbreiterung der Bemessungsgrundlage hat das ihre dazu beigetragen. Die hilfreichen Anreize und die kleinen, systematischen Korrekturen trugen dazu bei, dass bei niedrigeren Sätzen der Fiskus mehr Einnahmen erzielte ... Es geht also – und es muss weitergehen. Noch dümmer, als kraftvoll Falsches zu unternehmen wäre es, nachgewiesen Richtiges wieder zurückzunehmen. Ist Deutschland auf bestem Wege dazu?

V. Die Enteignung läuft ... – und die Freiheit weg?

Warum so viel Raum für die Beschreibung der Mechanismen der Wohlfahrtsstaatsexpansion und der maßgeblich dadurch verursachten Schuldenproblematik? Warum soll es so dringend so vieler Veränderung bedürfen? Was hat dies mit Freiheit und Eigentum zu tun? Leider mehr, als einem angesichts des Ausmaßes der Schuldenkrise lieb sein kann. Fassen lässt sich dies in einen simplen, alten Erfahrungssatz: Die Schulden von heute sind die Steuern von morgen. Und nicht nur das: Die Schulden von heute sind auch der staatliche Trickdiebstahl, die finanzielle Repression, die Renten-Expropriation und vor allem die Inflation von morgen. Kurz: Die schon anlaufende Enteignung auf kaltem Wege.

Diskutiert man im Jahr 2013 über die Bedeutung von Eigentum und Eigentumsrechten, dann geht es in der Regel nicht mehr um die große Auseinandersetzung des 20. Jahrhunderts, also Marktwirtschaft mit Privateigentum versus Plan- oder Zentralverwaltungswirtschaft mit Kollektiveigentum. Auch in westlichen Ländern scheinen die Zeiten vorbei, als mit offenem Visier um Eigentum gekämpft und beispielsweise im Frankreich der frühen 1980er Jahre unter Francois Mitterrand noch viel verstaatlicht wurde.

Die „Angriffe" auf das Privateigentum sind subtiler geworden und gehen, bei unverdrossener Eigentumsschutzrhetorik in politischen Reden, von einem Wohlfahrtsstaat aus, der sich selbst zu Zweck und Hauptsache erklärt hat und Marktwirtschaft nur als notwendiges Übel bzw. Einnahmequelle zu betrachten scheint: Anstatt Privateigentum zu verbieten oder die Menschen direkt zu enteignen, wählt der Wohlfahrtsstaat deutlich weniger Widerstand hervorrufende Wege. Oft versteckt er sich hinter Intransparenz oder setzt Mechanismen in

Gang, die kurzfristig angenehmes Regieren und dramatische Folgen für Freiheit und Eigentum erst dann verheißen, wenn die, die dies ausgelöst und politisch profitiert haben, schon lange nicht mehr im Amt sind.

Nur noch gelegentlich blitzt fast schon erfrischende Ehrlichkeit auf, zumindest an der Peripherie: Wenn ein Staat wie Zypern in der europäischen Schulden- und seiner eigenen Liquiditätskrise Krisenfolgekosten und Rettungslasten nicht in die Zukunft verschieben kann, sondern direkt z. B. auf einen Teil der Einlagen auf Bankkonten zurückgreift. Oder für Spanien erste Rechnungen angestellt werden, nach denen mit einer „Sparersteuer" von 8,5 Prozent ein Sechstel der Staatsschulden getilgt werden könnte. Allein die Diskussion darüber sorgte in Deutschland unter den Sparern für so viel Unruhe und Zweifel am Schutz des Eigentums, dass der deutsche Staat sich erst recht in seiner impliziten, unaus- und unabgesprochenen „Strategie" bestätigt sieht. Sie ist natürlich kein öffentliches Thema bei den politischen Akteuren in Bund, Ländern und Gemeinden, aber immer findet sich irgendwo einer, der in der jeweils nächsten homöopathischen Dosis diskret über neue Geldquellen für den nimmersatten Staat nachdenkt. Die „Strategie" des Staates in der Frage des Schutzes von privatem Eigentum also lautet: Verbal abwiegeln, ansonsten tarnen, tricksen, täuschen.

1. Steuern mit Steuern – in den Abgrund?

Ein offener, staatlicher Zugriff auf Eigentum generell würde das ganze Land in Wallung bringen. Eine Konfrontation Staat versus Gesamtheit der Bürger wäre schon im Ansatz eine Niederlage für Politik und Fiskus. Höchst effektiv und aus ihrer Sicht erfolgreich agieren beide da, wo sie Bevölkerungsgruppen gegeneinander ausspielen können, zum Beispiel bei der Besteuerung.

Steuern wie auch Sozialbeiträge zu erheben, hat, auch wenn das nicht nur in den Vereinigten Staaten von Amerika von manchen anders gesehen wird, mit Enteignung erst einmal nichts zu tun. Steuern sind eine unverzichtbare Grundlage des grundsätzlich gewollten Wirkens eines aufsehenden und ausgleichenden starken Staats. Steuern stoßen darum in Deutschland im Grundsatz zu Recht auf eine hohe gesellschaftliche Akzeptanz.

Unter Hinweis auf die soziale Verantwortung von Eigentum und das Leistungsfähigkeitsprinzip werden zum einen in der Addition hohe, teils progressiv ausgestaltete laufende Steuern und Abgaben gerechtfertigt. Damit ist es aber für viele, wie bei den staatlichen Einnahmen generell, nie genug. Davon künden im deutschen Wahljahr 2013 zahlreiche öffentliche Debatten über mehr (Verteilungs-)Gerechtigkeit und, daraus resultierend, über die Erhöhung von Einkommensteuerspitzensätzen, die Wieder-Einführung der hochgradig gestaltungsanfälligen und bürokratieträchtigen Vermögensteuer und Erhöhungen bei der Be-

steuerung von Erbschaften. Vermeintlich „leistungslos" erworbene Vermögen –
die Leistung fand bei Erbfällen, bereits versteuert, in einer anderen Generation
statt – und (Kapital-)Einkommen werden besonders kritisch gesehen, so dass
diesbezüglich permanent Forderungen nach einer besonders hohen Besteuerung
zu vernehmen sind.

Nochmals: Es ist richtig und bereits lange und in ausreichendem Maß geübte
deutsche Praxis, dass starke Schultern mehr tragen als schwache. Aber inwieweit sollte man der Kuh, die man weiter zu melken gedenkt, aus der Substanz
auch noch Fleischstücke entnehmen wollen? Kann das nachhaltig sein? Und
welchen Anreiz setzt man für das gute Tier, wenn es das Messer sieht? Oder
lässt es sich von dem bewährten, oft Erleichterung hervorrufenden politischen
Kommunikationsmuster täuschen, mit 30 Messern gleichzeitig herumzufuch-
teln und am Ende vermeintlich beruhigend 28 demonstrativ wegzulegen?

Problematisch ist nicht die Belastung von Eigentum und Einkommen per
se – Probleme entstehen vor allem dann, wenn die Abgabenlast auf Eigentum
und Einkommen zu hoch wird. An erster Stelle wirken sich die negativen An-
reizeffekte des Sozialstaats schädlich aus, von denen vor allem der Arbeitsmarkt betroffen ist. Insbesondere dann, wenn – wie beispielsweise in Deutschland – eine progressive Einkommensteuer mit lohnabhängigen Sozialabgaben
zusammentrifft, resultieren bereits bei durchschnittlichen Einkommen der „Mittelschicht" hohe Grenzbelastungen, die sich dämpfend auf das Arbeitsangebot
auswirken können. Verstärkt wird diese Problematik, wenn gleichzeitig ein
großzügiges Grundsicherungsnetz als soziales Auffangnetz besteht, und so das
Arbeitsangebot der Mittelschicht durch den Sozialstaat von zwei Seiten in die
Zange genommen wird.

Hohe Steuern auf Einkommen und Vermögen wirken sich aber nicht nur im
Hier und Jetzt negativ auf die Wirtschaftsaktivität aus, sie beeinflussen zudem
die intertemporalen Konsum- und Sparentscheidungen der Menschen negativ.
Dies kann sowohl auf einzelwirtschaftlicher Ebene negative Auswirkungen haben – z. B. in Form unterlassener kapitalgedeckter Vorsorge für das Alter – als
auch den gesamtwirtschaftlichen Kapitalstock, der eine wichtige Determinante
des Wirtschaftswachstums ist, beeinträchtigen.

Die Politik droht an dieser Stelle ohne ausreichenden verfassungsrechtlich
gebotenen und politisch respektierten Schutz von Eigentum in eine Zeitinkon-
sistenzfalle[21] zu laufen: Sofern in der Vergangenheit aufgebautes Vermögen
existiert, ist es für die Politik zwar kurzfristig attraktiv, dieses zu besteuern und
die resultierenden Einnahmen für hoffentlich im Interesse der Bürger liegende
Dinge zu verwenden. Langfristig, oder wenn die Wirtschaftssubjekte dieses Po-

---

[21] *F. Kydland/E. Prescott*, Rules Rather than Discretion: The Inconsistency of Optimal Plans, Journal of Political Economy, Vol. 85, 1977, S. 473–491.

litikverhalten bereits antizipieren, wäre eine solche Politikstrategie allerdings nicht optimal, da mit Verhaltensänderungen bei den wirtschaftlich Agierenden zu rechnen wäre und der Vermögensaufbau erst gar nicht oder nur in geringerem Umfang stattfände.

Neben diesem Zeitinkonsistenzproblem baut sich dabei auch ein Demokratieproblem auf. Im Namen von „Gerechtigkeit" entließ der Staat über Jahre eine wachsende Menge der teil- oder vollzeitarbeitenden Bevölkerung am unteren Rand der Einkommensskala über höhere Freibeträge aus der Einkommen-Steuerpflicht. Der Anstieg der Freibeträge weit über ein mit Inflation zu erklärendes Maß hinaus ist populär und gleichzeitig eine Entlastung der Finanzbehörden. Die stete Ausweitung der Freibeträge hat aber auch dazu geführt, dass viele Bürger den Staat nur noch als Goldesel wahrnehmen – sie kennen ihn nur als Auszahlungsstelle und haben das Gespür dafür, dass Geld auch erwirtschaftet werden muss, verloren. Der pädagogische Wert von Mehrwertsteuer und Mineralölsteuer ist jedenfalls überschaubar. Und wenn in Umfragen inzwischen über 50 % der repräsentativ Befragten Einkommensteuersenkungen ablehnen, kann das nicht überraschen, weil ja nur noch eine Minderheit der Deutschen überhaupt Einkommensteuer zahlt. Diese wird dann aber gleich richtig zur Kasse gebeten: Die Rede ist von den abhängig Beschäftigten aus der gesellschaftlichen Mitte mit höchst transparenten Einkommensverhältnissen, geringen Steuergestaltungsmöglichkeiten, ansehnlichem Brutto wie frustrierendem Netto, geschröpft noch durch die „kalte Progression" und den vorschnell erreichten Spitzensteuersatz, aber chloroformiert durch das trügerisch gute Gefühl, irgendwo auch einen kleinen Steuervorteil zu haben – z. B. in Form der Pendlerpauschale.

Im Ergebnis trägt diese Entwicklung dazu bei, dass bei der Besteuerung Mehrheiten von Nehmenden über Minderheiten von Zahlenden entscheiden. Für die Politik ist dies höchst attraktiv, weil via Neiddiskussionen über „Reiche" leicht Zustimmung für zusätzliches Steueraufkommen mobilisierbar ist. Dass am Ende eher die ihrerseits ebenfalls minoritäre steuerzahlende Mitte das Ganze trägt – die 2005 in Deutschland eingeführte „Reichensteuer", eine Erhöhung des Spitzensteuersatzes um drei Prozentpunkte ab einem Einkommen von 250.000 Euro bei Alleinstehenden, brachte gerade einmal 600 Millionen in den Bundeshaushalt – bleibt eher ohne politische Folgen bzw. Eruptionen. Die meisten der noch Steuern zahlenden Bürger ahnen und spüren allerdings schon lange, dass die Masse Kasse macht für den Fiskus.

2013 noch für eine kleine Minderheit, später vielleicht für mehr Bürger stellt sich angesichts einer scheinbar strukturellen Ohnmacht unter Umständen die Frage, ob sie mit den Füßen abstimmen. Was, bei gleichem Grundproblem der Inanspruchnahme der Minderheit durch die Mehrheit, ein Bundesland oder ein Eurozonen-Mitglied im EZB-Rat nicht tun kann, ist für Privatpersonen und Unternehmen eine Option. Das Frankreich des Francois Hollande mit dem 2012

beschlossenen Spitzensteuersatz von 75 % lässt grüßen. Gegen die einsetzenden Absetzbewegungen nützte schon die 2013 folgende Begrenzung des Ver-
fassungsgerichts auf 66,6 % Maximalbelastung – eine höhere Belastung käme
einer Enteignung gleich – nichts mehr. Zumal die Menschen um die Wankel-
mütigkeit der Justiz wissen: Schließlich hatte auch schon das Bundesverfassungsgericht für Deutschland einmal eine Besteuerung von 50 % als Obergren-
ze deklariert – um diese Jahre später wieder für obsolet zu erklären. Wo die Besteuerung aufhört und die Enteignung beginnt, bleibt also eine politische Frage.
Das muss nichts Gutes heißen.

2. Der Staat als Trickdieb

Gelegentlich bleibt steuerloyalen und -ehrlichen Bürgern ein Steuerberater-
spruch im Hals stecken: „Rechnen Sie Ihre Einkünfte zusammen und überwei-
sen Sie alles ans Finanzamt." Noch ist es nicht soweit, aber die gönnerhafte At-
titüde, mit der gelegentlich von offizieller Seite über Steuersenkungen gesprochen wird – wenn überhaupt – suggeriert durchaus: Eigentlich gehört oder gebührt alles dem Staat, aber ein wenig Netto darf der Bürger behalten – sofern er
konsumierend die Binnennachfrage steigert, nicht zu viel, aber das in staatlichen Papieren, spart und darüber hinaus investiert, wo es der weise und allwis-
sende Vater Staat, dokumentiert durch Steuernachlässe und Subventionen, für
richtig erachtet, gern beispielsweise in Handwerkerleistungen und Solarmodule.

Das Verhältnis von Brutto zu Netto wird mit jeder Gehaltserhöhung, Prä-
mienzahlung, Sondervergütung oder zusätzlichen Einnahme ungünstiger – aus
Sicht des Steuerzahlers. Das ist, wenn man die Steuerprogression grundsätzlich
für richtig hält, unabweisbar.

Nicht nachzuvollziehen ist allerdings die Selbstverständlichkeit, mit der
deutsche Finanzpolitiker in Bund und Ländern sich jenseits öffentlich diskutier-
ter Steuersätze und -kurven über Jahrzehnte zusätzliche Einnahmen in Höhe eines dreistelligen Milliardenbetrags verschafft haben – durch versteckte Steuer-
erhöhungen ohne Parlamentsbeschlüsse und „dank" einer zum Teil auch noch
selbst angeheizten Inflation.

Die sogenannte „kalte Progression" ist schlicht kalte Enteignung. Spätestens
hier beginnt die notwendige und reguläre Erhebung von Steuern in staatlichen
Trickdiebstahl überzugehen. Vor allem deshalb, weil der Staat, wo es um seine
eigenen fiskalischen Interessen geht, Jahr für Jahr die Inflationsentwicklung
ausgleicht: Beitragsbemessungsgrenzen für Sozialversicherungen und damit die
Beiträge der Versicherten steigen regelmäßig ohne Debatte – es wird einfach
abgebucht. Schon Steuerfreibeträge dagegen werden nur ab und an, eher willkürlich angehoben – und dies dann dem deutschen Wähler als großartiges Ge-
schenk verkauft.

Insbesondere beim Einkommensteuertarif aber hat das Ausnehmen des Steuerzahlers Methode, finden die notwendigen und gerechten Inflationsanpassungen schlicht nicht statt. Die Progressionskurve führt logischerweise dazu, dass von jedem weiteren verdienten Brutto-Euro weniger Netto bleibt. Ein Arbeitnehmer, der 2012 50.000 Euro verdiente, zahlte 25,7 Prozent Einkommensteuer. Bei zwei Prozent Inflation muss er 2013 schon 51.000 Euro verdienen, um keine Kaufkraft zu verlieren. Die „kalte Progression" sorgt nun aber dafür, dass sein um 1000 Euro verbessertes Gehalt mit 26 Prozent besteuert wird. Unter dem Strich hat der Bürger etwas verloren, der Staat gewonnen – still und heimlich. Das ist seit Jahrzehnten bekannt – umso ärgerlicher, dass ständig eine Korrektur versprochen, aber nichts getan wird. Warum auch – für Finanzminister ist das einfach zu schön: Mehr Einnahmen ohne mehr Ärger. Hier macht Masse richtig Kasse beim Fiskus: Über 50 Jahre hinweg haben sich die Gewichte in aberwitziger Weise verschoben: Zahlte man einst den (damals höheren) Spitzensteuersatz, wenn man das Zwanzigfache des Durchschnittslohns verdiente, reicht 2012 das eineinhalbfache. Lauter „Spitzenverdiener" im Land – und Spitzengeschröpfte. Auf der Ausgabenseite übrigens sind automatische Inflationsanpassungen inzwischen weniger ein Fremdwort – zum Beispiel in der Sozialen Pflegeversicherung oder bei den Hartz-IV-Empfängern, wo je nach Entwicklung des entsprechenden „Warenkorbs" Jahr für Jahr angehoben wird. Transferempfänger sind von der Inflation befreit, Steuerzahler nicht – eine für einen ausgeprägten Wohlfahrtsstaat nicht überraschende Prioritätensetzung.

Erleichtert wird dies durch nicht bewusst herbeigeführte, aber in ihren praktischen Vorteilen für den Fiskus wertgeschätzte Intransparenz. Was die Steuerzahler nicht so richtig verstehen, kann auch nicht für Unruhe sorgen. Steuervereinfachung ist schon deshalb ein Unwort für viele Politiker, weil dann Bürger wüssten, wie viel Prozent ihres zu versteuernden Einkommens nach aller liebevoll und verwirrend detailliert aufgeführten Hin- und Her-Rechnerei denn effektiv abgeführt wurden – und an wen und wozu: Kaum jemandem ist beispielsweise klar, dass 15 Prozent der vom Bürger gezahlten Einkommensteuer an die jeweilige Wohnsitzkommune gehen. Damit gar nicht erst Fragen zur Sinnhaftigkeit der Mittelverwendung, zur Verhältnismäßigkeit und Rechtmäßigkeit des Geleisteten aufkommen, bleibt der Steuerbescheid des Finanzamts in Deutschland ein wenig aussagendes Dokument staatlicher Ablenkung.

Unabhängig davon fordert der Staat zu Recht Rechtstreue von seinen Bürgern und setzt sie gerade im Bereich der Steuern seit Ende der 2000er Jahre auch mit allen, selbst illegal anmutenden Mitteln wie Anstiftung zum Datenraub in der Schweiz, um. Um dem Staat zu geben, was nach demokratisch beschlossener, gesetzlicher Maßgabe des Staates ist, bedarf es nicht mehr der „Kavallerie", mit der einst Finanzminister Peer Steinbrück dem Nachbarland Schweiz drohte. Umgekehrt darf vom Staat allerdings auch erwartet werden, dass er das hohe Gut der Rechtssicherheit pflegt und privates Eigentum seiner

Bürger respektiert. Genau das ist regelmäßig nicht der Fall, wenn vor allem bei der Unternehmensbesteuerung Gesetze rückwirkend geändert werden.[22] Vertrauensschutz und Eigentumsschutz gelten, ist man des Öfteren versucht zu schließen, nicht generell, sondern nach politischer Tagesstimmung und Kassenlage.

Ähnlich verhält es sich, wenn auch in der 17. Legislaturperiode des Deutschen Bundestages mit deutlichen Zeichen der Besserung, bei Entscheidungen der Justiz: Regelmäßig wurden aus Einzelfällen abgeleitete Urteilssprüche z. B. des obersten deutschen Finanzgerichts, des Bundesfinanzhofs, sofort flächendeckend umgesetzt bzw. angewandt, wenn sie dem Bundesfinanzministerium genehm und dem Fiskus zuträglich waren. Traf das Gegenteil zu, neigte man in der Berliner Wilhelmstrasse gern zu sogenannten „Nichtanwendungserlassen" an die Finanzverwaltung.

3. „Finanzielle Repression" – klingt grausam genug, um wahr zu sein

Auch in anderer Hinsicht trickst sich der Staat zu einer günstigeren und ergiebigeren Finanzierung seiner selbst. Dabei wird zumindest ein großer Teil der Bürger, dem er eigentlich auch dienen und für laufende Einzahlungen auf die öffentlichen Konten dankbar sein sollte, im Verborgenen enteignet.

„Finanzielle Repression" nennt sich dieses Phänomen. Das klingt grausam genug, um wahr zu sein, und gleichzeitig zu wissenschaftlich-bürokratisch, um von einer breiteren Öffentlichkeit wahrgenommen zu werden. Finanziell repressiv ist ein Handeln, das mit staatlichen Eingriffen in die Finanzmärkte Anleger quasi dazu zwingt, zur Finanzierung von Staatsschulden beizutragen und beispielsweise Staatsschuldtitel zu kaufen. All dies zu Bedingungen, vor allem Niedrigzinsen, unter denen normalerweise kein geistig klarer Anleger sein Geld einbringen würde. Es funktioniert vor allem dann hervorragend, wenn es wie in den Jahren 2012 und 2013 wenig Anlagealternativen gibt.

Gleich doppelter Gewinner sind die Finanzminister: Sie profitieren einerseits von der Liquidität, mit der die Notenbanken die Märkte fluten, durch Niedrigzinsen. Und können andererseits trotzdem ihre Staatsschuldtitel loswerden, die Bundesrepublik 2012 sogar mit negativer Verzinsung: Der Staat leiht sich 1000 Euro und zahlt Jahre später etwas weniger zurück. Der Investor wäre besser damit gefahren, die Scheine in einem Sparstrumpf zu deponieren. Das dürfen beispielsweise Lebensversicherungen aber nicht. Sie müssen „sicher" anlegen.

---

[22] So beispielsweise die Modifikation der Regelungen über die körperschaftsteuerliche Verlustnutzungsbeschränkung mit dem Jahressteuergesetz 2010 oder die rückwirkende Einführung der Gewerbesteuerpflicht auf Streubesitzdividenden durch Ergänzung der gewerbesteuerlichen Hinzurechnungsvorschrift 2001.

Was sicher ist, legt der Staat fest. Und der, Überraschung, hält Staatsanleihen für „besonders sicher" – trotz aller Erfahrungen der jüngeren Zeit. So werden die Unternehmen gezwungen, in schlecht rentierliche Papiere zu investieren – und können später die Zusagen an ihre Kunden kaum halten. Eine sanfte Enteignung mit verzögerter Wirkung – optimal für auf die Bewältigung der Gegenwart fixierte öffentliche Hände.

Weiter geht es bei den Banken, die als Reaktion auf die Finanzmarktkrise höhere Eigenkapitalanforderungen erfüllen müssen. Investieren sie in Aktien oder Immobilien, sind deren Werte mit Eigenkapital zu unterlegen. Kaufen sie dagegen Staatsanleihen, entfällt diese Anforderung. Denn diese sind ja, wie der Staat schon festzustellen geruhte, „besonders sicher". Auch Bankengeld wird also in Staatsanleihen getrieben.

Ein Korrektiv wäre, im Sinne des Schutzes des Eigentums von Sparern, Lebensversicherten und Riesterrentnern u. a., die Privilegierung von Staatsanleihen zu beenden und ebenso, deren Einstufung realitätsnäher auszugestalten[23]. Das wird allerdings kaum geschehen. Finanzielle Repression ist für die Politik in der Zeit schwindender Handlungsspielräume aufgrund der massiven Staatsschuldenlasten ein einfach zu verlockender Ausweg.

4. Die Renten-Expropriation: Der Vorsorgende könnte der Dumme sein

Eine weitere Versuchung könnte in etwas fernerer Zukunft locken, nämlich der Zugriff auf Sozialkassen oder Versorgungswerke und die Reduzierung, wenn nicht Streichung von 2013 noch verfassungsfest garantiert scheinenden Ansprüchen.

Viele Bürger glauben allen Ernstes, die staatliche Rente basiere in Deutschland auf einem Umlageverfahren und die Aktiven trügen die jeweils aktuellen Renten. Jahr für Jahr aber fließt ein großer Teil des Bundeshaushalts – 2012 27 Prozent – als Zuschuss in die unterfinanzierte Rentenversicherung, mit steigender Tendenz nicht nur wegen der Demographie: Auch im Wahljahr 2013 wollen sich fast alle Parteien dauerhaft auf neue Leistungen festlegen, denen keine Einzahlungen gegenüberstehen – z. B. für Kindererziehung. Und mit einer „Lebensleistungsrente" für Geringverdiener, die im Alter gut gemeint über der Grundsicherung liegen soll, wird ein tragendes, ordnungspolitisch fundiertes Prinzip der Rentenversicherung weiter ausgehöhlt: Rente nach Bedürftigkeit statt nach Leistung. Außerdem sollen frühere Absenkungen des Rentenniveaus rückgängig gemacht werden – obwohl sich an der Begründung dafür nichts ge-

---

[23] Vgl. Kronberger Kreis (2011), Systemstabilität für die Finanzmärkte, Studie, Nr. 53, Stiftung Marktwirtschaft, Berlin.

ändert hat. Demokratisches Gedächtnis ist mitunter kurz, und jede politische Generation muss offensichtlich die bekannten Dummheiten neu machen.

Eine mögliche Rezession? Schuldenbremse? Versteckte Lasten wie die sich bis 2020 annähernd verdoppelnden Beamtenpensionen? Euro-Rettungskosten? Wird alles verdrängt – es ist ja Bundestagswahl. Die, die dabei von „gerechten Renten" reden, dürften genau damit eine große, ganz andere Ungerechtigkeit verursachen, die an dieser Stelle in einem kurzen, gar nicht allzu fiktiven Szenario dargestellt werden soll.

Wenn die geburtenstarken Jahrgänge der 1960er Jahre vor der Rente stehen, wird es weniger Beitragszahler und keine Spielräume für zusätzliche Steuerfinanzierung geben. Die Ausgabenseite wird wie immer tabu sein, die Einnahmeseite bei 25 % Mehrwertsteuer, 60 % Spitzensteuersatz und nach Einführung der Vermögensteuer ausgereizt. Nachdem bereits 2015 eine Mindestrente für Geringverdiener und vor der Wahl 2021 ein Sicherungsniveau von 50 Prozent beschlossen worden waren, muss noch weit mehr als in früheren Jahren aus dem chronisch klammen Bundeshaushalt abgezweigt werden. Wer die auf den jeweiligen Jetzt-Horizont fixierten Handlungs-Muster der Politik versteht, ahnt, was geschehen wird: Spätestens im Bundestagswahlkampf 2029 wird eine neue „Gerechtigkeitslücke" ausgemacht. Es könne nicht sein, dass die einen Rentner in Saus und Braus lebten, andere aber, die auch lange gearbeitet hätten, benachteiligt seien. Daraufhin wird die Bundesregierung vorschlagen, dem Subsidiaritätsprinzip zu neuer Geltung zu verhelfen: Wer andere Altersversorgungsquellen habe und für sich sorgen könne, benötige die staatliche Rente nicht. Eine Kommission erarbeitet Vorschläge für eine gerechte Anrechnung sonstiger Einnahmen.

Fiktion? Alarmismus? Mitnichten. Erstens hat es grundsätzlich Vergleichbares in Deutschland schon gegeben: Nachdem die Politik jahrelang insbesondere für betriebliche Altersvorsorge als zusätzliches Standbein geworben hatte, wurde 2003 von der rot-grünen Bundesregierung im Zusammenspiel mit dem schwarz dominierten Bundesrat beschlossen, die Geschäftsgrundlage rückwirkend zu ändern: Es wurden davon Beiträge für die Gesetzliche Krankenkasse abgezogen, ein Sechstel der erhofften Summe, auf deren Grundlage Vereinbarungen, z. B. Betriebsrenten und Direktversicherungen, geschlossen worden waren, war weg.

Zweitens formulierte Gregor Gysi, Fraktionsvorsitzender der „Linken" im Deutschen Bundestag, schon 2012: „Der Millionär braucht keine gesetzliche Rente, aber die gesetzliche Rente braucht den Millionär." Nur die Zielgruppe benannte er irreführend: Von „Millionären" spricht man, die Mittelschicht trifft man. Ralf Stegner, führender Linker in der SPD, brachte den Gedanken auf, Gutverdiener könnten mit 43 % Rentenniveau zufrieden sein, „bedürftige Ruheständler" dagegen 47 % erhalten. Der Saar-SPD-Spitzenkandidat Heiko Maas hat bereits 2009 verkündet, Gutverdiener bräuchten die staatliche Rente nicht. Im Rahmen des bei wohlfahrtsstaatlichen Visionen üblichen Rosinenpickens verwies er auf die Schweiz, wo tatsächlich Besserverdienende mehr in die Rentenkassen einzahlen, aber nicht entsprechend mehr herausbekommen. Allerdings vergaß Maas, zu erwähnen, dass im Gegenzug in der Schweiz weder Krankenkassenbeiträge noch Steuersätze nach Einkommen unterschiedlich ausgestaltet sind.

Wer, wenn es so kommt, gegen diese mit dem Subsidiaritätsbegriff auch noch intelligent verbrämte Enteignung vorgehen will, sollte nicht auf das Bundesverfassungsgericht bauen: Schon 2003 deutete dessen damaliger Präsident an, Eigentum unterliege laut Grundgesetz einer Sozialpflicht und Rentenansprüche ergäben sich auch aus dem jeweiligen gesellschaftlichen Zusammenhang. Wenn die Menschen dies nicht antizipieren, nicht ihre Leistungsbereitschaft senken und die „Work-Life-Balance" verbessern, nicht zugunsten des Gegenwartskonsums die Zukunftsvorsorge reduzieren, nicht Goldbarren als dem Staat nicht bekannte und damit nicht anrechenbare persönliche Reserve unter dem Rosenbeet vergraben, könnten einmal mehr diejenigen, die vorgesorgt haben, die Dummen sein: Neben Progression – auch bei der in einigen Jahren vollständigen Rentenbesteuerung – und finanzieller Repression noch Renten-Expropriation.

5. Inflation: Der Taschendieb des kleinen Mannes

Nicht zu vergessen die Inflation – der Taschendieb des kleinen Mannes und für Deutsche bald ein Jahrhundert nach der dramatischen Geldentwertung 1923 ein in den Genen verankerter Albtraum. Dabei muss es gar keine galoppierende Inflation mit folgendem und in der Eurozone höchst unwahrscheinlichem Währungsschnitt sein.

Schon die ganz „normale" Inflation würde viele Bürger, wenn sie sich die Folgen vergegenwärtigten, unruhig schlafen lassen. 2 Prozent jährliche Geldentwertung sind der Zielwert der „Währungshüter" der Europäischen Zentralbank. 2 Prozent Geldentwertung pro Jahr waren auch der Durchschnitt der Teuerung in Deutschland zwischen 2002 und 2011. Politiker, vor allem Europapolitiker, loben das nicht ganz zu Unrecht – statistisch gab es in den letzten zehn Jahren der Deutschen Mark eine etwas höhere Inflation. Auch deswegen bezeichnet die europäische Notenbank in Frankfurt 2 Prozent offiziell als Stabilität. Selbst diese „Stabilität" hat allerdings zur Folge, dass über einen Zeitraum von zwanzig Jahren hinweg in bestimmter nominaler Höhe zugesagte Renten, Lebensversicherungsauszahlungen, Sparguthaben und vieles andere rund ein Drittel ihres Werts verlieren: Bei weiter 2 Prozent jährlicher Inflation wird eine 2033 ausgezahlte oder abgehobene Summe von 100.000 Euro nach Maßstäben des Jahres 2013 nur mehr eine Kaufkraft von 67.300 Euro aufweisen. Mögliche Erträge dürften sich auch dank der repressiven Finanzpolitik in Grenzen und unter der Höhe der Inflation halten, die 2033 zu zahlenden Mieten, Stromrechnungen und Krankenversicherungsbeiträge dagegen deutlicher steigen.

Bereits die besagten 2 Prozent aber könnten über einen längeren Zeitraum hinweg, wie dargestellt, zum Schulden„abbau" des Staates ohne Tilgung beitragen. Je höher die Inflation, desto größer der Hebel für den Staat, Schulden abzuschütteln, ohne zu tilgen. Wie wahrscheinlich ist es angesichts der bekannten, an Dramatik zunehmenden Haushaltsengpässe, dass die Politik der Versuchung widersteht, sich dies zu wünschen? Und wie sehr darf man sich auf die Europäische Zentralbank verlassen, gegebenenfalls dem Ruf der Politik zu widerstehen? Wie sehr kann man auf eine Notenbank bauen, die ganz offensichtlich nicht der Tradition der Bundesbank, sondern südeuropäischen Notenbankgepflogenheiten nahesteht? Deren Präsident sich ohne jede demokratische Legitimation als Gestalter und Politiker geriert?

Die Bekämpfung von Inflation ist nicht nur eine technische Frage, sondern ein Ergebnis politischen Willens. Wenn aber diejenigen, die Politik machen, wie geschildert von Inflation profitieren, liegt nahe, was kommen wird – und welche Konsequenzen es hat. „Vorsicht, Inflation! Die schleichende Enteignung der Deutschen", titelte der „Spiegel" im Herbst 2012, und formulierte weiter: „Die Notenbanken überschwemmen die klammen Industriestaaten mit Geld. Das hilft den Regierungen, ihre Schulden zu senken, raubt aber den Bürgern ihre Ersparnisse. Die Geschichte einer perfiden Umverteilung – von unten nach oben ... Die einfachen Bürger werden als Kreditnehmer ausgenommen – und als Sparer durch negative Realzinsen schleichend enteignet."[24]

Der „kleine Mann" ist nicht systemrelevant – und zu machtlos, um sich mit seinem Interesse im Spiel der „Systemrelevanten" Gehör zu verschaffen. Die fast schon zur Routine gewordenen Rettungsaktionen laufen immer nach dem gleichen Muster ab: Kurzfristig gibt es konkrete Gewinner und Gerettete, langfristig einen abstrakten Verlierer – den Steuerzahler. Wenn es zum Schwur kommt bzw. die Angst vor der nächsten Börsenöffnung oder Unsicherheit siegt, gelten alle vorherigen Versprechen und Zusagen nichts mehr, werden Schuldenprobleme mit neuen Schulden bekämpft und immer noch mehr Liquidität in Umlauf gebracht – um Zeit zu gewinnen, die dann keiner nutzt. Das Vertrauen ist bereits zerstört, nach Umfragen glaubt mindestens die Hälfte der deutschen Bevölkerung nicht den Beteuerungen von EZB-Offiziellen, es bleibe zentrale Aufgabe der Notenbank, Inflation zu verhindern.

---

[24] Der Spiegel, 8. Oktober 2012, S. 1, 75, 80.

Weiter soll an dieser Stelle nicht näher auf die europäische Schuldenkrise, Für und Wider von Gemeinschaftshaftung, Transferunion, Fiskalunion oder einfach nur Maastricht 2.0 in Form von Regeldisziplin und Vertragstreue eingegangen werden.[25] Wie auch immer sich die Schuldenkrise, der Euro und die Europäische Union weiterentwickeln mögen: Inflation wird diesen Weg begleiten – und stören wird das allenfalls ein paar Zentral- und Nordeuropäer.

Offen dürften somit nur der Beginn, natürlich die Höhe, der Verlauf und die Frage sein, inwieweit Inflation „kontrollierbar" wäre. Die entsprechende Grunderwartung an den Finanzmärkten jedenfalls bezeugen unter anderem der langjährige Boom inflationsindexierter Anleihen, die interessanterweise von den Staaten aber seit 2010 kaum noch ausgegeben werden, das Niveau z. B. des Goldpreises oder die Hausse beim „Betongold".

VI. Ausblick

Die Inflation kommt. Die Rentenexpropriation droht. Die finanzielle Repression läuft. Der staatliche Trickdiebstahl auch – und vom Steuern mit höheren Steuern werden am Ende alle Parteien nicht lassen können. Es muss nicht alles kommen, aber es wird auch nicht bei einem bleiben. Der Staat wird einen aus seiner Sicht intelligenten Mix an „Folterinstrumenten" ersinnen bzw. in der Summe jeweils tagespolitischer Entscheidungen wirken lassen. Alles wird wie eingeübt in homöopathischen Dosen erfolgen, unter schönfärbenden, solidarisch und gut klingenden Begriffen und weitgehend intransparent.

Egal, wie das Zusammenspiel letztlich aussieht: Der Staat enteignet so seine Bürger. Zumindest eine Minderheit, um sich selbst und seine Nutznießer zu finanzieren und eine Mehrheit von Abhängigen ruhig und bei Laune zu halten. Ganz offensichtlich ist, dass die im Grundgesetz niedergelegte Sozialpflichtigkeit von Eigentum neu und recht einfach ausgelegt zu werden beginnt. Damit legt der Staat aus kurzfristigen Erwägungen aber die Axt an die Wurzeln, die ihn auch langfristig nähren sollen. Das dürfte nicht lange funktionieren. Es würde zu Menschen führen, die in bequemer und bräsiger Abhängigkeit leben, wie der französische Philosoph Alexis de Tocqueville es weitsichtig und klar bereits vor annähernd 200 Jahren beschrieben hat:

„In den modernen Massendemokratien sind die Regierenden keine Tyrannen mehr, sondern Vormünder. Und die Regierten bewegen sich im Hamsterrad der kleinen Lüste und Vergnügungen – gleich, einförmig und rastlos ... Der demokratische Despotismus ist die Herrschaft der Betreuer, eine gewaltige, bevormundende Macht, die das

---

[25] Vgl. Kronberger Kreis (2012), Wie viel Koordinierung braucht Europa?, Studie Nr. 55, Stiftung Marktwirtschaft, Berlin; *Manfred J. M. Neumann*, Die europäische Zentralbank auf Abwegen, Argumente zur Marktwirtschaft und Politik, Nr. 116, Stiftung Marktwirtschaft, Berlin 2012.

Leben der vielen überwacht, sichert und vergnüglich gestaltet. Sie ist unumschränkt, ins einzelne gehend, regelmäßig, vorsorglich und mild. Sie wäre der väterlichen Gewalt gleich, wenn sie wie diese das Ziel verfolgte, die Menschen auf das reife Alter vorzubereiten; statt dessen aber suchen sie bloß, sie unwiderruflich im Zustand der Kindheit festzuhalten.

Die umfassend Betreuten brauchen gar keinen freien Willen mehr und empfinden die totale Vorsorge als Wohltat. Der demokratische Despotismus entlastet – vom Ärger des Nachdenkens genauso wie von der Mühe des Lebens ... Die Widerstrebenden werden nicht gezwungen, sondern entmutigt; sie werden nicht tyrannisiert, sondern zermürbt. So entsteht eine Art von geregelter ... Knechtschaft. Und niemand scheint sich an der Bevormundung, der Herrschaft der Betreuer zu stören, weil man sich ja einreden kann, die Vormünder selbst gewählt zu haben."[26]

Wo aus Subjekten Objekte werden, aus Handelnden Behandelte, wo Freiheit nicht täglich gelebt, gefordert, gefördert wird, sondern zur Fassade verkommt, wo Eigentum ein Negativum, eher Ungleichheit als Anreiz ist, stirbt beides, Eigentum und Freiheit. Nicht laut und plötzlich, sondern, langsam, still und leise: Tocquevilles große Sorge war der schleichende Verlust der Freiheit, durch zu viel Gleichheit und Gleichmacherei, durch die Bequemlichkeit der Menschen und die Neigung des Staates, sich nicht nur für die großen Linien verantwortlich zu fühlen, sondern sich um das Wohlergehen jedes Einzelnen kümmern zu wollen, darum, den Bürger „zu leiten und zu beraten, ja ihn notfalls gegen seinen Willen glücklich zu machen". Gleichheit führe immer zum Zentralismus, als Gegenmittel und Schutz von Freiheit sah Tocqueville Dezentralität, „Bürgersinn" und, rein funktional und ohne persönliche tiefe Bindung, Glauben.

Sie tragen auch heute noch zum Erhalt der Freiheit bei, ganz im Sinne des bekannten Diktums der früheren Bundesverfassungsrichters Wolfgang Böckenförde: „Der Staat lebt von Voraussetzungen, die er nicht selbst schaffen kann." Eigentum bleibt eine davon – und untrennbar mit dem Begriff der Freiheit verbunden: „Zum Personsein gehören Freiheit und Selbstbestimmung. Für eine biologische Lebensfristung genügte die bloße Nutzung der Güter ... Der Mensch ist jedoch mehr und etwas anderes als ein biologisches Lebewesen. Er bedarf der rechtlichen Verfügung über die in seinem Eigentum stehenden Güter. Das Privateigentum verleiht ihm die notwendige Unabhängigkeit und Freiheit, um sein Leben selbst zu gestalten."[27]

In der Eigentumsethik der Christlichen Gesellschaftslehre findet dies klaren Ausdruck:

„Das Privateigentum vermittelt so ,den unbedingt nötigen Raum für eigenverantwortliche Gestaltung des persönlichen Lebens jedes einzelnen und seiner Familie' und

---

[26] Zitiert nach *Norbert Bolz*, Diskurs über die Ungleichheit. Ein Anti-Rousseau, München 2009, S. 23/24.

[27] *Anton Rauscher*, Der innere Zusammenhang zwischen Freiheit und Eigentum, in diesem Band, S. 30.

muss ‚als eine Art Verlängerung der menschlichen Freiheit betrachtet werden'. Es spornt an ‚zur Übernahme von Aufgaben und Verantwortung' und zählt damit ‚zu den Voraussetzungen staatsbürgerlicher Freiheit' ...

Diese positive Begründung des Privateigentums, die vor allem von Johannes XXIII. 1961 in der Enzyklika *Mater et magistra* entfaltet wird ..., wird ergänzt durch eine Argumentation via negationis: das Fehlen des Privateigentums führe zu Trägheit, Unordnung, Bürokratie und Machtkonzentration, sozialem Unfrieden und einer Bedrohung der Freiheit und damit der Würde des Menschen ..."[28]

Deutschland wäre viel und bleibend geholfen, diskutierte man weniger über Umverteilung und unternähme mehr für Chancengerechtigkeit und Befähigung, käme man endlich weiter mit der Vermögensbildung in Arbeitnehmerhand und richtete sich der Sozialstaat konsequenter auf Hilfe zur Selbsthilfe aus statt Betroffene auf dauerhafte Abhängigkeiten ein. Auch mehr Leistungsanreize, z. B. ein ansehnlicher Selbstbehalt vom Selbstverdienten, eine geringere Transferentzugsrate hülfen weiter – damit eben nicht kommt, womit bei purem Fortschreiben bisheriger Entwicklungen zu rechnen wäre.

Manches im vorliegenden Beitrag klingt düster. Viele Fakten sind es ja auch. Ihre Nennung soll nicht zur Verzweiflung führen, sondern dazu aufrufen, sich an die Arbeit zu machen. Nur wenig, z. B. der demographische Wandel, kommt relativ zwangsläufig. Seine Bewältigung ist indes ebenso gestaltbar wie vieles andere. Es mangelt wahrlich nicht an Erkenntnis, nur an Umsetzung – und dem Mut dazu. Der wird schon durch die absehbaren Engpässe gefördert werden – mit dem Rücken zur Wand und in schwierigeren Zeiten gelingen Veränderungen leichter, weil bei den einen Einsicht und Courage, bei den anderen das Verständnis und die Akzeptanz wachsen.

Wie sagte Friedrich Hölderlin: „Wo aber Gefahr ist, wächst das Rettende auch." Letzteres muss man allerdings ergreifen und Ersteres erkennen wollen. Deshalb gilt es, die Dinge offener anzusprechen und gerne auch demokratisch zu streiten. Im Grundgesetz der Bundesrepublik Deutschland steht nicht, dass alle Parteien, von Arbeitslosenhilfe bis Zypern, einer Meinung sein müssen und sich nur über die liebevolle Ausgestaltung der dritten Stelle hinter dem Komma ein wenig unterscheiden dürfen.

Jean Cocteau mahnte einst: „Man darf die Wahrheit nicht mit der Mehrheit verwechseln." Vor allem sollte man nicht flüchtige bis fragwürdige Demoskopie und Umfrage„mehrheiten" mit demokratischen Wahlen und Entscheidungen des Souveräns verwechseln. Wenn auch „besser" oder „schlechter", „richtig" oder „falsch" im politischen Streit nicht absolute Kategorien sein mögen, kann man mindestens formulieren: Deutschland und Europa brauchen eine nachhaltigere Balance zwischen Sozial und Marktwirtschaft, zwischen Erwirt-

---

[28] Zitiert nach *Manfred Spieker*, Die universelle Bestimmung der Güter, in diesem Band, S. 62.

schaften und Konsumieren, zwischen Geben und Nehmen, zwischen Fordern und Fördern.

Zu beschreiben, was im Ergebnis nicht mehr richtig sein kann und gefährliche Trends zu extrapolieren, soll nicht Resignation oder gar Fatalismus befördern, sondern aufrütteln und Kräfte wecken. Im Sinne dessen, was Hans Jonas, der Vater des „ökologischen Imperativs", mit Geltung weit über den Erhalt der Schöpfung hinaus beschreibt[29]:

> „Handle so, daß die Wirkungen deiner Handlung verträglich sind mit der Permanenz echten menschlichen Lebens auf Erden ... Was aber die so nötige Verbesserung der Bedingungen betrifft, so ist es höchst notwendig, die Forderung der Gerechtigkeit, der Güte und der Vernunft vom Köder der Utopie freizumachen ... Dem erbarmungslosen Optimismus steht die barmherzige Skepsis gegenüber ... Der schlechten Prognose den Vorrang zu geben gegenüber der guten, ist verantwortungsbewußtes Handeln im Hinblick auf zukünftige Generationen ... Die Unheilsprophezeiung wird gemacht, um ihr Eintreffen zu verhüten, und es wäre die Höhe der Ungerechtigkeit, etwaige Alarmisten später damit zu verspotten, dass es doch gar nicht so schlimm gekommen sei: Ihre Blamage mag ihr Verdienst sein."

Zusammenfassung

Freiheit und Eigentum sind nicht zu trennen. Wo Eigentum nicht Schutz und Anerkennung erfährt, gehen über kurz oder lang auch zentrale Antriebskräfte für Wachstum und Wohlstand, persönliches Engagement und Verantwortung sowie am Ende die Freiheit verloren. Ohne es explizit zu wollen oder öffentlich zu diskutieren, ist der moderne (deutsche) Wohlfahrtstaat in der Summe seiner Bestrebungen, Instrumente, Begünstigungen und Wirkungen auf dem Weg dazu, seine Bürger zu enteignen, zu entmutigen und zu entmündigen. Durch sein stetes, inhärentes Wachstum und seinen Finanzbedarf höhlt er den Schutz des Eigentums und die Freiheit aus.

Summary

Freedom and Property cannot be separated. Without protection and social acceptance of individual property, a fundamental driving force for growth and prosperity, for individual commitment and responsibility is missing. In the end, freedom will get lost, too.

Although there has not been a clear-stated political will and not even a public discussion, the modern (German) welfare state – taking together the effects of all its attempts, policy-tools, measures and privileges to special interest groups – is on the way to expropriate, to discourage and to patronize its citizens. The continuous growth and the enormous financial needs of the welfare state endanger both the protection of property and individual freedom.

---

[29] *Hans Jonas*, Das Prinzip Verantwortung. Versuch einer Ethik für die technologische Zivilisation, Frankfurt 1979, S. 386.

Sparkassen in Deutschland – wichtige Partner des Mittelstands

Von Norbert Kleinheyer

I. Einleitung

Im Vergleich mit zahlreichen anderen Staaten haben die Krise an den internationalen Finanzmärkten und die darauf folgende Konjunkturschwäche nur zu vergleichsweise geringen Auswirkungen auf die deutsche Volkswirtschaft geführt. Im Zuge der später wieder einsetzenden wirtschaftlichen Erholung entwickelte sich Deutschland zur Konjunkturlokomotive innerhalb Europas. Viele Beobachter haben sich gefragt, wie dies möglich gewesen sei. Wesentliche Antworten darauf lassen sich aus den strukturellen Besonderheiten der deutschen Wirtschaft und des deutschen Bankwesens ableiten.

Einmal mehr erwies sich der unternehmerische Mittelstand als starkes, dynamisches und anpassungsfähiges Fundament der Wirtschaft in Deutschland. Hinzu kam das dreigliedrige Bankensystem, in dem die Sparkassen der wohl wichtigste kreditwirtschaftliche Partner mittelständischer Unternehmen sind und eine bedeutende Rolle bei der Bildung von privatem Eigentum spielen.

II. Die mittelständische Struktur der deutschen Wirtschaft

Das Wirtschaftssystem in Deutschland wird nachhaltig vom unternehmerischen Mittelstand geprägt. In Deutschland gilt der unternehmerische Mittelstand als „Rückgrat der Wirtschaft". Die nachfolgenden Ausführungen sollen verdeutlichen, was in Deutschland unter mittelständischer Wirtschaft im Allgemeinen verstanden wird und inwiefern der unternehmerische Mittelstand das starke und dynamische Fundament der deutschen Wirtschaft ist.

1. Quantitative Merkmale des unternehmerischen Mittelstands

Wenn man gemäß Definition des Instituts für Mittelstandsforschung (IfM) in Bonn vom unternehmerischen Mittelstand in Deutschland spricht, dann sind damit unabhängige kleine und mittlere Unternehmen gemeint. Eine gesetzliche

Definition des unternehmerischen Mittelstands gibt es in Deutschland nicht. Vielfach orientiert man sich an den quantitativen Kriterien, die vom IfM festgelegt worden sind. Demnach gelten Unternehmen als klein, wenn sie höchstens 9 Beschäftigte haben und weniger als 1 Mio. Euro Jahresumsatz erzielen. Von Unternehmen mittlerer Größe spricht das IfM, solange die Zahl der Beschäftigten zwischen 10 und 499 liegt und der Jahresumsatz mindestens 1 Mio. Euro aber weniger als 50 Mio. Euro beträgt. Demnach gelten Unternehmen als mittelständisch, solange sie maximal 499 Beschäftigte haben und der Jahresumsatz weniger als 50 Mio. Euro beträgt.[1]

Wenn in Deutschland vom „unternehmerischen Mittelstand" oder kurz „Mittelstand" die Rede ist, so werden neben quantitativen Kriterien auch qualitative Aspekte zur Begriffsbestimmung herangezogen. Das IfM verwendet ergänzend zu quantitativen Kriterien die qualitativen Kriterien Eigentum und Leitung für die Mittelstandsdefinition. Dem Mittelstand ohne Größenbeschränkung hinsichtlich Beschäftigte und Umsatz zugerechnet werden sogenannte Familienunternehmen. Um ein Familienunternehmen handelt es sich nach Auffassung des IfM, wenn mindestens die Hälfte der Stimmrechtsanteile von bis zu zwei Personen oder ihren Familien gehalten werden und diese Personen der Geschäftsführung angehören. Zum unternehmerischen Mittelstand werden auch Handwerksbetriebe und Freie Berufe gezählt, selbst wenn deren Umsatz- oder Mitarbeiterzahlen die genannten Größenwerte überschreiten.

In wichtigen Bereichen wird auf die Definition des IfM zurückgegriffen. So finden dessen quantitative Kriterien beispielsweise Verwendung beim Statistischen Bundesamt und bei der Vergabe von Fördermitteln.

2. Struktur und Bedeutung des Mittelstands in Deutschland

Mit einigen wenigen Zahlen soll die Struktur und Bedeutung des unternehmerischen Mittelstands in Deutschland verdeutlicht werden.

Auf Basis der quantitativen Definition des Mittelstands durch das IfM gehörten im Jahr 2009 in Deutschland 99,7 Prozent von insgesamt gut 3,5 Mio. aktiven Unternehmen mit steuerbarem Umsatz und/oder sozialversicherungspflichtig Beschäftigten zum Mittelstand. Sie beschäftigten 60,8 Prozent der gut 25 Mio. in Unternehmen sozialversicherungspflichtig beschäftigten Arbeitnehmer.

---

[1] Vgl. Institut für Mittelstandsforschung (2012): KMU-Definition des IfM Bonn, URL: http://www.ifm-bonn.org/index.php?id=89 (Stand: 28.06.2012).

Ihr Anteil am gesamten Umsatz aller Unternehmen in Höhe von knapp 5.000 Mrd. Euro erreichte 39,1 Prozent im Jahr 2009.[2]

Legt man das qualitative Kriterium Familienunternehmen zugrunde, so waren im Jahr 2006 95,3 Prozent aller Unternehmen Familienunternehmen. Sie vereinigten auf sich 41,1 Prozent aller Umsätze und 61,2 Prozent aller sozialversicherungspflichtig Beschäftigten.[3] Laut Umsatzsteuerstatistik hatten im Jahr 2010 mehr als 50 Prozent der mittelständischen Unternehmen in Deutschland einen Umsatz von 5 Mio. Euro oder weniger.[4] Die Rechtsform des Einzelunternehmers überwog mit 69,0 Prozent. Die Rechtsform der Gesellschaft mit beschränkter Haftung hatten 15,3 Prozent der mittelständischen Unternehmen gewählt. Die Rechtsform der Aktiengesellschaft traf nur für 0,3 Prozent der Unternehmen zu.[5]

Gemäß Umsatzsteuerstatistik waren im Jahr 2009 im Wirtschaftszweig Erziehung und Unterricht 99,98 Prozent der Unternehmen mittelständisch. Sie erzielten 92,1 Prozent des gesamten Umsatzes in diesem Wirtschaftszweig. Auch im Gastgewerbe waren 99,98 Prozent der Unternehmen von kleiner und mittlerer Größe. Ihr Umsatzanteil in diesem Wirtschaftszweig betrug 89,9 Prozent. Anders dagegen im Verarbeitenden Gewerbe. Dort waren zwar 98,53 Prozent der Unternehmen mittelständisch, diese erzielten aber nur 24,1 Prozent des Umsatzes. Noch auffälliger ist es im Wirtschaftszweig der Energieversorgung. 98,49 Prozent der Unternehmen waren mittelständisch. Diese hatten aber nur einen Umsatzanteil von 8,9 Prozent.[6]

3. Existenzgründungen als Ausdruck wirtschaftlicher Freiheit

Existenzgründungen sind ein Ausdruck wirtschaftlicher Freiheit. Die Motive von Existenzgründungen können sehr vielfältig sein. So ermittelte die Statista

---

[2] Vgl. Institut für Mittelstandsforschung (2012): Schlüsselzahlen des Mittelstands in Deutschland gemäß der KMU-Definition des IfM Bonn, URL: http://www.ifm-bonn. org/assets/documents/SZ-Unt&Ums&Besch_2004-2009&2010revSch_D_KMU_nach_ IfM-Def.pdf (Stand: 28.06.2012).

[3] Vgl. Institut für Mittelstandsforschung (2012): Schlüsselzahlen der Familienunternehmen nach IfM Bonn, URL: http://www.ifm-bonn.org/index.php?id=905 (Stand: 28.06.2012).

[4] Vgl. Institut für Mittelstandsforschung (2012): Umsatzgrößenstruktur laut Umsatzsteuerstatistik, URL: http://www.ifm-bonn.org/assets/documents/Ums_GrKl_2000-2010.pdf (Stand: 28.06.2012).

[5] Vgl. Institut für Mittelstandsforschung (2012): Unternehmen nach Rechtsform und Umsatzgrößenklassen laut Umsatzsteuerstatistik 2010, URL: http://www.ifm-bonn.org /assets/documents/Unt_RF_2000-2010.pdf (Stand: 28.06.2012).

[6] Vgl. Institut für Mittelstandsforschung (2012): Ergebnisse aus der Umsatzsteuerstatistik, URL: http://www.ifm-bonn.org/index.php?id=579 (Stand: 16.05.2012).

GmbH, Hamburg, im Jahr 2012, dass die Gründer in angelsächsischen Ländern mit einer Unternehmensgründung in erster Linie erhöhte Einkommenschancen verbinden.[7] Im deutschsprachigen Raum stehen andere Motive im Vordergrund. Das Institut für Gewerbe- und Handwerksforschung in Wien hat 1996 festgestellt, dass Unabhängigkeit und Selbstverwirklichung die beiden stärksten Motive von Unternehmensgründern waren. In Zeiten hoher Arbeitslosigkeit werden auch die fehlenden Erwerbsalternativen zu einem wesentlichen Gründungsmotiv. Als Hemmnisse gelten bei Existenzgründern oftmals die schwierige Kapitalbeschaffung und administrative Belastungen.

Die Konsumfreiheit des Einzelnen zählt zu den traditionellen menschlichen Grundfreiheiten. Nach Auffassung des ehemaligen deutschen Wirtschaftsministers und späteren Bundeskanzlers Ludwig Erhard muss das demokratische Grundrecht der Konsumfreiheit seine logische Ergänzung in der Freiheit des Unternehmers finden.[8] Die Freiheit des Unternehmers besteht insbesondere in der Möglichkeit, das zu produzieren oder zu vertreiben, was er unter Berücksichtigung des Marktes als Erfolg versprechend erachtet. In jeder Gesellschaft gibt es aber auch Grenzen der unternehmerischen Freiheit und Pflichten, denen Unternehmer nachkommen müssen. In dem Maße, wie unternehmerische Betätigung von staatlichen Auflagen, von Bürokratie und staatlicher Gängelung begleitet wird, ist der Umfang von Existenzgründungen auch ein Ausdruck für das Maß an wirtschaftlicher Freiheit.

III. Die enge Verbindung von Eigentum und Unternehmertum

Mittelständische Unternehmen können zahlreiche Vorteile aus der engen Verbindung von Eigentum und Unternehmertum ziehen. Hierzu gehören flache Hierarchien und kurze Entscheidungswege, die Entscheidungsprozesse im Vergleich mit großen Unternehmen beschleunigen können.

1. Schnelle Entscheidungen im unternehmerischen Mittelstand

Bei der Planung von Existenzgründungen stehen Gründer vor zahlreichen Aufgabenstellungen. Dazu gehören die Wahl der Rechtsform, des Standortes, die Entscheidung für ein Produkt- bzw. Dienstleistungsangebot, die Marktsegmentierung, die Finanzierung sowie die Aufbau- und Ablauforganisation. Bei

---

[7] Vgl. Statista (2012): Verteilung der Gründungsmotive in Deutschland von 2009 bis 2011, URL: http://de.statista.com/statistik/daten/studie/183864/umfrage/hauptsaechliche-gruendungsmotive-der-unternehmensgruender-in-deutschland/ (Stand: 09.07.2012).

[8] Vgl. *Ludwig Erhard*, Wohlstand für Alle, Düsseldorf 1957, S. 14.

der Überwindung der wirtschaftlichen Krise und bei Einsetzen der konjunkturellen Erholung in Deutschland erwiesen sich wichtige Strukturmerkmale mittelständischer Unternehmen in Deutschland wie die hierarchische Organisation, die Länge der Entscheidungswege und das Tempo der Entscheidungsumsetzung als Vorteil gegenüber großen Unternehmen und Konzernen. Flache Hierarchien, kurze Entscheidungswege und bürokratiearme Durchführung getroffener Entscheidungen ermöglichten es den Unternehmen, frühzeitig auf den anrollenden Konjunkturzug aufzuspringen. Zahlreiche kleine und mittlere Unternehmen sind typischerweise als Zulieferer für große Unternehmen tätig, beispielsweise in der Automobilindustrie oder im Maschinenbau. Für sie ist es wichtig, ihren Abnehmern stets einen Schritt voraus zu sein, um auf veränderte Marktgegebenheiten schnell reagieren zu können.

2. Institutionalisierte Prüfung von Entscheidungen in großen Unternehmen

Mittelständische Unternehmen unterscheiden sich vielfach gravierend von großen Unternehmen und Konzernen. Dies trifft einerseits vor allem beim internen Aufbau zu. Andererseits unterliegen große Unternehmen in höherem Maße einer institutionalisierten Überprüfung der unternehmerischen Entscheidungen, etwa durch einen Aufsichtsrat und eine Aktionärsversammlung (Hauptversammlung) bei börsennotierten Unternehmen. Für kleine, mittlere und große Unternehmen sowie für Konzerne gilt gleichermaßen: der wunde Punkt liegt nicht in den Fähigkeiten der Manager, sondern in den Entscheidungsstrukturen. Oftmals wären Führungskräfte zwar in der Lage Entscheidungen zu treffen, im Zusammenwirken großer Abteilungen, Teams und Koalitionen bleiben aber manche Entscheidungen hängen oder werden von anderen Beschlüssen gestoppt, torpediert oder egalisiert. Mit zunehmender Größe von Unternehmen sind Entscheidungsbefugnisse des Einzelnen zwar eindeutiger definiert, aber offenbar scheint gerade diese klare Zuweisung von Kompetenzen die Beschlussfassung und Umsetzung neuer Ideen eher zu verhindern als zu fördern. Das ergab eine Befragung von 560 deutschen Führungskräften durch die Akademie für Führungskräfte der Wirtschaft GmbH, Überlingen, im Jahr 2005.

Gerade in Unternehmen mit der Rechtsform Aktiengesellschaft kann durch den Aufsichtsrat und die Aktionärsversammlung maßgeblich auf die Führung eines Unternehmens und damit auf die Entscheidungen an der Unternehmensspitze eingewirkt werden. So sieht das Deutsche Aktiengesetz vor, dass grundlegende Entscheidungen von den Aktionären mittels Mehrheitsabstimmung in der Hauptversammlung abgesegnet werden müssen. Die Unternehmensleitung hat nur die Möglichkeit, im Rahmen der Meinungsbildung Einfluss auf das Abstimmungsergebnis zu nehmen. Darüber hinaus können Großaktionäre Sperrminoritäten erreichen und Entscheidungen des Vorstands blockieren. Grundsätzlich ist daher davon auszugehen, dass für eine Unternehmensführung das Maß der unternehmerischen Freiheit positiv korreliert mit dem Umfang des Eigentums an einem Unternehmen. Die Verbindung von Eigentum und Leitung gibt den mittelständischen Unternehmen und insbesondere den Familienunternehmen die Möglichkeit, wichtige Entscheidungen unabhängig von weiteren Entscheidungsträgern zu treffen.

Zudem werden an große Unternehmen strengere Rechnungslegungsanforderungen gestellt als an kleine Unternehmen. Größenunterschiede haben vor allem für die Publizitätspflicht Bedeutung hinsichtlich des Umfangs und Detaillierungsgrades, in welchem der Inhalt des Jahresabschlusses offenzulegen ist. Ab einer bestimmten Unternehmensgröße besteht gemäß Handelsgesetzbuch außerdem die Pflicht, den Jahresabschluss durch einen Abschlussprüfer prüfen zu lassen.

Die potenzielle Einflussnahme zahlreicher Anteilseigner auf Entscheidungen der Unternehmensleitung und die Publizitätspflicht können bei großen Unternehmen dazu führen, dass strategische Entscheidungen, die aufgrund aktueller Marktentwicklungen zu treffen sind, bestenfalls nur mehr Zeit beanspruchen. Die Flexibilität und Freiheit von Entscheidungen der Unternehmensleitung bringen der überwiegend mittelständisch strukturierten Wirtschaft in Deutschland also einen strategischen Vorteil im Wettbewerb.

3. Privateigentum fördert wirtschaftliches Denken

Es wurde schon erwähnt, dass gut 95 Prozent der Unternehmen Familienunternehmen sind, bei denen eine unmittelbare Verbindung von Eigentum und Geschäftsführung besteht. Das Recht der Unternehmer an ihrem Eigentum und der Schutz dieses Rechts sind gerade für die mittelständische Wirtschaft ein Anreiz, sich besonders zu engagieren. Die Eigentümer wissen, was sie vom Eigentum haben. Deshalb werden sie es hegen und pflegen, sie werden es nicht beschädigen, und sie werden es verteidigen. Eigentum fördert das wirtschaftliche Denken. Es veranlasst zu einem sorgsamen Umgang mit Wirtschaftsgütern und es motiviert zur Leistung. Das kann sich in gewisser Weise auch auf die Beschäftigten übertragen. Je besser die Mitarbeiter erkennen können, welchen Einfluss ihr eigenes Verhalten im positiven wie im negativen Sinn auf den Unternehmenserfolg hat, desto ausgeprägter wird auch das ökonomische Denken und Verhalten der Angestellten innerhalb des Unternehmens sein, etwa im Umgang mit betrieblichen Ressourcen.

IV. Sparkassen –
wichtiger Bestandteil des deutschen Finanzsystems

Die strukturelle Besonderheit der deutschen Wirtschaft war sicherlich ein Grund für die rasche konjunkturelle Erholung der vergangenen Jahre in Deutschland. Ein Grund dafür, dass Deutschland gut durch die Finanzkrise kam, ist im dreigliedrigen Bankensystem in Deutschland zu sehen, mit den Sparkassen als einer wesentlichen Stütze dieses Finanzsystems. Abgesehen von Erbschaften und Lotteriegewinnen setzt die Bildung von Eigentum grundsätzlich Sparen und Konsumverzicht voraus. Sparkassen bilden sowohl bei der Finanzierung des unternehmerischen Mittelstands als auch bei der Bildung von Vermögen breiter Bevölkerungsschichten in Deutschland eine ganz wichtige Rolle.

1. Sparkassen sind eng mit der wirtschaftlichen
Entwicklung in Deutschland verbunden

Das Bankwesen in Deutschland ruht auf drei Säulen: Private Großbanken, Genossenschaftsbanken und Sparkassen. Die Bezeichnung „Sparkasse" ist in Deutschland gemäß § 40 des Gesetzes über das Kreditwesen gesetzlich geschützt. Nur öffentlich-rechtliche Sparkassen und wenige sogenannte freie Sparkassen dürfen diese Bezeichnung führen.

Im Jahre 1778 wurde in Hamburg die erste Sparkasse gegründet. Hierbei handelte es sich noch um eine private Organisationsform. Ihre Gründer, wohlhabende Personen, verfolgten die Zielsetzung, Armut bei großen Teilen der Bevölkerung zu bekämpfen und zu vermeiden. Im Jahr 1801 kam es in Göttingen zur Gründung der ersten kommunal getragenen Sparkasse. Eine Kommune übernahm damit erstmals eine Garantie für die Verbindlichkeiten der Sparkasse. Nach der Niederlage Preußens gegen Napoleon im Jahre 1806 kam es in Preußen zu einer Reihe von Staats- und Verwaltungsreformen. Sie wurden von zahlreichen gesellschafts- und wirtschaftspolitischen Maßnahmen begleitet.[9]

Bezug nehmend auf die beiden Hauptinitiatoren der Reformen sind sie bekannt geworden als „Stein-Hardenbergsche Reformen". Im Zuge dieser Reformen wurde die kommunale Selbstverwaltung eingeführt. Kommunen erhielten mit ihnen mehr Freiraum für wirtschaftliche und soziale Gestaltung sowie Autonomie in der Finanzverwaltung. Das war ein wichtiger Schritt für die Entwicklung der Sparkassen, denn es gab der Gründung von Sparkassen einen großen Schub. In den darauf folgenden Jahren setzte eine Welle von Sparkas-

---

[9] Vgl. Deutscher Sparkassen- und Giroverband: Fakten, Analysen, Positionen, Nr. 45, Zur Geschichte der Sparkassen in Deutschland, Berlin 2010.

sengründungen ein. Bis zum Jahr 1900 stieg die Anzahl der Sparkassen auf rund 2.700 Institute. Ende 2011 waren es, bedingt durch Gebietsreformen der Kommunalen Träger und Fusionen, noch 427 Sparkassen. Aufgrund dessen, dass Sparkassen kommunal getragen sind, haben sie einen öffentlichen Auftrag zu erfüllen. Sie haben sicherzustellen, dass alle Bevölkerungsschichten in allen Regionen Deutschlands mit allen wesentlichen Finanzdienstleistungen zu fairen Preisen versorgt werden.[10]

2. Vorteile des Regionalprinzips von Sparkassen

Die Sparkassen in Deutschland unterliegen einem sogenannten Regionalprinzip, nach dem das Geschäftsgebiet einer Sparkasse mit dem Gebiet ihres kommunalen Trägers übereinstimmt. Das Regionalprinzip ist in Landesgesetzen geregelt. So heißt es in § 6 des Thüringer Sparkassengesetzes: *„Das Geschäftsgebiet der Sparkassen ist das Gebiet ihres Trägers … ".* Somit ist auch die geschäftliche Betätigung einer Sparkasse grundsätzlich auf ihr Geschäftsgebiet beschränkt. Die Erschließung attraktiver Geschäftspotenziale in anderen Regionen ist für eine Sparkasse somit nicht möglich. Für die Sparkassen bedeutet das einen Kundenkreis, der grundsätzlich auf die Region beschränkt ist. Durch das Regionalprinzip ist der Wettbewerb zwischen Sparkassen untereinander weitgehend ausgeschlossen. Kritiker des Regionalprinzips sehen darin eine Wettbewerbsverzerrung. Dem ist entgegenzuhalten, dass sich große Banken aus vielen Regionen bereits zurückgezogen haben. Da jede Sparkasse ihre Geschäftsaktivitäten auf eine Region beschränken muss und es in Deutschland viele Sparkassen gibt, wird auf diese Weise eine flächendeckende Präsenz der Sparkassen sichergestellt. Nur dadurch ist es vielen Menschen und vor allem mittelständischen Unternehmen auch in strukturschwachen Regionen noch möglich, Zugang zu Finanzdienstleistungen zu erhalten. Das ist gerade für die Entwicklung der vielen strukturschwachen Regionen in Ostdeutschland wichtig. Für die Sparkassen selbst führt die durch das Regionalprinzip verursachte Marktnähe zu einer besseren Kenntnis der eingegangenen Risiken und zu einer nachhaltigen Marktbearbeitung.

3. Der Marktanteil der Sparkassen
an der Unternehmensfinanzierung ist bedeutend

Zu den Aufgaben der Sparkassen gehört, die Realwirtschaft mit modernen Finanzdienstleistungen zu versorgen. Sie konzentrieren sich mit ihrem Kernge-

---

[10] Ebenda.

schäft auf mittelständische Firmenkunden und das breite Privatkundengeschäft. Ende 2010 betrug der Marktanteil der Sparkassen bei Krediten an Unternehmen und Selbständige 24,3 Prozent. Drei Viertel der Unternehmen führten ein Konto bei einer Sparkasse oder Landesbank und die Hälfte aller Unternehmen mit einem Umsatz bis zu 0,5 Mio. Euro unterhält seine Hauptbankverbindung bei einer Sparkasse. Durch ihr flächendeckendes und umfassendes Angebot an Finanzdienstleistungen sorgen die Sparkassen für die notwendige kreditwirtschaftliche Basis einer leistungsfähigen, mittelständischen Wirtschaftsstruktur. Hierzu zählt auch das Deutsche Handwerk. Zwei Drittel aller Handwerksbetriebe waren Ende 2010 Sparkassenkunden. Der Marktanteil der Sparkassen bei Krediten an das Handwerk betrug zu diesem Zeitpunkt 68,2 Prozent. Eine starke Marktstellung nehmen die Sparkassen aber nicht nur bei etablierten Unternehmen ein. Auch mit ihrem Engagement für Existenzgründer liegen Sparkassen deutlich über dem Branchendurchschnitt. Insgesamt begleiteten die Institute im Jahr 2010 mehr als 11.300 Gründungsvorhaben.[11]

4. Die Sparkassen-Idee ist nach wie vor aktuell

In Deutschland ermöglichen insbesondere Sparkassen seit mehr als 200 Jahren allen Bevölkerungsgruppen und kleinen Unternehmen eine kreditwirtschaftliche Teilhabe und Versorgung. Den wachsenden Ansprüchen ihrer mittelständischen Kunden und Privatpersonen an Umfang und Modernität von Finanzdienstleistungen entsprechend erweiterten die Sparkassen ihr Angebot. Sie spielten eine wichtige Rolle beim Aufbau in den fünf neuen Bundesländern nach dem Fall der innerdeutschen Grenze. In vielen Ländern der Erde gibt es heute Sparkassen. Massenarmut, Hunger, Kinderarmut, Ausbeutung und Landflucht sind Zustände, die wir in vielen Entwicklungsländern antreffen. Sie sind vergleichbar mit den Zuständen, die in Deutschland zur Zeit der industriellen Revolution anzutreffen waren. Sparkassen können dazu beitragen, Armut zu bekämpfen. Sie ermöglichen Menschen mit niedrigem Einkommen und Vermögen, geringe Geldbeträge sicher und verzinslich anzulegen, damit sie Rücklagen für Notzeiten bilden oder einen Kapitalstock für die Existenzgründung sammeln können.

---

[11] Vgl. Deutscher Sparkassen- und Giroverband: Informationen zum Firmenkundengeschäft, Berlin 2011.

V. Fazit

Eigentum ist eine Bedingung für die Entscheidungsfreiheit mittelständischer Unternehmen. Um dieses Eigentum zu erhalten, ist es notwendig, die mittelständischen Unternehmen in ausreichendem Maße bei der Kapitalbeschaffung zu unterstützen und sie mit modernen Finanzdienstleistungen zu fairen Preisen zu versorgen. Auch ist es wichtig, einer breiten Schicht von Menschen die Bildung von Vermögen und Eigentum zu ermöglichen, worauf wiederum Existenzgründer ihre Zukunft aufbauen können und damit für den Fortbestand der mittelständischen Wirtschaft in Deutschland sorgen. Die Sparkassen in Deutschland sind bei der Finanzierung der mittelständischen Wirtschaft und bei der Bildung von Privateigentum unverzichtbar.

Zusammenfassung

Deutschland kam verhältnismäßig gut durch die Finanzkrise und die davon ausgelöste Rezession dank seiner Wirtschaftsstruktur und der Sparkassen als Teil des Bankensystems. Die deutsche Wirtschaft ruht auf kleinen und mittleren Unternehmen. Der sogenannte „Mittelstand" zeichnet sich aus durch ein enges Verhältnis zwischen Eigentum, Unternehmertum, Wahlfreiheit und wirtschaftlichem Denken. In den verschiedenen Regionen in Deutschland gibt es kommunale Sparkassen. Auf sie entfällt ein großer Teil der Finanzierung der kleinen und mittleren Unternehmen. Seit mehr als 200 Jahren ist ihr Hauptgeschäft die preisgünstige Versorgung der kleinen und mittleren Unternehmen sowie der Bevölkerung mit den nötigen Bankprodukten.

Summary

Due to the structure of its economy as well as to the role of the savings banks in the German three-tiered banking system, Germany passed through the financial crisis and its related recession in relatively good shape. The German economy is founded on small and medium sized enterprises, freelance professionals and family businesses. The so-called "Mittelstand" is characterized by a close relationship between property, entrepreneurship, freedom of choice and economic thinking. Following the regional principle in Germany there are area-wide municipal savings banks. They make up a big portion of the financing for small and medium sized enterprises. They have stood the test of time for more than 200 years at the core of business activity by providing all kinds of banking products at competitive prices for both small and medium sized enterprises as well as for individual personal accounts.

Autorenverzeichnis

Aretz, Dr. phil. Jürgen, Historiker, Staatssekretär a. D., Generalbevollmächtigter a. D. der Thüringer Aufbaubank in Brüssel (Belgien), Bonn

Dobranski, Prof. Dr. Bernard, Dean Emeritus, Ave Maria School of Law, Naples, FL

Dougherty, Prof. Dr. Jude P., Dean Emeritus, School of Philosophy, The Catholic University of America, Washington, DC

Dougherty, Prof. Dr. Richard J., Department of Politics, University of Dallas, Irving, TX

Duffy, Mr. Robert M., Esq., Founding Partner and Shareholder, Duffy and Sweeney, Ltd, Providence, RI

Eilfort, Prof. Dr. Michael, Vorstand der Stiftung Marktwirtschaft, Berlin

Frank, Prof. Dr. William A., Department of Philosophy, University of Dallas, Irving, TX, Director of Leo XIII Center for Philosophy and Social Issues

Hillgruber, Prof. Dr. Christian, Lehrstuhl für Öffentliches Recht, Universität Bonn

Hittinger, Prof. Dr. John P., Department of Philosophy, University of St. Thomas, Houston, TX

Kleinheyer, Prof. Dr. Norbert, Geschäftsführer des Sparkassen- und Giroverbandes Hessen-Thüringen, Erfurt

Koons, Prof. Dr. Robert, Department of Philosophy, University of Texas at Austin, Austin, TX

Pinchuk, Mr. Nicholas T., Chairman and Chief Executive Officer of Snap-On, Inc., Kenosha, WI

Rauscher, Prof. Dr. Anton, em. Professor für Christliche Gesellschaftslehre an der Universität Augsburg, Direktor der Katholischen Sozialwissenschaftlichen Zentralstelle (KSZ) Mönchengladbach von 1963 bis 2010

Simpson, Prof. Dr. Peter, Professor of Philosophy and Classics, Graduate Center, City University of New York, NY

Spieker, Prof. Dr. Manfred, Professor für Christliche Sozialwissenschaften an der Universität Osnabrück

Stüwe, Prof. Dr. Klaus, Professor für Politische Systemlehre und Vergleichende Politik-wissenschaft an der Katholischen Universität Eichstätt-Ingolstadt

Vogel, Prof. Dr. Bernhard, Ministerpräsident a. D., Ehrenvorsitzender der Konrad-Adenauer-Stiftung e. V., Berlin